=

Abortion

Abortion

Moral and Legal Perspectives

Edited by Jay L. Garfield and Patricia Hennessey

The University of Massachusetts Press

Amherst, 1984

Acknowledgment is hereby made for permission to
reprint previously copyrighted material:
"The Juridical Status of the Fetus: A Proposal for
the Protection of the Unborn" by Patricia King is
reprinted by permission of the publisher from *The
Law and Politics of Abortion*, edited by Carl E.
Schneider and Maris A. Vinovskis (Lexington,
Mass.: Lexington Books, D.C. Heath and Co.) ©
1980 D. C. Heath and Co.
Portions of "Personhood and the Abortion Debate"
by Ruth Macklin originally appeared in "Person-
hood in the Bioethics Literature," Macklin, R. 1983.
*Milbank Memorial Fund Quarterly/Health and
Society* 61 (1): 35–57.
"A Human Life Statute" by Stephen Galebach is
reprinted by permission from *The Human Life
Review*, 150 East 35th St., New York, N.Y. ©
1981, the Human Life Foundation.
"Abortion and Self-Defense" by Nancy Davis
originally appeared in *Philosophy and Public Affairs*
13, no. 3 (1984) and is reprinted by permission of
Princeton University Press, © 1984 Princeton
University Press.

Publication of this book has been assisted by a
grant from the Civil Liberties and Public Policy
Program of Hampshire College.

Contents

=

Acknowledgments

Most of the essays in this volume were contributions to a conference, Abortion, Persons, Morality, and the Law, held at Hampshire College on the tenth anniversary of the Supreme Court's decision of *Roe* v. *Wade*, January 21–23, 1983. This conference was made possible by the generous support of A. Hans Huber, the Huber Foundation, the Boehm Foundation, and Hampshire College, through its Civil Liberties and Public Policy Program.

Additional thanks for help on this project are due to Adele Simmons, president of Hampshire College; Bruce Wilcox, director of the University of Massachusetts Press, for valuable suggestions and invaluable encouragement; two anonymous reviewers whose suggestions were incorporated; Dyan Sublett, for administrative and developmental support; Francine Lorenz, Christine Brooks, Ruth Hammen, and Leni Bowen, for secretarial support; Matthew Alexander, for research assistance; and to Blaine Garson and Jean Hennessey, for extraordinary moral and emotional support.

=

Introduction
Abortion: Persons, Morality, and the Law

Jay L. Garfield

PHILOSOPHY and legal theory are replete with difficult moral and legal problems which generate protracted and often bitter debate among scholars within these fields. Few of these issues, however, either attract the public's attention, or generate the public's passion. The question of the legal and moral status of abortion is an exception. The abortion issue is as alive and controversial in the body politic as it is in the academy and the courtroom. The issue is of pressing social concern, and because it is so complicated and difficult, rational resolution of the political questions it poses requires careful scholarly examination of the fundamental moral and legal questions into which the issue resolves.

The abortion issue is not only important politically and socially, though this importance alone would justify our serious attention. The question of the moral and legal status of abortion is also of considerable intrinsic philosophical and legal interest, inasmuch as it involves some of the most profound questions about the nature of persons, the boundaries of the state's power over persons, the connection between law and morality, and the nature of action. Moreover, the issue, lying as it does on the boundary between moral philosophy and legal theory, offers a splendid opportunity for interdisciplinary cooperation between these two fields.

So far we have been speaking of "the abortion issue" as though it is a single issue. This is misleading. In fact it is really a set of interrelated puzzles, each of substantial interest to the philosopher or legal theorist. The complete resolution of the abortion question arguably requires clarity with respect to each of these subproblems. One problem which is of pressing legislative and judicial concern in the United States is

that of the correct interpretation of the Supreme Court's 1973 landmark decision of *Roe* v. *Wade*, 410 U.S. 113. Understanding this decision is fundamental for the evaluation of any proposed national or
local legislation governing abortion. Unfortunately, it is far from clear
just what boundaries *Roe* establishes. In addition to this practical
judicial and political problem are several more fundamental issues:
that of the nature of personhood—just when in human development a
human organism becomes a person; that of the limits of legislative and
judicial enforcement of controversial moral standards; that of the distinction between actively killing and merely passively letting die; and
that of constitutionally guaranteed privacy.

The decision of *Roe* v. *Wade* invalidated nearly all then-existent
laws restricting abortion. The Court ruled unconstitutional any restriction on a woman's access to abortion during the first trimester of pregnancy, any restriction not based upon the protection of maternal
health during the second trimester, and any restriction which would
place maternal life in danger in the third trimester. This ruling was
based on the argument that such state intrusion into the doctor-patient
relationship and into a woman's decisions concerning procreation violates the right to privacy. In resting the decision on this right to privacy, the Court relied heavily on *Griswold* v. *Connecticut*, 381 U.S.
479 (1965), in which a Connecticut statute forbidding the use of contraceptive devices by married couples was struck down by appeal to
the right to privacy.

It was in *Griswold* that the right to privacy was first noted by the
Court. There is, of course, no such right explicitly recognized by the
Constitution. Rather, the Court inferred the existence of a "zone of
privacy," delimited by the right not to quarter soldiers, the right
against self-incrimination, the religious disestablishment clause, the
right to free speech and association, and the right against unreasonable
search and seizure. The intended joint effect of these several provisions, coupled with the Ninth Amendment's provision that the Bill of
Rights not be taken as exhaustive of personal rights, was held by the
Court to be the creation of a right of the individual "to be let alone"
by the government, at least where the government has no compelling
interest that could override such a right. The right to marital privacy,
the Court held, falls in the "penumbra" of that zone.

Once this "zone of privacy" was discovered by the *Griswold* court,
it seemed a short step for the *Roe* court to recognize that the right to
make decisions regarding childbearing, including the decision whether

to terminate or to continue a pregnancy, falls within that zone. But things get complicated. The very use of the term "penumbra" by the *Griswold* court shows the Court's awareness of the vagueness of the boundaries of the right to privacy. And if the boundaries are vague, it is even more unclear just when a competing state interest exists, or is strong enough to override this right. Recent cases have raised difficult questions for the interpretation of the *Roe* precedent: Does the right to abortion entail the right to Medicaid funding of abortion? Does the right to privacy preclude state laws protecting maternal or fetal health which may significantly restrict a woman's vocational pursuits or recreational activities? Does the right to privacy protect a woman against forced Ceasarean section if her life or the life of the fetus is in danger during childbirth? These issues of interpretation, as well as the foundational issues raised by *Roe* concerning fetal personhood, are addressed in the essays in "*Roe* v. *Wade*: A Retrospective," as well as by several in "The Limits of Legislative and Judicial Enforcement of Controversial Moral Standards," and in "Persons, Privacy, and Samaritanism."

The concept of a *Homo sapiens* is a biological one. If we want to know what it is for a thing to be a member of that species, we can find relatively determinate and uncontroversial criteria for answering this query. The concept of a person, however, belongs not to biology alone, but jointly to biology, ethics, metaphysics, and legal theory. None of these enterprises has yet developed an uncontroversial and perspicuous analysis of the concept. What is more, it may well be that these disciplines arrive at divergent analyses of the concept, given their divergent interests.

This is particularly troublesome if one believes, as many do, that the issue of the nature of personhood is the central issue in the abortion controversy. Proabortion and antiabortion theorists alike have staked their arguments on claims about the location of a threshold beyond which a fetus becomes a person. Advocates of an extreme antiabortion position have argued that a fertilized ovum is already a person in the moral and legal sense. Advocates of an extreme prochoice position have argued that even young infants are not yet persons, and so may be destroyed without committing homicide. The *Roe* court acknowledges the difficulty of the metaphysical and moral issues involved when Justice Blackmun, in delivering the majority opinion says, "We need not resolve the difficult question of when life begins. When those trained in the respective disciplines of medicine, philosophy, and theology are unable to arrive at any consensus, the judiciary, at this point in the development of man's knowledge is not in a position to speculate as to the answer" (410 U.S. 113, 159).

It is possible for something to be morally and metaphysically a person without being legally a person, e.g., a slave in a slave-owning society. At the same time it is possible for something to be legally a person without it being morally and metaphysically a person, e.g., a corporation in our own society. Although the Court could, in deciding *Roe*, afford to leave the moral and metaphysical portions of the personhood controversy alone, it could not do likewise for the legal question. For the State of Texas argued that the fetus is a legal person, and is hence subject to the protection of the state, and cannot be deprived of its life without due process, and certainly not by its mother. Roger Wertheimer's "Understanding Blackmun's Argument: The Reasoning of *Roe* v. *Wade*" explores the Court's strategy in resolving this issue.

The vexed nature of the moral and metaphysical aspects of the personhood question has not only generated considerable debate about the status of the fetus, but also about the very relevance of the status of the fetus to the abortion issue. Judith Thomson[1] argued that even if the fetus is a person, abortion is justifiable in a wide range of circumstances. Patricia King contends that there are sound arguments for offering the fetus certain protections which do not rely upon the premise that it is a person. Extending King's position, Ruth Macklin argues that the entire issue of fetal personhood is both unresolvable and irrelevant to the abortion controversy.

Like most facets of this controversy, the personhood issue is not self-contained. How it is resolved will determine, at least in part, the relevance of the right to privacy to the permissibility of abortion. For if the fetus is seen as a person, the privacy of the act comes into question, whereas if the fetus is not held to be a person, privacy doctrine appears to provide an especially compelling defense of the right to abortion, inasmuch as no harm could then be said to be done to the fetus. If the fetus is not a person, then the difficult issue of whether abortion is an act of killing or a case of passively letting die becomes irrelevant. If, on the other hand, the fetus is a person, this distinction, and the side of it upon which abortion falls, may be crucial for evaluating abortion's moral and legal status. Finally, our views about the right of government to protect the fetus by restricting access to abortion may in part depend on our view of the fetus's legal and moral status as a person. Because of this insinuation of the personhood issue through all aspects of the abortion question, many of the essays in this volume, not only those in the "Personhood" section, deal directly or indirectly with the issue of fetal personhood.

What is the proper relationship between the law and morality; between the law of a democratic society and the deeply held moral convictions of some segment of that society? On the one hand, we feel that the law must protect individuals against plainly immoral treatment by their fellows or by the state. To this end, we proscribe murder, assault, theft, perjury, unreasonable search and seizure, and a host of other wrongs. On the other hand, we have a firm conviction that some moral strictures are not the business of the state, and for this reason carefully separate church and state. Just how this tension in the relation between law and morality is to be resolved is critical for the resolution of the abortion controversy. At the same time, to resolve this issue in the particular context of the abortion controversy demands careful attention to the question of the personhood of the fetus.

If the fetus is a person from the moment of conception, or from some early stage in pregnancy, it would seem that however socially controversial the abortion question may be, it would be the state's duty to offer the fetus full legal protection. This is the line of argument often employed by those who press the analogy between antebellum slavery and abortion. They note that despite the fact that those who practiced slavery held it to be morally and legally permissible on the grounds that slaves were not fully persons, slavery was nonetheless justifiably outlawed, just because it represented the unjust treatment of beings who were in fact persons. Similarly, proponents of this argument continue that abortion—despite the fact that those who condone it do so on the grounds that fetuses are not fully persons—in fact represents the killing of persons; and so, the moral beliefs of pro-choice advocates notwithstanding, abortion is immoral; and furthermore, as a species of homicide, it ought to be illegal. Laurence Thomas's paper is a response to this position.

Others, including David A. J. Richards, regard this view of fetal personhood as essentially a religious position, and hence argue that any legal recognition of fetal personhood would constitute the establishment of a state religion, and would hence be unconstitutional. Between these two positions there is much room for maneuver. In several important pornography decisions, the Court has recognized the state's right to enforce prevailing community moral standards in certain instances. Just where the boundary between such legitimate moral enforcement and religious establishment lies, and how abortion stands with respect to this boundary is an open question in legal and political theory. This is the question addressed by the essays in "The Limits of Legislative and Judicial Enforcement of Controversial Moral Standards."

Judith Thomson argued that pregnancy is properly to be thought of as a situation of samaritanism, where the pregnant woman is giving supererogatory aid to the fetus. As in any case of samaritanism, this aid may be withdrawn at any time. Abortion, Thomson contends, is simply the withdrawal of this aid. To be sure, the fetus inevitably dies. But it does not follow that the fetus is killed. Rather, it is passively allowed to die. Hence, in the absence of any positive right to be kept alive—or, as Regan points out,[2] of any individual samaritan obligation on the part of the woman—abortion does not constitute the violation of the fetus's right to life, even supposing the fetus to have such a right.

This analysis of abortion and pregnancy has won much support in both philosophy and law, and harmonizes well with much of our thinking about samaritan obligation. But it is not without its problems. Difficulties with Thomson's position are raised by Nancy Davis, Philippa Foot, and Meredith Michaels in their articles. Foot disputes the passivity of the abortion act; Davis contends that even self-defense may be problematic as a defense of killing; Michaels argues that the samaritan analysis of pregnancy may be wholly inadequate to resolve the abortion issue, in that parallel arguments can be constructed on behalf of the fetus, and because Thomson's and Regan's claim that individuals never have samaritan duties toward other individuals is indeed mistaken. Depending upon how the personhood controversy is resolved, this debate on the status of pregnancy and the nature of the act of abortion could be critical in deciding abortion's moral and legal status.

Although the concept of privacy is an old one, its importance in legal theory and jurisprudence has only become fully apparent in the wake of *Griswold* and *Roe*. Consequently, relatively little philosophical attention has been devoted to its explication, despite the centrality of this notion to *Roe* and to subsequent decisions. Daniel Wikler offers an analysis of the right to privacy, resolving it into two subsidiary rights —the right to informational privacy and the right to autonomy privacy. He argues that antiabortion laws abridge the right to autonomy privacy. Specifically, he argues, the state, in determining when life begins, abridges the right to be autonomous in one's private moral beliefs.

Clearly, this issue interacts with the problem of the limits of the legislative and judicial enforcement of moral standards, and the problem of the nature of personhood. Any serious consideration of the nature of privacy, and its relation to the abortion question, must occur in the context of this matrix of overlapping problems.

These essays represent the joint endeavor of legal and philosophical scholars to raise the level of discussion on, and to clarify if not entirely to resolve, the host of interrelated moral, political, and legal problems comprised by the abortion controversy. They not only advance this significant debate, but demonstrate the vitality and importance of interdisciplinary research on this and similar social issues.

Part 1

Roe v. Wade: A Retrospective

ROE v. *Wade*, 410 U.S. 113 (1973) was one of the most important constitutional decisions rendered in the history of the United States Supreme Court. The subject of the decision—the legal status of abortion and the right to make the decision to abort—has been one of the most divisive social issues facing the country during the past quarter century. The first section of this book includes an edited version of the decision, and two analyses of its meaning and legacy.

Janet Benshoof's "*Roe* v. *Wade*: A Retrospective" discusses the legal underpinnings of the decision, specifically the constitutional right to privacy and the scope of the decision, and evaluates its meaning after ten years. She argues that the right to privacy is actually two rights: the individual's right not to have certain matters disclosed to the public or government, and the right to independence in making certain important and personal decisions, such as those pertaining to marriage and procreation. The abortion right, as defined by the Supreme Court encompasses both of these aspects of the privacy right.

Benshoof explains that the decision did not give women the right to abortion on demand, but rather, through an interest analysis, it carefully balanced the interests of the woman, the state, and the fetus, and allocated rights accordingly. In the end, the two interests the state might legitimately promote through legislation or regulation are maternal health and, in the third trimester, in limited circumstances, the interests of the fetus.

Catharine MacKinnon provides a highly original analysis and feminist critique of *Roe* v. *Wade* and challenges the assumption that the right to privacy developed in *Griswold* and *Roe* benefits women. She argues that the privacy right might in the long run be more harmful than beneficial to women's interests in protection from oppression. MacKinnon suggests that an aspect of the abortion issue insufficiently considered in most discussions is that of gender inequality as it pertains to sexual relations. She reasons, *contra* Benshoof, that the right to privacy creates a tension between, on the one hand, the interest in prohibiting the disclosure of private facts or decisions, and on the other, the interest in being protected in the personal sphere. MacKinnon argues that by restraining state action in the traditionally private spheres of marriage and procreation, and thereby barring such interference on behalf of women, the law protects and institutionalizes traditional patriarchal social values which harm women.

Her analysis also challenges the notion that the right to abortion grants a woman a right to control her own body. She proffers that such a notion is based on a liberal legal tradition which has falsely assumed that equality obtains between persons in relationships which the law defines as private. Given the falsity of this assumption, MacKinnon argues, the right to privacy protects men's ability to control women. The final section of MacKinnon's essay argues that it is precisely because the right to abortion was based on this type of privacy right that the Court could legitimately deny women the right to public funding for abortion.

Roe v. Wade: Majority Opinion
and Rehnquist Dissent

Roe et al. v. *Wade*, District Attorney of Dallas County
410 U.S. 113 (1973)

MR. JUSTICE BLACKMUN delivered the opinion of the Court.

This Texas federal appeal [presents a constitutional challenge] to state criminal abortion legislation. The Texas statutes under attack here are typical of those that have been in effect in many States for approximately a century. The Georgia statutes, in contrast, have a modern cast and are a legislative product that, to an extent at least, obviously reflects the influences of recent attitudinal change, of advancing medical knowledge and techniques, and of new thinking about an old issue.

We forthwith acknowledge our awareness of the sensitive and emotional nature of the abortion controversy, of the vigorous opposing views, even among physicians, and of the deep and seemingly absolute convictions that the subject inspires. One's philosophy, one's experiences, one's exposure to the raw edges of human existence, one's religious training, one's attitudes toward life and family and their values, and the moral standards one establishes and seeks to observe, are all likely to influence and to color one's thinking and conclusions about abortion.

In addition, population growth, pollution, poverty, and racial overtones tend to complicate and not to simplify the problem.

Our task, of course, is to resolve the issue by constitutional measurement, free of emotion and of predilection. We seek earnestly to do this, and, because we do, we have inquired into, and in this opinion place some emphasis upon, medical and medical-legal history and what that history reveals about man's attitudes toward the abortion procedure over the centuries. We bear in mind, too, Mr. Justice Holmes's admonition in his now-vindicated dissent in *Lochner* v. *New York*, 198 U.S. 45, 76 (1905):

"[The Constitution] is made for people of fundamentally differing views, and the accident of our finding certain opinions natural and familiar or novel and even shocking ought not to conclude our judgment upon the question whether statutes embodying them conflict with the Constitution of the United States."

I

The Texas statutes that concern us here are Arts. 1191–1194 and 1196 of the State's Penal Code.[1] These make it a crime to "procure an abortion," as therein defined, or to attempt one, except with respect to "an abortion procured or attempted by medical advice for the purpose of saving the life of the mother." Similar statutes are in existence in a majority of the States. . . .

II

Jane Roe,[4] a single woman who was residing in Dallas County, Texas, instituted this federal action in March 1970 against the District Attorney of the county. She sought a declaratory judgment that the Texas criminal abortion statutes were unconstitutional on their face, and an injunction restraining the defendant from enforcing the statutes.

Roe alleged that she was unmarried and pregnant; that she wished to terminate her pregnancy by an abortion "performed by a competent, licensed physician, under safe, clinical conditions"; that she was unable to get a "legal" abortion in Texas because her life did not appear to be threatened by the continuation of her pregnancy; and that she could not afford to travel to another jurisdiction in order to secure a legal abortion under safe conditions. She claimed that the Texas statutes were unconstitutionally vague and that they abridged her right of personal privacy, protected by the First, Fourth, Fifth, Ninth, and Fourteenth Amendments. . . .

V

The principal thrust of appellant's attack on the Texas statutes is that they improperly invade a right, said to be possessed by the pregnant woman, to choose to terminate her pregnancy. Appellant would discover this right in the concept of personal "liberty" embodied in the Fourteenth Amendment's Due Process Clause; or in personal, marital, familial, and sexual privacy said to be protected by the Bill of Rights or its penumbras, see *Griswold* v. *Connecticut,* 381 U.S. 479 (1965); *Eisenstadt* v. *Baird,* 405 U.S. 438 (1972); *id.,* at 460 (WHITE, J., concurring in result); or among those rights reserved to the people by the Ninth Amendment, *Griswold* v. *Connecticut,* 381 U.S., at 486 (Goldberg, J., concurring). Before addressing this claim, we feel it desirable briefly to survey, in several aspects, the history of abortion, for such insight as that history may afford us, and then to examine the state purposes and interests behind the criminal abortion laws.

VI

It perhaps is not generally appreciated that the restrictive criminal abortion laws in effect in a majority of States today are of relatively recent vintage. Those laws, generally proscribing abortion or its attempt at any time during pregnancy except when necessary to preserve the pregnant woman's life, are not of ancient or even of common-law origin. Instead, they derive from statutory changes effected, for the most part, in the latter half of the 19th century.

1. Ancient attitudes   These are not capable of precise determination. We are told that at the time of the Persian Empire abortifacients were known and that criminal abortions were severely punished.[8] We are also told, however, that abortion was practiced in Greek times as well as in the Roman Era,[9] and that "it was resorted to without scruple." [10] The Ephesian, Soranos, often described as the greatest of the ancient gynecologists, appears to have been generally opposed to Rome's prevailing free-abortion practices. He found it necessary to think first of the life of the mother, and he resorted to abortion when, upon this standard, he felt the procedure advisable.[11] Greek and Roman law afforded little protection to the unborn. If abortion was prosecuted in some places, it seems to have been based on a concept of a violation of the father's right to his offspring. Ancient religion did not bar abortion.[12]

2. The Hippocratic Oath   What then of the famous Oath that has stood so long as the ethical guide of the medical profession and that bears the name of the great Greek (460[?]–377[?] B.C.), who has been described as the Father of Medicine, the "wisest and the greatest practitioner of his art," and the "most important and most complete medical personality of antiquity," who dominated the medical schools of his time, and who typified the sum of the medical knowledge of the past? [13] The Oath varies somewhat according to the particular translation, but in any translation the content is clear: "I will give no deadly medicine to anyone if asked, nor suggest any such counsel; and in like manner I will not give to a woman a pessary to produce abortion," [14] or "I will neither give a deadly drug to anybody if asked for it, nor will I make a suggestion to this effect. Similarly, I will not give to a woman an abortive remedy." [15]

Although the Oath is not mentioned in any of the principal briefs in this case or in *Doe* v. *Bolton, post,* p. 179, it represents the apex of the development of strict ethical concepts in medicine, and its influence endures to this day. Why did not the authority of Hippocrates dissuade abortion practice in his time and that of Rome? The late Dr. Edelstein provides us with a theory:[16] The Oath was not uncontested even in Hippocrates' day; only the Pythagorean school of philosophers frowned upon the related act of suicide. Most Greek thinkers, on the other hand, commended abortion, at least prior to viability. See Plato, Republic, V, 461; Aristotle, Politics, VII, 1335b 25. For the Pythagoreans, however, it was a matter of dogma. For them the embryo was animate from the moment of conception, and abortion meant destruction of a living being. The abortion clause of the Oath, therefore, "echoes Pythagorean doctrines," and "[i]n no other stratum of Greek opinion were such views held or proposed in the same spirit of uncompromising austerity." [17]

Dr. Edelstein then concludes that the Oath originated in a group representing only a small segment of Greek opinion and that it certainly was not accepted by all ancient physicians. He points out that medical writings down to Galen (A.D. 130–200) "give evidence of the violation of almost every one of its injunctions." [18] But with the end of antiquity a decided change took place. Resistance against suicide and against abortion became common. The Oath came to be popular. The emerging teachings of Christianity were in agreement with the Pythagorean ethic. The Oath "became the nucleus of all medical ethics" and "was applauded as the embodiment of truth." Thus, suggests Dr. Edelstein, it is "a Pythagorean manifesto and not the expression of an absolute standard of medical conduct." [19]

This, it seems to us, is a satisfactory and acceptable explanation of the Hippocratic Oath's apparent rigidity. It enables us to understand, in historical context, a long-accepted and revered statement of medical ethics.

3. The common law   It is undisputed that at common law, abortion performed *before* "quickening"—the first recognizable movement of the fetus *in utero,* appearing usually from the 16th to the 18th week of pregnancy [20]—was not an indictable offense.[21] The absence of a common-law crime for pre-quickening abortion appears to have developed from a confluence of earlier philosophical, theological, and civil and canon law concepts of when life begins. These disciplines variously approached the question in terms of the point at which the embryo or fetus became "formed" or recognizably human, or in terms of when a "person" came into being, that is, infused with a "soul" or "animated." A loose consensus evolved in early English law that these events occurred at some point between conception and live birth.[22] This was "mediate animation." Although Christian theology and the canon law came to fix the point of animation at 40 days for a male and 80 days for a female, a view that persisted until the 19th century, there was otherwise little agreement about the precise time of formation or animation. There was agreement, however, that prior to this point the fetus was to be regarded as part of the mother, and its destruction, therefore, was not homicide. Due to continued uncertainty about the precise time when animation occurred, to the lack of any empirical basis for the 40–80-day view, and perhaps to Aquinas's definition of movement as one of the two first principles of life, Bracton focused upon quickening as the critical point. The significance of quickening was echoed by later common-law scholars and found its way into the received common law in this country.

Whether abortion of a *quick* fetus was a felony at common law, or even a lesser crime, is still disputed. Bracton, writing early in the 13th century, thought it homicide.[23] But the later and predominant view, following the great common-law scholars, has been that it was, at most, a lesser offense. In a frequently cited passage, Coke took the position that abortion of a woman "quick with childe" is "a great misprision, and no murder." [24] Blackstone followed, saying that while abortion after quickening had once been considered manslaughter (though not murder), "modern law" took a less severe view.[25] A recent review of the common-law precedents argues, however, that those precedents contradict Coke and that even post-quickening abortion was never established as a common-law crime.[26] This is of some importance because while most American courts ruled, in holding or dictum, that abortion of an unquickened fetus was not criminal under their received common law,[27] others followed Coke in stating that abortion of a quick fetus was a "misprision," a term they translated to mean "misdemeanor." [28] That their reliance on Coke on this aspect of the law was uncritical and, apparently in all the reported cases, dictum (due probably to the paucity of common-law prosecutions for post-quickening abortion), makes it now appear doubtful that abortion was ever firmly established as a common-law crime even with respect to the destruction of a quick fetus.

4. *The English statutory law*   England's first criminal abortion statute, Lord Ellenborough's Act, 43 Geo. 3, c. 58, came in 1803. It made abortion of a quick fetus, § 1, a capital crime, but in § 2 it provided lesser penalties for the felony of abortion before quickening, and thus preserved the "quickening" distinction. This contrast was continued in the general revision of 1828, 9 Geo. 4, c. 31, § 13. It disappeared, however, together with the death penalty, in 1837, 7 Will. 4 & 1 Vict., c. 85, § 6, and did not reappear in the Offenses Against the Person Act of 1861, 24 & 25 Vict., c. 100, § 59, that formed the core of English anti-abortion law until the liberalizing reforms of 1967. In 1929, the Infant Life (Preservation) Act, 19 & 20 Geo. 5, c. 34, came into being. Its emphasis was upon the destruction of "the life of a child capable of being born alive." It made a willful act performed with the necessary intent a felony. It contained a proviso that one was not to be found guilty of the offense "unless it is proved that the act which caused the death of the child was not done in good faith for the purpose only of preserving the life of the mother."

A seemingly notable development in the English law was the case of *Rex* v. *Bourne,* [1939] 1 K.B. 687. This case apparently answered in the affirmative the question whether an abortion necessary to preserve the life of the pregnant woman was excepted from the criminal penalties of the 1861 Act. . . .

5. *The American law*   In this country, the law in effect in all but a few States until mid-19th century was the pre-existing English common law. Connecticut, the first State to enact abortion legislation, adopted in 1821 that part of Lord Ellenborough's Act that related to a woman "quick with child." [29] The death penalty was not imposed. Abortion before quickening was made a crime in that State only in 1860.[30] In 1828, New York enacted legislation[31] that, in two respects, was to serve as a model or early anti-abortion statutes. First, while barring destruction of an unquickened fetus as well as a quick fetus, it made the former only a misdemeanor, but the latter second-degree manslaughter. Second, it incorporated a concept of therapeutic abortion by providing that an abortion was excused if it "'shall have been necessary to preserve the life of such mother, or shall have been ad-

vised by two physicians to be necessary for such purpose." By 1840, when Texas had received the common law,[32] only eight American States had statutes dealing with abortion.[33] It was not until after the War Between the States that legislation began generally to replace the common law. Most of these initial statutes dealt severely with abortion after quickening but were lenient with it before quickening. Most punished attempts equally with completed abortions. While many statutes included the exception for an abortion thought by one or more physicians to be necessary to save the mother's life, that provision soon disappeared and the typical law required that the procedure actually be necessary for that purpose.

Gradually, in the middle and late 19th century the quickening distinction disappeared from the statutory law of most States and the degree of the offense and the penalties were increased. By the end of the 1950s, a large majority of the jurisdictions banned abortion, however and whenever performed, unless done to save or preserve the life of the mother.[34] The exceptions, Alabama and the District of Columbia, permitted abortion to preserve the mother's health.[35] Three States permitted abortions that were not "unlawfully" performed or that were not "without lawful justification," leaving interpretation of those standards to the courts.[36] In the past several years, however, a trend toward liberalization of abortion statutes has resulted in adoption, by about one-third of the States, of less stringent laws, most of them patterned after the ALI Model Penal Code, § 230.3,[37] set forth as Appendix B to the opinion in *Doe v. Bolton, post,* p. 205.

It is thus apparent that at common law, at the time of the adoption of our Constitution, and throughout the major portion of the 19th century, abortion was viewed with less disfavor than under most American statutes currently in effect. Phrasing it another way, a woman enjoyed a substantially broader right to terminate a pregnancy than she does in most States today. At least with respect to the early stage of pregnancy, and very possibly without such a limitation, the opportunity to make this choice was present in this country well into the 19th century. Even later, the law continued for some time to treat less punitively an abortion procured in early pregnancy.

6. *The position of the American Medical Association*   The anti-abortion mood prevalent in this country in the late 19th century was shared by the medical profession. Indeed, the attitude of the profession may have played a significant role in the enactment of stringent criminal abortion legislation during that period.

An AMA Committee on Criminal Abortion was appointed in May 1857. It presented its report, 12 Trans. of the Am. Med. Assn. 73–78 (1859), to the Twelfth Annual Meeting. That report observed that the Committee had been appointed to investigate criminal abortion "with a view to its general suppression." It deplored abortion and its frequency and it listed three causes of "this general demoralization":

"The first of these causes is a wide-spread popular ignorance of the true character of the crime—a belief, even among mothers themselves, that the foetus is not alive till after the period of quickening.

"The second of the agents alluded to is the fact that the profession themselves are frequently supposed careless of foetal life. . . .

"The third reason of the frightful extent of this crime is found in the grave defects of our laws, both common and statute, as regards the independent and actual existence of the child before birth, as a living being. These errors, which are sufficient in most instances to prevent conviction, are based, and only based, upon mistaken and exploded medical dogmas. With strange inconsistency, the law fully acknowledges the foetus in utero and its inherent rights, for civil purposes; while personally and as criminally affected, it fails to recognize it, and to its life as yet denies all protection." *Id.*, at 75–76.

The Committee then offered, and the Association adopted, resolutions protesting "against such unwarrantable destruction of human life," calling upon state legislatures to revise their abortion laws, and requesting the cooperation of state medical societies "in pressing the subject." *Id.*, at 28, 78.

In 1871 a long and vivid report was submitted by the Committee on Criminal Abortion. It ended with the observation, "We had to deal with human life. In a matter of less importance we could entertain no compromise. An honest judge on the bench would call things by their proper names. We could do no less." 22 Trans. of the Am. Med. Assn. 258 (1871). It proffered resolutions, adopted by the Association, *id.*, at 38–39, recommending, among other things, that it "be unlawful and unprofessional for any physician to induce abortion or premature labor, without the concurrent opinion of at least one respectable consulting physician, and then always with a view to the safety of the child—if that be possible," and calling "the attention of the clergy of all denominations to the perverted views of morality entertained by a large class of females—aye, and men also, on this important question."

Except for periodic condemnation of the criminal abortionist, no further formal AMA action took place until 1967. In that year, the Committee on Human Reproduction urged the adoption of a stated policy of opposition to induced abortion, except when there is "documented medical evidence" of a threat to the health or life of the mother, or that the child "may be born with incapacitating physical deformity or mental deficiency," or that a pregnancy "resulting from legally established statutory or forcible rape or incest may constitute a threat to the mental or physical health of the patient," two other physicians "chosen because of their recognized professional competence have examined the patient and have concurred in writing," and the procedure "is performed in a hospital accredited by the Joint Commission on Accreditation of Hospitals." The providing of medical information by physicians to state legislatures in their consideration of legislation regarding therapeutic abortion was "to be considered consistent with the principles of ethics of the American Medical Association." This recommendation was adopted by the House of Delegates. Proceedings of the AMA House of Delegates 40–51 (June 1967).

In 1970, after the introduction of a variety of proposed resolutions, and of a report from its Board of Trustees, a reference committee noted "polarization of the medical profession on this controversial issue"; division among those who had testified; a difference of opinion among AMA councils and committees; "the remarkable shift in testimony" in six months, felt to be influenced "by the rapid changes in state laws and by the judicial decisions which tend to make abortion more freely available;" and a feeling "that this trend will continue." On June 25, 1970, the House of Delegates adopted preambles and most of the resolutions proposed by the reference committee. The preambles emphasized "the best interests of the patient," "sound clinical judgment," and "informed patient consent," in contrast to "mere acquiescence to the patient's demand." The resolutions asserted that abortion is a medical procedure that should be performed by a licensed physician in an accredited hospital only after consultation with two other physicians and in conformity with state law, and that no party to the procedure should be required to violate personally held moral principles.[38] Proceedings of the AMA House of Delegates 220 (June 1970). The AMA Judicial Council rendered a complementary opinion.[39]

7. *The position of the American Public Health Association* In October 1970, the Executive Board of the APHA adopted Standards for Abortion Services. These were five in number:

"a. Rapid and simple abortion referral must be readily available through state and local public health departments, medical societies, or other nonprofit organizations.

"b. An important function of counseling should be to simplify and expedite the provision of abortion services; it should not delay the obtaining of these services.

"c. Psychiatric consultation should not be mandatory. As in the case of other specialized medical services, psychiatric consultation should be sought for definite indications and not on a routine basis.

"d. A wide range of individuals from appropriately trained, sympathetic volunteers to highly skilled physicians may qualify as abortion counselors.

"e. Contraception and/or sterilization should be discussed with each abortion patient." Recommended Standards for Abortion Services, 61 Am. J. Pub. Health 396 (1971).

Among factors pertinent to life and health risks associated with abortion were three that "are recognized as important":

"a. the skill of the physician,

"b. the environment in which the abortion is performed, and above all

"c. the duration of pregnancy, as determined by uterine size and confirmed by menstrual history." *Id.*, at 397.

It was said that "a well-equipped hospital" offers more protection "to cope with unforeseen difficulties than an office or clinic without such resources. . . . The factor of gestational age is of overriding importance." Thus, it was recommended that abortions in the second trimester and early abortions in the presence of existing medical complications be performed in hospitals as in-patient procedures. For pregnancies in the first trimester, abortion in the hospital with or without overnight stay "is probably the safest practice." An abortion in an extramural facility, however, is an acceptable alternative, "provided arrangements exist in advance to admit patients promptly if unforeseen complications develop." Standards for an abortion facility were listed. It was said that at present abortions should be performed by physicians or osteopaths who are licensed to practice and who have "adequate training." *Id.*, at 398.

8. *The position of the American Bar Association*   At its meeting in February 1972, the ABA House of Delegates approved, with 17 opposing votes, the Uniform Abortion Act that had been drafted and approved the preceding August by the Conference of Commissioners on Uniform State Laws. 58 A.B.A.J. 380 (1972). . . .

VII

Three reasons have been advanced to explain historically the enactment of criminal abortion laws in the 19th century and to justify their continued existence.

It has been argued occasionally that these laws were the product of a Victorian social concern to discourage illicit sexual conduct. Texas, however, does not advance this justification in the present case, and it appears that no court or commentator has taken the argument seriously. The appellants and *amici* contend, moreover, that this is not a proper state purpose at all and suggest that, if it were, the Texas statutes are overbroad in protecting it since the law fails to distinguish between married and unwed mothers.

A second reason is concerned with abortion as a medical procedure. When most criminal abortion laws were first enacted, the procedure was a hazardous one for the woman. This was particularly true prior to the development of antisepsis. Antiseptic techniques, of course, were based on discoveries by Lister, Pasteur, and others first announced in 1867, but were not generally accepted and employed until about the turn of the century. Abortion mortality was high. Even after 1900, and perhaps until as late as the development of antibiotics in the 1940s, standard modern techniques such as dilation and curettage were not nearly so safe as they are today. Thus, it has been argued that a State's real concern in enacting a criminal abortion law was to protect the pregnant woman, that is, to restrain her from submitting to a procedure that placed her life in serious jeopardy.

Modern medical techniques have altered this situation. Appellants and various *amici* refer to medical data indicating that abortion in early pregnancy, that is, prior to the end of the first trimester, although not without its risk, is now relatively safe. Mortality rates for women undergoing early abortions, where the procedure is legal, appear to be as low as or lower than the rates for normal childbirth.[44] Consequently, any interest of the State in protecting the woman from an inherently hazardous procedure, except when it would be equally dangerous for her to forgo it, has largely disappeared. Of course, important state interests in the areas of health and medical standards do remain. The State has a legitimate interest in seeing to it that abortion, like any other medical procedure, is performed under circumstances that insure maximum safety for the patient. This interest obviously extends at least to the performing physician and his staff, to the facilities involved, to the availability of aftercare, and to adequate provision for any complication or emergency that might arise. The prevalence of high mortality rates at illegal "abortion mills" strengthens, rather than weakens, the State's interest in regulating the conditions under which abortions are performed. Moreover, the risk to the woman increases as her pregnancy continues. Thus, the State retains a definite interest in protecting the woman's own health and safety when an abortion is proposed at a late stage of pregnancy.

The third reason is the State's interest—some phrase it in terms of duty—in protecting prenatal life. Some of the argument for this justification rests on the theory that a new human life is present from the moment of conception.[45] The State's interest and general obligation to protect life then extends, it is argued, to prenatal life. Only when the life of the pregnant mother herself is at stake, balanced against the life she carries within her, should the interest of the embryo or fetus not prevail. Logically, of course, a legitimate state interest in this area need not stand or fall on acceptance of the belief that life begins at conception or at some other point prior to live birth. In assessing the State's interest, recognition may be given to the less rigid claim that as long as at least *potential* life is involved, the State may assert interests beyond the protection of the pregnant woman alone.

Parties challenging state abortion laws have sharply disputed in some courts the contention that a purpose of these laws, when enacted, was to protect prenatal life.[46] Pointing to the absence of legislative history to support the contention, they claim that most state laws were designed solely to protect the woman. Because medical advances have lessened this concern, at least with respect to abortion in early pregnancy, they argue that with respect to such abortions the laws can no longer be justified by any state interest. There is some scholarly support for this view of original purpose.[47] The few state courts called upon to interpret their laws in the late 19th and early 20th centuries did focus on the State's intereset in protecting the woman's health rather than in preserving the embryo and fetus.[48] Proponents of this view point out that in many States, including Texas,[49] by statute or judicial interpretation, the pregnant woman herself could not be prosecuted for self-abortion or for cooperating in an abortion performed upon her by another.[50] They claim that adoption of the "quickening" distinction through received common law and state statutes tacitly recognizes the greater health hazards inherent in late abortion and impliedly repudiates the theory that life begins at conception.

It is with these interests, and the weight to be attached to them, that this case is concerned.

VIII

The Constitution does not explicitly mention any right of privacy. In a line of decisions, however, going back perhaps as far as *Union Pacific R. Co. v. Botsford*, 141 U.S. 250, 251 (1891), the Court has recognized that a right of personal privacy, or a guarantee of certain areas or zones of privacy, does exist under the Constitution. In varying contexts, the Court or individual Justices have, indeed, found at least the roots of that right in the First Amendment, *Stanley* v. *Georgia*, 394 U.S. 557, 564 (1969); in the Fourth and Fifth Amendments, *Terry* v. *Ohio*, 392 U.S. 1, 8–9 (1968), *Katz* v. *United States*, 389 U.S. 347, 350 (1967), *Boyd* v. *United States*, 116 U.S. 616 (1886), see *Olmstead* v. *United States*, 277 U.S. 438, 478 (1928) (Brandeis, J., dissenting); in the penumbras of the Bill of Rights, *Griswold* v. *Connecticut*, 381 U.S., at 484–485; in the Ninth Amendment, *id.*, at 486 (Goldberg, J., concurring); or in the concept of liberty guaranteed by the first section of the Fourteenth Amendment, see *Meyer* v. *Nebraska*, 262 U.S. 390, 399 (1923). These decisions make it clear that only personal rights that can be deemed "fundamental" or "implicit in the concept of ordered liberty," *Palko* v. *Connecticut*, 302 U.S. 319, 325 (1937), are included in this guarantee of personal privacy. They also make it clear that the right has some extension to activities relating to marriage, *Loving* v. *Virginia*, 388 U.S. 1, 12 (1967); procreation, *Skinner* v. *Oklahoma*, 316 U.S. 535, 541–542 (1942); contraception, *Eisenstadt* v. *Baird*, 405 U.S., at 453–454; *id.*, at 460, 463–465 (White, J., concurring in result); family relationships, *Prince* v. *Massachusetts*, 321 U.S. 158, 166 (1944); and child rearing and education, *Pierce* v. *Society of Sisters*, 268 U.S. 510, 535 (1925), *Meyer* v. *Nebraska, supra.*

This right of privacy, whether it be founded in the Fourteenth Amendment's concept of personal liberty and restrictions upon state action, as we feel it is, or, as the District Court determined, in the Ninth Amendment's reservation of rights to the people, is broad enough to encompass a woman's decision whether or not to terminate her pregnancy. The detriment that the State would impose upon the pregnant woman by denying this choice altogether is apparent. Specific and direct harm medically diagnosable even in early pregnancy may be involved. Maternity, or additional offspring, may force upon the woman a distressful life and future. Psychological harm may be imminent. Mental and physical health may be taxed by child care. There is also the distress, for all concerned, associated with the unwanted child, and there is the problem of bringing a child into a family already unable, psychologically and otherwise, to care for it. In other cases, as in this one, the additional difficulties and continuing stigma of unwed motherhood may be involved. All these are factors the woman and her responsible physician necessarily will consider in consultation.

On the basis of elements such as these, appellant and some *amici* argue that the woman's right is absolute and that she is entitled to terminate her pregnancy at whatever time, in whatever way, and for whatever reason she alone chooses. With this we do not agree. Appellant's arguments that Texas either has no valid interest at all in regulating the abortion decision, or no interest strong enough to support any limitation upon the woman's sole determination, are unpersuasive. The Court's decisions recognizing a right of privacy also acknowledge that some state regulation in areas protected by that right is appropriate. As noted above, a State may properly assert important interests in safeguarding health, in maintaining medical standards, and in protecting potential life. At some point in pregnancy, these respective interests become sufficiently compelling to sustain regulation of the factors that govern the abortion decision. The privacy right involved, therefore, cannot be said to be absolute. In fact, it is not clear to us that the claim asserted by some *amici* that one has an unlimited right to do with one's body as one pleases bears a close relationship to the right of privacy previously articulated in the Court's decisions. The Court has refused to recognize an unlimited right of this kind in the past. *Jacobson* v. *Massachusetts,* 197 U.S. 11 (1905) (vaccination); *Buck* v. *Bell,* 274 U.S. 200 (1927) (sterilization).

We, therefore, conclude that the right of personal privacy includes the abortion decision, but that this right is not unqualified and must be considered against important state interests in regulation.

We note that those federal and state courts that have recently considered abortion law challenges have reached the same conclusion. . . . Although the results are divided, most of these courts have agreed that the right of privacy, however based, is broad enough to cover the abortion decision; that the right, nonetheless, is not absolute and is subject to some limitations; and that at some point the state interests as to protection of health, medical standards, and prenatal life, become dominant. We agree with this approach.

Where certain "fundamental rights" are involved, the Court has held that regulation limiting these rights may be justified only by a "compelling state interest," *Kramer* v. *Union Free School District,* 395 U.S. 621, 627 (1969); *Shapiro* v. *Thompson,* 394 U.S. 618, 634 (1969), *Sherbert* v. *Verner,* 374 U.S. 398, 406 (1963), and that legislative enactments must be narrowly drawn to express only the legitimate state interests at stake. *Griswold* v. *Connecticut,* 381 U.S., at 485; *Aptheker* v. *Secretary of State,* 378 U.S. 500, 508 (1964); *Cantwell* v. *Connecticut,* 310 U.S. 296, 307–308 (1940); see *Eisenstadt* v. *Baird,* 405 U.S., at 460, 463–464 (WHITE, J., concurring in result).

In the recent abortion cases, cited above, courts have recognized these principles. Those striking down state laws have generally scrutinized the State's interests in protecting health and potential life, and have concluded that neither interest justified broad limitations on the reasons for which a physician and his pregnant patient might decide that she should have an abortion in the early stages of pregnancy. Courts sustaining state laws have held that the State's determinations to protect health or prenatal life are dominant and constitutionally justifiable.

IX

The District Court held that the appellee failed to meet his burden of demonstrating that the Texas statute's infringement upon Roe's rights was necessary to support a compelling state interest, and that, although the appellee presented "several compelling justifications for state presence in the area of abortions," the statutes outstripped these justifications and swept "far beyond any areas of compelling state interest." 314 F. Supp., at 1222–1223. Appellant and appellee both contest that holding. Appellant, as has been indicated, claims an absolute right that bars any state imposition of criminal penalties in the area. Appellee argues that the State's determination to recognize and protect prenatal life from and after conception constitutes a compelling state interest. As noted above, we do not agree fully with either formulation.

A. The appellee and certain *amici* argue that the fetus is a "person" within the language and meaning of the Fourteenth Amendment. In support of this, they outline at length and in detail the well-known facts of fetal development. If this suggestion of personhood is established, the appellant's case, of course, collapses, for the fetus's right to life would then be guaranteed specifically by the Amendment. The appellant conceded as much on reargument.[51] On the other hand, the appellee conceded on reargument[52] that no case could be cited that holds that a fetus is a person within the meaning of the Fourteenth Amendment.

The Constitution does not define "person" in so many words. Section 1 of the Fourteenth Amendment contains three references to "person." The first, in defining "citizens," speaks of "persons born or naturalized in the United States." The word also appears both in the Due Process Clause and in the Equal Protection Clause. "Person" is used in other places in the Constitution: in the listing of qualifications for Representatives and Senators, Art. I, § 2, cl. 2, and § 3, cl. 3; in the Apportionment Clause, Art. I, § 2, cl. 3;[53] in the Migration and Importation provision, Art. I, § 9, cl. 1; in the Emolument Clause, Art. 1, § 9, cl. 8; in the Electors provisions, Art. II, § 1, cl. 2, and the superseded cl. 3; in the provision outlining qualifications for the office of President, Art. II, § 1, cl. 5; in the Extradition provisions, Art. IV, § 2, cl. 2, and the superseded Fugitive Slave Clause 3; and in the Fifth, Twelfth, and Twenty-second Amendments, as well as in §§ 2 and 3 of the Fourteenth Amendment. But in nearly all these instances, the use of the word is such that it has application only postnatally. None indicates, with any assurance, that it has any possible pre-natal application.[54]

All this, together with our observation, *supra*, that throughout the major portion of the 19th century prevailing legal abortion practices were far freer than they are today, persuades us that the word "person," as used in the Fourteenth Amendment, does not include the unborn. . . . This conclusion, however, does not of itself fully answer the contentions raised by Texas, and we pass on to other considerations.

B. The pregnant woman cannot be isolated in her privacy. She carries an embryo and, later, a fetus, if one accepts the medical definitions of the developing young in the human uterus. See Dorland's Illustrated Medical Dictionary 478–479, 547 (24th ed. 1965). The situation therefore is inherently different from marital intimacy, or bedroom possession of obscene material, or marriage, or procreation, or education, with which *Eisenstadt* and *Griswold, Stanley, Loving, Skinner* and *Pierce* and *Meyer* were respectively concerned. As we have intimated above, it is reasonable and appropriate for a State to decide that at some point in time another interest, that of health of the mother or that of potential human life, becomes significantly involved. The woman's privacy is no longer sole and any right of privacy she possesses must be measured accordingly.

Texas urges that, apart from the Fourteenth Amendment, life begins at conception and is present throughout pregnancy, and that, therefore, the State has a compelling interest in protecting that life from and after conception. We need not resolve the difficult question of when life begins. When those trained in the respective disciplines of medicine, philosophy, and theology are unable to arrive at any consensus, the judiciary, at this point in the development of man's knowledge, is not in a position to speculate as to the answer.

It should be sufficient to note briefly the wide divergence of thinking on this most sensitive and difficult question. There has always been strong support for the view that life does not begin until live birth. This was the belief of the Stoics.[56] It appears to be the predominant, though not the unanimous, attitude of the Jewish faith.[57] It may be taken to represent also the position of a large segment of the Protestant community, insofar as that can be ascertained; organized groups that have taken a formal position on the abortion issue have generally regarded abortion as a matter for the conscience of the individual and her family.[58] As we have noted, the common law found greater significance in quickening. Physicians and their scientific colleagues have regarded that event with less interest and have tended to focus either upon conception, upon live birth, or upon the interim point at which the fetus becomes "viable," that is, potentially able to live outside the mother's womb, albeit with artificial aid.[59] Viability is usually placed at about seven months (28 weeks) but may occur earlier, even at 24 weeks.[60] The Aristotelian theory of "mediate animation," that held sway throughout the Middle Ages and the Renaissance in Europe, continued to be official Roman Catholic dogma until the 19th century, despite opposition to this "ensoulment" theory from those in the Church who would recognize the existence of life from the moment of conception.[61] The latter is now, of course, the official belief of the Catholic Church. As one brief *amicus* discloses, this is a view strongly held by many non-Catholics as well, and by many physicians. Substantial problems for precise definition of this view are posed, however, by new embryological data that purport to indicate that conception is a "process" over time, rather than an event, and by new medical techniques such as menstrual extraction, the "morning-after" pill, implantation of embryos, artificial insemination, and even artificial wombs.[62]

In areas other than criminal abortion, the law has been reluctant to endorse any theory that life, as we recognize it, begins before live birth, or to accord legal rights to the unborn except in narrowly defined situations and except when the rights are contingent upon live birth. For example, the traditional rule of tort law denied recovery for prenatal injuries even though the child was born alive.[63] That rule has been changed in almost every jurisdiction. In most States, recovery is said to be permitted only if the fetus was viable, or at least quick, when the injuries were sustained, though few courts have squarely so held.[64] In a recent development, generally opposed by the commentators, some states permit the parents of a stillborn child to maintain an action for wrongful death because of prenatal injuries.[65] Such an action, however, would appear to be one to vindicate the parents' interest and is thus consistent with the view that the fetus, at most, represents only the potentiality of life. Similarly, unborn children have been recognized as acquiring rights or interests by way of inheritance or other devolution of property, and have been represented by guardians *ad litem.*[66] Perfection of the interests involved, again, has generally been contingent upon live birth. In short, the unborn have never been recognized in the law as persons in the whole sense.

X

In view of all this, we do not agree that, by adopting one theory of life, Texas may override the rights of the pregnant woman that are at stake. We repeat, however, that the State does have an important and legitimate interest in preserving and protecting the health of the pregnant woman, whether she be a resident of the State or a nonresident who seeks medical consultation and treatment there, and that it has still *another* important and legitimate interest in protecting the potentiality of human life. These interests are separate and distinct. Each grows in substantiality as the woman approaches term and, at a point during pregnancy, each becomes "compelling."

With respect to the State's important and legitimate interest in the health of the mother, the "compelling" point, in the light of present medical knowledge, is at approximately the end of the first trimester. This is so because of the now-established medical fact, referred to above at 149, that until the end of the first trimester mortality in abortion may be less than mortality in normal childbirth. It follows that, from and after this point, a State may regulate the abortion procedure to the extent that the regulation reasonably relates to the preservation and protection of maternal health. Examples of permissible state regulation in this area are requirements as to the qualifications of the person who is to perform the abortion; as to the licensure of that person; as to the facility in which the procedure is to be performed, that is, whether it must be a hospital or may be a clinic or some other place of less-than-hospital status; as to the licensing of the facility; and the like.

This means, on the other hand, that, for the period of pregnancy prior to this "compelling" point, the attending physician, in consultation with his patient, is free to determine, without regulation by the State, that, in his medical judgment, the patient's pregnancy should be terminated. If that decision is reached, the judgment may be effectuated by an abortion free of interference by the State.

With respect to the State's important and legitimate interest in potential life, the "compelling" point is at viability. This is so because the fetus then presumably has the capability of meaningful life outside the mother's womb. State regulation protective of fetal life after viability thus has both logical and biological justifications. If the State is interested in protecting fetal life after viability, it may go so far as to proscribe abortion during that period, except when it is necessary to preserve the life or health of the mother.

Measured against these standards, Art. 1196 of the Texas Penal Code, in restricting legal abortions to those "procured or attempted by medical advice for the purpose of saving the life of the mother," sweeps too broadly. The statute makes no distinction between abortions performed early in pregnancy and those performed later, and it limits to a single reason, "saving" the mother's life, the legal justification for the procedure. The statute, therefore, cannot survive the constitutional attack made upon it here. . . .

XI

To summarize and to repeat:

1. A state criminal abortion statute of the current Texas type, that excepts from criminality only a *lifesaving* procedure on behalf of the mother, without regard to pregnancy stage and without recognition of the other interests involved, is violative of the Due Process Clause of the Fourteenth Amendment.

(a) For the stage prior to approximately the end of the first trimester, the abortion decision and its effectuation must be left to the medical judgment of the pregnant woman's attending physician.

(b) For the stage subsequent to approximately the end of the first trimester, the State, in promoting its interest in the health of the mother, may, if it chooses, regulate the abortion procedure in ways that are reasonably related to maternal health.

(c) For the stage subsequent to viability, the State in promoting its interest in the potentiality of human life may, if it chooses, regulate, and even proscribe, abortion except where it is necessary, in appropriate medical judgment, for the preservation of the life or health of the mother.

2. The State may define the term "physician," as it has been employed in the preceding paragraphs of this Part XI of this opinion, to mean only a physician currently licensed by the State, and may proscribe any abortion by a person who is not a physician as so defined.

In *Doe* v. *Bolton, post,* p. 179, procedural requirements contained in one of the modern abortion statutes are considered. That opinion and this one, of course, are to be read together.[67]

This holding, we feel, is consistent with the relative weights of the respective interests involved, with the lessons and examples of medical and legal history, with the lenity of the common law, and with the demands of the profound problems of the present day. The decision leaves the State free to place increasing restrictions on abortion as the period of pregnancy lengthens, so long as those restrictions are tailored to the recognized state interests. The decision vindicates the right of the physician to administer medical treatment according to his professional judgment up to the points where important state interests provide compelling justifications for intervention. Up to those points, the abortion decision in all its aspects is inherently, and primarily, a medical decision, and basic responsibility for it must rest with the physician. If an individual practitioner abuses the privilege of exercising proper medical judgment, the usual remedies, judicial and intraprofessional, are available.

XII

Our conclusion that Art. 1196 is unconstitutional means, of course, that the Texas abortion statutes, as a unit, must fall. The exception of Art. 1196 cannot be struck down separately, for then the State would be left with a statute proscribing all abortion procedures no matter how medically urgent the case.

Although the District Court granted appellant Roe declaratory relief, it stopped short of issuing an injunction against enforcement of the Texas statutes. The Court has recognized that different considerations enter into a federal court's decision as to declaratory relief, on the one hand, and injunctive relief, on the other. *Zwickler* v. *Koota,* 389 U.S. 241, 252–255 (1967); *Dombrowski* v. *Pfister,* 380 U.S. 479 (1965). We are not dealing with a statute that, on its face, appears to abridge free expression, an area of particular concern under *Dombrowski* and refined in *Younger* v. *Harris,* 401 U.S., at 50. . . .

MR. JUSTICE REHNQUIST, dissenting.

The Court's opinion brings to the decision of this troubling question both extensive historical fact and a wealth of legal scholarship. While the opinion thus commands my respect, I find myself nonetheless in fundamental disagreement with those parts of it that invalidate the Texas statute in question, and therefore dissent.

I

The Court's opinion decides that a State may impose virtually no restriction on the performance of abortions during the first trimester of pregnancy. Our previous decisions indicate that a necessary predicate for such an opinion is a plaintiff who was in her first trimester of pregnancy at some time during the pendency of her lawsuit. While a party may vindicate his own constitutional rights, he may not seek vindication for the rights of others. *Moose Lodge* v. *Irvis,* 407 U.S. 163 (1972); *Sierra Club* v. *Morton,* 405 U.S. 727 (1972). The Court's statement of facts in this case makes clear, however, that the record in no way indicates the presence of such a plaintiff. We know only that plaintiff Roe at the time of filing her complaint was a pregnant woman; for aught that appears in this record, she may have been in her *last* trimester of pregnancy as of the date the complaint was filed.

Nothing in the Court's opinion indicates that Texas might not constitutionally apply its proscription of abortion as written to a woman in that stage of pregnancy. Nonetheless, the Court uses her complaint against the Texas statute as a fulcrum for deciding that States may impose virtually no restrictions on medical abortions performed during the *first* trimester of pregnancy. In deciding such a hypothetical lawsuit, the Court departs from the longstanding admonition that it should never "formulate a rule of constitutional law broader than is required by the precise facts to which it is to be applied." *Liverpool, New York & Philadelphia S. S. Co.* v. *Commissioners of Emigration,* 113 U.S. 33, 39 (1885). See also *Ashwander* v. *TVA,* 297 U.S. 288, 345 (1936) (Brandeis, J., concurring).

II

Even if there were a plaintiff in this case capable of litigating the issue which the Court decides, I would reach a conclusion opposite to that reached by the Court. I have difficulty in concluding, as the Court does, that the right of "privacy" is involved in this case. Texas, by the statute here challenged, bars the performance of a medical abortion by a licensed physician on a plaintiff such as Roe. A transaction resulting in an operation such as this is not "private" in the ordinary usage of that word. Nor is the "privacy" that the Court finds here even a distant relative of the freedom from searches and seizures protected by the Fourth Amendment to the Constitution, which the Court has referred to as embodying a right to privacy. *Katz* v. *United States,* 389 U.S. 347 (1967).

If the Court means by the term "privacy" no more than that the claim of a person to be free from unwanted state regulation of consensual transactions may be a form of "liberty" protected by the Fourteenth Amendment, there is no doubt that similar claims have been upheld in our earlier decisions on the basis of that liberty. I agree with the statement of Mr. Justice Stewart in his concurring opinion that the "liberty," against deprivation of which without due process the Fourteenth Amendment protects, embraces more than the rights found in the Bill of Rights. But that liberty is not guaranteed absolutely against deprivation, only against deprivation without due process of law. The test traditionally applied in the area of social and economic legislation is whether or not a law such as that challenged has a rational relation to a valid state objective. *Williamson* v. *Lee Optical Co.,* 348 U.S. 483, 491 (1955). The Due Process Clause of the Fourteenth Amendment undoubtedly does place a limit, albeit a broad one, on legislative power to enact laws such as this. If the Texas statute were to prohibit an abortion even where the mother's life is in jeopardy, I have little doubt that such a statute would lack a rational relation to a valid state objective under the test stated in *Williamson, supra.* But the Court's sweeping invalidation of any restrictions on abortion during the first trimester is impossible to justify under that standard, and the conscious weighing of competing factors that the Court's opinion apparently substitutes for the established test is far more appropriate to a legislative judgment than to a judicial one.

The Court eschews the history of the Fourteenth Amendment in its reliance on the "compelling state interest" test. See *Weber* v. *Aetna Casualty & Surety Co.,* 406 U.S. 164, 179 (1972) (dissenting opinion). But the Court adds a new wrinkle to this test by transposing it from the legal considerations associated with the Equal Protection Clause of the Fourteenth Amendment to this case arising under the Due Process Clause of the Fourteenth Amendment. Unless I misapprehend the consequences of this transplanting of the "compelling state interest test," the Court's opinion will accomplish the seemingly impossible feat of leaving this area of the law more confused than it found it.

While the Court's opinion quotes from the dissent of Mr. Justice Holmes in *Lochner* v. *New York,* 198 U.S. 45, 74 (1905), the result it reaches is more closely attuned to the majority opinion of Mr. Justice Peckham in that case. As in *Lochner* and similar cases applying substantive due process standards to economic and social welfare legislation, the adoption of the compelling state interest standard will inevitably require this Court to examine the legislative policies and pass on the wisdom of these policies in the very process of deciding whether a particular state interest put forward may or may not be "compelling." The decision here to break pregnancy into three distinct terms and to outline the permissible restrictions the State may impose in each one, for example, partakes more of judicial legislation than it does of a determination of the intent of the drafters of the Fourteenth Amendment.

The fact that a majority of the States reflecting, after all, the majority sentiment in those States, have had restrictions on abortions for at least a century is a strong indication, it seems to me, that the asserted right to an abortion is not "so rooted in the traditions and conscience of our people as to be ranked as fundamental," *Snyder* v. *Massachusetts,* 291 U.S. 97, 105 (1934). Even today, when society's views on abortion are changing, the very existence of the debate is evidence that the "right" to an abortion is not so universally accepted as the appellant would have us believe.

To reach its result, the Court necessarily has had to find within the scope of the Fourteenth Amendment a right that was apparently completely unknown to the drafters of the Amendment. As early as 1821, the first state law dealing directly with abortion was enacted by the Connecticut Legislature. Conn. Stat., Tit. 22, §§ 14, 16. By the time of the adoption of the Fourteenth Amendment in 1868, there were at least 36 laws enacted by state or territorial legislatures limiting abortion. While many States have amended or updated their laws, 21 of the laws on the books in 1868 remain in effect today. Indeed, the Texas statute struck down today was, as the majority notes, first enacted in 1857 and "has remained substantially unchanged to the present time."

There apparently was no question concerning the validity of this provision or of any of the other state statutes when the Fourteenth Amendment was adopted. The only conclusion possible from this history is that the drafters did not intend to have the Fourteenth Amendment withdraw from the States the power to legislate with respect to this matter.

III

Even if one were to agree that the case that the Court decides were here, and that the enunciation of the substantive constitutional law in the Court's opinion were proper, the actual disposition of the case by the Court is still difficult to justify. The Texas statute is struck down *in toto*, even though the Court apparently concedes that at later periods of pregnancy Texas might impose these selfsame statutory limitations on abortion. My understanding of past practice is that a statute found to be invalid as applied to a particular plaintiff, but not unconstitutional as a whole, is not simply "struck down" but is, instead, declared unconstitutional as applied to the fact situation before the Court. *Yick Wo* v. *Hopkins*, 118 U.S. 356 (1886); *Street* v. *New York*, 394 U.S. 576 (1969).

For all of the foregoing reasons, I respectfully dissent.

The Legacy of Roe v. Wade

Janet Benshoof

IN the history of this country no Supreme Court decision has been so important to women's liberty, equality, and health as the 1973 decision in *Roe* v. *Wade*, which declared and recognized that a woman's right to choose abortion is part of her fundamental right of privacy. In the last decade, *Roe* v. *Wade* has transformed abortion from a clandestine and dangerous ordeal into one of the safest medical procedures in the United States. The constitutional protection of abortion from governmental interference has meant that doctors can now treat pregnant patients according to their best medical judgment, and that women can now make decisions about their pregnancies that are best for their lives, their health, and their families.

Despite public health benefits and the obvious advances in granting women equal rights under law, resistance to *Roe* v. *Wade* has been similar to that following the Supreme Court decision outlawing segregated schools in *Brown* v. *Board of Education*. No issue is as hotly contested in the state and federal legislatures as is abortion. Since 1973, states and localities have passed over seventy-five pieces of legislation that have attempted to eviscerate the right to abortion by enacting criminal statutes that harass doctors and put obstacles in the path of women needing abortions. This controversy has naturally extended to the courts. In fact, the Supreme Court is currently deciding three cases that will clarify the exact scope of *Roe* v. *Wade* and decide whether courts must view abortion with the same degree of strict constitutional scrutiny with which they must view other fundamental constitutional rights, or whether abortion will be further singled out and treated as a lesser right under law.[1]

A focal point of the criticism surrounding *Roe* v. *Wade* over the last ten years has been that the Supreme Court, in a spirit of well-motivated judicial activism, fabricated a right to abortion from a Constitution that is notably silent about such matters. Antiabortion activists try to portray the Supreme Court decision as an aberration in constitutional law, rather than as the logical and inevitable corollary of other Court decisions on privacy. This perspective is wrong. *Roe* v. *Wade* has less to do with the granting of a new, affirmative constitutional right than it does with a consistent recognition that the Fourteenth Amendment guarantees of liberty restrict governmental interference in decisionmaking about personal matters. *Roe* v. *Wade* flows out of a history of constitutional recognition that certain intimate areas must be free from governmental intrusion.

This essay focuses briefly on the history of the right to privacy, and on the scope of *Roe* v. *Wade* and the evolution of the constitutional right to choose abortion subsequent to this case. It concludes by explaining how issues currently before the Supreme Court present the opportunity to alter substantially the constitutional guarantee now attached to the right to choose abortion, and to further segregate abortion from other constitutional rights.

Because the word "privacy" does not explicitly appear in the Bill of Rights, the right to privacy is less well defined than other fundamental constitutional rights. It is less understood as critical to our form of constitutional democracy and, accordingly, is given less respect by legislatures, courts, and the general public. Although the Bill of Rights guarantees certain rights to individuals, its enumeration of what rights we have is not complete, nor was it intended to be complete by the framers of our Constitution. The Constitution would not have been ratified without the promise that a Bill of Rights would be adopted, even though some of the framers considered such rights so obvious and implicit that additional guarantees were unnecessary. Other framers considered it imperative that it contain explicit legal limits on the power of government. The proponents of a Bill of Rights wanted to ensure that listing explicit rights, such as the guarantee against establishment of religion, would never be taken to imply that other rights are excluded. The Ninth Amendment thus make clear that "the enumeration in the Constitution, of certain rights, shall not be construed to deny or disparage others retained by the people." Therefore, although the Constitution never mentions a "right to privacy"—in those exact words—or a right to marry, or a right to raise one's children, these rights, as well as procreative rights, are protected as fundamental constitutional rights.

As early as 1891, the Supreme Court recognized that a guarantee of privacy exists under the Constitution. The Court's most comprehensive definition of this right is contained in a decision entitled *Whalen* v. *Roe*, 429 U.S. 589 (1977). The Court defined privacy as consisting of two distinct protections. First, privacy means an individual's right not to disclose certain matters to the public or to the government. Second, privacy means the independence to make certain kinds of important decisions, such as the right to have an abortion or the right to marry. In some cases, such as abortion, both kinds of privacy are involved. You not only have the right to make that decision, but you also have the right to make it anonymously, without governmental or public knowledge. It would violate your constitutional right to privacy if you could have an abortion but were required to register publicly that you were pregnant and to say publicly which choice you were making.

The Supreme Court has ruled that the right to privacy, which is basically a right to personal autonomy under our Constitution, is guaranteed by the Fourteenth Amendment, which ensures that an individual will not be deprived of liberty without due process of law. The importance of an individual's control over his or her own reproductive life was first recognized by the Court in 1942, in *Skinner* v. *Oklahoma*, 316 U.S. 535 (1942), when the Court invalidated an Oklahoma statute that mandated that certain felons be sterilized. This concept, that procreative decisions are protected by the right to privacy, was further developed when in *Griswold* v. *Connecticut*, 381 U.S. 479 (1965), the Supreme Court struck down a Connecticut law that prohibited the use of contraceptives even by married persons. In that decision, the Court declared that the state could not interfere with private decisions—that is, with decisions lying within the zone of privacy. In *Eisenstadt* v. *Baird*, 405 U.S. 438 (1972), the Court struck down a Massachusetts law forbidding contraceptives to unmarried persons, making clear that the right to privacy did not attach to the marital relationship, but to the individual. In that decision, the Court stated:

If the right to privacy means anything, it is the right of the *individual*, married or single, to be free from unwarranted governmental intrusion into matters so fundamentally affecting a person as the decision whether to bear or beget a child. [*Eisenstadt* v. *Baird*, 405 U.S. 438, 453 (1972)]

These two cases provided the critical precedents for the 1973 abortion decisions.

In 1973, the Supreme Court, by a 7–2 vote, ruled that a Texas criminal abortion statute and portions of a Georgia law were unconstitutional on the grounds that they violated a woman's right to privacy under the Fourteenth Amendment. These cases—*Roe* v. *Wade,* 410 U.S. 113 (1973), and *Doe* v. *Bolton,* 410 U.S. 179 (1973)—also established how courts were to review future abortion restrictions. It is important to examine these cases in some detail, because it is against these principles that the constitutionality of all related legislation is measured.

Justice Blackmun wrote the decision in *Roe* v. *Wade.* In writing the opinion of the Court, he made it clear that the right to privacy was broad enough to encompass a woman's decision of whether or not to terminate her pregnancy. However, *Roe* v. *Wade* does not give a woman the right to abortion on demand, nor does it grant an unqualified right to abortion. Justice Blackmun struggled to accommodate the different interests involved. It is neither an unqualified victory for women, nor an unqualified victory for doctors. The Court held that only two legitimate interests can be asserted to support state interference in the abortion decision: the state may claim a legitimate interest in maternal health in regulating abortions after the first trimester of pregnancy; and it can assert an interest in potential life, but only in the third trimester. In the first trimester, the decision to have an abortion must be between a woman and her doctor, and the state cannot interfere. Therefore, in the first trimester of pregnancy, the state should not be able to dictate where the abortion takes place, what the doctor tells the woman, how long the woman must wait, or what technique must be used.

A state may issue rules covering the second trimester of pregnancy, but only if they are tailored to promote women's health. For example, if a new abortion technique were developed that could endanger a woman's health if performed in the second trimester—in relation to other, equally available methods—it would be legitimate for the state to pass a law outlawing that technique in the second trimester.

In the third trimester, at which point the fetus is considered viable ("potentially able to live outside the mother's womb, albeit with artificial aid," *Roe* v. *Wade,* 410 U.S. at 160), the state may, if it chooses, regulate or proscribe abortion to protect fetal life. However, if a state does choose to outlaw third-trimester abortion, the law must contain an exception permitting abortion if a woman's health or life is at stake. Her right to bodily integrity must prevail over the state's interest in promoting fetal life.

Given this construct, and given the fact that about 90 percent of all abortions in this country are performed during the first trimester, it is clear that *Roe* v. *Wade* severely—indeed, almost completely—limits the state's ability to restrict abortion. During the first trimester of pregnancy, abortion cannot be prohibited or regulated for any reason. Laws may be passed which regulate the second trimester, but the laws must be strictly scrutinized by the courts to see that they are necessary to protect maternal health. And abortion cannot be prohibited even during the third trimester if a woman's life or health is at stake.

Many opponents of abortion insist that the Supreme Court has never ruled—or has never had the opportunity to rule—on whether the fetus is a human person. This is not true. In the 1973 cases, there was considerable evidence before the Court on fetal development and on the biological processes of life, evidence that was fully considered but was rejected by the Court as irrelevant to the constitutional question before it. The Court held that it did not need to resolve the difficult question of when life begins because the fetus is not a person under the Fourteenth Amendment. Even Justice Rehnquist, the most conservative member of the Court, conceded in his dissent that a right to privacy exists to a certain extent within the liberty guaranteed by the Fourteenth Amendment, for he stated that it would be unconstitutional for a legislature to protect fetal life at the expense of a woman's life.

In *Doe* v. *Bolton*, 410 U.S. 179 (1973), a companion case to *Roe* v. *Wade,* the Court examined a liberalized Georgia abortion statute that contained some procedural restrictions, such as a hospital requirement, a requirement that two doctors concur on the need for the abortion, and a Georgia residency requirement. The Court struck down these provisions on the grounds that they violated the right to privacy. Although in this decision the Court declared that abortion cannot be singled out and treated differently from other surgical procedures, the Court has subsequently retreated from that position and has tolerated singling out abortion from other medical procedures. In retrospect, *Roe* v. *Wade* did set the stage for a different treatment of abortion as a constitutional right, as opposed to other fundamental constitutional rights. First, abortion involves serious medical, ethical, social, and religious questions. The 1973 decisions did not answer any of these questions, nor did they prevent abortion from becoming the most politicized social controversy of the day. Second, *Roe* v. *Wade* is very unusual in constitutional law, in that it creates a standard of judicial review that permits laws to do different things at different points in pregnancy. The rationale for dividing a woman's pregnancy into three trimesters, and according different protections to each trimester, was medical safety; in 1973, abortions performed during the first trimester were much safer than childbirth, but during the second trimester the risks were about equal to those of childbirth. What we are now facing in the area of constitutional litigation is the fact that these medical predicates to the construct formulated in *Roe* v. *Wade* are changing. With new advances in medical technology, abortions are becoming increasingly safer. Legal abortion today is ten times as safe as it was in 1970. Although second-trimester abortions were as risky as childbirth in 1973, new abortion techniques have made most second-trimester abortions today twice as safe as childbirth. There is no longer the reason for second-trimester regulations that the Supreme Court found so compelling in 1973.

Examining the Supreme Court decisions on abortion subsequent to *Roe* v. *Wade* is important for two reasons. First, these decisions answer many of the legal questions left open in *Roe*. Second, by tracing the language—if not the actual rulings—of the various decisions by the Court since 1973, one can discern a subtle but definite trend, a retreat by the Court from its initially firm ruling that the right to an abortion enjoys absolute, fundamental constitutional protection. The change in language over the last ten years illustrates the fact that the Court is not immune to political pressure, even though, as in the case of abortion, the pressure exerted represents the views of only a minority of Americans. Despite this change, *Roe* v. *Wade* and *Doe* v. *Bolton* have remained surprisingly strong legal precedents and have repeatedly been reaffirmed by lower courts that have examined restrictive antiabortion statutes.

In *Planned Parenthood of Central Missouri* v. *Danforth*, 428 U.S. 52 (1976), the Court struck down many portions of a Missouri ordinance. It was held to be unconstitutional for a state to require a husband's consent before a woman could have an abortion; the Court reasoned that if the state cannot forbid a woman to have an abortion during the first trimester, the state couldn't delegate to her husband the power to do the same thing. Similarly, the Court invalidated a requirement that all minors, no matter how mature or under what circumstances, had to obtain at least one parent's consent. The Court used the same rationale, stressing that minors have a right to privacy, and that if a state can't eliminate that right for minors, it can't delegate to her parents the power to deny a minor's right to abortion. The Missouri statute also attempted to eliminate most second-trimester abortions by forbidding one particular kind of abortion, saline amniocentesis, which was the only technique available for second-trimester abortions in Missouri at the time. The Court also held this prohibition unconstitutional, finding that, despite the ostensible legislative reason, this regulation did not promote maternal health, in that it prohibited a technique widely accepted in the medical community and which was the only one available.

But this 1976 decision did step back from the language used in *Roe* v. *Wade* in that, for the first time, the Court ruled that Missouri could attach to abortion certain requirements, such as those involving record-keeping and informed consent, even though such requirements were not attached to comparable surgical procedures.

In another important decision, *Colautti* v. *Franklin*, 439 U.S. 379 (1979), the Supreme Court agreed with a lower court that a Pennsylvania statute was unconstitutional, in that it imposed criminal penalties on doctors who failed to use the abortion technique most likely to result in a live birth when a fetus was "viable" or "[might] be viable." The Court held that the statute was void because its vague language precluded good faith judgments by doctors. This decision reaffirms the principles in *Roe* and supports a doctor's ability to use discretion when making medical judgments. It also serves as a warning to all legislatures that they cannot promote fetal life by criminalizing the conduct of doctors, or by intimidating doctors from ever performing abortions if they think that their good faith medical judgments will be questioned.

Since 1973, there have been four cases dealing with minors' rights to abortion. Restrictions in this area are the most popular item on the agenda of antiabortion activists. The Supreme Court has indicated that you can more easily regulate a minor's access to abortion than you can regulate that of an adult woman. The majority of the justices in the Court have held that states can require minors to obtain the consent of their parents or to have their parents notified before they can have an abortion, *Bellotti* v. *Baird*, 443 U.S. 622 (1979); *H. L.* v. *Matheson*, 450 U.S. 398 (1981). However, any such statutes must establish a mechanism by which the minor can go to a state court and prove that she is mature and able to make her decision without her parents' knowledge, or, even if she is immature, that there are reasons why her parents should not know about the abortion. This kind of statute has passed in Massachusetts, Louisiana, Minnesota, Indiana, Utah, Arizona, North Dakota, Nebraska, and Missouri. In states whose laws present this kind of obstacle for minors, what we see is the survival of the fittest: minors who live in urban areas, who have boyfriends or older family members who can help them navigate through a court system; minors who have some money so that they can travel to a nearby state that doesn't have such a law—these are the minors who are still able to get safe, early abortions. But minors who live in rural Minnesota, where the judge down the street is a family friend; those who are far away from urban areas where they can't get counseling from Planned Parenthood; those who have no money, so that they would have to drive 500 or 600 miles across North Dakota to get to a states that does not have such a law—these are the minors who can't get abortions. In states that have implemented this kind of statute, about one-third fewer minors get abortions every year. The minors who do not get the abortions are the younger, more immature teenagers, those least prepared for the emotional and physical rigors of pregnancy and childbirth, which is their alternative.

Minors' rights to choose abortion are one serious retreat from the firm guarantees of *Roe* v. *Wade*. The second class of persons who are suffering from another retreat are poor women. In 1977, the Supreme Court decided three cases concerning abortion and indigents; two were Medicaid cases involving nonpayment for elective abortion, and one involved a public hospital in St. Louis (which was staffed by Jesuits from a nearby medical school) which refused to do any abortions for its poor patients. The Court held that in the context of a Medicaid program the state could pay for childbirth and not for abortion, and that such discrimination was legitimate and not a denial of equal protection. In 1980, in *Harris* v. *McRae*, 448 U.S. 297, the Court went even further and said that the Hyde Amendment—which eliminates federal Medicaid funding for poor women—was constitutional, even though the discrimination extended to Medicaid patients who sought *medically necessary* abortions. The argument in *Harris* v. *McRae* was that, in the context of the Medicaid program, which pays for every other medically necessary treatment for poor people, the equal protection clause precludes the state from singling out abortion and discriminating against poor women whose lives and health may be at stake because they are denied this one medical treatment. The Court rejected this argument and held that the state can promote childbirth/ fetal life in the context of using its spending power. This is a far-reaching and threatening decision, because it says that the power of the purse can influence our constitutional rights. If the states and the federal government can do with money what they cannot do with criminal statutes, to some people the result will be the same. Although in *Roe* v. *Wade* the Court stated very clearly that the government cannot promote fetal interests until the third trimester of pregnancy, and that even then it is limited in doing so, in *Harris* v. *McRae* the Court made clear that it is legitimate to promote those interests throughout pregnancy insofar as use of money is concerned. The fact that in *Harris* v. *McRae* they would uphold a promotion of fetal interests as a legitimate interest in the funding context, and hold that it is not legitimate in criminal statutes, sets forth a very dangerous constitutional demarcation between poor women and other adult women.

In 1983, ten years after the breakthrough abortion decisions, the Supreme Court decided three new abortion cases in which the scope of *Roe* v. *Wade* was defined, and which presented the Court with an opportunity to eviscerate the constitutional right to choose abortion. These three cases arise out of Missouri, Virginia, and Akron, Ohio, and involve challenges to various abortion restrictions, including the requirements that:

1. second-trimester abortion take place only in hospitals;
2. women must wait twenty-four hours between the time they are counseled by their physician and the time the abortion takes place;
3. doctors counsel their patients in a certain dictated way, providing actual medical misinformation, describing the fetus in detail (including statements about its sensitivity to pain), and making statements about abortion and human life which amount to ethical and religious statements, not medical statements, with which the doctor may or may not actually agree —all under the guise of informed consent;
4. minors' parents must consent to, or be notified of, their daughters' impending abortions.

These impediments to access to abortion, and these state-sponsored coercive efforts to make women feel guilty about choosing abortion, come before the Court at a time when the Court is under enormous pressure to give back to the states the leeway to harass women and doctors in order to promote a political goal. Furthermore, for the first time in history, the United States government has filed a brief in a case involving only state or local statutes, the Akron Ordinance case.

The Reagan Administration, in its brief filed by the Justice Department before the Supreme Court, asked that the entire constitutional standard of review be reversed insofar as abortion is concerned. Rather than treating abortion as a fundamental right, the Justice Department brief asked that abortion be considered a constitutional right with so little protection that it should fall when confronted face on by a legislative attempt to undercut it. The Justice Department termed the right to abortion a shadowy right, along with other elements of the right to privacy. If this position should be adopted by the Court, what we will have in effect will be a standardless standard. Local federal courts would not know how to rule on abortion cases, because abortion would have been singled out from other cases involving fundamental constitutional rights. The courts would be asked to weigh certain factors; to abandon the strict scrutiny test enunciated in *Roe* v. *Wade*; and to substitute an ad hoc balancing approach in which the burdens imposed by certain abortion restrictions would be weighed by the federal judges against an unlimited and unspecified number of state interests. This would leave local federal courts without clear guidance from the Supreme Court and would force local courts into policy-making rules each time they are faced with antiabortion legislation. In effect, the right to abortion would depend on where you live. This recipe for chaos came at a time when the Reagan Administration admitted in its brief that this is exactly what it believes would be most helpful. The administration stated that, in the interests of social experimentation, it would be fine if differing abortion laws applied in different places in the country. This position is not only extremely detrimental to women, in that it would undercut everything we have fought for in the last twenty years, but it is also a very radical position under our Constitution, because if the Supreme Court followed this proposal, the federal courts would lose their unique and critical role in our constitutional scheme—the power to review legislation in view of constitutional principles as the courts interpret them. By undermining the standard of judicial review, and by endorsing the idea that constitutional rights should depend on geography, the proposal by the Reagan Administration threatens the fundamental rights not only of abortion and of privacy, but also of all our fundamental rights which are not politically supported at this time.[2]

=

Roe v. Wade: A Study in Male Ideology

Catharine MacKinnon

In a society where women entered sexual intercourse willingly, where adequate contraception was a genuine social priority, there would be no "abortion issue." . . . Abortion is violence. . . . It is the offspring, and will continue to be the accuser of a more pervasive and prevalent violence, the violence of rapism. Adrienne Rich, *Of Woman Born*

THIS is a two-part feminist critique of *Roe* v. *Wade*. First I will situate abortion and the abortion right in the experience of women. The argument is that abortion is inextricable from sexuality, assuming that the feminist analysis of sexuality is our analysis of gender inequality.[1] I will then criticize the doctrinal choice to pursue the abortion right under the law of privacy. The argument is that privacy doctrine reaffirms what the feminist critique of sexuality criticizes: the public/private split. The political and ideological meaning of privacy as a legal doctrine is connected with the concrete consequences of the public/private split for the lives of women. This analysis makes *Harris* v. *McRae*, in which public funding for abortions was held not required, appear consistent with the larger meaning of *Roe*.[2]

I will neglect two important explorations, which I bracket now. The first is, What are babies to men? On one level, men respond to women's right to abort as if confronting the possibility of their own potential nonexistence—at *women's* hands, no less. On another level, men's issues of potency, of continuity as a compensation for mortality, of the thrust to embody themselves or their own image in the world, underlie their relation to babies (as well as to most everything else). To overlook these meanings of abortion to men as men, is to overlook political and strategic as well as fundamental theoretical issues, and is to misassess where much of the opposition to abortion is coming from. The second issue I bracket is one that, unlike the first, has been discussed extensively in the abortion debate: the moral rightness of abortion itself. My stance is that the abortion choice should be available and must be *women's,* but not because the fetus is not a form of life. In the usual argument, the abortion decision is made contingent on whether the fetus is a form of life. I cannot follow that. Why should not women make life or death decisions? This returns us to the first bracketed issue.

The issues I will explore have largely not been discussed in the terms I will use. What has happened instead, I think, is that women's embattled need to survive in a world hostile to our survival has precluded our exploring these issues as I am about to. That is, the perspective from which we have addressed abortion has been shaped and constrained by the very situation that the abortion issue requires us to address. We have not been able to risk thinking about these issues on our own terms because the terms have not been ours, either in sex, in life in general, or in court. The attempt to grasp women's situation on our own terms, from our own point of view, defines the feminist impulse. If doing that is risky, our situation also makes it risky not to. So, first feminism, then law.

Most women who seek abortions became pregnant while having sexual intercourse with men. Most did not mean or wish to conceive. In contrast to this fact of women's experience, the abortion debate has centered on separating control over sexuality from control over reproduction, and on separating both from gender. Liberals have supported the availability of the abortion choice as if the woman just happened on the fetus.[3] The political Right imagines that the intercourse which precedes conception is usually voluntary, only to urge abstinence, as if sex were up to women. At the same time, the Right defends male authority, specifically including a wife's duty to submit to sex. Continuing with this logic, many opponents of state funding of abortions, such as supporters of some versions of the Hyde Amendment, would permit funding of abortions when pregnancy results from rape or incest.[4] Thus, they make exceptions for those special occasions during which they presume women did not control sex. From all this I deduce that abortion's proponents and opponents share a tacit assumption that women significantly do control sex.

Feminist investigations suggest otherwise. Sexual intercourse, the most common cause of pregnancy, cannot simply be presumed coequally determined. Feminism has found that women feel compelled to preserve the appearance—which, acted upon, becomes the reality—of male direction of sexual expression, as if it is male initiative itself that we want: it is that which turns us on. Men enforce this. It is much of what men want in a woman. It is what pornography eroticizes and prostitutes provide. Rape—that is, intercourse with force that is recognized as force—is adjudicated not according to the power or force that the man wields, but according to indices of intimacy between the parties. The more intimate you are with your accused rapist, the less likely a court is to find that what happened to you was rape. Often indices of intimacy include intercourse itself. If "no" can be taken as "yes," how free can "yes" be?

Under these conditions, women often do not use birth control because of its social meaning, a meaning we did not create. Using contraception means acknowledging and planning and taking direction of intercourse, accepting one's sexual availability, and appearing nonspontaneous. It means appearing available to male incursions. A good user of contraception is a bad girl. She can be presumed sexually available and, among other consequences, raped with relative impunity. (If you think this isn't true, you should consider rape cases in which the fact that a woman had a diaphragm in is taken as an indication that what happened to her was intercourse, not rape. "Why did you have your diaphragm in?") From studies of abortion clinics, women who repeatedly seek abortions (and now I'm looking at the repeat offenders high on the list of the Right's villains, their best case for opposing abortion as female irresponsibility),[5] when asked why, say something like, "The sex just happened." Like every night for two and a half years. I wonder if a woman can be presumed to control access to her sexuality if she feels unable to interrupt intercourse to insert a diaphragm; or worse, cannot even want to, aware that she risks a pregnancy she knows she does not want. Do you think she would stop the man for any other reason, such as, for instance, the real taboo—lack of desire? If not, how is sex, hence its consequences, meaningfully voluntary for women? Norms of sexual rhythm and romance that are felt to be interrupted by women's needs are constructed against women's interests. Sex doesn't look a whole lot like freedom when it appears normatively less costly for women to risk an undesired, often painful, traumatic, dangerous, sometimes illegal, and potentially life-threatening procedure, than it is to protect oneself in advance. Yet abortion policy has never been explicitly approached in the context of how women get pregnant; that is, as a consequence of intercourse under conditions of gender inequality; that is, as an issue of forced sex.

Now we come to the law. In 1973, *Roe* v. *Wade* found that a statute that made criminal all abortions except those to save the life of the mother violated the constitutional right to privacy.[8] The privacy right had been previously created as a constitutional principle in a case that decriminalized the prescription and use of contraceptives.[7] Note that courts use the privacy rubric to connect contraception with abortion in a way that parallels what I just did under the sexuality rubric. In *Roe*, that right to privacy was found "broad enough to encompass a woman's decision whether or not to terminate her pregnancy." In 1977, three justices observed, "In the abortion context, we have held that the right to privacy shields the woman from undue state intrusion in and external scrutiny of her very personal choice." [8] In 1981, the Supreme Court in *Harris* v. *McRae* decided that this right to privacy did not mean that federal Medicaid programs had to cover medically necessary abortions. According to the Court, the privacy of the woman's choice was not unconstitutionally burdened by the government supporting her decision to continue, but not her decision to end, a conception. In support of this conclusion, the Supreme Court stated that "although the government may not place obstacles in the path of a woman's exercise of her freedom of choice, it need not remove those not of its own creation." [9] It is apparently a very short step from that which the government has a duty *not* to intervene in, to that which it has *no* duty to intervene in.

If regarded as the outer edge of the limitations on government, I think the idea of privacy embodies a tension between precluding public exposure or governmental intrusion on the one hand, and autonomy in the sense of protecting personal self-action on the other. This is a tension, not just two facets of one whole right. This tension is resolved in the liberal state by identifying the threshold of the state with its permissible extent of penetration (a term I use advisedly) into a domain that is considered free by definition: the private sphere. By this move the state secures what has been termed "an inviolable personality" by insuring what has been called "autonomy or control over the intimacies of personal identity." [10] The state does this by centering its self-restraint on body and home, especially bedroom. By staying out of marriage and the family, prominently meaning sexuality —that is to say, heterosexuality—from contraception through pornography to the abortion decision, the law of privacy proposes to guarantee individual bodily integrity, personal exercise of moral intelligence, and freedom of intimacy.[11] What it actually does is translate traditional social values into the rhetoric of individual rights as a means of subordinating those rights to specific social imperatives.[12] In feminist terms, I am arguing that the logic of *Roe* consummated in *Harris* translates the ideology of the private sphere into the individual woman's legal right to privacy as a means of subordinating women's collective needs to the imperatives of male supremacy.

This is my retrospective on *Roe* v. *Wade:* reproduction is sexual, men control sexuality, and the state supports the interest of men as a group. *Roe* does not contradict this. So why was abortion legalized; why were women even imagined to have such a right as privacy? It is not an accusation of bad faith to answer that the interests of men as a social group converge with the definition of justice embodied in law in what I call the male point of view. The way the male point of view constructs a social event or legal need will be the way that social event or legal need is framed by state policy. For example, to the extent possession is the point of sex, illegal rape will be sex with a woman who is not yours unless the act makes her yours. If part of the kick of pornography involves eroticizing the putatively prohibited, illegal pornography—obscenity—will be prohibited enough to keep pornography desirable without ever making it truly illegitimate or unavailable. If, from the male standpoint, male is the implicit definition of human, maleness will be the implicit standard by which sex equality is measured in discrimination law. In parallel terms, abortion's availability frames, and is framed by, the conditions under which men, worked out between themselves, will grant legitimacy to women to control the reproductive consequences of intercourse.

Since Freud, the social problem posed by sexuality has been perceived as the problem of the innate desire for sexual pleasure being repressed by the constraints of civilization. Inequality arises as an issue in this context only in women's repressive socialization to passivity and coolness (so-called frigidity), in women's so-called desexualization, and in the disparate consequences of biology, that is, pregnancy. Who defines what is sexual, what sexuality therefore is, to whom what stimuli are erotic and why, and who defines the conditions under which sexuality is expressed—these issues are not even available for consideration. "Civilization's" answer to these questions instead fuses women's reproductivity with our attributed sexuality in its definition of what a woman is. We are defined as women by the uses to which men put us.

In this context it becomes clear why the struggle for reproductive freedom has never included a woman's right to refuse sex. In this notion of sexual liberation, the equality issue has been framed as a struggle for women to have sex with men on the same terms as men: without consequences. In this sense the abortion right has been sought as freedom from the unequal reproductive consequences of sexual expression, with sexuality defined as centered on heterosexual genital intercourse. It has been as if biological organisms, rather than social relations, reproduce the species. But if your concern is not how more people can get more sex, if instead your concern is who defines sexuality—hence pleasure and violation—then the abortion right is situated within a very different problematic: the social and political problematic of the inequality of the sexes. As Susan Sontag said, "Sex itself is not liberating for women. Neither is more sex. . . . The question is, what sexuality shall women be liberated to enjoy?" [13] To be able to address this requires rethinking the problem of sexuality, from the repression of drives by civilization to the oppression of women by men.

Arguments for abortion under the rubric of feminism have rested upon the right to control one's own body—gender neutral. I think that argument has been appealing for the same reasons it is inadequate: Socially, women's bodies have not been ours; we have not controlled their meanings and destinies. Feminists tried to assert that control without risking the pursuit of the idea that something more might be at stake than our bodies, something closer to a net of relations in which we are (at present unescapedly) gendered.[14] Some feminists have noticed that our right to decide has become merged with an overwhelmingly male profession's right not to have his professional judgment second-guessed by the government.[15] But most abortion advocates argue in rigidly and rigorously gender-neutral terms.

Thus, for instance, because Judith Jarvis Thomson's celebrated abducted violinist had no obligation to be somebody else's life support system, women have no obligation to support a fetus.[16] Never mind that no woman who needs an abortion—no woman period—is valued, no potential a woman's life might hold is cherished, like a gender-neutral famous violinist's unencumbered possibilities. Not to mention that in that hypothetical, the underlying parallel to rape—the origin in force, in abduction, that gives the hypothetical its weight while confining its application to instances in which force is recognized as force —is seldom interrogated in the abortion context for its applicability to the normal case. And abortion policy is to apply to the normal case. So we need to talk about sex, specifically about intercourse in relation to rape in relation to conception. By avoiding this issue in the abortion context liberal feminists have obscured the unequal basis on which they are attempting to construct our personhood.

The meaning of abortion in the context of a sexual critique of gender inequality is its promise to women of sex with men on the same terms as promised to men—that is, "without consequences." Under conditions in which women do not control access to our sexuality, this facilitates women's heterosexual availability. In other words, under conditions of gender inequality, sexual liberation in this sense does not free women, it frees male sexual aggression. The availability of abortion thus removes the one remaining legitimized reason that women have had for refusing sex besides the headache. As Andrea Dworkin puts it, analyzing male ideology on abortion: "Getting laid was at stake." [17] The Playboy Foundation has supported abortion rights from day one; it continues to, even with shrinking disposable funds, on a level of priority comparable to its opposition to censorship.

Privacy doctrine is an ideal vehicle for this process. The democratic liberal ideal of the private holds that, so long as the public does not interfere, autonomous individuals interact freely and equally. Conceptually, this private is hermetic. It *means* that which is inaccessible to, unaccountable to, unconstructed by anything beyond itself. By definition, it is not part of or conditioned by anything systematic or outside of it. It is personal, intimate, autonomous, particular, individual, the original source and final outpost of the self, gender neutral. It is, in short, defined by everything that feminism reveals women have never been allowed to be or to have, and everything that women have been equated with and defined in terms of *men's* ability to have. It contradicts the liberal definition of the private to complain in public of inequality within it. In this view, no act of the state contributes to —hence should properly participate in—shaping its internal alignments or distributing its internal forces. Its inviolability by the state, framed as an individual right, presupposes that it is not already an arm of the state. In this scheme, intimacy is implicitly thought to guarantee symmetry of power. Injuries arise in violating the private sphere, not within and by and because of it.

In private, consent tends to be presumed. It is true that a showing of coercion voids this presumption. But the problem is getting anything private to be perceived as coercive. Why one would allow force in private—the "why doesn't she leave" question raised to battered women—is a question given its urgency by the social meaning of the private as a sphere of choice. But for women the measure of the intimacy has been the measure of the oppression. This is why feminism has had to explode the private. This is why feminism has seen the personal as the political. The private is public for those for whom the personal is political. In this sense, there is no private, either normatively or empirically. Feminism confronts the fact that women have no privacy to lose or to guarantee. We are not inviolable. Our sexuality is not only violable, it is—hence, we are—seen *in* and *as* our violation. To confront the fact that we have no privacy is to confront the intimate degradation of women as the public order.

In this light, a right to privacy looks like an injury got up as a gift. Freedom from public intervention coexists uneasily with any right which requires social preconditions to be meaningfully delivered. For example, if inequality is socially pervasive and enforced, equality will require intervention, not abdication, to be meaningful. But the right to privacy is not thought to require social change. It is not even thought to require any social preconditions, other than nonintervention by the public. The point for the abortion cases is not that indigency—which was the specific barrier to effective choice in *McRae* —is well within the public power to remedy, nor that the state is hardly exempt in issues of the distribution of wealth. The point is rather that *Roe* v. *Wade* presumes that government nonintervention into the private sphere promotes a woman's freedom of choice. When the alternative is jail, there is much to be said for this argument. But the *McRae* result sustains the meaning of privacy in *Roe*: women are guaranteed by the public no more than what we can get in private— that is, what we can extract through our intimate associations with men. Women with privileges get rights.

So women got abortion as a private privilege, not as a public right. We got control over reproduction that is controlled by "a man or The Man," an individual man or the doctors or the government. Abortion was not decriminalized, it was legalized. In *Roe*, the government set the stage for the conditions under which women gain access to this right. Virtually every ounce of control that women won out of legalization has gone directly into the hands of men—husbands, doctors, or fathers—or is now in the process of attempting to be reclaimed through regulation.[18] This, surely, must be what is meant by reform.

It is not inconsistent, then, that framed as a privacy right a woman's decision to abort would have no claim on public support and would genuinely not be seen as burdened by that deprivation. Privacy conceived as a right from public intervention and disclosure is the opposite of the relief that *McRae* sought for welfare women. State intervention would have provided a choice women did *not* have in private. The women in *McRae*, women whose sexual refusal has counted for particularly little, needed something to make their privacy effective.[19] The logic of the court's response resembles the logic by which women are supposed to consent to sex. Preclude the alternatives, then call the sole remaining option "her choice." The point is that the alternatives are precluded *prior to* the reach of the chosen legal doctrine. They are precluded by conditions of sex, race, and class—the very conditions the privacy frame not only leaves tacit, but which it exists to *guarantee*.

When the law of privacy restricts intrusions into intimacy, it bars change in control over that intimacy. The existing distribution of power and resources within the private sphere will be precisely what the law of privacy exists to protect. Just as pornography is legally protected as individual freedom of expression—without questioning whose .freedom and whose expression and at whose expense—abstract privacy protects abstract autonomy, without inquiring into whose freedom of action is being sanctioned, at whose expense. It is probably not coincidence that the very things feminism regards as central to the subjection of women—the very place, the body; the very relations, heterosexual; the very activities, intercourse and reproduction; and the very feelings, intimate—form the core of privacy doctrine's coverage. From this perspective, the legal concept of privacy can and has shielded the place of battery, marital rape, and women's exploited labor; has preserved the central institutions whereby women are *deprived* of identity, autonomy, control and self-definition; and has protected the primary activity through which male supremacy is expressed and enforced.

To fail to recognize the meaning of the private in the ideology and reality of women's subordination by seeking protection behind a right *to* that privacy is to cut women off from collective verification and state support in the same act. I think this has a lot to do with why we can't organize women on the abortion issue. When women are segregated in private, separated from each other, one at a time, a right *to* that privacy isolates us at once from each other and from public recourse. This right to privacy is a right of men "to be let alone" to oppress women one at a time.[20] It embodies and reflects the private sphere's existing definition of womanhood. This instance of liberalism —applied to women as if we *are* persons, gender neutral—reinforces the division between public and private that is *not* gender neutral. It is at once an ideological division that lies about women's shared experience and mystifies the unity among the spheres of women's violation. It is a very material division that keeps the private beyond public redress and depoliticizes women's subjection within it. It keeps some men out of the bedrooms of other men.

Part 2

Personhood

THE question of the personhood of the fetus is widely perceived to be the single central question in the abortion controversy. In *Roe* v. *Wade* the Supreme Court decided that a fetus is not a person for the purposes of the Fourteenth Amendment to the Constitution. Yet the Court acknowledged the complexity and importance of the arguments concerning fetal personhood:

Texas urges that, apart from the Fourteenth Amendment, life begins at conception and is present throughout pregnancy, and that, therefore, the state has a compelling interest in protecting that life from and after conception. We need not resolve the difficult question of when life begins. When those trained in the respective disciplines of medicine, philosophy, and theology are unable to arrive at any consensus, the judiciary, at this point in the development of man's knowledge, is not in a position to speculate as to the answer. [*Roe* v. *Wade*, 410 U.S. 113, 159 (1973)]

The essays in this section reject the notion that, even if it is possible to determine the answer to the personhood question, the answer would in turn resolve the abortion controversy.

In "The Juridical Status of the Fetus: A Proposal for Legal Protection for the Unborn," Patricia King argues that resolving the question of the fetus's personhood is not necessary in order to resolve any important issue about the legal status of the fetus, and that the *Roe* decision with its trimester structure does not provide sufficient guidance for resolving problems concerning the interests of fetuses.

The second section of King's essay presents a careful examination of historical reliance on birth as the point at which legal protections associated with personhood attach. She argues that the most important factor in adopting this threshold was the recognition of the capacity for independent existence. But, she argues, a more appropriate threshold is now the point of fetal viability.

The consequences of the facts of fetal development and of the adoption of a viability criterion are examined in the final two sections of King's essay. She concludes that the viability criterion strikes a fair balance between the competing interests of mature and developing humans, and that whereas it may necessarily represent a shifting threshold as medical technology develops, it is still a criterion supported by the weight of legal and ethical argument.

Ruth Macklin's "Personhood and the Abortion Debate" follows King in arguing that inquiry into the nature of personhood and the question of the threshold of its possession by the fetus is useless. She begins by reviewing definitions of personhood and accounts of fetal personhood from the bioethical literature, concluding that these criteria and their applicability to fetuses is a matter of decision rather than one of discovery—that one's prior intuitions about the abortion issue determine both one's account of personhood and one's decision as to whether the fetus is a person. Macklin examines a number of proposed criteria of personhood and rejects each as incapable of settling the debate from an independent, noncontroversial vantage point.

Finally, Macklin notes that the law offers no more help in clarifying this question. She agrees with King that questions about fetal protection and about the status of and access to abortion must be answered independently of questions concerning the personhood of the fetus.

The Juridical Status of the Fetus:
A Proposal for Legal Protection
of the Unborn

Patricia A. King

WHAT claims to protection can be asserted by a human fetus? That question, familiar to philosophy and religion, has long haunted law as well. While the philosophical and theological issues remain unresolved, and are perhaps unresolvable,[1] I believe that we can no longer avoid some resolution of the legal status of the fetus. The potential benefits of fetal research,[2] the ability to fertilize the human ovum in a laboratory dish,[3] and the increasing awareness that a mother's activities during pregnancy may affect the health of her offspring[4] create pressing policy issues that raise possible conflicts among fetuses, mothers, and researchers. This essay probes the juridical status of the fetus, assessing what it should be in light of recent developments in case law,[5] legislation,[6] medicine, and technology.[7]

Section I reviews the Supreme Court's landmark decision in *Roe* v. *Wade*[8] and assesses its helpfulness in defining fetal status. I contend that, while the Court's opinion leaves many issues unresolved,[9] it provides a sketchy base upon which to construct a definition. *Roe* is useful because it relies on the biological stages of fetal development, especially viability, rather than attempting a philosophical determination of when human life begins. I argue, however, that *Roe* furnishes inadequate guidance for reconciling fetal interests with conflicting interests of the mother. In particular, it fails to illuminate the resolution of arguable claims on behalf of the previable fetus. Should fertile women be permitted to work in environments that might endanger the health of their offspring? In attempting *in vitro* fertilization, followed by transfer of the fertilized ovum into a mother's womb, should the physician be able to use several eggs and discard those fertilized ova that are not implanted?[10] Moreover, *Roe* fails to define adequately what protection should be afforded viable fetuses before birth. Does *Roe* permit abortion of a viable fetus when the mother asserts that continued pregnancy would cause her great mental anguish? [11]

Section II examines the historical reliance on birth as the point at which legal protection vests in the developing human. I contend that that reliance was due to the perceived significance of birth as the moment at which a developing human became capable of independent existence, not to any special importance of physical separation. Since a fetus today becomes capable of independent existence—viable —before birth, I argue that the law should recognize fetal claims to legal protection.

Section III compares fetuses with newborn children, identifying relevant similarities and differences. Like children, fetuses may develop into rational adults. I contend that the ability to interact with humans other than the mother—possessed by children but not by fetuses—is not a relevant distinction. This contention is supported by an examination of society's treatment of the interests of the dead.

Section IV studies whether fetuses at all stages of development should have the same protection, and concludes that they should not. Previable fetuses should remain legally distinguishable from viable fetuses. I argue that the viability criterion strikes a fair balance between the competing interests of developing and mature humans.

Section V examines the practical implications of choosing viability as a developmental stage of special significance for legal protection. It responds to some of the difficulties created by a standard that shifts with medical technology and shows them inadequate to overcome the logical and ethical arguments in favor of the viability criterion.

I. *Roe* v. *Wade* Reexamined

Jane Roe, unmarried and pregnant, wanted an abortion. Because her life was not threatened by continuing pregnancy, she could not get an abortion legally in her home state of Texas.[12] Moreover, she could not afford to travel to another jurisdiction for a legal abortion.[13] She therefore sued on behalf of herself and all similarly situated women. Roe contended that she had a constitutionally guaranteed right of privacy that included the right to terminate her pregnancy.[14] In defense of its statutes, Texas contended that it could protect fetal life constitutionally from the time of conception, and that Roe therefore had no right to an abortion.[15] A three-judge district court panel held that the Texas criminal abortion statutes were void on their faces, but they abstained from granting the plaintiff's request for an injunction.[16] Roe appealed to the Supreme Court,[17] Texas cross-appealed, and the Court had to determine the constitutionality of the Texas statutes.

The Court agreed with Roe that a woman has a constitutional right of privacy that "is broad enough to encompass [her] decision whether or not to terminate her pregnancy."[18] Yet the Court emphasized that the state might have "important" and "legitimate interests" that could limit that right. Mind you, not any interest would do—the interest had to be a " 'compelling state interest.' "[19] Nonetheless, the woman's right of privacy was definitely qualified.

The issue was thus whether the state had any "compelling" interests that could justify criminal abortion statutes. The Court engaged in a lengthy examination of the historical bases for such statutes. It observed that three justifications could be offered—discouraging immoral conduct, safeguarding the health of pregnant women, and protecting fetal life[20]—but quickly dismissed the first justification because Texas had not proffered it, and because neither courts nor commentators had ever considered it seriously.[21]

The second justification, paternalistic concern for the safety of pregnant women, grew from the historical dangers of the abortion technique. The information available to the Court regarding the safety of contemporary abortion procedures was contradictory. Roe, relying on data about abortions in New York City, argued that mortality rates for childbirth are higher than mortality rates for induced abortions.[22] Amici supporting Texas laws challenged the reliability of the New York data and pointed to evidence showing higher abortion mortality rates when abortions are performed late in pregnancy.[23] In the face of these conflicting presentations, the Court concluded that abortions can be performed more safely today than when criminal abortion laws were first enacted,[24] and that, at least at some stages of pregnancy, modern abortions are as safe as childbirth.

The Roe court held that the state's interest in protecting a woman's health becomes compelling—at the point where the risk of death from an abortion is not less than the risk of death from a normal childbirth, roughly the end of the first trimester of pregnancy.[25] After that point, "a State may regulate the abortion procedure to the extent that the regulation reasonably relates to the preservation and protection of maternal health." [26] Before that point, the state's interest in her health is insufficient to override the woman's decision in consultation with her physician.[27]

The third justification for criminal abortion statutes, the state's interest in protecting prenatal life,[28] was potentially the most complex. The medical and scientific data before the Court were inconclusive on all the details of fetal development, except for general consensus that a fetus has a separate genetic identity at or soon after conception.[29] On the other hand, the common law had traditionally been stingy in awarding rights to the unborn, and where it had grudgingly made such awards, it had, with few exceptions, made them contingent upon the fetus's live birth.[30] The Court first held that "the word 'person,' as used in the Fourteenth Amendment, does not include the unborn." [31] But the Court did not and could not stop there. Texas was arguing that, whether or not a fetus was a " 'person' as used in the Fourteenth Amendment," the state could take a legitimate, even compelling interest in its well-being. After noting that in other areas of the law, legal protection vests at the moment of birth, the Court equivocated on a central issue:

We need not resolve the difficult question of when life begins. When those trained in the respective disciplines of medicine, philosophy, and theology are unable to arrive at any consensus, the judiciary, at this point in the development of man's knowledge, is not in a position to speculate as to the answer.[32]

That statement was more than a little disingenuous. Only a few pages later, the Court did decide "when life begins," at least for the purpose of limiting the moment at which a state may bestow full legal protection. The Court held that a state acquires a compelling interest in the potential human life of the fetus at the moment the fetus becomes viable—"potentially able to live outside the mother's womb, albeit with artificial aid." [33] After that time, a state may prohibit all abortions that are not necessary to protect the life or health of the mother.[34]

Later in this essay, I suggest that the Roe decision's indirect implications regarding legal protection of fetal interests—indirect because they express those interests as those of the state rather than of the fetus—are justifiable in history and in reason. Before doing so, it is useful to discuss some of the ambiguities and logical flaws that weakened the Roe opinion.

One ambiguity rests with the Court's definition of viability. The statement that a fetus is "potentially able to live" can be interpreted in at least two ways. It could be merely a contingent prediction: the fetus is now alive and will continue to live unless something alters its environment. Viability in this sense depends on a continuing, unaltered relationship between mother and child. But viability has a second meaning: the level of developmental maturity at which a fetus will continue to live and develop even if physically separated from its mother. Clearly the Court intended this latter sense, which includes the possibility that artificial aid might be needed. It referred to a specific stage of development (twenty-four to twenty-eight weeks)[35] and refused to recognize a compelling state interest in potential human life before then.[36] If the Court intended "viable" to be understood in the first sense, it would have had to recognize a compelling state interest at the moment of conception, since from that time on fetuses are "potentially able to live" *if* they are not separated from their mothers.

The comment that viability "is usually placed at about seven months (twenty-eight weeks) but may occur earlier," [37] created a second ambiguity. Undoubtedly the Court wished to reflect present knowledge of premature survival rates. Although most fetuses are capable of surviving at twenty-eight weeks, some fetuses are not able to survive independently until some later point, and a few fetuses survive as early as twenty-four weeks after conception.[38] The moment when a particular fetus can survive is affected by such factors as race, medical care, nutritional health of the mother and fetus, genetic composition, and availability of neonatal facilities.[39] General predictions about fetal survival do not consider these personal traits; at best, they describe only the typical case, and suggest a range of probability rather than a specific developmental point. But although the Court's range of weeks may have been an accurate generalization about available medical information, it left unsettled whether a state's compelling interest attaches at twenty-four weeks—when it is possible, but not likely, that the individual fetus can survive—or at whatever point the fetus can in fact survive, but in no event later than twenty-eight weeks.[40]

The Court's *Roe* discussion contains further ambiguities. It includes a statement that the state's compelling interest in potential life attaches at viability "because the fetus then presumably has the capability of meaningful life outside the mother's womb." [41] What did the Court mean by the word "meaningful"? Did it mean that human life must have some special, unarticulated quality before it is entitled to protection by the state? Did it mean that fetuses with genetic diseases are excluded from the domain of legitimate state interests? This seems unlikely. Even at the time of *Roe*, it was usually possible to diagnose genetic disease before the twenty-four to twenty-eight week period used by the Court,[42] and there was nothing special about the twenty-four to twenty-eight period for purposes of diagnosis. Moreover, the greatest strides in development of prenatal diagnostic techniques have been made since the *Roe* decision.[43] It is far more likely that the Court meant the word "meaningful" to exclude only the class of fetuses that lack the minimal integrative physiological equipment and therefore could not survive for a significant period of time—more than a few minutes—if separated from their mothers by existing medical techniques.[44]

Although the *Roe* court took a reasonable position on fetal status, its holding stood upon notably weak reasoning. The Court chose viability as the critical point in fetal development "because presumably the fetus has the capability of meaningful life outside the mother's womb." [45] As Professor Ely eloquently observed, "the Court's defense seems to mistake a definition for a syllogism": [46] the definition of viability for a syllogism demonstrating that a compelling interest arises at viability. The Court found that, until a fetus is viable, neither it nor the state has a compelling interest that can override the constitutionally protected rights of the mother to obtain an abortion. After viability, except where the life and health of the mother are at issue, the state can vindicate its interests in fetal life and deny a woman an abortion. The Court offered no justification for this conclusion, perhaps because any justification would have exposed the thinness of its claim that it was taking no position on when life begins.

The remainder of this essay examines the suitability of the *Roe* framework for resolving legal and public policy issues involving the unborn. I believe that although the opinion was inadequately reasoned, its framework is broadly acceptable if properly modified and rooted in the reasons developed below.

II. The Reasons for the Traditional Live Birth Requirement for Granting Legal Protection

A. *The historical perspective* At the time *Roe* was decided, the case law typically bestowed legal protection at birth, a determination that suggests at least two possible explanations: only then was the fetus physically separate from the mother, and only then was the fetus traditionally capable of surviving independently of the mother.[47] The cases are unclear about which of those explanations was more central, largely because there was no reason to decide. Live birth was an adequate and uncomplicated standard, and courts rarely needed to discuss its significance.

Yet two types of cases provide clues to the value underlying the live birth standard. The first type involves a premature infant who exhibits some signs of life, but who expires shortly after birth. The second type involves an infant born after a normal gestation period, but who expires before all physical connections to the mother have been severed.

Although few early American cases concerned premature births, the first case to consider whether one may inherit through a stillborn child, *Marsellis* v. *Thalhimer*,[48] discussed the problem of prematures in dictum. The question presented was whether a widow, pregnant at the time of her husband's death, could inherit the share of her husband's estate allocable to her unborn child, when that child was subsequently stillborn. The law was clear that, had the fetus been born alive, it would have taken the share.[49] A child born alive qualifies for an inheritance even if it was only a fetus *in utero* at the testator's death. What was unclear was whether another person could benefit from the existence of a fetus *in utero* that was not subsequently born alive. After examining the civil law, the source of the rule permitting inheritance by a child who was *in utero* at the death of the testator,[50] the *Marsellis* court concluded that "children born dead, or in such an *early state of pregnancy as to be incapable of living, although they be not actually dead at the time of their birth,* are considered as if they had never been born or conceived." [51] Thus, a third party could not inherit through a stillborn child; a live birth of a mature baby was necessary to secure property interests. The dictum also suggests that a person claiming through a premature child had to prove that the child was capable of continued existence.[52] Since *Marsellis*, other cases have reinforced its implications that the live birth criterion was important not as a sign of physical separation, which could occur at any time during the gestational period, but as verification of a capacity for continued life.[53]

Cases involving fetuses born after a full gestation period, but who died before they were completely separated from their mothers, offer other clues. In *State* v. *Winthrop*, the issue was whether the killing of such a fetus was homicide—the killing of a person.[54] The trial court instructed the jury as follows:

If the child is fully delivered from the body of the mother, while the after birth is not, and the two are connected by the umbilical cord, and the child had independent life, *no matter whether it has breathed or not, or an independent circulation has been established or not,* it is a human being. . . .[55]

Because that instruction looked solely to the fact of physical expulsion in defining personhood, the Supreme Court of Iowa reversed.[56] According to the court, the instruction "would tell the jury . . . that they might find independence of life in utter disregard of the conditions in which alone, it could exist." [57] The high court held that potential independence was not enough; the state needed to show actual independence in order to sustain a conviction for homicide.[58] Thus, the state had to prove that the victim had an independent circulation, that the umbilical cord had been severed, and that the newborn had breathed on its own before the killing.[59] To be a "person," the infant needed to be capable of survival; mere physical separateness was not determinative.

Other cases agree with *Winthrop*'s view of when a fetus becomes a person and reject mere physical separation in favor of other factors, factors suggesting a capacity for continued independent life. The indices of live birth that courts have used include independent circulation,[60] severance of the umbilical cord,[61] and physical expulsion from the uterus.[62] Secondary signs have also been offered, such as vocal cries[63] and heartbeat.[64] The most widely used criterion, however, has been independent respiration.[65]

B. *The effect of recent medical advances on the case law*   Two developments in medicine have eroded the adequacy of the live birth criterion. First, as the *Roe* court acknowledged, modern biological studies have verified that the fetus is *genetically* a separate entity from a point at or near conception.[66] Second, advances in medicine have made it possible for a fetus that is too young for normal birth to survive apart from its mother.[67] These developments directly called into question the selection of live birth as *the only* relevant moment for distributing legal protection.

The verification and acceptance of the fetus's genetic separation from the mother at or near conception significantly influenced tort law. As early as 1946, the court in *Bonbrest* v. *Kotz*[68] awarded damages to a child for injuries suffered *en ventre sa mere*.[69] The court specifically rejected the contention that a fetus is only a "part" of its mother and therefore not entitled to an independent claim, calling such notion "a contradiction of terms." By 1967, every state had followed *Bonbrest's* lead and permitted recovery for fetal injury if the fetus was subsequently born alive.[70]

The second modern medical development—a fetus's ability to exist independently of its mother at about twenty-eight weeks—helped some courts even before *Roe* to award fetuses full legal protection at the moment of viability.[71] *Verkennes* v. *Corniea*, decided in 1949, initiated this trend: it was the first case to allow recovery for injuries to a viable fetus that resulted in stillbirth.[72] The Supreme Court of Minnesota reasoned, "There is no question here about the viability of the unborn child, or its capacity for a separate and independent existence. . . . [W]here independent existence is possible and the life is destroyed through a wrongful act a cause of action arises." [73] By relying on a capacity criterion—a finding that the fetus was capable of continued independent existence—the court endorsed the view that I discussed above: capacity was the key reason for the traditional reliance on birth. Because the fetus was sufficiently mature to grow and develop even if separated from its mother, the court saw no reason to treat it differently from a newborn infant. The view first expressed in *Verkennes* has now been adopted in a substantial number of states.[74]

The criminal law of at least one state has developed similarly.[75] In *Keeler* v. *Superior Court*, the Supreme Court of California held that a viable fetus was not a human being within the meaning of the state homicide statute.[76] The California legislature responded by revising the general homicide statute to read: "Murder is the unlawful killing of a human being, *or a fetus*, with malice aforethought." [77] In 1976, a court of appeals in California construed the revised statute in a case involving the death of a fetus twelve to fifteen weeks in development.[78] Such a fetus was "previable": it had not reached the stage where it was capable of living independently of its mother. In construing the statute the court concluded that its protection was coextensive with the capability for independent human life, and thus existed only from the point of viability.[79]

Thus, birth was traditionally the point at which the fetus was entitled to full legal protection of its interests *because birth was once synonymous with viability*. Now that the concepts are distinct, courts have begun to abandon birth as the central criterion in both tort and criminal law. The next sections of this essay analyze the arguments for retaining birth as the event that heralds legal protection and the related question of whether the law should provide the same protection to fetuses at different stages of development.

III. The Case for Recognizing Legal Protection for the Unborn: The Analogies to Children and to the Dead

To determine whether the unborn should be able to claim legal protection, we must ascertain what qualities determine who is entitled to such protection. The United States Constitution only protects "persons." [80] At least since the passage of the post-Civil War amendments, all born of human parents have been regarded as persons.[81] The Constitution protects persons by granting them rights that the state must respect. But not all persons have the same rights.[82] For example, public officials, soldiers, and prisoners have constitutional rights, but they may have fewer rights than citizens-at-large. Moreover, although two persons may have similar rights, the law does not always permit them to assert those rights in identical ways.[83] The differences between the legal rights of adults to make reproductive decisions and those of children illustrate that fact of American life.

Competent adults may, subject to compelling state interests, determine whether and under what circumstances they will reproduce.[84] The Supreme Court has stated: "If the right of privacy means anything, it is the right of the *individual*, married or single, to be free from unwarranted governmental intrusion into matters so fundamentally affecting a person as the decision whether to bear or beget a child." [85] This recognition of rights pertaining to childbearing began with *Griswold* v. *Connecticut*, a case addressing married persons' use of contraceptives.[86] The recognition continued with *Eisenstadt* v. *Baird* [87] (contraception), *Roe* v. *Wade*[88] (abortion) and *Planned Parenthood* v. *Danforth*[89] (abortion), and it culminated recently in *Carey* v. *Population Services International*.[90] In *Carey*, the Court invalidated a statute that permitted only licensed pharmacists to distribute nonprescription contraceptives:

Griswold may no longer be read as holding only that a State may not prohibit a married couple's use of contraceptives. Read in light of its progeny, the teaching of *Griswold* is that the Constitution protects individual decisions in matters of childbearing from unjustified intrusion by the State.[91]

Children, too, have constitutional rights entitling them to make reproductive decisions.[92] However, the cases hold that the state may regulate the child's right to make decisions about reproductive matters more extensively than it may an adult's right.[93] The issue is not whether children are capable of having rights in all respects equivalent to those of adults,[94] but rather whether the state's interest in regulating the activities of children may permit it to limit those rights more than it limits those of adults. The issue "is a vexing one, perhaps not susceptible to precise answer." [95] Although the Supreme Court has overturned statutes prohibiting persons from distributing contraceptives to minors under the age of sixteen[96] and statutes requiring parental consent to abortion for unmarried women under eighteen,[97] those decisions also suggest that the state may regulate a child's right to make reproductive decisions more extensively than an adult's right. *Carey*, which invalidated New York's blanket prohibition of contraceptive sales to minors,[98] did not foreclose less burdensome restrictions on such sales and did not give minors a full constitutional right to have sexual relations.[99] In *Bellotti* v. *Baird*, the Court held unconstitutional a Massachusetts statute that did not permit a mature minor to make an independent decision about abortion and required parental consultation and notification for all minors.[100] However, four Justices suggested that a court could determine that an abortion was not in the best interests of an immature minor.[101]

Both adults and children, then, may claim constitutional protections. On what basis do we distinguish the scope of their respective rights? Why, in the area of reproductive decisions, do we treat children differently from adults?[102] Traditionally there has been concern for a minor's ability to evaluate risks. Some states protect children from the risks associated with medical procedures by declaring that children are incapable of consenting to those procedures.[103] States have also limited a child's right to engage in other activities, such as driving, making contracts, and purchasing alcoholic beverages. These restrictions all manifest the state's concern for a child's ability to make mature judgments.[104]

While protecting the child from the consequences of immature decisions, the state has played an active role in rearing children, especially in matters that might contribute to a child's future ability to make judgments. State laws on compulsory education and on rehabilitation of juvenile delinquents are two examples of state efforts toward that end. Such efforts presume that a child must be carefully instructed and educated in order to assume adult responsibilities, and that during the education period it must be protected from the adverse consequences of its own behavior and from the harmful actions of others. Competent adults are not afforded similar nurture and protection. It is thought that they possess a level of maturity and capability for rational action that children lack. They are presumed capable of making responsible, mature, and reasoned decisions, fully appreciating the possible consequences.

If children cannot make rational decisions, why do we give them any rights at all? We do so to increase the likelihood that they will be regarded as persons rather than property.[105] Giving children rights also makes it easier for the state to protect them from the harmful acts of parents or third parties. Long ago, the Supreme Court said, "It is in the interest of youth itself, and of the whole community, that children be both safeguarded from abuses and given opportunities for growth into free and independent well-developed men and citizens." [106] Ultimately, it may be this last trait that truly motivates courts and legislatures to give children rights—the potential to grow into mature, competent, well-developed adults.[107] Although we realize that they are "not possessed of that full capacity for individual choice" that is essential to exercise of the broadest rights,[108] we know that children are potentially capable, and we nurture that potentiality.

The unborn are like children in their potentiality to become rational adults. Notwithstanding the *Roe* holding that the unborn are not persons within the meaning of the Fourteenth Amendment, that critical similarity between fetuses and children is convincing evidence for giving fetuses and children at least some legal protection. Neither fetuses nor newborn infants are capable of making rational judgments; both can develop that capacity. Professor Feinberg has remarked that a newborn infant "lacks the traits necessary for the possession of interests, but he has the capacity to acquire those traits, and his inherited potentialities are moving quickly toward actualization even as we watch him." [109] The identical statement could be made of the unborn.[110]

What differences there are between a fetus and a newborn are not of the sorts that the law has found material in awarding legal protection. Although it is true that the newborn infant is conscious and the fetus is not, comatose adults do not forfeit their constitutional rights. Not even the most arguably relevant difference between the newborn and the unborn—the ability to interact with other humans—is persuasive. Birth is certainly the point at which other humans see, touch, and communicate with the developing infant. But is there something unique about the characteristic of human interaction that should prevent recognition of legal protection at some earlier point in human development? I would argue not. Both the dead and the unborn lack that capacity to interact, yet the law respects the interests of the deceased; the incapacity to interact should be no greater barrier to legal protection for the unborn.

A brief digression to probe the forms and purposes of legal deference to the dead will prove enlightening. At first, the idea that the dead deserve legal protection seems strange. Physically, after all, they are mere decaying matter. They are incapable of making promises or of fulfilling responsibilities.[111] Yet, in a significant sense, they may be said to rule from the grave. This is especially true in property law; where testamentary dispositions change the lives of the living according to the whims of those no longer with us.[112] And it is true elsewhere in the law as well. For the most part, the wishes of the deceased concerning disposition of his corpse prevail, even though at English common law the corpse was not property[113] and was therefore not subject to testamentary direction.[114] In the United States, the strict English rule has been relaxed to the extent that, although there is no commercial property right in a dead body and it is not part of a decedent's estate,[115] a "quasi-property" right exists.[116] In some states a person's right to ordain the manner of disposition of his own body has been specifically conferred by statute.[117] The general American rule is that, while the decedent's wishes or directives concerning his interment are not technically testamentary and legal compulsion may not necessarily attach to them, they are entitled to respectful consideration and have been allowed great weight.[118]

The terms of the Uniform Anatomical Gift Act[119] also respect the wishes of the deceased. That act provides that any individual of sound mind and eighteen years or more of age may donate all or part of his body for transplant or for medical research by testamentary directive or by execution of a properly attested nontestamentary document,[120] even over opposition by his family.[121]

Why have we so frequently respected the deceased's desires concerning their remains, enforced their promises, and permitted their desired disposition of property? As living, existing persons we have many interests, most of which we can assert while we remain alive. But some interests cannot be asserted and fulfilled during our lifetimes; they must survive death if they are to be recognized and enforced. Yet, our legal system protects them. Does that protection imply that the dead have rights? Are we protecting those interests for the exclusive benefit of the dead? Probably not. Do we do it for the good of us all? Probably so. Most of us desire assurance that our wishes about the world we shall leave behind are recognized. We wish to take care of our families. We wish to leave nothing to certain people. It is a continuation of the responsibilities we assumed while living. By recognizing the claims of all dead people, we hope that our own desires will be accorded similar respect and deference. Giving legal protection to the dead thus serves two purposes. It gratifies people who are now alive by encouraging their present hopes that their own preferences will be satisfied after they are gone. Moreover, it affirms the importance to our society of human life generally: continued respect for the wishes of those who were once persons bolsters respect for the wishes of those who are still persons.

What relevance does consideration of the interests of the deceased have to the interests of the unborn? First, it makes clear that ability to interact with other humans is not a prerequisite for recognizing legal protection in our society. Second, the reasons that motivate our society to protect the dead have analogies in the realm of the unborn. Corresponding with the gratification felt by mature adults at the thought that their own wishes will be significant after they die is a gratification at the thought that their wishes were significant even before they were born. They can thereby escape whatever insecurity may be aroused by the notion that at one time in their prenatal existences they were deemed wholly undeserving of legal respect. Similarly, it can bolster societal appreciation of human life generally, by assuring that at no time during the development of any person alive today was that person wholly beyond legal concern.

To say that a fetus should have legal protection is not to delineate the contours of that protection.[122] It does not imply that the protection must be coextensive with that given children, any more than newborns must have rights equivalent to those of teenagers. I assert only that the unborn fetus, the newborn child, and the mature adult are all at different stages of development, and the fact that a fetus is not conscious or socially responsive should not preclude all legal protection.

IV. What Legal Protection for the Unborn? The Case for Distinguishing Between the Previable and the Viable Fetus

Even if, as has been argued above, there is no justification for denying the unborn all legal protection, we must still confront another problem: Should we give the same degree of legal protection to all humans at every stage of development, or should we recognize some specific point on the continuum of potentiality at which the legal protection becomes substantially greater than it was before? This problem is particularly acute when the interests of a fully matured individual conflict directly with those of a human at an earlier stage of biological development. In such a situation, it is impossible to resolve the conflict satisfactorily without subordinating the interests of one of the parties. For example, should the interests of a fertilized ovum be accorded the same, lesser, or greater legal protection than those of an infertile woman who desires to have a child through a procedure that involves fertilization outside of the womb? In such a procedure, physicians may destroy unused fertilized ova in an effort to impregnate the mother. In my view, the fetus should not be entitled to the same degree of protection at every stage of development. We should distinguish between the legal protection afforded the viable and the previable fetus just as we once distinguised between legal protection furnished before and after birth.

In exploring the contours of a revised view of legally cognizable fetal interests, we should consider the available medical and biological data concerning human development. Current medical understanding indicates that the meeting of sperm and ova results in the creation of a zygote possessing a totally independent genetic package of twenty-three chromosome pairs.[123] Within a week of fertilization, the zygote implants itself in the uterine wall [124]—a significant event, because only after implantation can we diagnose pregnancy.[125] "Twinning," and occasionally recombination, takes place during the first fourteen days after fertilization.[126] This suggests that although fertilization creates a new genetic grid, conception occurs over an extended time period. Moreover, fertilization does not necessarily indicate that genetic individuality has been accomplished. Thus, it may be impractical to recognize legal protection on the entire continuum of fetal existence if for no other reason than that we are not sure when "existence" begins.

Early fetal development continues through the eighth week of pregnancy, after which all organs of the fetus exist in rudimentary form and we can detect readable but not understandable brain activity. Subsequent development consists of growth and maturation of structures formed during the embryonic period.[127] Somewhere between the twelfth and sixteenth weeks, "quickening"—fetal movement perceptible to the mother—occurs.[128] Given current medical knowledge and technology, the fetus is viable somewhere between the twentieth and twenty-eighth weeks.[129]

In addition to better information about the stages of fetal development, modern science has acquired knowledge that is useful to prevent, ameliorate, or cure some fetal disabilities. We should also consider that information carefully in evaluating fetal interests. It suggests that some fetal interests deserve some legal protection at all stages of development. We have developed new and better methods of caring for neonates (infants four weeks old or younger).[130] Greater numbers of prematures are surviving, and they are surviving at earlier periods of development.[131] We have also developed a variety of techniques for observing individual fetuses. It is possible, for example, to detect and accurately diagnose in utero some disabilities and anomalies resulting from genetic conditions.[132] We can determine the sex of the fetus, hear fetal heartbeats, diagnose multiple fetuses, and obtain an outline of fetal structure.[133] Indeed, recent research has garnered so much knowledge about the fetus and its environment that we can view the fetus as a "second patient." [134]

We are only beginning to develop the capacity to administer therapy to fetuses in utero. One noteworthy achievement treats Rh incompatibility between mother and fetus: we can now give transfusions to the fetus in utero.[135] Current research suggests that administering certain drugs to mothers can prevent or minimize respiratory distress in newborns.[136] Moreover, contemporary animal reseach is expected to develop additional therapeutic techniques.[137]

This review of the medical data suggests a number of points in fetal development at which one might recognize a strong claim for significantly increasing the legal protection given a developing human. I would argue that, absent powerful countervailing considerations, the point selected should reflect the fundamental principles underlying the present legal system—principles that warrant revised rules to keep pace with recent medical advances.

As I noted earlier, the law has traditionally considered the acquisition of a capacity for independent existence to be the significant point in human development. Traditionally, birth was the point at which the capacity criterion was satisfied. Today viability precedes birth, and therefore birth is no longer the event most appropriately satisfying the capacity criterion.[138] Viability is preferable to birth, because, as we saw earlier, there is no relevant difference between a viable fetus and a newborn.[139] Explicit substitution of viability for birth as the point at which important legal protections vest would not establish a new principle. It would adhere to the traditional principle, invoking a more precise formulation of the standard in response to modern medical information and capabilities.

But we should not content ourselves with the law's traditional application of a capacity criterion. Before applying that criterion in the light of new developments, we must ask why it is an appropriate standard. Why should it be preferred to another principle, such as genetic individuality? Traditional acceptance alone is inadequate justification. I would argue that we should continue to use the capacity criterion because it represents a careful balance among powerful, complex, and perplexing societal concerns.

Society is naturally prone to protect most securely the interests of its most mature and responsible members. This instinct reveals itself whenever the interests of those members conflict with the interests of less mature or less responsible citizens. Preferring the interests of a "remote" potentiality in cases of conflict would be perceived as an intolerable incursion on the interests of the fully matured. Accordingly, we tend to favor the interests of parents over the interests of children when those interests collide.

Yet society has never wholly disregarded the interests of those less mature. It has always sought to strike a fair balance and has typically done so at that point in development where the entity shows a significant likelihood of becoming a mature, contributing member. That point has, logically, been the moment at which the entity is capable of independent existence—the capacity criterion. The criterion is thus a rational one—it represents a societal commitment to bestowing rights on those likely to contribute to its advancement. It naturally follows the societal instinct for self-perpetuation. It explains the early common law property rule that one had to be alive at the time of a testator's death to inherit; otherwise no one would fulfill the feudal responsibilities.[140] Similarly, modern law gives rights to artificial entities such as corporations only when they are capable of bearing responsibilities.[141]

Thus, the capacity criterion is a rational principle, and the viability standard is a rational application of that principle to the modern world. Yet that should not obscure the arguments in Section IV above: Although principal rights should be bestowed at viability, the previable fetus should still receive some protection. Where the protectable interests of fully mature members do not conflict with those of less mature members, there is no justification for ignoring the latter's claims. The *Roe* opinion was correct in recognizing a state's legitimate interest in protecting the previable fetus. In tort, property, and criminal law, when that interest does not oppose a protected interest of the mature mother, the state should not hesitate to vindicate it.

V. Some Implications of the Viability Criterion

I have argued that medical data and common-law theory strongly support a viability criterion as one of central significance. There is today no inherent legal obstacle to giving viable fetuses legal protection fully equivalent to that given the newborn. But is it practical? Will it help to resolve disputes between fetuses and mothers? Or between fetuses and third parties?

The first difficulty with the viability criterion is the extraordinary complexity of determining a particular fetus's viability.[142] Estimates of gestational age have a two-week margin of error. Moreover, even if we could always determine precisely the gestational age of a fetus, that datum would not be sufficient to tell us whether the fetus was in fact viable.[143] To apply the viability criterion in today's world we must resort to estimates of the probability of viability drawn from statistics on premature births. Using those estimates, we must then create a rebuttable legal presumption of viability or nonviability associable with each gestational age. The presumption chosen is vitally important, for in many cases it will not be feasible to marshal the evidence necessary to rebut it.

In *Roe*, the Court said that viability usually occurs at twenty-eight weeks, adopting what it believed to be the consensus of the medical profession that at least 40 to 50 percent of fetuses born at twenty-eight weeks of gestation survive.[144] But the Court did not stop there. It acknowledged that some fetuses beat the odds and survive at fewer than twenty-eight weeks of gestational age, possibly as early as twenty-four weeks. As I mentioned above, this left interpreters of the *Roe* opinion with a difficult ambiguity—when did the Court intend the presumption of viability to arise? At twenty-eight weeks, when most fetuses survive, or at twenty-four weeks, when some fetuses survive?

I would contend that states should be permitted to assert a compelling interest in potential life at the earliest point at which there has been verified fetal survival—at twenty-four weeks under *Roe*.[145] Such an assertion would certainly be within the language of *Roe*. Moreover, it would be consistent with the reasons for giving fetuses legal protection in the first place. If we want to ensure that no human being is denied fair consideration by entitling every fetus to legal protection as soon as it is viable, then we should err on the safe side by protecting all who might have such an entitlement. In fact, given the margin of error in estimating gestational age, one could at least argue for a compelling state interest in any potential human estimated to be within two weeks of the age of the youngest fetus known to have survived. Especially when we know that the concerned mature persons have had a chance to protect their interests earlier in pregnancy, we should draw the line to maximize protection for those who may be viable.[146]

Despite the logic of such an approach, the Supreme Court's post-*Roe* opinions strongly suggest that statutes adopting a presumption at twenty-four weeks would be unconstitutional.[147] In *Planned Parenthood* v. *Danforth*[148] the Court stated, "[I]t is not the proper function of the legislature or the courts to place viability at a specific point in the gestation period. [T]he determination of whether a particular fetus is viable is, and must be, a matter for the judgment of the responsible attending physician." [149] The Court expressly affirmed this view in *Colautti* v. *Franklin*.[150] Thus, a reading of *Roe*, *Danforth*, and *Colautti* might suggest that the states' compelling interest in potential life arises clearly at twenty-eight weeks, and earlier only if an individual physician so determines.[151]

If that is how the Court intends to resolve the problem of determining individual viability, its approach is not convincing. The medical profession is not of one mind concerning the conclusion that the fetus does not have a reasonable likelihood of survival until twenty-eight weeks. Some would argue that the point of reasonable likelihood of survival occurs earlier. In the Court's own words,

[E]ven if agreement may be reached on the probability of survival, different physicians equate viability with different probabilities of survival, and some physicians refuse to equate viability with any numerical probability at all. In the face of these uncertainties, it is not unlikely that experts will disagree over whether a particular fetus in the second trimester has advanced to the stage of viability.[152]

The Court's extraordinary deference to the medical profession regarding what constitutes a reasonable likelihood of survival seems unwarranted. Physicians do have some competence to tell us the probabilities of survival at each stage of development. They do not, however, have peculiar competence to decree that a specific probability of survival is the critical one for determining when a state's interest in potential life becomes compelling. That decision is important to all of society.

Moreover, the Court's apparent refusal to permit states to assert a compelling interest at the earliest moment of known fetal survival sacrifices the objectivity and ease of administration which that system offers. Under the Court's system, a physician could reasonably abort a fetus that other physicians consider viable. All physicians called upon to estimate the odds will do so subjectively under circumstances that make it impossible to ignore the powerful motives of the parties. One must question the justice of imposing such a difficult question of values on a profession that neither wants to answer it nor is especially competent to do so.

Although I have stressed the importance of the presumption of viability or nonviability, the manner of rebutting it should not be ignored. The question of a fetus's viability often arises when it is delivered stillborn after a traumatic event that occurred near the time of viability. For example, a fetus might be injured through another's negligence during the twenty-sixth week of pregnancy. After stillbirth, the question might arise of whether a wrongful death suit on its behalf could be brought in those states that require that the fetus be viable when injured. Under my approach, it would be presumed viable from the twenty-fourth week onward. To rebut the presumption, a doctor would have to examine the fetus after birth to find peculiar characteristics known to affect the time of viability. The difficult factual issue need not be any tougher than those already presented by efforts to separate the birth process from the moment of birth.

A second problem with giving full legal protection at viability stems from the fetus's physical attachment to the mother. Given this fact, how should we resolve conflicts between the interests of mothers and of viable, attached fetuses? The Court in *Roe* suggests that the mother's interest predominates, at least when her life and health are at stake.[153] It offered no justification for this value preference and did not attempt to reconcile it with the fact that a state's compelling interest in potential life otherwise attaches at viability. Moreover, it offered no guidance for other conflicts of interests, such as where a mother's treatment of her own body might hurt her unborn child. If it could be demonstrated that the intake of alcohol or drugs during pregnancy is likely to harm the fetus, could we prohibit a pregnant mother from drinking or taking drugs? [154] These are difficult issues, which should perhaps be distinguished according to whether the fetus is viable or previable.

I submit that the Court in *Roe* was not justified in assuming that the mother's interest in her life or health predominates over the identical interests of the viable fetus. The interests of mother and viable fetus should be weighed equally in resolving conflicts between them. We should strike a fair balance between their competing interests[155] on an issue-by-issue basis, considering the gestational age of the fetus, the severity of possible harm to the fetus, and the severity of possible harm to the mother's interests. If continued pregnancy threatens a mother's life[156] or health[157] at a time when her unborn child is viable, we should first consider separating them by a procedure designed to minimize the risks to both. Such a step is often difficult and is sometimes impossible, but in situations of clear danger to the mother, it may prove the fairest reconciliation of their competing interests. In other circumstances, that reconciliation might go more directly against the interests of the mother. It may require her to submit to activities she finds objectionable, such as blood transfusions, where they are necessary to save the life of the unborn fetus.[158] In such a case, that seems an appropriate balance between the mother's nonabsolute right to free exercise of religion and the fetus's life-or-death concern.

Where the mother's personal activities—smoking, drinking, using medication, or working, to give a few examples—endanger the fetus, resolution of conflicts should consider how much control the mother actually has over her actions, the severity of possible damage to the fetus, the nature of the conduct engaged in, and the invasion of the mother's interests. For example, if the mother were a heroin addict, the newborn could be born addicted—a serious injury. Her conduct would be involuntary, but her use of heroin illegal. It would certainly be justifiable to compel her to undergo treatment; we might even consider more severe sanctions.[159] If society may punish an addict for giving drugs to her children, it may consistently punish her for causing her unborn child to become addicted.[160] The more difficult cases involve smoking, drinking, or working in environments hazardous to fetuses. Perhaps resolution of those conflicts ought to turn on the risk of harm to the fetus. We should consider how likely it is that the risk will come about and the severity of damage if it occurs. Such conflicts may be difficult. But certainly the difficulty is not sufficient to force a retreat from the viability criterion or to warrant disregarding the fetus whenever a mother asserts some interest in her own lifestyle or health.

Viability poses another dilemma. It is not biologically fixed at some permanent time.[161] It will arrive earlier in gestation as new and better techniques are developed for sustaining existence outside the womb. The Supreme Court noted this possibility in *Danforth* when it stated: "[W]e recognized in *Roe* that viability was a matter of medical judgment, skill, and technical ability, and we preserved the flexibility of the term." [162] It is precisely the fact that viability is not forever fixed in time that gives rise to the strongest criticism of its use as a criterion. Some would object to granting legal protection at different moments in the gestational period for different generations; such critics would prefer to choose an unvarying point in fetal development. But since viability strikes a balance of competing interests with a standard that applies fairly to all humans, striking that balance at different times for different people is not morally offensive. And viability is not subject to the type of arbitrariness that lurks in vague formulations of "personhood." It is a biological concept that would minimize the possibility of discriminatory treatment of different human lives.

The shifting moment of viability would not create an undue problem under the standard for establishing the viability presumption that I espoused above. It is relatively easy to keep track of the age of the youngest known successful birth and to advance it with each new "miraculous" premature survival. Nonetheless, it would create difficulties in assessing the appropriate way to rebut that presumption in an individual case. Surely the standards for that assessment will have to be revised periodically in light of new medical knowledge and advances. Who should make that revision and who should have the responsibility for verifying the earliest known survival? The National Commission for the Protection of Human Subjects of Biomedical Behavioral Research has recommended giving a federal agency responsibility for monitoring new developments.[163] Legislatures and courts could then be guided by that agency's reports. Another possibility would be to give some organized arm of the medical profession responsibility for issuing guidelines that summarize the most recent knowledge about the specific factors affecting viability. This would be a less satisfying resolution, however, for such guidelines would operate without the imprimatur of government approval. If the responsibility were lodged in a government agency, all interested concerns, including the medical profession, could participate in the formulation of the guidelines.[164]

The shifting moment of viability suggests another possible concern. Physicians currently can diagnose certain genetic conditions and complications *in utero* in time to perform an abortion under *Roe* standards.[165] If viability were to move to an earlier point in gestation, abortion of a defective fetus might not be allowed. Yet the problem is really not new. Whether one may kill a human, either because it will enjoy a quality of life below some minimal level or because its parents do not wish a severely handicapped child, is not a question peculiar to the use of viability as a standard.[166] We should treat viable, defective fetuses in the same way we treat defective newborns. The problem, in short, should be viewed as one of euthanasia and not one uniquely affecting legal protection of fetuses.

A final potentially troublesome aspect of viability is that it is a moment in development whose achievement is not readily apparent to lay persons, or even to physicians. This problem also afflicts the current debate over shifting the traditional legal definition of death, which looks to heartbeat cessation, to a definition that looks to brain activity. Neither brain death nor viability is readily understood. Moreover, there is often lay resistance to the use of criteria that are technologically determined and can be used only by professionals. This is more a political problem than a legal or ethical one. We are therefore fortunate that, as a practical matter, the need to determine the point of viability, just as the need to use brain death definitions, is infrequent. In most abortion cases, we will have a termination of the pregnancy long before viability. In most other cases there will be a live birth. Achievement of live birth will adequately prove a separate and independent existence, to the satisfaction of professional and lay persons alike.

VI. Conclusion

Most legal and philosophical literature about the fetus concerns abortion, and in recent years moral philosophers have thought the critical preliminary issue in resolving the morality of abortion to be whether the fetus is a person. In *Roe* v. *Wade*, the Supreme Court also approached the abortion issue through the question of personhood. The

Court held that the fetus is not a person, a holding that has been criticized for inadequate analysis.

I submit that whether the fetus is a "person" is irrelevant to whether it should have legal protection. The personhood debate has only obscured the decisive issues. The juridical status of developing humans has historically depended upon their capacity for a separate and independent existence. It is not necessary to abandon that traditional understanding; we must only revise its application in the context of greater scientific knowledge. Today, capacity to have independent existence points to viability instead of birth as the determinative moment in development. There are no serious legal problems to recognizing legal protection of viable fetuses equal to that already afforded newborns. The standard presents some problems that birth does not, but none that is sufficiently serious to challenge the thesis that all fetuses merit some protection and that viable fetuses merit all protection currently given the newborn infant.

Personhood and the Abortion Debate

Ruth Macklin

INTRODUCTION   As if the ongoing debate surrounding abortion were not sufficient to sustain moral controversy, a second layer of debate has become entrenched with almost as much fervor. That layer of debate encompasses conceptual, epistemological, and ethical issues pertaining to 'personhood'. Numerous adversaries on both sides of the abortion controversy have taken the notion of personhood as a key to resolving the dispute: if only we could determine the status of the fetus (at some stage or other in its development) as a person, we would then have the answer to the moral permissibility of abortion. That the task of determining the personhood of the fetus has proved as intractable as the abortion question itself seems not to deter those who believe this line of inquiry to be fruitful.

The fact that most discussions of personhood are found within the context of the abortion debate should prompt the recognition that the concept of personhood is not value neutral, so there can be no value-free inquiry into this subject. Indeed, the most apparent reason for the continuing controversy, and the slim likelihood of ever reaching an agreement, is that the values writers antecedently embrace determine the definition or criteria they arrive at by way of conclusion. This is true no matter which definition of personhood is adopted, and no matter what the context in which the discussion takes place. As a result, appeal to the concept of personhood is entirely unhelpful in any effort to resolve the fundamentals of the abortion controversy. Writers either choose a definition of personhood that comports with the moral view they already hold on the abortion issue; or else they attempt to show that the personhood of the fetus is quite irrelevant to settling moral and legal aspects of abortion.

This essay will explore the uselessness of inquiry into personhood as a means of settling questions about the ethics of abortion. To that end, I will pursue two different strategies. The first approach surveys the bioethics literature on personhood. That review seeks to demonstrate, first, that the difficulty of arriving at an agreed-upon set of criteria for personhood is at least as great as that of resolving the abortion controversy itself; and second, that even reaching some agreement about whether or not the fetus is a person is of little help in drawing conclusions about the permissibility of abortion. The second strategy shows that at least in the legal sphere, and probably in the moral arena as well, the question of the personhood of the fetus can be completely bypassed even when the intention is to afford the fetus certain protections while *in utero*. Let me begin with a review of personhood in the bioethics literature, focusing almost exclusively on the concept as it relates to the abortion issue.

Personhood in the Bioethics Literature

Attempts to define 'personhood' or to arrive at a set of criteria for its correct application almost always embody an underlying value stance regarding the substantive moral issue under scrutiny. That value stance is the main determinant of where along the spectrum of possibilities the personhood line will be drawn. Writers who reveal a feminist bias, arguing within the context of the abortion debate, argue that at no stage of development does the fetus meet criteria of personhood (Warren, 1973). And writers from the religious tradition, largely if not entirely opposed to abortion, offer a standard of personhood that can be met by a zygote (Ramsey, 1971; Noonan, 1970, 1974). For ease of reference, I shall refer to one set of criteria for personhood that allows a zygote or blastocyst to qualify as a "low standard" for personhood, and to another set that enables, minimally, a neonate, but more typically, an infant of beyond a few months or a year to qualify as a "high standard" for personhood.

Before examining the nature of the dispute and the modes of argument, one characteristic of the literature on personhood is worth noting: the almost total absence of attempts to demonstrate a strictly scientific basis for determining when personhood begins. This is in sharp contrast to the wording of the proposed human life bill in the United States Congress (1981), and to the efforts of political anti-abortion forces to call expert witnesses and obtain scientific testimony regarding the beginning of human life. Although scientific findings are sometimes brought in as relevant to a determination of personhood (the presence of the full genetic code and encephalographic readings being the chief candidates), the bioethics literature can boast no seriout proponents of a strictly scientific criterion for personhood. Various proposals rely on scientific advances to lend support for age-old views: modern genetics—supplying knowledge about the unique genetic structure of every fertilized ovum—is used to provide biological backing for theological teachings (Ramsey, 1971; Noonan, 1970, 1974) by proponents of the view that conception is the moment when personhood begins. But insofar as those orthodox religious views antedated the modern science of genetics, it could hardly be hailed as a scientific "discovery" to cite conception as the inception of personhood. In this case, as in the case of encephalographic activity—the criterion proposed by Brody (1974)—scientific developments afford a convenient source of objective data used to support antecedently held views. My study of the bioethics literature did not reveal a single proponent of the view that when personhood begins is a straightforward scientific question. It remains, however, to explore a related point to which we shall return later. At least one writer (Brody, 1974) denies that the determination of personhood is a matter for decision, rather than discovery. But if it is not a matter of *scientific* discovery, as the senators who sought expert testimony would have us believe, what plausible candidates are there, and what methodology can be employed?

The Nature of the Dispute and Modes of Argument

All efforts to define 'person' are prescriptive, rather than descriptive. Most of those who have tried to arrive at a satisfactory definition would probably agree with this observation, in that there is little basis for continuing disagreement over the acceptance of a purely descriptive concept. Descriptive definitions capture the accepted meaning or general usage of a word or concept, as does a good dictionary. This is perfectly compatible with the view that living languages continue to evolve, and that natural languages are irreducibly "open-textured" (Hart, 1961). But although a term can be ambiguous—that is, it can have multiple meanings, all of which are correct—and whereas it can have a vagueness at the penumbra, a definition can be descriptive if its core meaning is widely accepted and at least roughly understood by users of the language as referring to the same type of entity, event, or state of affairs. That there remains such intractable and wide disagreement over the meaning of 'person', about the criteria for its correct application, and about the truth conditions for its proper use in practice, demonstrates beyond doubt that the definitions proposed in the literature are prescriptive rather than descriptive.

Substantial agreement exists among contributors to the bioethics literature who are explicit in acknowledging that personhood is a value-laden concept (Tooley, 1972; Gustafson, 1973; Warren, 1973; Wertheimer, 1971). This agreement exists even among those who disagree radically on where to draw the line between persons and nonpersons. Michael Tooley (1972) sets a very high standard for personhood, adopting the following criterion.

An organism possesses a serious right to life only if it possesses the concept of a self as a continuing subject of experiences and other mental states, and believes that it is itself such a continuing entity. [Tooley, 1972, in Gorovitz et al., p. 302]

Tooley identifies being a person with having a serious moral right to life, and is explicit in treating the concept of a person as a normative one: "I shall treat the concept of a person as a purely moral concept, free of all descriptive content" (Ibid., p. 299). At the other end of the continuum, John Noonan (1970) sets a very low standard for personhood, adhering to the traditional Roman Catholic position that "if you are conceived by human parents, you are human" (Noonan, 1970, in Gorovitz et al., p. 292). (Noonan treats humanity, or being human, as equivalent to personhood, whereas most other writers sharply distinguish these two notions.) Yet even though he locates the boundaries of personhood at the opposite end of the spectrum from Tooley, Fletcher, Warren, and others who set a very high standard of personhood, Noonan nonetheless treats the concept as largely a moral one:

To recognize a person is a moral decision; it depends on objective data but it also depends on the perceptions and inclinations and ends of the decision makers; it cannot be made without commitment and without consideration of alternative values. [Noonan, 1974, in Beauchamp and Walters, p. 214]

Explicit acknowledgment that personhood (and humanhood, when held to be synonymous with personhood) is at least a value-laden concept, if not a purely moral one, can also be found in the religiously based writings of James Gustafson. He poses the question, "What constitutes the distinctively human?" and replies that "a simply *descrip-*

tive answer to that question would not be sufficient" (Gustafson, 1973, in Williams, p. 49). And in the secular, philosophical tradition, Mary Anne Warren asserts that "the concept of a person is in part a moral concept; once we have admitted that x is a person we have recognized . . . x's right to be treated as a member of the moral community" (Warren, 1973, in Beauchamp and Walters, pp. 224–25).

Although I believe most writers who do not explicitly say so would agree with those who readily acknowledge that personhood is a normative concept, at least some would strongly disagree if that claim were couched in different terms—to wit, that arriving at a definition of personhood is a matter of *decision*, not a matter of *discovery*. Brody (1974) discusses this claim, and asserts his own position that it is not a matter for decision, arguing against those who espouse the opposite view (O'Connor, 1968, and Wertheimer, 1971, in particular). But if arriving at a set of criteria for personhood is a matter for discovery, what sort of discovery is it? Brody does not characterize the type of inquiry that would yield such a discovery, but he does offer some persuasive arguments against the opposing view. If, as I will argue, all proposed definitions of 'person' are prescriptive rather than descriptive, it follows that arriving at a satisfactory concept of personhood is a matter of decision, not discovery.

To indicate the nature and scope of disagreements surrounding personhood, it is useful to provide a list of issues on which writers in the field of bioethics disagree. The intractable nature of the problem is easier to understand when one sees that a mixed bag of subdisputes underlies what may at first seem to be the only "real" issue: arriving at criteria for personhood or determining when personhood begins.

1. Equivalence of meaning between 'human' and 'person'. Some writers sharply distinguish the terms 'human' and 'person', whereas others hold them to be equivalent in meaning. Although this may appear to be merely a question of semantics, philosophers have long noted that what seems to be a simple verbal quibble turns out to be an underlying conceptual disagreement of larger importance. Those writers whose disagreement does not reduce to a preference for one locution over another ('personhood' versus 'humanhood' versus 'distinctively human life', etc.) hold different positions on the ontological status of the fetus in the abortion controversy (Beauchamp, 1978, in Beauchamp and Walters, pp. 188–91). In that questions of ontology are metaphysical questions, we cannot expect ontological disputes to be settled by an appeal to factual considerations or to moral concerns—

although both may be relevant to metaphysical arguments designed to draw conclusions about the ontological status of an entity.

2. *Indeterminacy of the status of the fetus as a person.* Some authors offer bold prescriptions for defining personhood, whereas others devote their writings to analyzing the views of others. Within the second group, some writers explicitly state that it is impossible to secure agreement on the concept of a person (Wertheimer, 1971; Gustafson, 1973; English, 1975), and others are silent on that point. The sharpest disagreement, then, is between those who offer criteria for personhood and those who deny the feasibility of the entire enterprise.

3. *The importance of personhood for efforts to resolve the moral debates surrounding abortion.* Inasmuch as the majority of writings on personhood occur within the context of the abortion debate, it is not surprising that the widest variation of claims made in this connection concern the relevance and importance of defining 'personhood'. At least the following positions can be distinguished:

a. To settle the abortion issue once and for all, some agreement must be reached about whether the fetus is a person, and if so, when in its development personhood begins (Engelhardt, 1974; Tooley, 1972; Noonan, 1970; Brody, 1974; Warren, 1973).
b. Settling the abortion issue has little or nothing to do with when personhood begins, because abortion may be morally justified even if it is acknowledged that the fetus is a person from the moment of conception (Thomson, 1971).
c. Whether the fetus is a person is irrelevant to whether it should have legal protection; concerns about the health of the fetus create pressing policy issues regardless of whether or not the fetus is granted the status of a person (King, 1979).
d. Because it is impossible to provide a set of necessary and sufficient conditions for personhood, and therefore impossible to secure agreement on the criteria for personhood, that issue must be viewed as entirely irrelevant to solving the abortion controversy (English, 1975; Wertheimer, 1971).

Note that whereas (b), (c), and (d) all treat the issue of personhood as separable from the question of the justifiability of abortion, each draws a different conclusion: (b) justifies abortion *even if* the fetus is a person, by holding that one person's rights take precedence over the rights of another person (the rights of the mother override the rights of the fetus); (c) is compatible with holding that even if the fetus is *not* a person, it *still* deserves protection under the law; and (d) claims that the abortion issue *must* be addressed separately from the problem of personhood, inasmuch as the latter problem is insoluble.

4. *The importance of personhood linked to the need to ascribe rights.* Most writers accept without question a strong link between being a person and being the bearer of rights, especially the right to life. Yet at least one author denies the need for rights language altogether (Fletcher, 1972, 1974, 1979), and a second minimizes the importance of the link by allowing that even a being with rights, including a right to life, may have to yield to the overriding rights of another (Thomson, 1971).

In the above list, I intentionally omitted the most obvious points of disagreement: disputes about the properties an entity must have in order to satisfy the criteria of personhood. As a reminder of just which properties have been proposed as the defining characteristics of persons, the following candidates are selected from those writers who set a very high standard of personhood. Interestingly, authors who choose a lower standard most often present their criterion for personhood entirely within the context of the abortion controversy—as in the case of Brody (1974), whose proposed criterion is the onset of encephalographic activity, and Noonan (1970), who regards being conceived by human parents as the definitive condition. Brody considers it an advantage of his criterion that it can consistently be used as the determining condition for both the beginning *and* end of personhood, whereas most writers who confine their analysis to the abortion issue do not address the question of personhood in other moral contexts. The following examples of high standards are more significant as *general* proposals regarding personhood than most other candidates, in that the majority of the latter regard one or another stage of fetal development as the point at which personhood begins.

Tooley's criterion   Tooley does not offer a set of properties or characteristics, but rather, a criterion couched in the language of mental states and mental events: "An organism possesses a serious right to life [is a person] only if it possesses the concept of a self as a continuing subject of experiences and other mental states, and believes that it is itself such a continuing entity" (Tooley, 1972, in Gorovitz et al., p. 302). This is usually referred to as the "self-consciousness requirement," one that is an ingredient in the other two high standards of personhood discussed below. It is as obvious to Tooley as to his readers that this criterion justifies infanticide if it justifies abortion.

Tooley accepts this consequence of his argument, although he is reluctant to specify any precise point, based on his criterion, at which personhood begins. His acceptance of the consequences for infanticide may cause abhorrence in some readers, but Tooley dismisses such abhorrent reactions as emanating from irrational cultural taboos instead of from reasoned arguments:

The typical reaction to infanticide is like the reaction to incest or cannibalism, or the reaction of previous generations to masturbation or oral sex. The response, rather than appealing to carefully formulated moral principles, is primarily visceral. When philosophers themselves respond in this way, offering no arguments, and dismissing infanticide out of hand, it is reasonable to suspect that one is dealing with a taboo rather than with a rational prohibition. [Ibid., p. 229]

Warren's criteria   Mary Anne Warren suggests the following as "the traits which are most central to the concept of personhood, or humanity in the moral sense":

1. Consciousness (of objects and events external and/or internal to the being), and in particular the capacity to feel pain;
2. Reasoning (the developed capacity to solve new and relatively complex problems);
3. Self-motivated activity (activity which is relatively independent of either genetic or direct external control);
4. The capacity to communicate, by whatever means, messages of an indefinite variety of types, that is, not just with an indefinite number of possible contents, but on indefinitely many possible topics;
5. The presence of self-concepts, and self-awareness, either individual or racial, or both. [Warren, 1973, in Beauchamp and Walters, p. 224]

Warren is not altogether conclusive on how many of these traits need be present for the bearer to count as a person, nor is she entirely clear on whether they are to serve as necessary conditions, sufficient conditions, or both. She holds that (1) and (2) alone might be sufficient for personhood, "and quite probably (1)–(3) are sufficient." And "(1) and (2) look like fairly good candidates for necessary conditions, as does (3) ..." (Ibid.). Warren's criteria appear to be a detailed specification of Tooley's more simply stated proposal, but a further observation is worth making. Recognizing the same consequence for infanticide as noted above regarding Tooley's condition, Warren is nonetheless unhappy with that result of applying her criterion. But rather than weaken the criterion for personhood, she chooses to stand by her list and to hold that despite the fact that killing a newborn infant would not be murder, infanticide is nevertheless *not* permissible.

Warren offers two reasons in support of this moral judgment:

> In the first place, it would be wrong, at least in this country and in this period of history . . . to kill a newborn infant, because even if its parents do not want it and would not suffer from its destruction, there are other people who would like to have it, and would, in all probability, be deprived of a great deal of pleasure by its destruction. . . .
>
> Secondly, most people, at least in this country, value infants and would much prefer that they be preserved, even if foster parents are not immediately available. Most of us would rather be taxed to support orphanages than allow unwanted infants to be destroyed. So long as there are people who want an infant preserved, and who are willing and able to provide the means of caring for it, under reasonably humane conditions, it is, *ceteris paribus*, wrong to destroy it. [Ibid., p. 227]

It is not my purpose to assess these reasons, or to evaluate the adequacy of Warren's criteria for personhood in light of this moral stance concerning infanticide. I raise the issue to illustrate the response of an author who is unhappy about at least one of the logical consequences of the concept of a person she has articulated. Unlike Tooley, who is prepared to accept the consequence that infanticide is morally permissible, Warren seeks reasons to conform to her intuitions or moral sentiments to the contrary. But notice that she does not find infanticide wrong for reasons that refer even to the interests (much less to the rights) of the baby; the wrongness stems, instead, from the pleasures adults would be deprived of by virtue of the infant's destruction, or by the discomfort adults would experience in knowing that babies are being killed rather than placed in orphanages. Warren does not acknowledge an infant's "right to life," and so she remains consistent with her position regarding personhood and the status of the fetus as a nonperson. Perhaps this demonstrates the limits of rights language in the moral domain, even with respect to so rights-oriented a topic as abortion and infanticide. When an analysis couched in the language of rights fails to square with the moral judgments a philosopher would like to reach, one strategy is to abandon that language in favor of a consequentialist justification.

Compare Warren's attempted resolution with that of Thomson. Warren claims that neither a fetus nor an infant is a person, so neither has a right to life; nonetheless, it is permissible to kill a fetus but wrong to kill an infant (*ceteris paribus*, of course). Thomson argues that even if a fetus is a person, and therefore has a right to life, it is still permissible to kill a fetus because of the overriding rights of the mother. If appealing to the concept of a person in moral arguments about abortion yields a pair of conclusions such as these, it provides a good reason to doubt the value of that concept for the purpose of reaching an ethically acceptable solution to problems in bioethics.

Fletcher's criteria   In several essays, written over a period of years, Joseph Fletcher proposes criteria or indicators of humanness (1972, 1974, 1979). The following list is taken from the last of these writings, and consists only of Fletcher's headings, without his ensuing remarks that explicate the titles. The list consists of fifteen positive propositions and five negative ones:

1. Minimum intelligence
2. Self-awareness
3. Self-control
4. A sense of time
5. A sense of futurity
6. A sense of the past
7. The capability to relate to others
8. Concern for others
9. Communication
10. Control of existence
11. Curiosity
12. Change and changeability
13. Balance of rationality and feeling
14. Idiosyncrasy
15. Neocortical function

The five negative propositions are:

1. Man is not non- or antiartificial
2. Man is not essentially parental
3. Man is not essentially sexual
4. Man is not a bundle of rights
5. Man is not a worshipper [Fletcher, 1979, pp. 12–18]

Fletcher intends his list to be applicable across the board in bioethics —to problems of abortion, euthanasia, and decision making in gynecology, obstetrics, pediatrics, general surgery, and medicine. He is the one writer on this topic who denies the helpfulness or even relevance of the language of rights for finding solutions to problems in bioethics that give rise to discussions of personhood ('humanhood' is his preferred term).

Moreover, from his other writings it is clear why Fletcher rejects an approach to ethical issues based on the concept of rights. He is a straight-out consequentialist, one who, in the eyes of his critics, takes the tenets of consequentialism to an ethically questionable extreme. This may be the most telling example of an author's nonmoral values influencing the moral stance adopted with regard to personhood. A wholesale adherence to consequentialism has a direct bearing on moral issues, but the position is not itself a normative one. It is, however, a metaethical position and therefore falls within the domain of philosophical ethics, broadly construed. Ultimately grounded in a Christian ethics of love, Fletcher's brand of consequentialism is indistinguishable in practice from the much-maligned and oft-misunderstood theory of utilitarianism. But inasmuch as even the most enlightened form of utilitarianism must admit at least some cases in which the sacrifice of one or more human beings is required to achieve the greater good, adherence to that doctrine implies the unsavory result that it is sometimes necessary to kill human beings (or allow them to die) in order to do what is morally right. That result is rendered less unsavory by defining the individuals to be sacrificed as nonpersons or as subhuman.

It is worth mentioning some additional strategies of argumentation regarding personhood which foster strong disagreement in the bioethics literature. The chief strategies are: the use of the potentiality principle; the use of analogies; and the use of artificial cases (this last strategy is probably a subcategory of the use of analogies, but it is worth distinguishing because of the special character of the analogies employed).

The potentiality principle   This is the well-known strategy of taking the moment of conception as the beginning of personhood because of the potentiality of the fertilized ovum to develop into a full-fledged adult human being. Two writers who explicitly accept the argument from potentiality are Noonan (1970) and Kluge (1975), and those who argue directly against that strategy are Fletcher (1979), Tooley (1972), Brody (1974), and Warren (1973). Thomson offers no argument, but hurls the following barb: "Similar things might be said about the development of an acorn into an oak tree, and it does not follow that acorns are oak trees, or that we had better say they are.... A newly fertilized ovum, a newly implanted clump of cells, is no more a person than an acorn is an oak tree" (Thomson, 1971, in Beauchamp and Walters, p. 199). Thomson's remark is an example of mixed strategies, for she rejects the use of the potentiality principle by way of analogy with acorns and oak trees. Although those who accept the potentiality principle typically hold that personhood begins at conception, writers who reject its use accept the beginning of personhood at various later points: Brody at the onset of brain waves, Thomson somewhere prior to birth (she doesn't say when), Warren and Tooley at some point after infancy. It seems fair to conclude that an appeal to the potentiality principle is made only by those whose criterion of personhood, taken by itself, is so implausible it requires the use of some such principle in order to construct a reasoned argument. The only other alternative would be simply to accept religious dogma on the matter of personhood, which few contributors to the bioethics literature are inclined to do.

The use of analogies and artificial cases   Analogical reasoning is a powerful mode of argument, but for an analogy to be sound, the items compared must be similar in relevant respects. The trick, of course, is to agree on which respects are relevant, and which are not. Artificial cases appear to nonphilosophers as less similar to the case under consideration than real cases might be, despite the ingenuity philosophers display in cooking up compelling examples. I discuss these two strategies together here, because I think they are both aspects of the same type of argument.

Without supplying all the imaginative details, I remind the reader of two notable examples of cases concocted by way of analogy with the concerns of personhood and abortion. The first is Thomson's fanciful case of a famous violinist hooked up to your kidneys, which he needs to sustain his own life for a period of nine months, after which he will have recovered. The violinist is a person, and so he has a right to life. Your life is not endangered, but your freedom to move about for nine months is drastically inhibited. We are supposed to consider the violinist an appropriate analogue to a fetus, and you and your kidneys as analogous to a pregnant woman and her life supports for the fetus. If your right to disconnect yourself from the violinist overrides his right to life, the argument goes, shouldn't it follow that a woman's right to terminate her pregnancy overrides the fetus's right to life? One can admire Thomson's philosophical imagination, yet reject the soundness of the analogy on a number of different counts. Arguing in general against the use of artificial cases, Noonan writes about this one: "The similitude to pregnancy is grotesque. It is difficult to think of another age or society in which a caricature of this sort could be seriously put forward as a paradigm illustrating the moral choice to be made by the mother" (Noonan, 1974, in Beauchamp and Walters, p. 210). And Warren, who adopts a very high standard of personhood, and thus an extremely permissive stance on abortion, criticizes Thomson's analogy on the grounds that it is too weak to do the work required in the abortion argument: ". . . the Thomson analogy can provide a clear and persuasive defense of an abortion only with respect to those cases in which the woman is in no way responsible for her pregnancy, e.g., where it is due to rape" (Warren, 1973, in Beauchamp and Walters, p. 221).

The second example is hypothesized by Tooley in his attack on the potentiality principle (another example of a mixed strategy). Imagine we have a chemical that, if injected into a kitten, would enable it to develop into an adult cat having the intellectual and psychological abilities of a human adult. Tooley relies on the reader's intuition that it would not be wrong to kill a kitten injected with this chemical, and reasoning by analogy, he rejects the potentiality principle as applied to the human fetus (Tooley, 1972, in Gorovitz et al., pp. 314–15). Noonan responds to this artificial case in a fashion similar to his reaction to Thomson's example. A problem with the use of artificial cases as a strategy for arguing a moral point is that the debate shifts to a discussion of the preposterousness of the example, and hence to the adequacy of the analogy, leaving the real issue aside.

In analogical reasoning real cases have the advantage of being rooted in reality, yet the same problems exist regarding their similarity to the case at hand. The personhood debate variously uses an analogy that treats minority groups as nonpersons or as subhuman. Rejecting various tacks taken by proponents of abortion to show that the fetus is not a person, Noonan writes:

Feeling is notoriously an unsure guide to the humanity of others. Many groups of humans have had difficulty in feeling that persons of another tongue, color, religion, sex, are as human as they. . . . Experience shows that sight is even more untrustworthy than feeling in determining humanity. By sight, color became an appropriate index for saying who was a man, and the evil of racial discrimination was given foundation. . . . Finally, a distinction is sought in social visibility. . . . If humanity depends on social recognition, individuals or whole groups may be dehumanized by being denied any status in their society. [Noonan, 1970, in Gorovitz et al., pp. 293–94]

For a related yet somewhat different purpose, Brody also argues by way of analogy using minorities. In defending his view that the humanity of the fetus must be a matter of *discovery* of some sort, against O'Connor's that it is a matter for *decision*, Brody says:

This seems to place the matter of human rights open to too many objectionable decisions. After all, there are all types of people with all types of prejudices about what is or is not required for being a living human being. And would we want to say that members of some minority group are really not living human beings just because they fail to meet the criterion of humanity established by some prejudiced majority, where the criterion in question reflected the prejudices of that majority group? [Brody, 1974, in Beauchamp and Walters, p. 232]

Brody pursues the same line against Wertheimer, who defends a position similar to O'Connor's. Wertheimer (1971) himself raises the problematic issue of treatment of minorities based on perceptions of their humanity (pp. 86–87), but Brody still finds his account open to the same objections as O'Connor's position, and concludes that "neither Wertheimer nor O'Connor have been able to meet the problem of the prejudiced society" (Brody, 1974, in Beauchamp and Walters, p. 235). This conclusion leads Brody to adopt the alternative view, namely, that personhood and the ascription of rights are matters of discovery, not decision.

If it were necessary to arrive at suitable criteria for personhood before attempting to resolve the abortion controversy, it would be crucial to adjudicate the discovery versus decision debate. For present purposes, however, it is necessary only to indicate the problems with both approaches. Suppose that determining the criteria for personhood is a matter for decision. We are immediately confronted with the inability of many thoughtful people to reach a consensus on the definition of personhood. If it were a matter for political decision, the absurd consequence would follow that the definition of personhood would be contingent on which political faction is more powerful at any given time—antiabortionists or proabortionists. If it is a matter for moral decision, we are thrown back into the quagmire in which the most carefully reasoned moral arguments leave opponents unmoved. If it is a matter for religious decision, we are confronted with the facts of pluralism in our society and with the constitutionally mandated separation of church and state. This leaves only a matter for individual decision, which entails the absurdly mistaken view of language that people can use words to mean whatever they want them to mean.

Suppose, then, the determination of personhood is a matter for discovery. If so, what kind of discovery? No one in the bioethics literature seriously maintains that it is a purely scientific discovery, although as mentioned at several points, some scientific data are taken to be relevant to the problem. But the very fact that *different* bits of scientific evidence are marshalled (presence of the full genetic code, for one definition, and onset of encephalographic activity, for another), shows that just which scientific data are taken as relevant itself depends on antecedently held views about personhood.

Is it, then, a question to which metaphysics can provide answers? The discovery would then have to be either religious or philosophical. The epistemological difficulties of religious knowledge are well known, and this mode of inquiry would be wholly unacceptable to those who do not believe in the supernatural, or who do not follow whatever particular religious dogma is alleged to provide the source of relevant information. As for some metaphysical discovery that might follow from philosophical analysis, the evidence displayed herein reveals the futility of that approach. One can, nevertheless, continue in the quest for a Holy Grail or a Fountain of Youth, despite the failures of one's predecessors and based on the triumph of hope over experience.

Personhood Is Not a Useful Concept for Resolving Dilemmas in Bioethics

After this gallop through the literature on personhood, it is probably gratuitous to conclude that personhood is not a useful concept for resolving dilemmas in bioethics. It is striking that so much of the literature discusses personhood solely in the context of abortion, but I suspect that if a different topic absorbed as much public attention and was an equally pressing issue in public policy, the locus of debate would be lodged there.

If two people hold conflicting views on an issue in bioethics that allegedly involves the problem of personhood, is one of them likely to be convinced by the other's arguments regarding the proper standard for personhood? The answer is decidedly not. Let us take one last look at the writings featured in the discussion to this point.

Consider, first, Warren's stated expectations about how her proposed criteria will be received by the foes of abortion. She writes: "It is possible to show that, on the basis of intuitions which we may expect even the opponents of abortion to share, a fetus is not a person, and hence not the sort of entity to which it is proper to ascribe full moral rights" (Warren, 1973, in Beauchamp and Walters, p. 218). Warren is, of course, well aware of the views of other writers who have discussed the humanity or the personhood of the fetus, including those of John Noonan. Yet so confident is she of the correctness of her five criteria for personhood, and of the likelihood of their universal acceptance by any thinking person, that she writes:

All we need to claim, to demonstrate that a fetus is not a person, is that any being which satisfies *none* of (1)–(5) is certainly not a person. I consider this claim to be so obvious that I think anyone who denied it, and claimed that a being which satisfied none of (1)–(5) was a person all the same, would thereby demonstrate that he had no notion at all of what a person is—perhaps because he had confused the concept of a person with that of genetic humanity. [Ibid., p. 224]

Now it may well be the case that some naive individuals confuse the concept of a person with that of genetic humanity. It is because of the possibility of such confusion that Tooley proposes avoiding the term 'human' altogether in such discussions, noting that to use the terms 'person' and 'human being' interchangeably tends to lend covert support to antiabortionist positions (Tooley, 1972, in Gorovitz et al., p. 300). Among those whom Tooley cites as falling prey to the same confusion Warren describes are Brody, Thomson, and Wertheimer. A related error, committing the fallacy of equivocation, is the charge English levels against unnamed opponents:

Some have mistakenly reasoned from the premise that a fetus is human (after all, it is a human fetus rather than, say, a canine fetus), to the conclusion that it is a human. Adding an equivocation on 'being', we get the fallacious argument that since a fetus is something both living and human, it is a human being. [English, 1975, in Beauchamp and Walters, p. 242]

It is entirely possible, however unlikely it may be, that able philosophers like Brody, Thomson, and Wertheimer unwittingly confuse personhood with the property of being genetically human. But it is surely false that Noonan (1974) is a victim of such slipshod semantics or logic, for he explicitly provides reasons for considering that which is genetically human to be a person, discussing the proposals of others who choose a different locus for the beginning of personhood from the early point Noonan himself accepts. If there is any confusion here, it is to be laid at the door of those like Warren who, apparently forgetting her avowal that the concept of a person is in part a moral concept, treats it as a purely descriptive notion: "The concept of a person is one which is very nearly universal (to people), and that it is common to both proabortionists and antiabortionists, even though neither group has fully realized the relevance of this concept to the resolution of their dispute" (Warren, 1973, in Beauchamp and Walters, p. 224). What antiabortionists are doing, on the contrary, is *proposing* that the fetus be considered a person, and therefore, a creature to be treated as a member of the moral community.

Tooley, likewise, should not be at all surprised that some writers choose to call 'persons' those entities Tooley himself would consider genetically human but not persons. In that he acknowledges at the outset that he is using the term 'person' as a purely moral concept, it is reasonable to expect that others' use of the term is similarly influenced by their antecedently held moral values. Because of the wide range of positions regarding the permissibility of abortion, and the fact that all of the writers Tooley refers to discuss personhood entirely within the context of abortion, it is not in the least surprising to find them using the term 'person' in a prescriptive way that follows directly from their views about the morality of abortion.

As a reminder of the lack of consistency concerning this topic, consider Thomson's essay. Although she argues at length for the position that the rights of the mother override the rights of the fetus, and although she admits at the end of her article that "we have only been pretending throughout that the fetus is a human being from the moment of conception," she asserts that in some cases "resort to abortion is even positively indecent" (Thomson, 1971, in Beauchamp and Walters, pp. 208, 209). At the very end, Thomson concludes: "A *very early abortion* is surely not the killing of a person, and so is not dealt with by anything I have said here" (Ibid., p. 209; emphasis added). This suggests, at least by way of contrast, that Thomson is prepared to agree to the proposition that a very late abortion *is* the killing of a person. When not speaking hypothetically about the fetus as a person, Thomson ventures her own (tentative) view: "I am inclined to think also that we shall probably have to agree that the fetus has already become a human person well before birth. Indeed, it comes as a surprise when one first learns how early in its life it begins to acquire human characteristics" (Ibid., p. 199). If, in spite of these acknowledgments, Thomson nonetheless maintains that abortion is morally permissible (although in some cases indecent?), what further evidence is needed to show the irrelevance or the ad hoc nature of arguments about person-hood in bioethics?

Protecting the Interests of the Fetus

The analysis thus far has intended to show both the intractability of debates about the concept of personhood and also the fruitlessness of attempting to resolve the abortion controversy by appealing to that concept. In this concluding section, the view put forward by Patricia King (1979) will serve as our point of departure.

Recall that King authored one of four different positions regarding the importance of personhood in resolving the abortion controversy. According to King, whether the fetus is a person is irrelevant to whether it should have legal protection; concerns about the health of the fetus create pressing policy issues regardless of whether or not the fetus is granted the status of a person:

Most legal and philosophical literature about the fetus concerns abortion, and in recent years moral philosophers have thought the critical prelimi-nary issue in resolving the morality of abortion to be whether the fetus is a person. In *Roe* v. *Wade*, the Supreme Court also approached the abor-tion issue through the question of personhood. The Court held that the fetus is not a person, a holding that has been criticized for inadequate analysis.

I submit that whether the fetus is a "person" is irrelevant to whether it should have legal protection. The personhood debate has only obscured the decisive issues. [See King, above, pp. 79–80]

That a fetus can have interests (construing that notion very broadly) even prior to the time at which many writers ascribe to it the status of personhood is illustrated by the following considerations:

1. Damage to the fetus can occur in the early weeks after conception. In the case of a wanted pregnancy, responsible women do (and should) take steps to prevent or minimize the possibility of such harm. The increasing number of known or suspected toxic or harmful agents in-clude tobacco, alcohol, caffeine, and other drugs consumed by the preg-nant woman; various occupational and environmental hazards believed to cause birth defects, including X-rays and various gases used as anes-thesia; rubella and other diseases contracted by the mother that may affect the fetus. Because damage leading to birth defects can occur during the period in fetal development when none—except those who accept the very lowest standard—consider the fetus to be a person, it

is clear that the fetus has interests that stand in need of protection.

One may object that these are more properly viewed as the interests of the prospective parents, or of the pregnant woman, in having a normal, healthy baby. But it seems reasonable to describe the situation as one of identity of interests between the fetus and the prospective parents. This is entirely consistent with a decision to abort a fetus discovered to be defective or damaged. Inasmuch as the decision to abort in many cases is based on fetal abnormalities discovered through prenatal diagnosis, it is not inconsistent to hold that a fetus ought to be protected from hazards and potential damage while *in utero,* and at the same time to maintain that abortion is morally permissible if such precautions prove ineffective.

2. The emerging techniques of fetal therapy pose a new dilemma for a group that holds one of the many possible positions on the moral permissibility of abortion. The advent of *in utero* therapy is mistakenly viewed by some as having broad implications for the abortion debate. However, the concern should properly be confined to those who view abortion as ethically acceptable only in cases where defects are detected *in utero* (Ruddick and Wilcox, 1982). For those who hold that abortion is permissible whatever the condition of the fetus, and for those who take the opposite extreme—that abortion is never allowable, the emergence of *in utero* therapeutic techniques should make no difference. But for a third group, one that holds abortion to be morally permissible only in cases of demonstrable defects in the fetus, a new dilemma arises. Ruddick and Wilcox note, "For people such as these, the techniques of fetal repair may poses a serious moral question: How many options are morally permissible? Before such techniques there were two—abortion or birth of a defective child. Are there now three, two, or only one (treatment)?" (p. 12).

Discussions of the ethical issues surrounding fetal therapy are now taking place without essential reference to the status of the fetus as a person, although some writers raise the subject indirectly by posing questions about the rights of the fetus when *in utero* treatment is available (Robertson, 1982; Bowes and Selgestad, 1981). Curiously, a new focus on the status of the fetus as a *patient* makes an appearance in recent writings on fetal surgery and other modes of therapy (Fletcher, 1981; Canty and Wolf, 1982; Clewell et al., 1982). The relationship between patienthood and personhood has not yet become a widely discussed topic, although Ruddick and Wilcox offer a hypothetical argument linking these concepts. These authors deny that we are compelled to consider the fetus a person even if we grant it the status of a patient: "Some patients are not persons—for example, patients who are brain-dead, anencephalic, or animal" (p. 13).

Also undecided at present is the question of whether there will be a legal obligation to treat a defective fetus once these therapeutic techniques are no longer in their experimental stages, even if that requires overriding objections by the pregnant woman (Robertson, 1982). The point to emphasize for our purposes here, however, is the irrelevance of the personhood of the fetus for addressing these moral and legal concerns. Because the detection of correctable defects may occur before such time as personhood is ascribed (at least by the majority of writers on this subject), a decision to intervene therapeutically on behalf of the fetus is independent of its status as a person.

3. Legal recognition of the unborn varies considerably according to different circumstances. One article summarizes the legal situation as follows:

Now permitted clear discretion, under the U.S. Constitution, to take an interest in the viable unborn child, a state must nevertheless provide a common law or statutory basis for including the unborn child within the class of persons or objects over whom courts have jurisdiction. The threshold question of whether unborn children are "persons" for any purpose of the law has been answered differently for different legal matters. For example, the United States Supreme Court has decided (*Roe* v. *Wade*) that an unborn child is not a "person" under the 14th Amendment to the United States Constitution. This ruling does not mean that states cannot define an unborn child as a person, within constitutional guidelines. Also, deciding that the unborn is not a "person," does not totally prevent action on behalf of the unborn. In property, tort and probate law, moreover, there are a considerable number of cases recognizing unborn children as persons. [Bross and Meredyth, 1979, p. 645]

These variations in the law regarding the status of the unborn may prompt charges of inconsistency, but a different view invites us to explore the purposes the law is meant to serve.

Further reflection on the problems of looking too closely at what the law has ordained serves to remind us that the Supreme Court has held that corporations were to be considered "persons" coming under the protection of various provisions of the Constitution, including the Fourteenth Amendment. Regarding this example, in a discussion of various occurrences of the concept of person in the law, one writer asks:

Why has the Court done this? Is it because the members of the Court have adopted some theory that ensoulment occurs at the moment of incorporation? Is it because they were shown ultrasound images of a corporation that revealed a startlingly human form? Of course, the answer is "no." The real basis, even though the Court may not always be so clear about it, is in the social consequences that the Court can see will flow from a failure to apply the particular law to corporations. [Baron, 1982, pp. 6–7]

Baron finds the same variation in the law regarding the personhood of the unborn as noted in the earlier quotation from Bross and Meredyth: "We find the law generally evidencing the same sort of flexibility and pragmatism in ascribing personhood. For some purposes, the fetus is a person. For some it is not. And the stage at which it is granted personhood varies from one area of the law to another" (Ibid., p. 11).

Thus, any hope of receiving clear guidance from the law on the status of the fetus as a person is dimmed by these considerations. But this is no doubt as it should be. Consistency is indeed a virtue, in law as well as in morality. But its interpretation in this situation must be viewed in terms of consistency with the purposes the law is meant to serve. Variation in laws pertaining to recognition of the unborn affords additional evidence for the position that personhood is a matter for decision, not for discovery. Whether that issue is best left *undecided* in the controversy surrounding abortion is a question about which reasonable people disagree. However, inasmuch as unresolved legal issues concerning the fetus may be settled without first deciding whether the fetus is a person, it would be well to seek an approach that totally bypasses the question of personhood. This is the approach adopted by Patricia King who writes:

[W]e can no longer avoid some resolution of the legal status of the fetus. The potential benefits of fetal research, the ability to fertilize the human ovum in a laboratory dish, and the increasing awareness that a mother's activities during pregnancy may affect the health of her offspring create pressing policy issues that raise possible conflicts among fetuses, mothers, and researchers. [King, above, p. 57]

Although moral issues embodied in the law are often couched in terms of rights and duties—where appeal can be made to judicial precedents and statutes—questions of rights and duties are much less clear in the moral arena considered apart from the law. Appeals to fetal rights, especially the putative right to life, have had little effect on arguments directed at proponents of reproductive freedom. That the debate pits fetal rights against the rights of pregnant women has not helped either side in the ongoing abortion controversy. Intruding the concept of personhood into this impasse has accomplished nothing by way of resolution.

Invoking the interests of the fetus may be a more promising approach in confronting the broad range of moral concerns in the area of reproduction. There is good reason to seek protection of a wanted fetus, or one that will likely come to term, both for its own sake in the future and that of the parents. But in order to attribute interests to a fetus that will most likely become an infant at a later stage of development, it is not necessary to ascribe to it the status of personhood. Nor is it necessary to assign rights to a fetus, while still a fetus, in order to recognize that the likelihood of its becoming an infant places it in need of certain protections while still *in utero*. Given the disarray in the literature on personhood as it relates to abortion, the burden of proof lies with those who hold that the concept is fruitful or necessary for addressing moral and legal concerns in the area of reproduction.

=

Part 3

The Limits of Legislative and Judicial
Enforcement of Controversial Moral Standards

Roe v. *Wade* sets the current boundaries of judicial and legislative decision making on the abortion issue. These boundaries appear restrictive indeed. Yet since 1973, more than seventy-five pieces of local, state, and federal legislation have been introduced, many enacted, but most enjoined by state and federal courts.

It is undisputed that significant legal and moral questions remain unresolved in the wake of *Roe*. Some issues were explicitly left open by the *Roe* court. Others arise from ambiguities or incompleteness in the Court's reasoning. Some of these issues have been addressed by the Court in abortion rulings subsequent to *Roe*. Yet significant questions still remain, involving not only the propriety of specific legislative proposals or judicial decisions, but also the roles of the three branches of government with respect to abortion and the scope of the liberty defined by the *Roe* court. The essays in this section address some of these most difficult issues.

Roger Wertheimer's "Understanding Blackmun's Argument: The Reasoning of *Roe* v. *Wade*" examines Blackmun's majority opinion. Wertheimer offers a reconstruction of arguments he suggests are suppressed in the opinion, to produce an argument that is coherent and compelling. He articulates the interests at issue in the case, and shows how considerations of burden of proof, presumptions of rights, and *stare decisis* shaped the *Roe* decision.

Wertheimer takes issue with some aspects of the opinion, specifically the account of permissible state interests in maternal health and in the protection of viable fetuses. He argues that the correct understanding of Blackmun's argument denies the fetus any legal status, even granted the state's right to prohibit abortion in some circumstances.

Stephen Galebach's "A Human Life Statute" argues that a federal human life statute would be constitutional. He agrees with the *Roe* court's finding that the judiciary is not competent to rule on the issue of fetal personhood, and that given the current legal situation, it would be incorrect to view the fetus as a person for the purposes of the Fourteenth Amendment. He suggests, however, based upon past uses of the Fourteenth Amendment, that it is within Congress's purview to determine just what and who is to count as a person for the purposes of Fourteenth Amendment protection. Further, he suggests that the function of the legislative branch generally is to arrive at difficult legislative classifications. Hence, he argues, Congress would be well within its power to determine that fetuses are persons for the purposes of Fourteenth Amendment protection, and to extend such protection to them.

David A. J. Richards's "Constitutional Privacy, Religious Disestablishment, and the Abortion Decisions" provides a novel legal and moral analysis of the abortion issue grounded in a philosophical interpretation of the First Amendment's prohibition of the establishment of religion. Richards first discusses the development of privacy theory in law, political theory, and philosophy, and concludes that as developed by the Court, privacy theory provides insufficient support for the abortion decisions.

Richards then offers an alternative argument for grounding the abortion decisions in the right to privacy, based upon the antiestablishment clause. He approaches this argument through considerations raised by John Stuart Mill, as well as through the history of the use of the antiestablishment clause both within and outside the context of the abortion controversy.

Understanding Blackmun's Argument:
The Reasoning of *Roe* v. *Wade*

Roger Wertheimer

We need not resolve the difficult question of when life begins. When those trained in the respective disciplines of medicine, philosophy, and theology are unable to arrive at any consensus, the judiciary, at this point in the development of man's knowledge, is not in a position to speculate as to the answer.[1]

THESE words of Justice Blackmun, speaking for the majority in *Roe* v. *Wade*, bid fair to be among the most oft-quoted sentences of any Supreme Court opinion. Their fame derives from their having defined the pivotal premises for a ruling that all would deem epochal and many would damn as apocalyptic. But an aura of infamy now hangs round them, for to many trained minds they seem, in context, duncically paradoxical. Though the ruling has many friends, virtually all of them seem embarrassed by this particular reasoning; scholarly apologists defend their endorsement of the ruling with explanations notably independent of—if not inconsistent with—any argument in which those propositions figure.[2] And embarrassment has turned to chagrin as so-called pro-life advocates have interpreted those words as a license to undermine the ruling by means of congressional legislation or constitutional amendment. In brief, Blackmun's judicial epoche has induced every condition from perplexity to apoplexy, except ataraxy.

Though I shall later list some of my misgivings with other parts of the Blackmun opinion, my main message is that the greatest shortcoming of those two notorious sentences is that there are only two of them. Whereas the claims they proffer are correct and consistent with the rest of the opinion, some of the structure of suppositions requisite for understanding Blackmun's reasoning is neither obvious nor asserted, and thus uncertainty remains regarding the propriety of the Court's decision. To this extent the Court did not completely succeed in fulfilling its solemn responsibilities, which include not merely reaching just decisions and doing so for good and sufficient reasons, but also adequately informing the nation's citizenry, legislators, and lower courts of the rationale for the legal order it imposes. With all the fierce passions surrounding and sometimes beclouding the abortion controversy, that shortcoming is regrettable. Still, it is remediable. The explanations needed to render manifest the coherence of Blackmun's reasoning can be supplied by weaving his words into the structure of the argument I recommended two years prior to the *Wade* decision.[3]

Those notorious two sentences have been subject to three critical responses. First, those sentences state that there is a difficult question that the Court did not have to ("need not"), cannot ("is not in a position to"), and thus presumably should not try to answer. The unvoiced but unobviable implication is that the Court did not, expressly or otherwise, answer this difficult question. Yet, according to Blackmun's own analysis of the salient issues of the case, it appears that the Court had to and did endorse an answer. Second, the second sentence says that the Court's incapacity is connected with the presence of some disagreement among experts regarding this difficult question ("those trained in the respective disciplines of medicine, philosophy, and theology are unable to arrive at any consensus"). Yet, courts daily resolve questions upon which expert opinion is divided; that is one of the functions of a court. Third, the second sentence predicates this incapacity only of the judiciary. This leaves open the possibility that some other part of the government could properly resolve the question and thereby nullify the Court's ruling. In brief, the first criticism concerns the *internal consistency* of Blackmun's implicit denial that the Court answered the difficult question; the second criticism concerns the *justification* of his claim that the judiciary is incapable of answering that question; and the third criticism concerns the implications of that last claim for the *propriety of any governmental decision* on the question. Let us begin examining these matters in that order; eventually it will become apparent that the issues are intertwined.

Blackmun continually (and perhaps pointedly) refers to the difficult question as the "question when life begins." He also uses the expression "when a new human life is present,"[4] and he would assuredly accept the formulation, "Whether and when a human conceptus is a living human being." However, such rephrasing cancels only the crudest misconstruals.

Blackmun's disavowal of an answer is, at minimum, paradoxical. He unequivocally asserts that "if it is established" that "the fetus is a 'person' within the language and meaning of the Fourteenth Amendment," then "the appellant's [i.e., the pro-choice] case, of course, collapses, for the fetus's right to life is then guaranteed specifically by the Amendment." [5] And he unequivocally denies that antecedent clause: "The word 'person,' as used in the Fourteenth Amendment, does not include the unborn." [6] And, more generally, he concludes that "the unborn have never been recognized in the law as persons in the whole sense." [7] Further, of course the pro-choice case did not "collapse": the Court ruled that abortion may not be prohibited before viability (but only regulated in its medical aspects to protect the mother's health),[8] so the Court must have held that a fetus is not a person. Indeed, strictly speaking the Court appears committed to holding that personhood is not acquired before live birth, because the Court ruled that even after viability, an abortion necessary to preserve the life or health of the mother may not be prohibited.[9] (This latter point is almost as forceful as the former in light of Blackmun's footnote 54, wherein he questions where abortion prohibitions which contain some exceptions—as they all do, if only for the purpose of protecting the life of the mother —could be consistently based on a person's Fourteenth Amendment right to life.)

Evidently Blackmun must be presuming some distinction between the question of whether, within the meaning of the law, a fetus is a person, and the "difficult question" of whether it is a human life. Clearly the Court must and did answer the former question, if only because the law (e.g., the Fourteenth Amendment) explicitly speaks of persons and secures them a right to life, a right which would supersede a mother's rights. The problem, then, is whether and how Blackmun could separate these two questions so as to answer the former without answering the latter.

In light of the philosophical literature of the last decade, it is necessary to state that in none of the *Wade* opinions do any of the justices contemplate separating these questions by invoking that novel theory proclaimed to be self-evident by numerous contemporary philosophers: to wit, that the question of whether something is a living human being is utterly irrelevant—logically, morally, and metaphysically—to the question of whether that thing is a person, just as one's race and sex are irrelevant to one's being a person. That is, Lord knows, a lunatic theory, but, like many another theory only lunatics live by, it properly interests philosophers if only because its rebuttal requires an examination of a matrix of profound assumptions.[10] In any case, whatever its merits as pure moral theory, it is utterly irrelevant to the political and legal realities confronted in *Wade*. A Court endorsement of such a theory would be lunacy, because it would enrage a monolithic majority of the populace and legislators, not coincidentally, because it would grossly violate our most well-established legal principles. No philosophical theory that purports that a living human being must acquire certain cognitive, volitional, or affective capacities to be a person has a speck of respectable legal precedent in its favor.[11] For Blackmun, the operative contrast is between the born and the unborn, not between the presence and the absence of some psychological capacities. His opinion supplies no fuel for the hysteria of antiabortionists anxious about legalizing infanticide. Within the bounds of our legal tradition no court could rule that an unborn child is not legally a person while recognizing it as a living human being in every sense in which a born child is.

On the other hand, throughout his opinion Blackmun carefully distinguishes his talk about persons from his talk about life, human life, human beings, and so on. (The sole apparent exception occurs while he is describing some ancient and medieval discussions that "approached the question . . . in terms of when a 'person' came into being." [12] Here Blackmun is clearly not endorsing this terminology.) The crucial point here is that the laws relevant to this case are formulated with the term "person," not with such terms as "human being" or "human life." Yet, again, nothing Blackmun says implies a rejection of the principle that a living human being is a person. On the contrary, he does not rule out the argument for the personhood of the fetus based on "the well-known facts of fetal development" as being irrelevant or a non sequitur.[13]

But, then, if he accepts that principle as relevant, how could he say that he need not answer the "difficult question"? And if he did not reject that principle while denying that a fetus is a person, how could he implicitly say that he did not deny that a fetus is a human being? A key to solving both of these questions is that following the lead of the district court,[14] Blackmun put the burden of proof on the state to establish that a fetus is a person; he did not put it on the individual,

Roe, to establish that a fetus is not a person. The onus of proof ultimately lies with the state because our theory of government is premised on the principle that government derives its legitimate powers
from the consent of the governed—which means that governmental
acts infringing on their rights or frustrating their interests must be
justifiable to them. Thus, the individual is not compelled to justify her
exercise of her rights and capacities for action; rather, it is the state
that must justify its coercive acts. In *Wade* the adversaries were not
two persons (or a person and an alleged or putative person) with competing claims of rights; the adversaries were a person and the State of
Texas. This is so, not because the case arises from the violation of a
criminal statute which pits a woman as a defendant against the state
as prosecutor, but because the abortion statute at issue severely limits
the woman's "fundamental" right of privacy.[15] It is crucial that a governmental ruling to the effect that a fetus is a person is not an abstract
intellectual thesis; it is itself a limitation of the rights of pregnant
women. So the issue before the Court was not, Is the fetus, in some
scientific, metaphysical or moral sense, a person? Rather, it was, Can
the state provide sufficient justification for limiting the rights of the
pregnant woman by categorizing a fetus as a person? Thus, when
Blackmun had determined that the state failed to carry its burden, he
formulated his conclusion on this whole issue by saying, "In view of
all this, we do not agree that, by adopting one theory of life, Texas
may override the rights of the pregnant woman at stake." [16]

As that concluding remark suggests, Blackmun countenanced no
support of the suggestion made by others that the legislature or the
judiciary is empowered to define the category of person to suit public
policy.[17] No trace of a dubious theory of legal positivism or pragmatism is in evidence here.[18] Certainly classification by fiat is a common legislative and judicial activity elsewhere, but Blackmun does not
treat the category of person as susceptible to governmental discretion.
And rightly so, for the bestowal or denial of that status is not only
awesome in its consequences but also profound in its presuppositions.
A theory of government such as ours, predicated on the idea that government is an instrument for protecting the rights and furthering the
interests of persons, cannot coherently deny that the nature of personhood and the fundamental rights inhering in it are anterior to governmental acts. To deny the status of person to those who rightfully
possess it is a howling injustice. And bestowing that status upon those

who don't rightfully possess it is hardly less an injustice, inasmuch as that bestowal inevitably involves gross abridgments of the rights of those who rightfully possess that status.[19]

Still, a legal category is perforce distinct from its "natural" or nonlegal counterpart simply because it functions within an essentially distinct (albeit generally similar) system of epistemological norms. Although the defining criteria of the legal and nonlegal category may be the same so that the concepts are coextensive, the epistemological norms governing their application may permit or require the detachment of the legal category from its nonlegal counterpart. In the natural, nonlegal context wherein laymen (or "those trained in ... medicine, philosophy and theology") debate their questions—whether the questions be about the personhood or humanhood of the fetus, or whatever—there are no constraints on the debate comparable to the special rules of evidence and inference recognized by our courts. In particular, there is nothing comparable to an *onus probandi* assigned to one disputant. In a nonlegal context, the failure to prove that a fetus is a person or human being does not entail that it is contradictory, and the failure to prove that a fetus is not a person or human being does not entail that it is. Yet in a legal context an *argumentum ad ignorantium* need not be a fallacy. There, a failure to meet a burden of proving that x is y may permit and require the inference that x is not y. As a consequence, a legal question can be resolved while and even because its nonlegal counterpart remains moot.

What ought to be the epistemological rules employed by a court is a debatable matter of legal theory. But it appears sufficiently certain that a legal system must employ principles somewhat different from those in a noninstitutional context, and that Blackmun does not rely on any controversial principles of legal epistemology. Legal reasoning is practical: a decision must be reached, and even if avoided, the status quo is in effect sustained. Placing the onus of proof on some party is necessary and is often sufficient to insure that a decision is made. In a criminal trial we place that burden on the prosecution. For different but not unrelated reasons, in deciding an issue of constitutional law, the burden is placed on the state. However, these two situations are not completely parallel. When a criminal court finds a defendant innocent because the presumption of innocence has not been defeated, it is presupposing and applying but not defining the notion of innocence, and its "finding" does not alter the truth of the proposition that the defendant is really guilty, nor does it detach its sense from the ordinary, nonlegal interpretation of that claim. But in a case such as *Wade*, though the Court is presupposing and applying a notion of person, the Court is also specifying its application in law, defining it subject to constraints on legal reasoning that may cause that legal concept to be detached from its nonlegal interpretation. Thus, the Court's decision that a fetus is not legally a person need not imply an answer to the question of whether a fetus is, in some nonlegal sense, a person or a human being; it need not imply any more than that an affirmative answer was not sufficiently proven.

Blackmun need not have answered the question in another sense, for he can and does reach his denial of the personhood of the fetus quite independently of whether it is a human life. He does so by employing another legal epistemological principle that philosophers and scientists would not use for their comparable questions: viz., *stare decisis*, the authority of legal precedent. Yet here too the burden of proof plays a major role. Blackmun's tendentious deployment of legal precedent—his narrow reading of the law's use of the term "person" ("persons in the whole sense") and his interpretation that *any* divergence in the law's treatment of the unborn from that of the born is evidence that the law has not regarded the unborn as persons[20]— should, I believe, be understood as having been guided by an assumption that a rather severe burden of proof lies on the state because of the "fundamental" character of the woman's right at stake.[21]

Yet, presumably, Blackmun could have arrived at his ruling even if precedent were against it (as arguably much of it is), for the law is not, except in a trivial and innocuous sense, what the judges have said or do say it is.[22] Properly, the law is what the judges *ought* to say it is. Certainly Blackmun does not treat precedent as the sole and automatically decisive consideration. Although he argues against the unborn being persons for purposes of the Fourteenth Amendment solely by reference to precedent, he does not reject the facts of fetal development as irrelevant even for that restricted but crucial issue. Moreover, upon concluding his reading of the Fourteenth Amendment, he acknowledges that "this conclusion, however, does not of itself fully answer the contentions raised by Texas, and we pass on to other considerations." [23] He then confronts the Texas contention "that, apart from the Fourteenth Amendment, life begins at conception and is present throughout pregnancy, and that, therefore, the State has a compelling interest in protecting that life from and after conception." [24]

Up to this point it appears that Blackmun could have embraced the

Texas "theory of life" and found antiabortion legislation constitutional, and also that he could have denied that a fetus is a human being ("in the whole sense") and ruled against such legislation despite the substantial precedent behind it. He might have done either, but instead at this point he enters his claim that the Court need not and could not affirm or deny that "theory of life."

Thus far we have explained two senses in which Blackmun need not answer the difficult question: First, independent of any argument on the question, the weight of precedent alone could have decided whether the unborn are persons; Second, independent of the truth of an answer to the question, inasmuch as the state had the burden of proof and had no other line of argument, the mere failure of the state to demonstrate the truth of its theory of life would imply that the unborn are not persons and that its legislation is unconstitutional. What still needs explaining is why the Court did not need to (i.e., was not compelled by logic to) deny that a fetus is a human being while maintaining both that a fetus is not a person and that a human being is a person. To understand why the Court was under no necessity in this last and crucial respect we must move to the issue of why it could not answer the difficult question.

The Court cannot be compelled to answer a question that it cannot answer, and here "the judiciary . . . is not in a position to speculate as to the answer." But why not? After all, private individuals, including justices as private citizens, are in a position to speculate, for everyone has the First Amendment freedom to speculate about this or anything. Everyone, that is, except a justice, an authority whose mere opinions are law imposing constraints on others. For someone in that position, merely to pronounce an opinion is to impinge upon the legitimate interests of others. Here freedom of expression is limited. Indeed, even freedom of thought is restricted because a court has no unexpressed opinions: the mind of a court exists only in its pronouncements. Expressing an opinion is an action, and an authority may not act when it would thereby violate the principles which legitimate its authority.

Blackmun described the instant circumstances this way: "Those trained in the respective disciplines of medicine, philosophy and theology are unable to arrive at any consensus." He did not say—nor is it credible that he could possibly mean—that whenever a question lacks a consensus of expert opinion the judiciary is not competent to make a legal finding on the matter. Rather, he refers specifically to the extraordinary fact that, with this difficult question, presumptively expert opinion is divided within science *and* philosophy *and* religion. By contrast, when pathologists present opposed explanations of a wound, or psychiatrists disagree over the mental competence of an agent, theologians and philosophers have no expert opinion on the issue, no more than a chemist has much of interest to say about transubstantiation or logical atomism. Few questions arise in all three domains, and with those that do, the main disputes occur between different domains and perhaps within one domain, but not within and between all three. Some questions of cosmology and evolution may be debated within each domain, but in that case typically the premises, methods, and conclusions differ in kind for each domain. Yet with the question of when a human life begins we find the specialists of each discipline agreeing on and appealing to much the same subsidiary data and arriving at the same wide divergence of conclusions. In fact, aside from the disagreements on the answer itself, virtually the only matter debated within any discipline here is debated within all three—and that is the question of whether this question is scientific, religious, or philosophical (e.g., moral or conceptual). And surely, when the presumed experts are in utter disarray over what kinds of expertise are even relevant to a question, a judicious man might well be wary.

When Blackmun then proceeded "to note briefly the wide divergence of thinking on this most sensitive and difficult question," [25] he did not dwell on the disagreements about the character of the question. But then he hardly needed to, inasmuch as he had already taken judicial notice of the troublesome character of the question with these extraordinary introductory remarks:

We forthwith acknowledge our awareness of the sensitive and emotional nature of the abortion controversy, of the vigorous opposing views, even among physicians, and of the deep and seemingly absolute convictions that the subject inspires. One's philosophy, one's experiences, one's exposure to the raw edges of human existence, one's religious training, one's attitudes toward life and family and their values, and the moral standards one establishes and seeks to observe, are all likely to influence and to color one's thinking and conclusions about abortion.[26]

This might be dismissed as rhetorical window-dressing, inconsequential platitudes. Yet Blackmun deemed it worth saying, despite being keenly aware of how thoroughly unorthodox—and perhaps unique—such remarks are in the context of a Supreme Court opinion. A decade later he declared:

I believe everything I said in the second paragraph of that opinion, where I agonized, initially not only for myself, but for the Court. Parenthetically, in doing so publicly, I disobeyed one suggestion Hugo Black made to me when I first came here. He said, "Harry, never display agony. Never say that this is an agonizing, difficult decision. Always write as though it's clear as crystal." [27]

Why then did he preface his whole opinion this way? After all, great passions commonly surround the controversies coming before the Court. Blackmun must mean that the "emotional nature of the abortion controversy" is special—and presumably not (just) in degree, in that many of the momentous, fiercely contested Court cases have obviously been no less emotional in most senses of the word.

Blackmun's brief remarks do not constitute a theory about the emotional character of the controversy. They only highlight certain key features. For example, he does not deny that there is a question of empirical fact here: his stressing that even physicians hold vigorous opposing views would be pointless if their empirical expertise were not pertinent. However, he emphasizes "the deep and seemingly absolute" character of the convictions on this subject. Here he may be alluding to such phenomena as that the different claims concerning the time of hominization are typically not put forward as *hypotheses*, conjectures genuinely open to falsification by new empirical findings. Rather, people generally seem to be either in a quandary, with no clear sense of what they might learn that would relieve their doubts, or else they hold to their datings with a sense of obviousness, of being immediately justified by the most basic, uncontroverted and uncontrovertible facts of reproduction. He then rightly emphasized that both our conclusions and the thought processes by which we reach them seem to be a function of a great stew of factors—philosophical, religious, moral, experiential, intellectual, and attitudinal.[28]

Blackmun quickly contrasted this situation with another: "Our task, of course, is to resolve the issue by constitutional measurement free of emotion and predilection." [29] Of course. This may sound like a mere judicial piety, more window-dressing, and yet, again, Blackmun saw some need to affirm a platitude here. He continued: "We seek earnestly to do this, and because we do, we have inquired into, and in this opinion place some emphasis upon, medical and medical-legal history and what that history reveals about man's attitudes toward the abortive procedure over the centuries." [30]

With this as his preface, Blackmun first efficiently handled the preparatory issues and then devoted over one-fourth of the entire opinion and about one-half of his central argument to a review of that history.[31] It is a curiously inconclusive review whose structure and selection of contents seem determined by various motives. Putting aside any doubts about the accuracy or biases in that review, there remains the puzzle: What is it that Blackmun thinks this history "reveals about man's attitudes toward the abortive procedure"? What lesson does he think is to be learned from this history or his inquiry into it?

Blackmun concluded that the judiciary is not in a position to speculate as to when life begins. That conclusion seems justified on the plausible assumption that the character of the "emotional nature" of that question is such that the question cannot be resolved "by means of constitutional measurement free of emotion and predilection." That is, when a judge thoroughly takes on the disinterested, impartial, emotionally detached, utterly unbiased attitude required by his role, he assumes a cognitive standpoint from which no answer will seem correct. It is only within a fully embodied, emotionally engaged human life that the question has a relevant determinate sense and appears to have a determinate answer. In fact, there is no correct answer. Any one of a range of answers may appear to us (normal human beings) to be right, even obviously right, but in the blindness of total dispassion no answer at all appears.

To be sure, Blackmun did not explicitly advance this epistemological thesis, let alone argue for it in detail. (But then, consider how extraordinary it would be for a justice to expound a novel epistemological theory.) Nevertheless, that thesis is not only consistent with both the letter and the spirit of the whole opinion, but it also renders the opinion's central argument coherent and compelling. Moreover, attributing some version of the thesis to Blackmun is hardly far-fetched insofar as its core idea, in however vague or inchoate a form, has been shown by some polls to be among the most common views regarding the difficult question.[32] (It seems plainly irrelevant that most people who feel that the question has no objectively correct answer lack the knowledge of logic to appreciate and work out the formal implications of that idea.)

Of course, the truth of this epistemological thesis is another matter, but I am afraid that the arguments for it are too complex to do much more here than refer you to my writings for a more involved presentation.[33] Yet the essential idea is simple enough: for a belief to be objectively true or false there must be the possibility of intersubjective agreement on its truth value; we have, I think, good reason to believe that the requisite preconditions for agreement do not exist in this case. We can say that some answers to the question are flatly wrong—e.g., that an unfertilized egg or sperm is, by itself, a human being, or that hominization occurs substantially after birth. But between conception and partuition there seems to be no consensus as to when human life begins, for there seems to be nothing in logic or nature that would compel agreement on the matter.[34] The crucial point is not that people do do in fact disagree, but rather that we have no sound basis for supposing that disagreement here must be due to some cognitive defect.

That Blackmun accepted the epistemological thesis is further suggested by his denying the judiciary the capacity even to "speculate" as to the answer. Mere speculation requires less evidentiary backing than rendering an opinion, and, unlike the latter, it is not even a category of official judicial action. This description of the Court's incapacity suggests a more radical kind of nescience than the mere lack of information requisite for making a proper judicial determination. On the other hand, when Blackmun qualified the Court's incapacity with the clause, "at this point in the development of man's knowledge," he seems to allow the possibility that the Court's incapacity is due to some form of ignorance that could be remedied, perhaps in ten years, perhaps tomorrow. There are, however, more plausible possibilities. Blackmun speaks here of "man's knowledge," something much broader than embryological knowledge or even scientific knowledge, something that might encompass epistemological knowledge, self-knowledge, an understanding of our thinking on this question and the norms governing our thinking. The judiciary's position could conceivably be altered by, for example, a change in our conception of what constitutes a prejudicial bias regarding the question, or in our conception of what influences on our convictions are perversions of our cognitive activity. Consider the following: One's disposition to react to the human form with sympathetic and identificatory responses is, I assume, emotional, but do we really know whether it is a prejudicial "predilection" we must be free of to be able to resolve the question?

Again, although we could conceivably come to believe that the question of when human life begins has an objectively correct answer, we can not now substantiate such beliefs. Hence, in this situation, the Court should not try to answer the question; and when it denies that the unborn are persons, it need not abandon the principle that a human being is a person in order to refrain from denying that a fetus is a human being.

The epistemological thesis aside, Blackmun surely could not have meant that the judiciary's inability to resolve the question was due to some incapacity that did not affect a legislature. The whole thrust of his opinion is that a state legislature is not empowered to deprive a woman of her fundamental rights by endorsing some theory of life; nothing in that opinion suggests that the impotence of a state legislature here is due to its lacking some power possessed by the federal legislature. A woman's rights—which an abortion prohibition restricts —includes the right against interference by *any* level or branch of government.

But if the epistemological thesis is implicit in Blackmun's opinion, then that opinion presents a decisive argument against even a constitutional amendment to nullify the *Wade* ruling, not to mention a congressional enactment to that effect. The argument as presented thus far has been tailored to fit Blackmun's phrases, but the essence of the argument can readily be reformulated so as to be utterly free of any peculiarities of the judiciary. Indeed the argument is far simpler when divested of the forms internal to the judiciary to which a Court opinion must conform. First, the burden of proof is on the government. It must justify its coercive acts to its coerced subjects, because government derives its legitimacy from the consent of the governed. Second, any full-scale abortion prohibition (e.g., any that prohibited abortion from conception on, except to protect the mother's health, or in cases of rape) so severely limits a woman's liberties and damages the interests of parents that it could be justified only if the unborn are human beings (i.e., in the same sense that the born are human beings). Thus, a government may legitimately impose such a prohibition only if it can demonstrate that the unborn are human beings. Third, the epistemological thesis that the unborn are human beings is, *in principle*, undemonstrable; it cannot even be shown to be probable in that it is neither genuinely true nor false. Thus, no authority can legitimately demand that people respect such a prohibition, because no reason can be given as to why they should respect it.

Again, Blackmun's argument is more complicated, simply because a judicial ruling must be the result of reason referring to and restrained by existing rules and concepts of the legal system. For example, Blackmun was not free to finesse the term "person," as the simplified argument above did, for our legal forms fix that term in a way that makes it the focal term in this case. So too, inasmuch as the logic of the legal *onus probandi* legitimates an *argumentum ad ignoratium*, the epistemological thesis is inapplicable to the legal term, "person." Natural, nonlegal language is not so constrained, so if the epistemological thesis applies to "the unborn are human beings," and if a human being is *ipso facto* a person, then that thesis applies as well to the natural language claim that the unborn are persons. Further, though the epistemological thesis was introduced here in the context of discussing the judicial stance of disinterestedness and emotional detachment, the claim was not that the judicial perspective is epistemically inferior, restricting a judge from seeing something any competent observer can see. Quite the contrary, the restriction of detachment is required of a judge precisely so that his judgments and opinions can command the respect of any reasonable person. To be sure, we do not expect or require such detachment of citizens and legislators when they vote, for we think that generally the wishes of the majority should prevail over those of a minority. But we also think that majority rule should be limited so as to protect the rights of individuals. Of course, depriving some people of some of their rights by amending the Constitution would not be illegal; no such amendment could be voided by the Supreme Court. It would merely be unjust, a violation of the principles legitimating government, and incapable of commanding the respect of the governed.

But note now, none of this implies that Blackmun's ruling is fully justified in all its particulars. The analysis so far confirms Blackmun's argument only up to the notorious two sentences. There remains the question of how he gets from here to the holding. The answer is: very, very quickly indeed. Throughout, Blackmun recognized only two relevant state interests that could be compelling enough to warrant some state regulation of abortion. The first, protection of the mother's health, seems to put abortion in the same category as other medical procedures. Yet Blackmun provides no rationale for imposing, as a matter of constitutional law, special restrictions on the state regulation of this medical procedure. But, having contended that the state's right to regulate was actuated by the increased peril to maternal health after the first trimester, the Court cannot easily deny the reasonableness of regulations requiring that after the first trimester,[35] the decision to abort be subject to procedures ensuring that the decision be well informed. The Court seems to have recognized at least a prima facie reason for a woman not to abort after the first trimester, a reason that a state has a legitimate interest in having her act upon. When the dangers to her health are certain and severe enough, I presume the state has here whatever power it has elsewhere to proscribe self-destructive activity. But where the dangers are not so certain or severe, the state could, without infringing upon the woman's liberty, require her to engage in a supervised deliberative process. That process need not be confined to a discussion of the health risk, because the purpose of the deliberation is that she be justifiably certain that she has sufficiently sound reasons for putting her health at risk. Certainly, there is considerable room for controversy over what here constitutes reasonable regulations, but my interest is with the general principle and not the details. However, one detail is worth stating: the principle would warrant exempting from the deliberative procedure women who are certified by a physician to require an abortion to protect their own health.

Blackmun refers to the other state interest, the crucial one, as "an interest in protecting the potentiality of human life." He says that it "grows in substantiality as the woman approaches term" and that it becomes "compelling" at viability "because the fetus then presumably has the capability of meaningful life outside the mother's womb." [36] This, he says, provides "both logical and biological justifications" [37] for the holding that

for the stage subsequent to viability the State, in promoting its interest in the potentiality of human life, may, if it chooses, regulate, and even proscribe, abortion, except where it is necessary, in appropriate medical judgment, for the preservation of the life or health of the mother.[38]

Manifestly this is underargued. Justice White seems correct in calling this "an exercise in raw judicial power," for there is "nothing in the language or history of the Constitution to support the Court's judgment" here.[39] Precedents for a more conservative decision are plentiful. Though the meaning of "potentiality for life" and the nature of the legitimate state interest in it have little history of legal interpretation, arguably the whole history of the laws restricting abortion provides massive precedent for holding that the state's interest in the potentiality for life is compelling long before viability. Yet, whether this, the crucial part of the *Wade* decision, is "an improvident and extravagant exericse of the power of judicial review," [40] as White claimed, is another matter. Leaving aside the vexed questions of legal precedent, and approaching the argument "philosophically," it seems a mixed bag, far too large for me to unpack completely and do it justice. I shall briefly focus on a few salient points.

First, the mind boggles when Blackmun tells us that the holding has multiple justifications, one logical and one biological. Neither the principles of logic nor the facts of biology could individually yield a justification; only by combining the two can even an enthymatic argument be produced. Anyway, the cited premise—"the fetus then presumably has the capability of meaningful life outside the mother's womb"—is not a bit of biology or logic, but only a bare definition. "Viability" applied to a fetus means its capability for living outside the mother's womb. Biology, in conjunction with available medical technology, determines when viability occurs, not what the word means. And a definition is more a prelude to than a premise of reasoning, let alone a justification on its own.

Presumably what Blackmun has in mind here harks back to that key distinction between the born and the unborn. Though sometimes, as in Part VII, he seems to treat the term "potential life" as though it were interchangeable with "prenatal life," elsewhere, particularly in his conclusion, he seems pulled by the term's obviously distinct connotations. A prenatal life is the life of a fetus, but the life referred to by the term "potential life" is clearly that of a born human being. A fetus has an actual prenatal life but is only potentially a living born human being. And, I take it, Blackmun presumes that the legitimate state interest in the life of the prenatal derives wholly from its interest in the life of the postnatal. Further, it is natural (if not necessary) to construe potentiality as linked to capability in such a way that to be a potential human life at some moment is to have the capability of living as a born human being at that moment. This, I believe, is the reasoning behind Blackmun's finding viability to be the compelling point. It has some plausibility, but I would not wish to endorse it. If it is the rationale, then little sense can be given to Blackmun's claim that the state's interest in protecting the potentiality of human life "grows in substantiality as the woman approaches term." That claim rings hollow in any case, inasmuch as that substance has no detectable legal effect prior to viability.

Still, I would not deny that the use of viability as a "compelling" point is defensible and reasonable, though I defy anyone to show it to be uniquely so. Nor would I deny the propriety of abortion to prevent the mother's death or injury to her health if the state's interest in protecting maternal health is superior to its interest in protecting potential life. Of course, many will protest when Justice Douglas informs us in his concurring opinion, which refers to the *Vuitch* decision, that "health" must here be construed to "give full sweep to the 'psychological as well as the physical well-being' of women patients." [41] With that construal, a woman who wants a late-term abortion will usually be able to find a physician willing to certify it as necessary for her health.

Yet the broad interpretation of maternal health as justification for an abortion is not itself so worrisome, or would not be if it were not for two further factors. First, when the Court said, not that a state must, but that it "may, if it chooses . . . proscribe abortion," and that it may do so only in the state's interests, not the fetus's, the Court moved from denying that the fetus is a person "in the whole sense" to denying it any constitutional standing altogether, leaving it without any legally enforceable interests. Nothing in Blackmun's opinion provides a rationale for this or rules out the alternative implicit in the history of abortion regulation, of recognizing the existence of a legal status peculiar to the fetus.

Yet, even this would be primarily of symbolic importance and not of great practical consequence, if, in *Wade* or later, the Court had properly distinguished abortion—the termination of pregnancy—from the termination of the child's life. That distinction would seem of obvious intrinsic importance no matter what event the Court had picked as triggering legitimate state regulation. But when the Court finds some inherent significance in the condition of viability, its position seems threatened with incoherence if it then denies significance to the distinction between abortion and feticide, for there seems to be nothing significant about viability independent of its being the condition in which the distinction between abortion and feticide is practical and meaningful. I do not say that the significance of viability is constituted by that distinction, but only that the former is not independent of the significance of the latter. Pro-choice radicals may insist that a woman's right to privacy extends to her acting on an intention to kill her unborn child, not only when unavoidable to liberate herself from it physically, but also as something desired in itself or perhaps as a means of psychologically liberating herself from the child. But that surely is a distinctive and highly tendentious thesis. At minimum, even if a woman has a right to decide the fate of a viable fetus, that right is not directly entailed by her right to an abortion. Nothing in Blackmun's opinion precludes the Court from ruling that a state may—or even must—require that a viable fetus may not be endangered, any more than is necessary to remove it from the mother without endangering the mother's physical health. With that requirement the state would have little reason to prohibit any abortion of a viable fetus, except for those abortions that are not necessary for the mother's life or health and do significantly imperil the fetal life. In my judgment, the grave moral and political reasons in this issue demand that the High Court consider the abortion controversy with utmost care.

A Human Life Statute

Stephen H. Galebach

The Congress finds that present day scientific evidence indicates a significant likelihood that actual human life exists from conception. Upon the basis of this finding, and in the exercise of the powers of the Congress, including its power under Section 5 of the Fourteenth Amendment to the Constitution of the United States, the Congress hereby declares that for the purpose of enforcing the obligation of the States under the Fourteenth Amendment not to deprive persons of life without due process of law, human life shall be deemed to exist from conception, without regard to race, age, health, defect, or condition of dependency; and for this purpose "person" shall include all human life as defined herein.

OES Congress have constitutional power to enact such a statute? If Congress were to enact a statute of this sort, should the Supreme Court uphold it?

The Supreme Court's 1973 abortion decision in *Roe* v. *Wade* has received trenchant criticism for its defective legal reasoning as well as its consequences.[1] For the growing number of citizens unwilling to tolerate the consequences of *Roe* v. *Wade*, the answer has appeared to lie in a constitutional amendment to protect unborn life. While such an amendment may well afford the surest protection for unborn children, it will require an extraordinary consensus and a protracted ratification effort.

Until the time when an amendment could be ratified, are there any interim answers that a simple majority of Congress could provide, consistent with the Constitution and with Supreme Court precedent? In fact there are. The Constitution was not designed to leave any form of human life unprotected. Nor do Supreme Court precedents, as we shall see, prevent or discourage Congress from acting in this area.

Both the Fifth Amendment and the Fourteenth Amendment protect human life. The Fifth Amendment protects life against acts of the federal government: "No person shall be . . . deprived of life, liberty, or property, without due process of law." In similar language the Fourteenth Amendment limits the action of states: "nor shall any State deprive any person of life, liberty, or property, without due process of law."

These provisions reflect the belief, expressed in our Declaration of Independence, that the right to life is sacred and inalienable.[2] Whether unborn children enjoy those rights to life already contained in the Constitution depends on how life is defined. If life begins at conception, these rights logically extend to unborn children. If life begins only at birth, unborn children enjoy no protection from the Constitution as it now stands. The beginnings of life thus pose a crucial question for those branches of the federal government that enforce the Fifth and the Fourteenth amendments.

I. Determining When Life Begins

An inappropriate task for the courts   The judicial branch confronted the issue of when life begins in *Roe* v. *Wade,* when the state of Texas invoked the Fourteenth Amendment's protection of life as a justification for the state's antiabortion statute. In rejecting this justification, the Supreme Court did not define unborn children as nonlife or nonhumans. Instead it refused to decide when human life begins and whether unborn children are human life. With this issue unresolved, the Court found nothing to indicate that unborn children are persons protected by the Fourteenth Amendment. Justice Blackmun concluded for the Court that "the word 'person,' as used in the Fourteenth Amendment, does not include the unborn." [3]

The Court's refusal to decide when life begins was central to the outcome of *Roe* v. *Wade.* Without a decision on this question, there was no way to show that Fourteenth Amendment protection logically extends to unborn children. Although the state of Texas asserted its own definition of when life begins, the Supreme Court held that the state had no authority to adopt "one theory of life." [4] With the Supreme Court and the state legislatures both unable to define when life begins, the state had no way to demonstrate that unborn children are human persons deserving protection. As a result, the state had no compelling interest sufficient to justify its antiabortion statute. The

Supreme Court therefore struck down the statute as an unjustified infringement of the mother's right of privacy to decide whether to "terminate her pregnancy," a right newly discovered in this case.[5]

The result of *Roe* v. *Wade* would have been entirely different, however, if any branch of government had been able constitutionally to examine when life begins and to resolve the question in favor of unborn children. If in enforcing the Fourteenth Amendment, a branch of the federal government had been able to declare that the unborn are human persons, then any state could invoke that declaration as a compelling state interest for prohibiting abortions. The Supreme Court acknowledged this in *Roe* v. *Wade*: "If the suggestion of personhood is established, the appellant's case, of course, collapses, for the fetus's right to life would then be guaranteed specifically by the Amendment."[6]

It may seem odd that the Supreme Court refused to address the issue of the beginnings of life, when that issue is so fundamental to the scope of the Fourteenth Amendment and to the state's power to prohibit abortions. But the Court explained its refusal, and its explanation is very important. On the beginnings of life, the Court observed, there is a "wide divergence of thinking." The question is "sensitive and difficult."[7] For such questions the judiciary has no suitable evidentiary standards to determine an answer. A judge could only "speculate" on this difficult question. In short, the question stands outside the scope of judicial competence: "When those trained in the respective disciplines of medicine, philosophy, and theology are unable to arrive at any consensus, the judiciary, at this point in the development of man's knowledge, is not in a position to speculate as to the answer."[8]

Thus the failure of the Fourteenth Amendment to afford protection for the unborn, under *Roe* v. *Wade*, results from the institutional limitations of the judicial branch. Without a decision that the unborn are human life, it is not clear that the Fourteenth Amendment protects unborn children. And the Supreme Court gave strong reasons for abstaining from this question. But this does not end the matter. The Constitution gives Congress, as well as the courts, a role in the enforcement of the Fourteenth Amendment. If the question of when life begins can be addressed by Congress, and if Congress has a legitimate role in enforcing the Fourteenth Amendment's protection of life, then Congress can resolve the fundamental issue from which the Supreme Court abstained in *Roe* v. *Wade*.

An appropriate task for Congress   The Fourteenth Amendment provides: "The Congress shall have power to enforce, by appropriate legislation, the provisions of this article." [9] In enforcing the Amendment's protection of life, as in many other matters, Congress does not suffer from the same institutional limitations as the judiciary. Resolving sensitive and difficult policy questions, deciding between conflicting interests, making speculative judgments where no judicial standards can offer guidance—these are functions inherent in Congress's role and appropriate for Congress to perform.

To decide when human life begins involves the sort of considerations that are appropriate for Congress but not the courts. Any attempt to resolve the issue, as the Court observed, involves the examination of inconclusive evidence and the weighing of divergent views. By the nature of their position, congressmen are often called upon to reflect the views of divergent constituencies on matters that cannot be resolved by conclusive evidence. Congress routinely weighs divergent views on questions that admit of no "correct" answer from a court's perspective: whether to tax one person to support another, whether to protect various species endangered by governmental or private activities, whether to require the use of safety precautions that protect people while causing them inconvenience. Legal standards provide no answers to these questions; in such matters, decisions "are and should be undertaken only by those directly responsible to the people whose welfare they advance or imperil." [10]

One can best appreciate the legislative nature of deciding when life begins by considering the issue as it confronts the decision maker. He must first examine the divergent views and conflicting evidence, mentioned by the *Roe* v. *Wade* opinion, to see if they provide an answer. If this step leaves him uncertain whether the unborn are human life, then he faces an especially delicate and complex issue of legislative policy: Should one extend protection if human life is *probably* at stake? Or only *possibly* at stake? What degree of possibility does one require before deciding to extend constitutional protection by deeming the unborn to be human life for purposes of the Fourteenth Amendment?

The legislative nature of this issue is further confirmed by the "political question" doctrine. The Supreme Court has developed this doctrine as a means to identify those issues that are appropriately resolved not by the courts, but rather by Congress, the president, or the states. Although the Court did not invoke the political question doctrine in refusing to decide when life begins, the Court's reasoning could easily be explained by that doctrine. Political questions, according to Supreme Court precedent, are questions that are "delicate" and "complex," questions "of a kind for which the judiciary has neither aptitude, facilities nor responsibility." [11] Two of the major criteria for identifying a political question could be applied directly to the question of when life begins: "A lack of judicially discoverable and manageable standards for resolving it; or the impossibility of deciding without an initial policy determination of a kind clearly for nonjudicial discretion." [12] Questions of this sort, the Court has said, are "wholly confided by our Constitution to the political departments of the government, Executive and Legislative." [13]

The political department most appropriate to decide when life begins is Congress. The enforcement clause of the Fourteenth Amendment expressly grants power to Congress. When a term of the Fourteenth Amendment cannot be defined by the judiciary in concrete application to a category of beings—here the unborn—then the definition of that term by Congress is appropriate legislation to enforce the amendment.

If it appears strange that Congress should be able to play such a major role in formulating a national policy on the issue of abortions, that is only because the federal courts have gone to such great lengths to take control of this issue into their own hands. But when the courts have declared themselves incapable of resolving the beginnings of human life, it should be very hard for them to insist on taking this particular part of the abortion controversy out of Congress's hands and into their own. Before the Supreme Court stepped into this arena with its *Roe* opinion, former Justice Clark had recognized the legislative nature of the controversy:

It is for the legislature to determine the proper balance, i. e., that point between prevention of conception and viability of the fetus which would give the State the compelling subordinating interest so that it may regulate or prohibit abortion without violating the individual's constitutionally protected rights.[14]

The Supreme Court, moreover, has recently acknowledged that Congress has a proper role in protecting human life. In its 1980 decision on the public funding of abortions, the Court recognized the "legitimate congressional interest in protecting potential life." [15] If Congress has an interest in protecting potential human life, it certainly has a legitimate interest in protecting what it considers likely to be *actual* human life. If Congress is to make fully informed decisions to protect life, it must also have power to examine and answer such questions as what is actual life, what is potential life, what is likely to be actual life, and what protection should be extended to something that appears likely to be actual life.

If Congress decides that unborn children are human life for the purpose of the Fourteenth Amendment's protection of life, it follows logically that for this purpose they are "persons" as well. By common usage of language, any human being must be recognized as a person. The Supreme Court has interpreted "person" in the Fourteenth Amendment more broadly than common usage, to include corporations.[16]

Statements of the framers of the Fourteenth Amendment make it clear that "person" cannot include less than every human being. Congressman Bingham, author and sponsor of Section 1 of the amendment, spoke of the right to equal protection and the right to life, liberty, and property for "every human being." [17] The framers had good reason to contemplate unborn children as part of the human race, since in the decade leading up to the Fourteenth Amendment,[18] physicians responded to new evidence about conception by calling for protection of human life from that point.[19]

A determination that unborn children are human life, therefore, fully justifies the correlative determination that they are persons. The latter determination, however, collides with the Supreme Court's holding in Roe v. Wade that the unborn are not persons. But that holding makes sense only in light of the Court's inability to decide whether the unborn are human life. Informed by a congressional determination that life begins at conception, the Court might well reach a different conclusion. Still, the potential conflict raises serious constitutional questions. Does the Roe v. Wade holding as to "person" deprive Congress of power to pass contrary legislation? If Congress does pass legislation declaring unborn children to be human life and persons, should the Court defer to Congress's determination?

II. Congress as Co-enforcer of the Fourteenth Amendment

Supreme Court decisions have recognized that the Court does not have the only say in applying the Fourteenth Amendment. Under its Section 5 enforcement power Congress can apply, and has applied, Fourteenth Amendment terms in ways that differ from and even contradict Supreme Court interpretations. The Court has consistently upheld such legislation in the past two decades, often giving sweeping approval to Congress's expansive role. The precise extent of Congress's power to apply the Fourteenth Amendment independent of the Court, and the degree of deference the Court gives to such congressional actions, have been central issues in a number of Supreme Court decisions.

Interplay between the Supreme Court and Congress on issues of interpretation and application of constitutional rights has arisen most prominently in the area of state tests for voter qualification. Of the leading cases on Congress's power to enforce the Fourteenth and Fifteenth Amendments, three cases have involved literacy tests for voting. Literacy tests have been challenged under the Fifteenth Amendment[20] as well as the Fourteenth; the enforcement power of Congress is the same under both amendments.[21]

Just as in the abortion area, the Supreme Court pronounced its constitutional interpretation concerning literacy tests before Congress took up the issue. In 1959 the Court held, in *Lassiter v. Northampton County Board of Elections*,[22] that literacy tests did not violate the Equal Protection Clause of the Fourteenth Amendment or abridge the right to vote on account of race contrary to the Fifteenth Amendment.[23] The *Lassiter* opinion expresses a clear judgment that literacy tests, considered in general, have no inherently discriminatory character: "Literacy and illiteracy are neutral on race, creed, color, and sex, as reports around the world show." [24] Only with evidence that a particular literacy test was actually employed to promote discrimination would the *Lassiter* court find it to be a violation of the Fourteenth or Fifteenth Amendment.[25]

In the Voting Rights Act of 1965, however, Congress used its enforcement power to apply the Fourteenth and Fifteenth Amendments to state literacy tests in ways different from the Supreme Court in *Lassiter*. Section 4(a)–(d) of the act suspended all voter qualification tests in those states or counties in which fewer than 50 percent of the voting-age residents registered or voted in the 1964 presidential election. For such states Congress found that literacy tests and similar voting qualifications abridged the right to vote on account of race.[26]

The Supreme Court upheld this part of the act as an appropriate exercise of Congress's power to enforce the Fifteenth Amendment. In *South Carolina v. Katzenbach*[27] the Court held that Congress had complied with the *Lassiter* holding by making extensive, detailed legislative findings that literacy tests have been used to promote discrimination in most of the areas covered by the act.[28] For those areas in which

Congress had not found direct evidence of discriminatory use of the tests, the Court was satisfied that Congress had inferred or could infer a "significant danger" of discrimination.[29] By striking down those literacy tests that had actually been employed to promote discrimination, Congress did not depart from the *Lassiter* interpretation of the Fifteenth Amendment.[30] The further application of Section 4(a)–(d) to the other areas, in which there was a "significant danger" that tests would be applied discriminatorily, represented a slight modification of the *Lassiter* standard; this application was appropriate as a preventive measure to combat discrimination.[31]

Another provision of the act, however, represented a sharp departure from *Lassiter's* interpretation of the Fourteenth Amendment. Section 4(e) struck down the use of English literacy tests in New York to exclude voters who had completed the sixth grade in Puerto Rican schools.[32] For this section Congress did not provide legislative fact-finding to show discriminatory application of New York's literacy test.[33] Without such evidence the *Lassiter* holding would of course indicate that New York's use of a literacy test was constitutionally valid. Congress could only strike down New York's use of the test by applying a standard different from *Lassiter*.

Nevertheless, in *Katzenbach* v. *Morgan*[34] the Supreme Court upheld Section 4(e). The Court held that Congress enjoys broad authority to interpret the provisions of the Fourteenth Amendment independent of the judicial branch. As the Court framed the issue: "*Without regard to whether the judiciary would find that the Equal Protection Clause itself nullifies New York's English literacy requirement as so applied,* could Congress prohibit the enforcement of the state law by legislating under § 5 of the Fourteenth Amendment?" [35]

The *Morgan* opinion answered this question in the affirmative. The Court gave two equal and alternative reasons for holding that Congress could prohibit enforcement of the literacy test. First, Congress could have struck down the literacy requirement in order to help the Puerto Rican community gain sufficient political power to secure nondiscriminatory treatment in the provision of public services. This rationale rests on the principle that Congress enjoys the same broad powers under Section 5 that it exercises under the Necessary and Proper Clause.[36] Congress may take any action that is "plainly adapted" to the objective of securing the guarantees of the Fourteenth Amendment.[37] Under this rationale, Congress may strike down an act of a state that does not in itself violate the Fourteenth Amendment, so long as Congress's action tends to protect some Fourteenth Amendment right against infringement by the state.[38]

As a second rationale, the Court held that Congress could rationally conclude that New York's use of a literacy test was invidious discrimination not justified by any compelling interest of the state—and was therefore a violation of equal protection.[39] Unlike *South Carolina* v. *Katzenbach*, the *Morgan* opinion did not require any legislative findings of fact to show discriminatory use of the literacy test. Instead, the Court was willing to let Congress conclude that a literacy test by its nature, with no evidence of its actual effects, violates the Fourteenth Amendment. The Court did not even require Congress to express its reasons for reaching a conclusion opposite to the *Lassiter* holding: "It is enough that we perceive a basis upon which Congress *might* predicate a judgment that the application of New York's English literacy requirement . . . constituted an invidious discrimination in violation of the Equal Protection Clause." [40] The broadly deferential attitude of the majority in *Morgan* toward Congress evoked a dissent from Justices Harlan and Stewart, which will figure prominently in our later discussion.

Both rationales of the *Morgan* opinion appeared to give Congress authority virtually to overrule the *Lassiter* holding. The Court emphasized the broad discretion of Congress to determine what legislation is appropriate to carry out the ends of the Civil War amendments.[41] Citing historical evidence of the framers' intent, the Court observed that the Fourteenth Amendment primarily enlarges the power of Congress rather than the judiciary.[42] Commentators recognized *Morgan* as a broad endorsement of congressional power to interpret the substantive guarantees of the Fourteenth Amendment in ways that differ from or contradict prior interpretations of the Supreme Court.[43]

Four years after *Morgan*, Congress completed the process of undoing *Lassiter*. Title II of the Voting Rights Act Amendments of 1970 struck down all remaining state literacy tests.[44] The Supreme Court unanimously upheld Title II in *Oregon* v. *Mitchell*,[45] despite the lack of specific evidence of discriminatory application of these tests by states that still used them.[46] The Court relied on evidence available to Congress, showing that literacy tests are likely to have racially discriminatory effects wherever in the nation they may be used.[47] To say that literacy tests are likely to be discriminatory anywhere in the country is essentially the same as to say they are discriminatory by nature—a direct contradiction of the *Lassiter* holding.

Although *Oregon* v. *Mitchell* endorsed a congressional interpretation of the Fourteenth Amendment at variance with the *Lassiter* holding, it left some uncertainty over the scope of Congress's power to apply the amendment independent of the courts. The 1970 Voting Rights Act amendments had also invoked Section 5 of the amendment as a justification for Congress to lower the voting age in federal and state elections. A divided Supreme Court in *Oregon* v. *Mitchell* allowed Congress to lower the voting age for federal elections but not for state elections. Four justices opted for a very broad view of congressional power under Section 5 to strike down the states' 21-year-old voting age requirements; four justices espoused a narrower view; and Justice Black cast the deciding vote on grounds divorced from the Section 5 power. Justice Brennan, joined by Justices White and Marshall, endorsed a broad scope of congressional power, emphasizing "proper regard for the special function of Congress in making determinations of legislative fact." [48] Justice Stewart took the narrower view in an opinion which we shall discuss later.

The ambiguity left by the divided Court in *Oregon* v. *Mitchell* has been largely resolved quite recently. Two Supreme Court decisions expressly followed the *Morgan* view of Congress's power to enforce the Fourteenth and Fifteenth Amendments. *Fullilove* v. *Klutznick* followed the *Morgan* view that Congress's enforcement power is as broad as the Necessary and Proper Clause.[49] *Fullilove* specifically endorsed the broad power of Congress "in determining whether and what legislation is needed to secure the guarantees of the Fourteenth Amendment." [50]

The other case, *City of Rome* v. *United States*,[51] approved the *Morgan* holding in the context of Congress's equivalent power to enforce the Fifteenth Amendment. *City of Rome* especially illuminates the first rationale of *Morgan*. The case arose from the application of the Voting Rights Act of 1965 to prohibit electoral changes made by the city of Rome, Georgia.[52] There was evidence that Rome's voting practices had racially discriminatory effects, but no evidence of any discriminatory intent.[53] For purposes of deciding the case, the Supreme Court assumed that the Fifteenth Amendment prohibits only purposeful discrimination and not actions with only discriminatory effects.[54]

Nevertheless, *City of Rome* held that Congress could prohibit Rome's changes in electoral practices. The Court acknowledged that Congress may enforce the Fifteenth Amendment by prohibiting practices that in themselves do not violate the Fifteenth Amendment. The

Court required only that the prohibition of actions discriminatory in their effect be an "appropriate" and "proper" means to prevent the "risk of purposeful discrimination."[55] This reasoning builds on the first rationale of the *Morgan* opinion: Congress may strike at a constitutionally proper state action, in order to protect against a risk or likelihood of state infringement of a Fourteenth or Fifteenth Amendment right.

Supreme Court precedents, then, support a prominent role for Congress to enforce the Fourteenth Amendment in ways differing from the courts. Under the first rationale of *Morgan*, Congress was able in the *City of Rome* case to strike down electoral practices that a court could not have struck down without evidence of discriminatory intent. By following the second rationale of *Morgan*, Congress can also interpret the Fourteenth Amendment in ways that a court might not adopt.

Both rationales permit Congress to include unborn children within the protections of the Fourteenth Amendment, without regard to whether the judiciary would find them to be persons. The second rationale allows Congress to liberalize the scope of the term "person" if it has reason to do so. If Congress determines that life begins at conception, or that life possibly begins at conception, this presents a good reason—indeed, a compelling reason—to deem unborn children to be persons. For Congress to examine evidence and draw conclusions on a matter unresolved and unresolvable by the Supreme Court is among the strongest bases imaginable for acting under the second rationale of *Morgan*. If the Fourteenth Amendment primarily enlarges the power of Congress and not the judiciary, then it surely gives Congress power to interpret a matter as to which Congress is competent and the courts are not.

Congress could also take action to extend the Fourteenth Amendment's protection to unborn children under the first rationale of *Morgan*. Even if Congress leaves undisturbed the *Roe* v. *Wade* holding that the Fourteenth Amendment protects only postnatal "persons," Congress can still protect the unborn under this rationale. First, Congress can examine the unanswered question of when life begins. Next, it can reasonably determine that at conception a life has come into being—a specific, individual life in terms of chromosomal structure and many consequential identifying characteristics. This individual life would probably proceed to enjoy the status of "person" with life protected by the Fourteenth Amendment *but for* the act of abortion. Therefore, in order to protect the unborn child against the risk that state action will prevent him or her from enjoying the right to post-natal life guaranteed by the Fourteenth Amendment, Congress may appropriately protect the unborn child's life between conception and birth. State-supported deprivation of unborn life may not be (for pur-poses of argument) a violation of the Fourteenth Amendment; but Congress can prohibit it in order to prevent the risk that individuals may be deprived by the state of an opportunity to enjoy a right to post-natal life guaranteed by the Fourteenth Amendment.

This line of reasoning from the first rationale of *Morgan* may appear at first glance too much like a debater's trick. But a concrete example helps to show the merit in this reasoning. Suppose that a state under-takes a program, in cooperation with expectant mothers, to eliminate a genetically identifiable group that is unwanted—for instance, chil-dren with Down's Syndrome (mongolism), to take an example not far removed from the realm of possibility. Under the holding of *Roe v. Wade*, the Fourteenth Amendment by its own force does not protect unborn mongoloid children. Thus the state might be able to identify all unborn mongoloid children through the use of amniocentesis tech-niques, and eliminate them by abortion. Could not Congress, then, declare unborn mongoloid children to be human life and persons un-der the Fourteenth Amendment, in order to protect them against the risk that their right to a life after birth may be deprived by state action?

It is difficult to deny that Congress has power to include unborn children within the scope of the Fourteenth Amendment's protection of life. For Congress to use this power would represent only a narrow and restrained exercise of Congress's authority to enforce the Four-teenth Amendment. To define "life" and "person" is only the first and smallest step that must be taken if any branch of the federal govern-ment is rationally to determine what scope of human life falls within the protection of the Fourteenth Amendment. Indeed, in *Morgan* the Court expressed dissatisfaction with the idea of limiting Congress's en-forcement power to the "insignificant role" of "merely informing the judgment of the judiciary by particularizing the 'majestic generalities' of § 1 of the Amendment." [56] It is an even narrower role for Congress to inform the judiciary of the precise meaning of less general terms such as "life" and "person" in light of contemporary evidence on these matters.

Professor William Cohen has discussed whether Congress has power in "marginal cases" to enlarge the meaning of due process and equal protection, so long as it does not adopt interpretations or applications not reasonably within the scope of the constitutional terms.[57] He observes that Congress has especially solid justification to act on marginal questions of constitutional interpretation when they "involve drawing difficult lines that could best be drawn by legislatures." [58] Congress's power to adopt "arguable" interpretations expanding Fourteenth Amendment rights should not vary, he reasons, simply because the Supreme Court has expressed an opinion on the meaning of the constitutional term at issue: "Obviously, congressional power should neither depend upon whether Congress or the Court was first in the race to cope with the issue, nor vary with the voting breakdown when the Court finishes first." [59] Cohen concludes that theories which limit Congress to interpreting *only* in marginal cases are "not viable"—that Congress's enforcement power, in other words, should extend well *beyond* this narrow realm.[60]

The definition of "life" and "person" involves this sort of interpretation on the "margin." An interpretation of "life" and "person" that includes the unborn could not be held unwarranted by the language of the Fourteenth Amendment; the Constitution does not define either term. The framers of the Fourteenth Amendment did not try to specify concrete definitions of terms that are susceptible to varying interpretations. Instead, they chose "language capable of growth." [61] "Life" and "person" are among the most concrete and particular terms in the Fourteenth Amendment. Yet even these terms permit some degree of interpretation on the margin. Both terms are "capable of growing" to reflect a more liberal view of the scope of human existence.

The task of adjusting the meaning of "life" and "person" to accord with changing evidence and views of life is properly a task for Congress. Not only is the line between life and nonlife a difficult one, more appropriately drawn by the legislature than by the courts; it is also a line that the *Roe v. Wade* opinion itself explicitly declared the courts unable to draw. If Congress draws the line at conception, the courts have no independent basis on which to draw a line different from that drawn by Congress. Under the approach of *Katzenbach v. Morgan*, the Court's prior definition of "person" in *Roe v. Wade* poses no greater barrier to congressional enforcement action than the *Lassiter* holding posed to Congress's nationwide prohibition of literacy tests.

Our review of these Supreme Court precedents has mentioned dissents to the majority view. There is indeed a consistent minority view, first expressed by Justice Harlan's dissent in *Katzenbach v. Morgan,* next developed by Justice Stewart's opinion in *Oregon* v. *Mitchell*, and most recently espoused by Justice Rehnquist. To arrive at a balanced assessment of the wisdom of congressional action to protect unborn life, we must pay close attention to these dissents as well as to the majority opinions.

The dissenting view emphasizes the distinction between the legislative and the judicial role. Justice Harlan maintained in *Katzenbach* v. *Morgan* that it was ultimately for the judicial branch to determine the substantive scope of the Fourteenth Amendment.[62] Justice Stewart objected in his *Oregon* v. *Mitchell* opinion that Congress does not have power to determine the substantive scope and application of the Equal Protection Clause.[63] And in *City of Rome*, Justice Rehnquist argued that Congress cannot "effectively amend the Constitution" by interpreting the Fifteenth Amendment independently and escaping judicial review.[64]

At some points these dissents might be read as saying that Congress has no role whatever in interpreting the Fourteenth Amendment, that Congress is limited to providing remedies after the courts interpret the amendment and identify violations of it. But the dissents do not go quite that far. Justice Harlan left open a legitimate though limited role for Congress to interpret the substantive scope of the Fourteenth Amendment: "To the extent 'legislative facts' are relevant to a judicial determination, Congress is well equipped to investigate them, and such determinations are of course entitled to due respect." [65]

Justice Harlan's view, repeated in essence by Justices Stewart and Rehnquist, is that the judiciary must make the final determination of the constitutional issue in light of the congressional findings of fact. These findings may of course influence the Court, and may change its mind. But Justice Harlan's view requires facts sufficient to justify a new constitutional interpretation, not just sufficient to afford some slight rational basis to Congress's interpretation of Fourteenth Amendment terms.

In *Oregon* v. *Mitchell* it is safe to say that Congress could not provide facts sufficient to convince Justice Harlan or Justice Stewart that the 21-year-old voting age requirement violated the Equal Protection Clause.[66] Similarly in *City of Rome*, Congress came forth with no evidence to persuade Justice Rehnquist that the city had done anything in violation of the Fifteenth Amendment.[67] But in *South Carolina* v. *Katzenbach* Congress had set forth voluminous findings of fact that persuaded Justices Harlan and Stewart—among others—that literacy tests in some areas did violate the Fifteenth Amendment.[68] Similar evidence convinced both justices again in *Oregon v. Mitchell* that Congress could strike down all literacy tests because they were thought to be discriminatory, despite the *Lassiter* holding.

Justice Harlan's recognition of a congressional role in this area is based on his observation that "questions of equal protection and due process are based not on abstract logic, but on empirical foundations." [69] How strongly Congress will influence the Court by legislative fact-finding depends on the relative competence of Congress and the courts to decide the particular empirical question. Both Justice Harlan and Justice Stewart recognized some matters on which Congress was at least as competent as the courts to express an opinion. For such matters these justices not only held that Congress has power to declare its views, but also held that the courts should give great deference to Congress.

Justice Harlan, writing for the Court in *Glidden Co. v. Zdanok*,[70] allowed a congressional declaration to overturn two earlier Supreme Court decisions on a matter of constitutional interpretation. The earlier decisions had held that the United States Court of Claims and the United States Court of Customs and Patent Appeals were courts created under Article I rather than Article III of the Constitution.[71] Subsequent to those decisions, Congress examined the historical evidence surrounding the creation of the two courts, and declared that they were created under Article III.

Justice Harlan's opinion in the *Glidden* case acknowledged Congress's competence to declare its views on this matter, even though the issue was one of "constitutional dimension" rather than statutory construction.[72] Deferring to Congress's declaration, Justice Harlan refused to follow the two earlier decisions because at the time they were decided, "the Court did not have the benefit of this congressional understanding." [73] To allow Congress to change the Court's mind did not violate Justice Harlan's theory of the judicial and legislative roles: "To give due weight to these congressional declarations is not of course to compromise the authority or responsibility of this Court as the ultimate expositor of the Constitution." [74]

Justice Stewart has endorsed the power of Congress to declare its interpretation of terms in the Thirteenth Amendment. This amendment, which prohibits slavery and involuntary servitude, confers on Congress an enforcement power parallel to that conferred by the Fourteenth and Fifteenth Amendments.[75] Justice Stewart's opinion for the Court in *Jones* v. *Alfred H. Mayer Co.*[76] allowed Congress to enforce the Thirteenth Amendment by broadening the scope of its prohibitions to include particular acts of racial discrimination, on grounds that they are "badges and incidents" of slavery.[77] So long as its determinations are rational, Congress has authority to "determine what are the badges and the incidents of slavery" and to "translate that determination into effective legislation." [78]

The *Jones* decision had been accepted as binding precedent by all the justices, whether they take the broad or the narrow view of Congress's power to enforce the Civil War amendments. In *Runyon* v. *McCrary*,[79] the justices disagreed over how far to extend *Jones*, but all the opinions in that case accepted *Jones* as binding precedent.[80] In a concurring opinion to *Fullilove* v. *Klutznick*, Justice Powell relied on *Jones* to show that Congress is competent to decide what types of racial discrimination come within the scope of the prohibitions of the Civil War amendments.[81]

Jones establishes that Congress has some role in interpreting terms of the Thirteenth, Fourteenth, and Fifteenth Amendments. Terms such as "slavery," "involuntary servitude," "life," and "person," are more concrete and particular than open-ended phrases such as "due process" and "equal protection." Yet even the more concrete terms admit of some ambiguities. In areas of ambiguity Congress may give these terms a broader scope than the Supreme Court has given them. Thus *Jones* supports Congress's authority to interpret "on the margin," as the *least* that Congress is empowered to do in enforcing the Civil War amendments.

Our discussion has already shown that the scope of "life" and "person" is an appropriate matter for Congress to interpret on the margin, in light of a determination of when life begins. For Congress to inform the courts of its determination of when life begins is appropriate under Justice Harlan's view of proper judicial and legislative roles. Indeed, a matter on which Congress is competent to decide and the courts are not is the most appropriate of all circumstances for Congress to express its judgment and for the courts to defer to Congress. Concerning such matters Justice Harlan has said: "I fully agree that judgments of the sort involved here are beyond the constitutional competence and constitutional authority of the judiciary. . . . They are pre-eminently matters for legislative discretion, with judicial review, if it exists at all, reasonably limited." [82]

Because the question of when life begins is a matter for legislative discretion, and because the courts are not competent to resolve this matter, the courts should exercise great deference in reviewing any congressional declaration that the Fourteenth Amendment shall include unborn human persons in its protection of life against state action. Such deference would not compromise the Supreme Court's role as ultimate arbiter of the Constitution; it would simply comport with judicial limitations already recognized in *Roe v. Wade.* Thus, whether the Court follows the standard of the *Morgan* majority, or the stricter review standard of the minority, the result in this case is the same: the Supreme Court's interpretation of "person" in *Roe v. Wade* does not bar Congress from taking a different view based on its determination that human life begins or is likely to begin at conception.

When Congress has greater competence than the courts, Congress *should* take the lead in defining the content of Fourteenth Amendment rights.[83] Had Congress done so more frequently in the past, it could have alleviated some of the most troubling institutional problems in constitutional interpretation. For example, the Supreme Court's decision in *Brown v. Board of Education*[84] produced a result widely applauded today, but doubts still remain about the propriety of the Supreme Court's making the sociological judgments involved in that decision. What if Congress had taken the lead to enforce the Fourteenth Amendment by declaring its judgment, based on legislative fact-finding, that separate schooling is inherently unequal and contrary to the Equal Protection Clause. Such action could have placed the issue in the branch of government best suited to resolve it. And would we really want to argue that the Supreme Court's endorsement of "separate but equal" in *Plessy v. Ferguson*[85] would have barred such action by Congress?

III. Possible Objections to a Human Life Statute

Our examination of Supreme Court opinions, both majority and dissenting, suggests that Congress does have power to enforce the Fourteenth Amendment by enacting a statute similar to that set forth at the beginning of this article. There are additional arguments, however, that might be raised against such a statute. Several of them deserve close attention, though none is persuasive.

First, it might be argued that the same divergence of views that persuaded the Court in *Roe v. Wade* not to decide when life begins, also makes it impossible for Congress rationally to arrive at an answer. The crucial point, however, is that Congress does not need to be *certain* of an answer before it declares a national policy on when human life begins.

Throughout the cases on Congress's enforcement power, the Supreme Court has held that Congress need only predicate its action on a *danger* to Fourteenth or Fifteenth Amendment rights, on a *likelihood* that particular circumstances might constitute a violation of protected rights. *South Carolina* v. *Katzenbach* allowed Congress to strike down South Carolina's literacy test even though the record contained no evidence that South Carolina had applied its voter qualification tests in any discriminatory way.[86] Sufficient for the Court was Congress's inference from various facts that South Carolina *might* use its literacy test to discriminate.[87] In *Katzenbach* v. *Morgan* as well, there was no certainty that disenfranchisement of Puerto Ricans would deprive them of equal provision of government services; the mere likelihood of deprivation of rights was enough.[88] The *City of Rome* decision allowed Congress to prevent electoral changes that created only "the *risk* of purposeful discrimination." [89] In order to define the unborn as persons, therefore, Congress need only find a likelihood that life begins at conception.

This standard makes perfectly good sense. If Congress discerns a likelihood or possibility that human life may be endangered by state action, it should certainly be able to take immediate action, rather than wait until the state of knowledge advances to the point that we can say for certain that it really is human life that we have been eliminating. Congress has often taken action to protect life when the uncertainties were at least as great as in the matter of abortions. Regulating the use of new, relatively untested drugs, regulating or refusing to regulate the use of tobacco, requiring passive restraint devices in cars—all such actions involve a calculation of the risk that human life will be lost without federal action, combined with a rough weighing of how much we value the possible risk of loss of human life. In all these decisions the protection of life conflicts with the convenience of many people. Sometimes, as for instance with drugs, the protection of persons from possible harmful effects conflicts directly with the grave medical needs of other persons. Decisions related to possible risks to human life are not only appropriate for Congress, they are far *more* appropriate for Congress than for the courts.

Second, it might be argued that Congress may not decide anything about the beginnings of life because the issue is inherently religious. To enact a statute for purely religious reasons, the argument goes, is to violate the Establishment Clause of the First Amendment. Professor Tribe advanced this argument in 1973 in an attempt to provide a rationale for *Roe* v. *Wade*.[90] Even if the argument were good constitutional law, it is by no means clear that it would properly apply to the issue of abortion. Certainly one does not have to hold any religious beliefs in order to be able to examine biological evidence on the development of unborn children—or to look at an aborted child—and conclude that the unborn are likely to be human life.

The argument fails even more decisively as a general rule of constitutional law. Professor Tribe himself subsequently retracted it as a rationale for the abortion cases, recognizing that it would impede the free expression of religious beliefs in the political arena.[91] Finally, the Supreme Court settled the issue when it ruled that legislation related to abortions does not violate the Establishment Clause just because it "happens to coincide or harmonize with the tenets of some or all religions." [92]

Third, one might argue that no branch of government should decide when life begins or decide whether abortions are acceptable; these decisions should instead be left to private individuals. For a court to espouse this view, however, *would* represent a decision as to when life begins. No society that values human life could permit private individuals to have the final say on the taking of innocent life. A court that rules out any role for Congress, the executive, and the judiciary in protecting the unborn cannot pretend to be taking a neutral stand. If no branch of the government decides that the unborn are worth protecting, then the government implicitly decides that they are *not* human life. Since a decision must inevitably be made, the real question is which branch of government should make the decision. The answer to this question, as we have already seen, is the Congress.

A fourth argument against congressional action on this issue might proceed from the so-called ratchet theory. Justice Brennan's opinion for the Court in *Katzenbach* v. *Morgan* set up a ratchetlike standard: Congress may expand Fourteenth Amendment rights but not restrict them. The enforcement clause of each Civil War amendment, under this theory, "does not grant Congress power to exercise discretion in the other direction and to enact 'statutes so as in effect to dilute equal protection and due process decisions of this Court.' " [93] The Court did not explain why Congress is so limited, except to assert: "We emphasize that Congress's power under § 5 grants Congress no power to restrict, abrogate, or dilute these guarantees." [94]

Some congressional actions to enforce Fourteenth Amendment protection for unborn children might be thought to run afoul of the ratchet theory by abrogating the right to privacy.[95] The most simple and straightforward action Congress could take in this area, however, would not present this difficulty. Congress could simply declare that "life" is deemed to commence at conception and that "person" includes all human life, for purposes of the Fourteenth Amendment's protection of life. In effect the Fourteenth Amendment would then read: No state shall deprive any person (including unborn children) of life (which begins at conception) ... without due process of law.

By its terms this type of legislation would bring about an *expansion* of Fourteenth Amendment rights. Such legislation would exert a collateral effect on the right to privacy, but it would not abrogate or infringe that right as the Supreme Court has interpreted it. Congress's action would impose limits only on what *states* may do—it would limit the ability of states to perform abortions in institutions owned or operated by states and their subdivisions, and it would restrict funding of abortions by states. The Supreme Court has already held, however, that statutory limitations on government funding of abortion do *not* infringe the right to privacy.[96] The privacy right to "terminate a pregnancy" does not require the government to fund or provide any abortions.[97] Thus a statute such as the one proposed here, preventing states from continuing to fund abortions, does not abrogate or infringe on the right to privacy. Such legislation would not prevent women from obtaining abortions, since privately performed abortions are not state action. While it can be debated whether Congress *may* reach private action as well as state action when it enforces the Fourteenth Amendment,[98] it is clear that both the Fourteenth Amendment and the statute suggested here, by their direct terms, apply only to state action and not to private acts of abortion.

It is true, of course, that the suggested statute would create a situation in which states have a compelling state interest in the protection of unborn life, sufficient to justify antiabortion statutes should states choose to enact them. Once the unborn child's status as human life and as a person is established by a branch of the government exercising power to enforce the Fourteenth Amendment, the states then have a constitutional standard of "life" and "person" to which they can refer. As the Supreme Court acknowledged in *Roe* v. *Wade*, the state then has a valid interest in protecting unborn life, and any challenge to a state's antiabortion statute collapses.[99]

To create a situation in which states have a compelling interest in protecting human life, however, would not constitute an abrogation of the right to privacy by Congress. Any state might then choose to protect the unborn child's life at the expense of the right to privacy, but no state would be compelled by Congress's action to do so. In effect, the proposed statute would make it clear that the privacy right to "terminate a pregnancy" conflicts with the life of the unborn child. This is not in itself a contraction of rights, but merely a recognition of reality. The fact is that the decision to abort an unborn child *does* conflict with the life of the unborn child. If the Supreme Court chooses to recognize a right to privacy in deciding whether to "terminate a pregnancy," and Congress decides that human life begins at conception, then of course the right to privacy will conflict with the right to life.

Some supporters of *Roe* v. *Wade* have acknowledged the underlying conflict between the two rights, and have recognized that the real constitutional issue comes down to a choice between them. Justice Douglas observed: "The interests of the mother and the fetus are opposed. On which side should the State throw its weight?"[100] In *Roe* v. *Wade*, however, the Court did not face the choice between these rights, because it refused to decide when life begins. Once Congress decides that life begins at conception, or is likely to begin at conception, the basic choice is squarely presented. The choice, whichever branch of government makes it, should not depend on the fortuity of which branch was first in the race to express its opinion.[101] Instead, the choice should turn on whether the life of the unborn child is more important than the right of the mother to decide whether or not to terminate her pregnancy. The proposed statute leaves this choice to the states, informed by Congress's judgment that unborn children are human life and human persons.

Whether the choice between these rights is eventually made by state legislatures, by Congress, or by courts, the fact remains that the statute suggested here does nothing more than expand the Fourteenth Amendment's protection of life to make it clear that indeed we do face a conflict of rights. A contraction of the scope of life under the amendment —by congressional or judicial action—would of course be grounds for the utmost concern. But an *expansion* threatens only to err on the side of compassion and justice, as Senator Hatfield has well remarked: "It is difficult to bring to mind an advocate of justice whom history has condemned for a too 'liberal' view of the range of human life and personhood." [102]

A fifth possible objection to this statute is the argument that Congress may not delegate its power to the states. Congress does have unquestionable authority, however, to take many actions within its delegated powers, which indirectly result in giving the states powers they would not otherwise possess. Cases arising from the Commerce Clause provide an example. Such cases arise typically after the Supreme Court has declared a state unable to regulate a particular type of commerce because of the need for national uniformity. Congress then passes a statute declaring the particular subject matter to be of the type that states *may* regulate. As a result of the statute, the state can exert a power from which it otherwise would be foreclosed. The Supreme Court interprets this not as Congress delegating its power, but rather as Congress removing an obstacle to the state's exercise of its constitutional powers.[103]

In the area of abortions, the state's exercise of its police power to protect health and safety is blocked by an obstacle consisting of the lack of any compelling state interest for outlawing abortions. This obstacle exists only because neither the state nor the courts in *Roe* v. *Wade* were competent to define when human life begins. Once Congress performs this task under its Fourteenth Amendment power, no obstacle any longer exists to prevent the state from exerting its police power. Congress has not delegated any of its power—the police power was not its to delegate in the first place—but it has removed an obstacle to state exercise of a state power, just as in the Commerce Clause cases. This result is fully consistent with precedent. Congress and the states "were not forbidden to cooperate or by doing so to achieve legislative consequences, particularly in the great fields of regulating commerce and taxation, which, to some extent at least, neither could accomplish in isolated exertion." [104]

As a sixth objection, it might be argued that a mere declaration is not appropriate action to enforce the Fourteenth Amendment. But Congress may indeed choose to achieve its ends by declaration. It need not exert the full scope of its available power to enforce declared rights directly; it can leave implementation instead to the courts through the institution of legal action by other parties. For example, Section 10 of the Voting Rights Act of 1965 merely declared Congress's belief that poll taxes violate the Constitution. Congress did not require states to discontinue the use of poll taxes, but instead left implementation to the courts and authorized the attorney general to file suits as appropriate.[105]

Congress has good reason to act by declaration without further enforcement in the matter of protecting unborn life under the Fourteenth Amendment. The only reason that many states are today depriving unborn children of life—by funding or providing abortions on demand—is that no branch of government has successfully defined when life begins. Once Congress declares that life is deemed to commence at conception, one can reasonably expect many states not only to halt state action that deprives the unborn of life, but also to invoke the compelling state interest in the protection of unborn persons, in order to prohibit private abortions.

It is appropriate, therefore, for Congress initially to trust the good faith of the states to implement a congressional declaration that "person" and "life" include the unborn. Congress could well choose to delay any further enforcement action until it sees the extent of state compliance. Such a restrained action by Congress is well within Congress's discretion to decide "whether and what legislation is needed to secure the guarantees of the Fourteenth Amendment." [106]

The reasonableness of such action can perhaps best be seen by leaving the issue of abortion for a moment to consider a hypothetical. Suppose a federal court were to repeat the holding of *Dred Scott* today and decide that members of the black race do not have rights enforceable in court. Would it be unreasonable for Congress simply to declare that blacks are persons under the Fourteenth Amendment? Congress would not *have* to take specific measures to insure state compliance; it could simply assume that the states will act in good faith once the judicially created obstacle to justice is removed.

That Congress chooses not to use the full scope of its powers against a perceived constitutional violation does not in any way undermine the validity of a declaratory statute. It might be argued that the proposed statute is irrational because it defines life and person for purposes of protection of life by the Fourteenth Amendment's Due Process Clause, but not for purposes of the Equal Protection Clause or the protection of liberty and property in the Due Process Clause. Congress does have power, though, to act in piecemeal fashion. On the issue of abortion it may be especially appropriate to do so.

Imagine this problem from the perspective of a congressman who believes there is a likelihood that life begins at conception, but who is not certain. He might not see any urgent need to protect property and liberty rights which the unborn child cannot yet enjoy and which do not have the same paramount importance as the right to life. Further, the congressman might not wish to extend to unborn children a guarantee of equal protection, which has no concrete meaning and will turn out to mean whatever the courts say it means. On the other hand, his perception that unborn children are likely to be human life becomes a much more compelling and urgent guide for public policy when the issue is the protection of life itself. Any legislator might rationally decide to protect against the risk that a human being may be deprived of life, even while refusing to protect immediately against an equal risk that a human being may be deprived of other rights. Further, he might choose to protect unborn children from state action under the Fourteenth Amendment, before addressing the issue of protection under the Fifth Amendment against federal governmental action.[107] In choosing this approach, the legislator would find firm support in statements by the Supreme Court that "a statute is not invalid under the Constitution because it might have gone farther than it did," [108] that a legislature need not "strike at all evils at the same time," [109] and that "reform may take one step at a time, addressing itself to the phase of the problem which seems most acute to the legislative mind." [110]

IV. Conclusion

All the constitutional considerations suggest that Congress would be well within the bounds of its authority were it to pass a Fourteenth Amendment enforcement statute defining "person" and "life" to include the unborn. The relative competence of the courts and Congress to decide when life begins suggests that Congress not only *can* do this, but *should*. It is because of the courts' limitations as fact-finders and policy-makers that they have left the nation without any answer to the question of when life begins. Since Congress does not share these limitations, it is positioned to fill this gap by serving as the proper institution to reflect and express society's answer to this question. By taking this initiative Congress could put an end to the great anomaly of our country's abortion policy since *Roe* v. *Wade,* a national policy founded on a nonanswer to the most fundamental question underlying *any* abortion policy.

We should not delude ourselves, however, that the constitutional merit of such legislation assures its survival in the courts. For the past decade federal judges have not been noted for their reluctance to stretch the law in favor of abortions. Better than a statute would be an amendment to insure that our Constitution recognizes the unborn as human life.

Even an ironclad guarantee of status for the unborn as human persons, however, would not be foolproof protection against judges who are not committed to the idea that the worth of innocent human life is inviolable. One court, for instance, was willing to accept a legislative definition of unborn children as human beings, but nevertheless concluded that the state does not have a strong interest in protecting unborn human life. The court argued quite openly that "population growth must be restricted, not enhanced and thus the state interest in pronatalist statutes such as these is limited." [111] The same judge was willing to belittle the worth of human life in "a fetus likely to be born a mental or physical cripple." [112]

For a judge who employs such reasoning and refuses to acknowledge the equal worth of all human life, it is just as easy to circumvent a constitutional amendment as a statute declaring the unborn to be human. That is one good reason to insure that federal judges are men and women who either respect the limitations of the judicial role enough to refrain from imposing their views of population control or eugenics on the rest of us. At the same time we should not delay in enacting whatever legislation is within Congress's constitutional powers, to protect the lives of the unborn. Although we cannot hope to cure at once all the mischief caused by courts in the area of abortions, we must at least take those actions that currently lie within our power.

Constitutional Privacy, Religious Disestablishment, and the Abortion Decisions

David A. J. Richards

THIS essay examines a problem about punishment which intersects the theory and practice of both constitutional and criminal law in the United States. It comes as no surprise to an American, though it would to citizens of other liberal democracies, that a central issue of justice in punishment—namely, the just limits on the application of the criminal sanction—should take the form not only of public debate over legislative policy but of arguments of principle over the meaning of constitutional values. In this study, I explore why and how these questions properly interconnect for us, and propose a novel account within political and constitutional theory of the terms in which they should be connected. My aim is to identify and explore what I take to be the seminal injustice in American criminal law—namely, overcriminalization. It is seminal in the sense that it is the predicate on which many of the other injustices of American criminal law depend—for example, the abuse of discretion, wasteful and often barbarous use of police and prison resources, the distortion of the dignity of criminal justice by the prejudices of race, class, gender, and the like. If we could become clearer in our collective understanding of this seminal injustice, we could redirect the forms and scope of the criminal sanction to their properly limited and humane purposes and deal with other national problems in ways more sensible and more consistent with both social justice and respect for human rights.

I address this subject through the prism of intellectual focus on two interconnected puzzles at the core of contemporary political and constitutional controversy: first, the status and provenance of the elaboration by the Supreme Court of the constitutional right to privacy; and second, the application of that right to abortion in *Roe* v. *Wade*,[1] the failure of its application to consensual adult sexuality by the Supreme Court,[2] its application thereto by state supreme courts,[3] and other controverted issues. After addressing the various perspectives that may justify these developments, I shall urge the fertility of a mode of analysis, neither deeply addressed in the philosophical or legal literature nor coherently developed by the judiciary. The analysis involves a philosophical interpretation of the moral value of respect for persons. The right to this respect is central to the reasonable elaboration of the values of the religion clauses of the First Amendment. My objective is to urge the utility and promise of fundamental philosophical and historical work in support of the further elaboration of this mode of analysis.

We begin with the reigning conundrum of contemporary constitutional jurisprudence: how, if at all, consistent with sound principles of constitutional interpretation, the Supreme Court can justifiably have elaborated the constitutional right to privacy in general. An affirmative resolution of this conundrum, favorable to the legitimacy of constitutional privacy, would not, *pari passu*, justify all the forms of the Supreme Court's application or refusals of application of constitutional privacy to particular cases. The elaboration of constitutional privacy as a critical doctrine may be justified, even required, and yet particular applications of the doctrine (to abortion, for example) may be justified, and particular refusals of application (i.e., to consensual homosexuality) may be unjustified. Let us begin, then, with the general conundrum, and then turn to the examination of particular applications of the right.

The conundrum of constitutional privacy is familiarly posed by the critics of constitutional privacy in a twofold challenge: first, how can a right like constitutional privacy, which is not textually rooted in any clause of the written Constitution, be inferred consistent with judicial fidelity to the interpretation of the terms of the Constitution?; and second, assuming the right is textually based in some form, how can such textual inference be squared with basic premises of the political theory of democratic self-rule which sharply limit the scope of proper judicial invalidation of majority rule? This latter challenge is sharply posed by John Hart Ely in his *Democracy and Distrust*.[4] Ely argues that the first prong of the conundrum—the interpretivist challenge to the judicial elaboration of constitutional privacy—is much overstated in the constitutional literature: the Privileges and Immunities Clause of the Fourteenth Amendment, adapted from the comparable clause of Article IV, may reasonably be textually and historically interpreted to include rights of the kind encompassed by constitutional privacy. For example, assume that the Privileges and Immunities Clause of the Fourteenth Amendment or the reservation clause of the Ninth Amendment contemplated unenumerated basic human rights which would be enforceable on a par with enumerated rights. In this case one such basic human right—clearly stated in the literature that influenced the remarkably learned generation which wrote the United States Constitution and Bill of Rights—was what Hutcheson called "the natural right each one to enter into the matrimonial relation with any one who consents." [5] Indeed, historical materials suggest that the right may properly be more abstractly stated. For example, James Witherspoon, in lectures Madison heard when a student at Princeton, follows Hutcheson in listing as a basic human and natural right, the "right to associate, if he so incline, with any person or persons, whom he can persuade (not force)—under this is contained the right to marriage." [6] So, the historical material would reasonably support a basic human right of association, including intimate associations, of which marriage is one central, but nonexclusive example.[7] Ely concedes that this historical record reasonably bears some such interpretation of a kind clearly central to the elaboration of the constitutional right to privacy (which, in *Griswold* v. *Connecticut*,[8] protects the marriage relationship from coercive state prohibition of contraception use). So, his objection to constitutional privacy does not rest on history or textual interpretation (both are consistent with the doctrine). Rather, Ely rests his critical case—against constitutional privacy in general and the abortion cases in particular—on the second prong of the challenge: textually and historically sustainable inferences from the written Constitution should be rejected when inconsistent with the sound political theory of constitutional democracy.

For Ely, this political theory holds that a working democracy must secure fair representation to all relevant interests, so that judicial review of majoritarian legislation is justified if it secures on balance a fairer representation of interests than majority rule unqualified by judicial review. On this theory, the heart of the justification of judicial review is the demonstration of a suspect classification requiring strict scrutiny under the Fourteenth Amendment. This amendment critically assesses and invalidates legislation that stigmatizes racial and other stereotypes which manifest themselves in popular prejudices contemptuous of and hostile to the interests of the stereotyped groups. Thus, fair democratic weight is not accorded to those interests. Whatever the textual or historical warrant for constitutional privacy, the doctrine is unjustified because it does not secure fairer representation in the way democratic political theory requires: the constitutional privacy extended to contraceptive use, for example, does not protect an insular minority, but a large majority of contraceptive-using Americans. If there is good reason to allow these Americans to use contraceptives without liability to criminal sanctions, as Ely would surely concede there is, that reason should justify political action in the normal democratic way, not the special intervention of the countermajoritarian judiciary which is here not called for or justified. The abortion cases are, for Ely, wrong *a fortiori*. For by extending to pregnant women an absolute right to terminate pregnancy during the first trimester, not only is an insular minority left unprotected from unfair representation, but arguably a quite insular minority indeed (the unborn fetuses) is also, by virtue of the abortion decisions themselves, exposed to constitutional invidious prejudice.[9]

Ely's form of argument is surely correct in refocusing debate over constitutional privacy from text and history to political theory, for much in the text and history of the Constitution would support, indeed require, the general doctrine of constitutional privacy. Indeed, there is more text and history than even Ely adduces, as discussed in my treatment below of the religion clauses. But, it would be a vapid victory for the living faith of constitutional morality if only textual or historical argument controlled. For, if arguments of text or history were to require what is forbidden by a sound political theory of democratic constitutionalism, how could we fault a conscientious judge who gave primacy to the latter in limiting the force of text or history? For example, Learned Hand, one of America's Herculean judges, appeared to believe that the ideas of human rights explicit in the text and history of the Constitution were roughly as defensible, to a critical modern mind like Hand's, as the witchcraft beliefs of the Azande.[10] If this were true, as a certain Benthamite skepticism about rights or more general value skepticism might have led Hand reasonably to believe, how could a judge or lawyer or citizen of any measure of integrity allow the work of justice to be tainted by such ideas? Surely, on such a basis, Hand's skeptical attack on judicial review cannot be faulted: that political theory should control text and history is manifestly just. Hand's political theory is, of course, deplorably wrong, and thus his attack on judicial review is jerrybuilt.[11] But the primacy Hand gives to political theory, assumed also by Ely, supports a sound methodology in constitutional theory of giving central place to political theory which, inevitably, controls, rearranges, and recasts other arguments. Consistent with this methodology, our discussion of the legitimacy of constitutional privacy should focus on the prior question: what political theory, if any, would justify the form of argument which constitutional privacy is? If we can resolve this issue favorably to this form of argument on grounds of political theory, the constitutional issue may be resolved at the same time, or at least more easily.

Three general arguments are worth exploring as forms of political theory that might justify constitutional privacy: first, the argument from shifting moral consensus; second, the harm principle, seminally stated by John Stuart Mill in *On Liberty;*[12] and third, the religion clauses of the First Amendment, suitably interpreted. Each perspective has problems both as general political theory and as background theory for constitutional privacy. I submit that the most promising strategy in understanding constitutional privacy in general and the abortion cases in particular is grounded in a certain interpretation of the religion clauses.

1. The Argument from Changing Moral Consensus

The argument from changing moral consensus grounds privacy argument on putative shifts in the conventional moral values held in the society-at-large and thus regarded as the traditional basis for concepts of public morality. In that the values of the public morality supply the relevant standards for criminal law, and in that the aim of criminal law is the public enforcement of minimal moral standards of decency, any shift in conventional moral values toward irregarding certain forms of conduct as morally wrong would justify forms of decriminalization of the conduct in question. However, there is a lag time between the shift in moral consensus and the associated decriminalization: conventional social morality no longer regards certain conduct as wrong (for example, use of contraceptives, or abortions, or consensual homosexual relations), and yet such conduct is still the object of criminal sanctions. Arguments of privacy arise in the interstices between shifts in moral consensus and unchanged criminal sanctions: conduct is immunized from criminal sanction by invocation of a right to privacy or, more accurately, a right of personal autonomy when the moral basis for the criminal sanction is no longer supported by moral consensus.

If the argument from moral consensus is interpreted in a certain natural way, it is trivially true almost by definition, which may account for the continuing popular attraction of this form of argument. In that the criminal law or its essential purposes rests on definitions of certain forms of moral wrongdoing, conduct which is not morally wrong in the required way should not be criminal. So far, so good.

But the argument from moral consensus is not confined to this trivially true interpretation. It is supposed to say something informative about the real basis for criminalization and the appropriate grounds for substantive shifts in the scope of application of the criminal sanction, either by way of contraction or expansion. As such, it wrongly describes the phenomenon it purports to explain, and certainly renders incoherent any theory of constitutional privacy as a judicially enforceable right.

This informative interpretation of the argument from changing moral consensus appeals to a conception of conventional morality as the basis for criminal law, but, in so doing, it fails to explain how changes in moral consensus occur or how, normatively, we should assess their justifiability. It is by now a philosophical banality in decriminalization controversy—in the recurrent forms of the Mill-Stephen[13] or Hart-Devlin[14] debates—that the controversy centers on different interpretations of what public morality is and may properly demand through social convention. Serious arguments for decriminalization standardly controvert traditional moral conventions for failing to satisfy certain independently desirable criteria of rationality or critical morality; standard answers of moral conservatives question the possibility of such internal moral reforms given the inextricable web of moral conventions alleged by them to define the public morality. As Devlin quite clearly argues,[15] forms of decriminalization alleged to reflect a changing moral consensus may treasonably rend the very fabric of social unity. The argument from shifts in moral consensus fails to address the substance of such disagreements between advocates of and dissenters to proposed forms of decriminalization, suppressing precisely the issue in dispute—namely, the proper interpretation and assessment of conventional morality—in the name of the question-begging assertion controlled by shifting moral consensus.

From the perspective of the traditional liberal concern for a program of decriminalization, the argument from shifting moral consensus fails to capture the dynamic of critical moral assessment fundamental to the explanation of shifts in moral consensus. No serious moral critic, liberal or not, has ever regarded conventional morality *simpliciter* as the measure of moral criticism;[16] indeed, the whole enterprise of enlightened moral reform assumes that ethics is not conventional morality. From the liberal perspective, the argument from shifting moral standards is especially dubious: It proves too little—allowing moral reform only on the basis of moral consensus; or too much—requiring moral reform when, from the perspective of enlightened values, the shift in moral consensus is morally corrupt, regressive, or atavistic.

If the informative form of the argument from shifting moral standards is a bad political theory of decriminalization, it appears incoherent as a justification for judicial enforcement of an argument for decriminalization. Thus, the argument from shifting moral standards rests on the lag time between shifts in moral consensus and decriminalization reflecting such shifts. But, if there has been a massive shift in moral consensus (as, for example, regarding permissible use of contraceptives), why cannot such massive public support reasonably express itself through the normal democratic processes without the need of intervention by a countermajoritarian judiciary? At most, judicial intervention may here accelerate the rate of legal change, but it does so at the real cost of diverting the issue from democratic politics, thereby enervating the capacity of democratic majorities to use politics to achieve their rightful ends. Indeed, the argument from shifting moral consensus, as a purported justification for judicial elaboration of the right of constitutional privacy, counterintuitively would justify the intervention of the countermajoritarian judiciary when it appears least morally needed (the shift in moral consensus is popularly widespread in large majorities of the population). And it would withhold its intervention when the judiciary's capacity for independent moral judgment may be most ethically required (i.e., the shift in moral consensus, legitimating nonprocreational sex in its popular heterosexual forms, has not consistently been extended to an isolated and stereotypically despised homosexual minority). On this theory, *Griswold* v. *Connecticut*[17] would be correct (contraceptive use was popular); *Roe* v. *Wade*[18] perhaps dubious (the shift in moral consensus at the time may have been unclear); *Doe* v. *Commonwealth's Attorney*[19] correct (homosexuality unpopular). Perhaps some of the Supreme Court's more startlingly inconsistent decisions may be explained in this way (*Naim* v. *Naim;*[20] *Doe*[21]). But, such an explanatory thesis, under which the Supreme Court supinely tracks majoritarian moral consensus in order, perhaps, to preserve its institutional capital, hardly rises to the dignity of a political theory of constitutional principle. Indeed, any theory which would dignify such cases with a mantle of high constitutional principle compromises the central values of constitutional government —that the judiciary must be available to test the validity of government action against its independent articulation of constitutional principle, precisely where large democratic majorities have lost their constitutional sanity.[22]

2. The Harm Principle

The argument based on the harm principle draws inspiration from the classic statement of this argument in a book of genius, John Stuart Mill's *On Liberty*.[23] Mill's complex argument has two objectives, which have come to define two central planks in the political program of liberalism as a self-conscious political theory: first, the primacy of freedom of expression as a political value uncompromisable in trade-offs with other values;[24] and second, a defense of a right of personal autonomy which, within its defined limits, justifies a general right to act in certain ways without coercive interference by either the state or by society in general.[25] The argument for constitutional privacy reflects Mill's defense of a right of personal autonomy.

Mill's argument rests on an extended and complex form of moral criticism of the degree to which a certain form of conventional morality has unreflectingly been permitted to require forms of state punishment through the criminal law, and larger patterns of social condemnation enforced through informal mechanisms of social control. The form of conventional morality at issue reflects this structure of argument: Any form of conduct may be subject to state or social condemnation if an ordinary person, reflecting some statistical normalcy of sentiment and opinion of the society-at-large, would experience deep revulsion and offense at the thought of the action in question *simpliciter*. Mill argues that the Anglo-American conception of public morality, reflected in the work of the purity reformers and others, rests on this form of the argument of conventional morality; if the argument from conventional morality is seriously defective—and Mill argues it is —the effective conception of public morality must also fall.

Mill's argument for the inadequacy of conventional morality as the measure of legal and social enforcement rests on the stark failure of the relevant standard (the offense taken by an ordinary person at the thought of _____) to advert to any impact of the conduct in question on any interests of persons. Forms of conduct are to be legally and socially condemned solely because an ordinary person would take offense at the thought of certain conduct, *without more*—in particular, without any required form of inquiry into the reasons why such conduct is condemned, the degree to which the conduct frustrates or advances human interests, the justifiability of requiring all persons similarly situated so to act, and so on. But, so understood, conventional morality will mandate legal and social prohibitions to narrow the range of permissible actions to those simply of the most unquestioned popular prejudices reflecting crude stereotypes, elementary failures of moral and human imagination, crass group stupidity, and bigotry. Following De Tocqueville,[26] Mill suggests that if the achievement of democratic government leads to the unquestioned dominance of conventional morality so understood, the deepest values of the political theory of democracy will be betrayed: a tool intended to liberate human capacities for the enlightened pursuit of interests on terms fair to all will become an instrument for the crudest oppression of the varieties of the pursuit of happiness into Procrustean and stupid convention—rigid, unintelligent, willful.

In order to obviate this betrayal of basic democratic values, Mill argues that conventional morality as such must be rejected as the basis for legal and social condemnation. In its place he offers the harm principle. In contrast to the standard of conventional morality, which allows anything in principle to be the object of legal and social condemnation (depending on the feelings of offense of the ordinary person), the harm principle imposes determinate constraints on the degree to which legal and social condemnation may be applied to acts. Focusing for our present purposes on constraints on criminal sanctions, Mill's formulation limits the scope of the criminal law—subject to a background theory of just distribution and of moral duties of fair contribution (Mill is no libertarian)—in the following ways:

1. Acts may properly be made criminal only if they inflict concrete harms on assignable persons.
2. Except to protect children, incompetents, and "backward" [27] peoples, it is never proper to criminalize an act *solely* on the ground of preventing harm to the agent.
3. It is never proper to criminalize conduct solely because the mere thought of it gives offense to others.

Mill argues that the harm principle states a form of reasoning which democratic majorities must observe in order justly to impose criminal sanctions—in the same way that justice in punishment requires that the definition and imposition of criminal sanctions must observe certain basic principles of legality, proportionality, concurrence of *actus reus* and *mens rea*, and the like.[28]

Mill's argument for the harm principle correctly seeks to dispel the superficial appeal of conventional morality as the most democratic way for a society to establish enforceable moral values. For how, it may be supposed, could a society more democratically decide these issues than by a kind of populist appeal to the felt values which unite democratic majorities as a people? Mill's arresting and provocative response is a profound political theory of the values fundamental to republican democracy. In such a democracy, populist moral romanticism—on which the appeal of conventional morality rests—does not depend on the sound values which make democracy a defensible form of government. Rather it rests on an older, indeed ancient, conception of public tribal morality antecedent to the elaboration and embodiment of the values of equality and liberty in working constitutional democracies, and indeed in tension—if not outrightly inconsistent—with many of these values (for example, the primacy of religious toleration and freedom of conscience).[29] The values distinctive of democracy are, Mill argues, precisely values of the liberation of human capacities for the enlightened pursuit of interests on terms fair to all. The enforcement of the tribal conception of conventional morality frustrates these values in deep and damaging ways. Accordingly, an alternative conception of an enforceable public morality—the harm principle—is required by democratic political theory.

Mill's arguments in *On Liberty* are a great advance in political theory because they connect in a philosophically profound way arguments for both the priority of free speech and the harm principle to a deep and plausible general theory of constitutional democracy. Nonetheless, the form of Mill's defense of liberalism suffers from the intractable internal tension between his sympathy for rights-based arguments of principle and his doctrinal utilitarianism. Thus, although Mill's harm principle places a constraint on the criminal law comparable to the one embodied in the French Declaration of Rights, Mill did not justify the constraint on the basis of the human rights paradigm, as did the French Declaration. Rather, Mill appealed to a general utilitarian argument, derived from Jeremy Bentham, that failing to follow the harm principle reduces the aggregate surplus of pleasure over pain. Mill was less doctrinaire in his opposition to the language and thought of rights than Bentham, and some find in *On Liberty* rights-based arguments of personal autonomy. But, although Mill did give great weight to preserving the capacity of persons to frame their own life plans independently, he appears—in accordance with his argument in *Utilitarianism*[30]—to have incorporated this factor into the utilitarian framework of preferring "higher" to "lower" pleasures. Thus, the argument of *On Liberty* is utilitarian: the greatest aggregate sum by which pleasure exceeds pain, taking into account the greater weight accorded by utilitarianism to higher pleasures, is secured by granting free speech and observing the harm principle as the measure of criminalization.

But, to the extent that the harm principle appears to be at least a good first approximation to a significant constraint of justice on permissible criminalization, there appear to be grave objections to grounding this perception of justice on utilitarian argument.[31] The harm principle is not a necessary corollary of utilitarian tenets; quite the contrary. The basic desideratum of utilitarianism is to maximize the surplus of pleasure over pain. If certain plausible assumptions about human nature are made, however, utilitarianism would require the criminalization of certain conduct in violation of the harm principle. Assume, for example, that an overwhelming majority of people in a community take personal satisfaction in their way of life and that their pleasure is appreciably heightened by the knowledge that conflicting ways of life are forbidden by the criminal law. Suppose, indeed, that hatred of the nonconforming minority, legitimated by the application of criminal penalties, reinforces the pleasurable feelings of social solidarity, peace of mind, self-worth, and achievement in a way that tolerance, with its invitation to self-doubt, ambivalence, and insecurity, could not. In such circumstances, the greater pleasure thus secured to the majority may not only outweigh the pain to the minority but, as compared to the toleration required by the harm principle, may result in a greater aggregate of pleasure; accordingly, utilitarianism would call for criminalization in violation of the harm principle. From this perspective, James Fitzjames Stephen may be a more consistent utilitarian than Mill in perceiving that a utilitarian analysis does not cohere with the stringent requirements of the harm principle.[32]

To the extent that recent Mill scholars have attempted to reconstruct his argument on utilitarian grounds,[33] they propose an interpretive structure which is not properly utilitarian, but rather explicatory of central neo-Kantian values of the independence and integrity of the person. For, to the extent that scholars tinker with utilitarian assumptions in order to yield anything as demanding as the harm principle, they confirm one's suspicions that, for them, the harm principle is a more secure moral judgment than any utilitarian rationale or assumption designed to justify it (cf. the familiar utilitarian use of a dubious empirical assumption, declining marginal utility, to justify beliefs in egalitarian distribution whose moral foundations are certainly more secure than our beliefs in diminishing marginal utility).[34] If so, as C. L. Ten suggests,[35] we should explicate an alternative moral theory which will ground the harm principle more directly and securely and which, in any event, Mill appears to assume, albeit through a glass darkly.

If the harm principle were only properly grounded in utilitarian argument, this would pose special justificatory difficulties for constitutional privacy as a judicially enforceable right. The utilitarian cast which Mill gives his arguments is understandable in a nation like Great Britain, where Mill makes his argument to a parliament that enjoys constitutional supremacy. In the United States, however, arguments of this kind are made not only to legislatures but also to countermajoritarian courts empowered with judicial supremacy in the elaboration of a charter of human rights, who have evolved the constitutional right to privacy to give expression to something like the harm principle. It is difficult to reconcile the notion of privacy rights that these cases embody with the utilitarian policy arguments that decriminalization proponents like Mill and his Anglo-American progeny generally use. Indeed, as we have already seen, the status and rationale of the constitutional right to privacy are at the center of contemporary controversy over constitutional theory and practice. Critics argue, for example, that the right to privacy is policy-based, legislative in character, and non-neutral, and therefore may not properly be enforced by courts, whose decisions must be grounded not in utilitarian policy but governed by neutral principles of justification.[36] If the deployment of constitutional privacy in these cases must be construed in utilitarian terms, such objections may be conclusive, and decriminalization arguments would be properly directed only to legislatures, not to courts.

Finally, even assuming that the harm principle were a justifiable standard which countermajoritarian courts could justly enforce, the judicial interpretation of the application of the principle is subject to doubt and controversy: the interpretation of what counts as a "harm" within the contemplation of the principle in many cases may simply

replicate the moral controversies over the proper scope of criminalization which the harm principle was supposed to clarify. Abortion may
be a striking example. Advocates of the criminalization of abortion
argue that abortion is not a victimless or complaintless crime: the
unborn fetus is harmed in a straightforward sense—its life is terminated. Opponents of such criminalization respond that no harm is
done to anyone here (in that there is no moral person killed), but
rather a great good is granted to a woman through the ability to control her reproductive autonomy. The simple notion of "harm," perhaps
very useful in some areas of decriminalization controversy, appears in
such cases as abortion only to carry the level of debate one step backward. The harm principle, often a useful starting point in decriminalization controversy, is not always the best ending point. In order to
probe more deeply at the crucial points (including background assumptions about upholding and supporting just institutions), we must in-
quire into a plausible background theory which may sensibly interpret
what "harm" should mean without collapsing into a utilitarianism unable to capture either the force or the sense that the harm principle
intuitively carries with it.

3. Respect for Persons and the Religion Clauses

In order to introduce my own constructive moral and constitutional
proposal for understanding constitutional privacy, consider the form of
such an argument, based on the antiestablishment of religion clause,
suggested by Louis Henkin in his important article, "Morals and the
Constitution: The Sin of Obscenity." [37] Henkin, focusing his argument
against the criminalization of the publication and use of obscene materials and consensual homosexual acts, argues that the values of antiestablishment clause require that the state not endorse in any way
purely religious values. In terms of the current trio of tests used by the
Supreme Court in antiestablishment cases (the legislation must have
a secular purpose, neither aid nor inhibit religion, and not promote
excessive entanglement between religious authorities and the state),[38]
Henkin places central emphasis on the requirement that laws must
have a secular purpose, not being supported by essentially religious
premises. The criminalization of obscene materials and consensual
homosexuality violate this requirement, Henkin argues, because, on
analysis, the rationale for such laws does not rest on empirically ascertainable secular harms. Instead it rests on premises unique to religious

traditions rooted in interpretations of certain texts and traditions having a religious authority shared neither by other religions nor by those of no religious persuasion. The argument grants that, historically, many fundamental ethical values may once have been interpreted as having religious sanction as well, and this fact, in itself, would not invalidate criminal laws (like those against homicide) which can be traced to such historical roots. It would, of course, be a rather blatant form of the genetic fallacy to suppose that an explanation of origins must determine essential purpose or justification. The proper interpretation of antiestablishment clause values requires us to avoid this fallacy by separating the question of religious origins from the question of how today certain laws and practices can be justified, in view of contemporary evidence and forms of ethical argument. If the policy of a law can no longer be grounded in any empirically ascertainable secular harm but only in a purely religious interpretation, then enforcement of the law is a constitutionally forbidden establishment of religion. The prohibitions of obscene materials and consensual homosexuality are unconstitutional on this ground because their justifications do not rest on secular harms. To the contrary, prohibition of obscene materials may not only harm consenting adults who want them, but it may also increase the incidence of ancillary harms (sex crimes);[39] and the prohibition of consensual homosexuality inflicts irreparable harm in an area of intimate personal life of the deepest moment and significance to consenting adults.[40] If contemporary assessment of such laws reveals empirical mistakes about matters of fact, as well as ethical failures of seeing persons as stereotypes, not as persons, the residual religious justification for such laws, which alone support them, must constitutionally condemn them.

If Henkin's establishment of religion argument seems a promising strategy in analyzing constitutional privacy, it raises, nonetheless, great puzzles of general principle as well as specific problems in understanding the legitimacy of *Roe* v. *Wade*. To take the last point first, while the antiestablishment approach may explain the constitutional difficulties which surround or should surround prohibitions both of obscene materials and consensual homosexuality, it does not justify *Roe* if, on examination, the criminalization of abortion does not rest on purely religious, but rather on more general, ethical premises. Henkin, for example, appears himself to believe this.[41] And the federal courts adopted this view when considering the argument that the Hyde Amendment, which deprived women of Medicaid funding for most abortions, constituted a constitutionally forbidden establishment of religion. Judge Dooling, in denying the antiestablishment argument, found that the relevant enactments "reflect a traditionalist view more accurately than any religious one, a view that was reflected in most state statutes of a generation ago." [42] And Justice Stewart, speaking for the Supreme Court, affirmed Dooling's rejection of the antiestablishment argument, observing:

That the Judaeo-Christian religions oppose stealing does mean that a State or the Federal Government may not, consistent with the Establishment Clause, enact laws prohibiting larceny.... The Hyde Amendment, as the District Court noted, is as much a reflection of "traditionalist" values towards abortion, as it is an embodiment of the views of any particular religion.[43]

If good constitutional theorists and federal judges concur that abortion is not a felicitous case for application of the antiestablishment argument, our investigation into alternative grounds for constitutional privacy may appear again nugatory. The problem appears to be that the argument has been understood as focusing on the nature of the groups who currently advocate certain legislation. This focus appears to draw the line between religious and secular purposes, for establishment clause purposes, in a way that makes the clause unfairly hostile to the important and benign role that political advocacy by religious groups has played in the elaboration of both American constitutional values and general values of justice and humanity.

In view of these difficulties, I propose a constructive reinterpretation of the connection of constitutional privacy to the values of the religion clauses, one which may enable us better to address the ways in which controversy over the application of the right may properly be conducted. I propose that we interpret constitutional privacy as a reflection of two complementary considerations: first, as grounded in one or another fundamental human right, supported by good moral argument and historical understanding[44]—for example, an abstract right of association, including a right of intimate association, of which marriage is one example; and second, in addition to the heavy burden of justification that any abridgement of a fundamental right would, as such, require, a special form of constitutionally compelled scrutiny of such grounds for abridgement in light of the natural elaboration of the primacy of religious toleration under American constitutional law.

By the primacy of religious toleration, I mean to describe or explicate the special, indeed unique, place that American constitutional law gives to the inalienable right to conscience—namely, that the state must express the greatest equal respect, consistent with a like respect for all, for the higher-order capacity of persons to exercise their independence and rationality in forming, expressing, and revising their basic systems of values and theories of living. In my judgment, respect for this background right explains the coordinated purposes of the free exercise and antiestablishment clauses of the First Amendment: the free exercise clause forbids state coercion of the expression of conscience inconsistent with this respect, and the antiestablishment clause insists on equal respect for the ways in which persons form and revise their consciences.[45] This primacy of religious toleration has naturally been elaborated in ways that bear on development of constitutional privacy under our law. In order to see the dynamic of this elaboration, consider three underlying, quite reasonable shifts of thought which have led the Supreme Court to expand the application of the values of the religion clauses of the First Amendment.

First, there has been an erosion of the sharp dichotomy, deployed in the early Mormon cases,[46] between belief (protected by the religion clauses) and action motivated by those beliefs (unprotected). Thus, although Mormon worship and belief could not, as such, be forbidden, the forms of polygamy, then religiously mandated, could be forbidden by the state because according to this view, the religion clauses extended only to belief, not action. More recently, the Supreme Court has abandoned this dichotomy, requiring that, when the state infringes a religiously motivated action, it must do so only in the pursuit of a compelling secular purpose reasonably pursued.[47] In this, the Court has, I believe, articulated a form of the harm principle inchoate in Locke's classic argument for religious toleration[48] and Jefferson's stark remark: "The legitimate powers of government extend to such acts only as are injurious to others. But it does no injury for my neighbor to say there are twenty gods, or no god. It neither picks my pocket nor breaks my leg." [49] The principle of this elaboration of religion clause values is philosophical in nature, reflecting, I believe, a deep modern skepticism about the kind of mind-body dualism implicit in the limitation of the religion clauses to the mind alone, as if only the mind must be guaranteed moral independence, but the body may remain a kind of enslaved hostage to conventional bigotry and intolerance.[50] If we come reasonably to believe that the maintenance of such a dichotomy, as the measure of constitutional law, is itself inconsistent with the required constitutional neutrality, then the protections of the religion clauses must radiate to encompass action, as Locke and Jefferson appear to have seen.

Second, beginning around World War II, there has been a striking shift in the Supreme Court's thinking about the constitutional acceptability of regarding religion as a kind of neutral proxy for the state's promotion of appropriately neutral purposes of public morality.[51] Skepticism about the necessity or inevitability of the link between morality and religion is not unknown to advocates of toleration; indeed, forms of such skepticism pervade almost all serious thought about the primacy of religious toleration both by Catholics (Italian humanists, Erasmus, Montaigne),[52] Protestants (Bayle,[53] Locke,[54] Roger Williams[55]), and others (Acontius, Castellio).[56] But the idea that religion as such does not track ethics (in contrast to the weaker claim that theological differences about the terms of theism do not track ethical differences) is much less common. Nonetheless, the Western philosophical tradition, at least since Plato's *Euthyphro*,[57] has taken seriously the idea of the conceptual independence of ethical and religious concepts, and the idea had become an important feature of religious thought about the nature of God's goodness, in eighteenth-century thought, through Shaftesbury, Butler, and Hutcheson.[58] Even Madison's teacher, the orthodox Calvinist Witherspoon,[59] assumes a form of the idea, which indicates its pervasiveness during the period that gave birth to the philosophy of the religion clauses and their radical embodiment of the primacy of religious toleration. Accordingly, the idea of the independence of ethics and religion cannot reasonably be supposed to be unknown to the American constitutional tradition; consider Jefferson's statement, in the Act for Religious Freedom, "that our civil rights have no dependence on our religious opinions, more than our opinions in physics or geometry." [60] But the dominant view, echoing Locke's exclusion of atheists from his principles of toleration,[61] and even Bayle's weaker exemption of them from full protection,[62] was that religion—and, more specifically, in nineteenth-century America, Protestant Christianity—was the central vehicle for the moral values of constitutionalism. The great Justice Story, for example, speaks early in this period of Protestant Christianity as the *de facto* established church of the republic, its values being, for this purpose, moral values as such.[63] When one begins to question the necessity or inevitability of the link between ethics and religion and, *a fortiori*, between ethics and Protestant Christianity, then the use of religion as a neutral proxy for moral argument and values as such becomes questionable. This leads naturally to the school prayer cases[64] and to the battles over teaching Darwin in the public schools,[65] and, more generally, to growing constitutional concern that, consistent with neutrality values, the state not enforce an illegitimately nonneutral conception of ethical values (as, for example, in the nativist prohibitionism which foisted ideological Protestant perfectionism on Catholics and Jews).[66]

Third, there has been a natural expansion in the concept of constitutionally protectable religious activity, especially for purposes of the protection of religious free exercise. In *Torcaso v. Watkins*,[67] for example, Justice Black, speaking for the Court, declared unconstitutional a state requirement that state officials must swear belief in God, on the ground that the constitutional conception of religious neutrality extended to belief systems without a God. And, in the conscientious objector cases, the Supreme Court, undoubtedly to avoid background questions premised on religious clause constitutional neutrality, interpreted the congressional statutory exemption from military service of religious conscientious objectors to all wars as extending to all forms of conscientious objection as such.[68]

These three developments in thought—the expansion of toleration values from thought to action, the closer scrutiny of religion as a neutral proxy for ethics, and the expansion in the constitutional concept of religion for free exercise and other purposes—lead to growing constitutional concern for any form of state coercion, including, of course, criminal penalties, which is applied to conscientiously motivated action in the absence of compelling state purposes. The inference may be put as follows: (1) constitutional protection under the free exercise clause cannot, consistent with constitutional neutrality, be withheld from independent conscience as such; (2) protection under the free exercise clause extends to criminal penalties applied to actions, motivated by conscience, as well as to beliefs; (3) criminal penalties applied under (2) to actions must be shown to rest on a neutral conception of enforceable values; (4) religion is not a proxy for ethics, so that the justification for coercion of conduct on religious grounds alone, without adequate support in independently neutral ethical considerations or arguments, will not constitute a legitimately neutral state interest under (4); (5) indeed, the attempt to impose such a religious nonneutral value under (4) may independently violate the antiestablishment clause. In short, through a natural elaboration of argument rooted in the evolving values of the religion clauses, we find that the conception of toleration there embodied radiates naturally to toleration of certain forms of life, which harm no one measured by neutral ethical argument, and whose prohibition by the state rests on precisely the kind of content-based hatred which is denied expression in law by the First Amendment. The doctrine known as constitutional privacy arose in the area of conscientious activity expressive of independently specified fundamental rights (the abstract right of voluntary association, including intimate relations), where state prohibition could not satisfy the constitutional burden thus required. As such, constitutional privacy was and is, in my judgment, a wholly natural, indeed constitutionally required, development best understood as a constitutional argument reflecting, in part, the religion clauses through a glass very, very darkly.

The form of argument, required to apply the principle of constitutional privacy thus understood, is undoubtedly complex, involving nothing less than sustained inquiry into history, sound moral argument, social and psychological facts, and the like, all of which bear on our collective critical self-consciousness of the justice or injustice of our traditional practices. In fact, all the privacy decisions reflect deep moral controversy within American society over which aspects of our collective moral traditions can and cannot justly be retained. Our moral practices as a community are not inextricably homogeneous: on critical reflection, we retain certain basic principles in them (for example, treating persons as equals), but change lower order conventions which we come to believe inconsistent with the reflective ethical core of our moral and constitutional values. Accordingly, the appeal to "morality and decency," [69] without more, falsely begs the central issue in dispute, supposing precisely the kind of homogeneity in moral values belied by the general history of Western ethics and specific history of constitutional privacy. It is a valued and admirable distinction of Western ethics and law that they have changed, open to critical reflection on their own history and to new empirical and normative perspectives. The right to constitutional privacy expresses this kind of reassessment, one certainly constitutive of the best impulses in Western culture to legitimate continually our values, to ground them in a more empirically grounded conception of fact and a more impartially ethical conception of value. In contrast to a form of this argument earlier discussed, no part of the present argument depends on the nature of the group who advocates certain claims. Religious groups in the United States were central in the abolitionist movement and many of the civil rights movements: their ethical aims were not, therefore, illegitimately nonneutral. Prohibitionism in the United States may have been supported by many nonreligious groups, or antiabortion laws mainly by medical, not religious groups;[70] their ethical aims may not today be any the less nonneutral in nature. The argument rather rests on inquiry into whether nonneutral values are, in fact, central in sustaining a certain policy—an inquiry which is complex and difficult.

Nonetheless, there may be clear cases—for example, the original application of constitutional privacy to the use of contraceptives by married couples.[71] Marriage is, clearly, a fundamental human right both in fact and in law, but it is one we are prepared to subject to state coercion if the appropriate burden of harm prevention is met. Thus, we do not object to the application of the criminal law to forbid intrafamilial murder or battery or child abuse (and should not, in my judgment, to rape laws thus applied). But, the ground for the prohibition of contraceptives meets no neutral burden of harm to others (indeed, such contraceptive use may allow better control of population) or of harm to self. Contraceptives have, if anything, enormously enhanced the rational dignity of women in separating and regulating their sexual and procreative lives, for the first time in human history making possible forms of personal sexual lives, unburdened by remorselessly procreative self-conceptions, which previously had been available only to men. The remaining justification for these laws (namely, that sexual activity must always be procreational because nonprocreative sex is a kind of homicide)[72] is a nonneutrally religious doctrine which could not, consistent with basic values of respect for persons who reject these doctrines, be enforced by law. As such, it was properly found to be the kind of justification for criminal sanctions which cannot, in principle, satisfy the kind of justificatory burden required for the abridgement of fundamental human rights.

In contrast to Mill's grounding of the harm principle in doctrinal utilitarianism, this account explicates the principle as a consequence of the value of respect for persons fundamental to the proper understanding of the First Amendment's religion clauses (and much else in American constitutional law, or so I would argue). The account of "harm" here does not depend on a notion of utilitarian aggregation, but on the deontological idea of equal respect for the basic demands of persons for freedom and rationality, which define the kinds of interests the violation of which gives a sense to, on this alternative view, what "harm" means or should mean. Mill was correct, I believe, to root the harm principle in a political theory of the values of constitutional democracy, but his doctrinal utilitarianism is not the best theory of these values, *inter alia*, not capturing, as I earlier noted, the force of the harm principle in intuitive moral and political thought. A better theory of these values starts from the intuitive conception of a new political order that the English moral philosopher Richard Price perceived in the aspirations of the American revolutionaries, and which Price, in opposition to Bentham, defended—namely, that in this new political order, the central idea would be: "every man his own legislator." [73] The political ideal is, of course, one of institutional organization according to principles which secure that persons may perceive the demands of law and community as expressive of their capacities, as free and rational persons, for self-legislation, broadly understood: what Rousseau meant by the general will,[74] and Kant by the mutual respect of membership of the kingdom of ends.[75] Such a political ideal of mutual respect explains, or so I earlier suggested, the place in religion clause jurisprudence of constitutionally entrenched guarantees of state respect for the capacity of persons, as free and rational persons, to form, develop, express, and revise independent conscience and to structure a life consistent with this capacity, consistent with a like capacity for all. The free exercise and antiestablishment clauses effectuate this principle in different ways and at different points: the free exercise clause forbids coercion and undue burdens on the expression of independent conscience both in thought and action; the antiestablishment clause prohibits any form of state involvement with the formation and revision of independent conscience inconsistent with the underlying equal respect. The interpretation of the latter antiestablishment principle requires that an operative distinction be made between respect for the minimum conditions requisite for the formation and revision of capacities for freedom and rationality in forming one's conscience (which is, of course, consistent with, indeed required by, the principle) and the contempt for the capacity for rational independence shown by state endorsement of values inconsistent with the required respect. The latter form of forbidden state-endorsed contempt occurs whenever the state endorses one set of values as alone legitimate when, in fact, equal respect for rational independence is consistent with other values and not always consistent with those endorsed.

The secular purpose requirement of establishment clause jurisprudence is an attempt, I believe, to articulate the relevant distinction which the background political ideal of respect for persons requires.

Correctly understood, the requirement does not forbid all state impositions of values, a result which would have the remarkable conclusion—drawn by William Godwin on utilitarian grounds and more recently by Robert Paul Wolff on Kantian grounds—that criminal law and punishment are, in principle, illegitimate.[76] On the other hand, it would be equally remarkable and unjustified to claim that the substantive scope of the criminal law is not constrained by any values rooted in the democratic ideal of respect for persons. For one thing, if the endorsement of certain kinds of values by the state is forbidden by the values underlying the antiestablishment clause, the controlling influence on making things criminal not otherwise criminal would be as significant an imposition of such values as any could be, and thus would violate the clause. For another, as I earlier argued, the very imposition of criminal sanctions on activity expressive of independent conscience calls for close scrutiny under the values of the free exercise clause, even more so where the actions involve an independently fundamental human right like voluntary association; such scrutiny must be even more exacting than the antiestablishment clause alone would require—absent these free exercise and fundamental right considerations—for the state imposition here occurs at *all* constitutionally relevant stages of belief formation, expression, and revision. This convergence of considerations provides solid foundation for a form of the harm principle as a constitutionally required constraint on just criminalization, only now the harm principle appears not as the consequence of utilitarian aggregation, but of an antiutilitarian political ideal of respect for free and rational persons who are bound by law and community only on the terms specified by principles expressive of this respect. Such equal respect for persons, which insures the basic liberties to form different religious, philosophical, and political allegiances, requires that the scope of the criminal law must itself express such respect for persons, in particular, by the protection and vindication only of those neutral goods all would require to lead their lives as free and rational persons, irrespective of other ideological differences in basic religious or other commitments.

In order to judge the fertility and explanatory value of this approach to understanding the just limits of the criminal sanction, let us consider abortion, where, earlier, we found Mill's approach unhelpful at crucial points.

In my judgment, both Judge Dooling and Justice Stewart err in

McRae when they argue that abortion funding restrictions do not trench upon antiestablishment values because they reflect "traditionalist" [77] values toward abortion, not a particular religious view. The issue, properly framed, is not the question-begging assertion that legislation is valid because traditional (so, one might add, are anticontraception laws); traditional laws may or may not raise problems of violating the harm principle depending on analysis of their essential grounds. Rather, the inquiry must be into the form of argument offered in defense of antiabortion legislation, in particular, whether it rests on values inconsistent with the kind of equal respect of the state for religions which is constitutionally required. Antiabortion laws do violate this principle, not because their political advocacy is today led by certain religious groups but because, on examination, the grounds for such laws are nonneutral in the constitutionally forbidden way in an area at the core of the fundamental human right of intimate association.

Contemporary debates about the morality of abortion center on two different kinds of issues: first, whether the fetus is a moral person throughout pregnancy, so that the usual proscription on homicide would fully apply; and second, assuming the fetus is a person, whether any feature of the abortion situation would support some form of justification or excuse applicable to killing in general, or specially applicable to the abortion context. Moral argument of the second kind, aimed at showing that abortion is not wrong, perhaps uncontroversially justifies abortion in the case where the abortion saves the mother's life; even here, however, the insistence by Catholic moral theology that this is legitimate only when observing the double effect doctrine may, to the extent other reasonable people extend the justification beyond double effect, raise establishment clause problems.[78] More general arguments of the second kind, showing that abortion is not wrong in general, are often ethically problematic: the analogies drawn to ordinary self-defense or necessity principles, for example, are often weak.[79] Other arguments, specially designed for the abortion situation of imposing undue burdens on a woman to support life, focus on the extraordinary good samaritan obligations thus imposed on women not consistent with the limited good samaritan obligations of Anglo-American law and, perhaps, morality.[80] But, such arguments appear to apply only to certain kinds of nonculpably accidental pregnancies, not to all abortions.[81] If these arguments were the only ones available to justify abortion, the prohibition on abortion might be sufficiently connected to uncontroversially neutral moral argument not to violate establishment clause values (except in the double effect context earlier discussed).

However, antiabortion argument appears crucially to turn on the truth of two assumptions: first, that the fetus is in all stages of pregnancy a moral person on a par with normal persons;[82] and second, that having sex without procreational purposed effect is always wrong. Inasmuch as the latter assumption (which underlies anticontraception laws as well) is clearly an unacceptably nonneutral argument which cannot be enforced on society-at-large (as I earlier discussed), the residual ground for antiabortion views is the first one, the personhood of the fetus. But, apart from certain religious or other assumptions not reasonably shared at large, this claim does appear unfounded. The claim of Catholic moral theory, which departs from its earlier Thomistic tradition and is not uniformly shared by Catholic theologians even today,[83] rests on the potentiality principle of genetic individuality: once a genetic individual exists, after fertilization or wherever, the individual is "life" subject to the homicide proscription on killing persons.[84] But it simply does not reasonably follow, absent other implicit premises, that a potential person is a person, or should ethically be treated as a person, when it lacks relevant characteristics of being a person—at a minimum, the capacity for self-consciousness, agency, and the like.[85] The implicit premises, which naturally bridge the gap from potentiality to actuality, surely are specifically religious or metaphysical assumptions about the fetus at all points having an individual soul: the soul requiring baptism for release from original sin (so that killing prior to birth has disastrous religious consequences for the soul); the radical innocence of the life; the moral obligation for sexual activity to lead to procreation (which leads to anticontraceptive policies as morally obligatory); the naturalness of the maternal burdens of birth; the historical association of the Church's adoption of the potentiality view with the dating of the Immaculate Conception[86] with its associated model of ideal maternity, and the like. From the religious perspective of vital belief in these assumptions, abortion in the potentiality stage is as wrongful, perhaps more wrongful, than ordinary homicide: the fetus is radically innocent and vulnerable, the woman murderously unnatural in her betrayal of her role as mother. But outside the metaphysics of natural processes and divine will underlying these assumptions, the potentiality principle is simply fallacious; an argument which requires specifically religious or other assumptions to bridge the gap, assumptions not shared by many other religious and nonreligious people (which may even be internally incoherent within its own religious tradition),[87] is exactly the kind of endorsement of nonneutral values by the state which the religion clauses forbid.

Indeed, the required burden of justification on the state in this case is even stronger than the usual antiestablishment case; for the issue here is the application of criminal penalties to a form of conscientious act at the core of the fundamental human right of intimate association.[88] The only assumption which could satisfy this burden—namely, the personhood of the fetus—cannot, on examination, do so. Indeed, our examination of this assumption, with its familiar link to the exclusively procreational model of legitimate sexual expression, suggests further reasons for the constitutional illegitimacy of allowing these assumptions to justify the application of coercive sanctions: at some deep level, the assumptions fail to take seriously the moral independence of women as free and rational persons, giving the force of law to ideas of biological naturalness and necessity which precisely degrade women's moral freedom to establish the meaning of their sexual and reproductive life histories. The underlying conception appears to be not discontinuous with the familiar idea that women's bodies are not their own, but the property of others, namely, men or their masculine God, who may use their bodies for the greater good. If we, as a self-reflective community, increasingly see that freedom of mind and of thought cannot coexist with slavery of the body, the right of women to center their lives in a body image which is their own would appear to require the kind of reproductive autonomy that *Roe* v. *Wade* guarantees.[89]

Two ethical arguments may be urged against my argument against the potentiality principle as a ground for coercive sanctions: first, the slippery slope argument about line-drawing; second, the argument about prophylaxis against mistakes. Neither is valid.

The slippery slope argument rests on a fallacy about the concept of similarity: if a is similar to b, and b to c, . . . etc., and y to z, then a is similar to z. Thus, because the early fetus is at one point similar to the fetus at a later point, etc., the early fetus is so similar to the late fetus or born child that they should be assimilated; otherwise, we are on the slippery slope to genocide, infanticide, senicide, etc. But, the concept of similarity is not transitive in this way: a continuum of similarities may yield dissimilarities between things at either end of the continuum; and a criterion of dissimilarity may be formulable to sort out the cases without the slip starting at all. It is, of course, true that some philosophers have denied that the neonate is a person, and thus that infanticide violates anyone's natural right to life.[90] But, first, their view is not an inevitable consequence of rejection of the potentiality principle: one may reasonably argue that the capacity for self-consciousness and agency occur in late pregnancy.[91] And, second, their view is often associated with good consequentialist arguments justifying in contemporary circumstances a moral and political practice which forbids infanticide and, indeed, draws the line of permissible abortion-on-demand late in pregnancy.[92]

The argument about prophylaxis against mistakes rests on the superficially attractive claim that, when in doubt about the morality or immorality of the consequences of one's activity, guard against the possibility of being mistaken about morality by playing safe: not doing the dubious deed. The implicit analogy is to the case where when on the verge of firing a gun at what looks like a target but which one believes to be a person, one should play safe and not fire. But, the analogy is fallacious: the supposed mistake in the abortion context is not that a thing known to be a person may look like something else (a target) but that a thing reasonably believed to be a target may be a metaphysical person, which is, morally, a totally different case. Moral people are not required to guide their moral conduct according to metaphysical assumptions they do not reasonably believe, for, in that case, Hindu reincarnation and vegetarianism (animals are metaphysical persons in some stage of their reincarnation) would morally impose vegetarianism on non-Hindus. Moral persons are not in this way hostage to beliefs they do not reasonably entertain.

The common belief (Henkin, Dooling, Stewart) that the prohibition of abortion rests on neutral moral values is, I have suggested, wrong. In order to do this, I argued for an alternative conception of the harm principle grounded in respect for the independence and rationality of persons, which cannot, consistent with this respect, be put at the hazard of the kind of tyrannous moral conventions which Mill anatomizes in On Liberty. Criminal laws, resting on normative and other assumptions which many reasonable persons would not accept, degrade moral independence. They make the lives of persons hostage to beliefs they do not and would not conscientiously or reasonably affirm, a form of moral slavery inconsistent with the central political ideals of constitutional democracy. Precisely the same considerations which debar the power of the state to homogenize religion or thought or speech, requiring rather the broadest toleration for independent and diverse formation of belief and attitude, require as well institutional respect for the diverse ways of life consistent with underlying equal respect for persons. The harm principle specifies, in part, the terms of this just social contract among free persons committed to such political ideals: just punishment must be limited—subject to background principles of justice and duties of fair contribution, and so on—to forms of conduct which threaten the neutrally understood goods which self-respecting persons demand, for example, security of life, bodily integrity, property. Punishment not directed against harms thus understood or suitably analogous thereto is, in principle, wrong.

My remarks have been fairly abstract, and I would not want to be taken to suggest that these principles easily resolve many difficult cases, nor that decriminalization argument in general is coextensive with constitutional privacy. Certainly, the exploration of the meaning and appropriate institutional embodiment of the harm principle often require legislative action and study of a kind inappropriate for courts (i.e., in the area of commercial sex and regulation of drug use and certain decisions about death).[93] But there is a significant overlap in the appeal to common principles, and the Supreme Court has, I believe, correctly seen that these principles are of constitutional dimensions. Finally, although I believe some of the Court's privacy decisions are monstrously wrong (*Doe* v. *Commonwealth's Attorney*),[94] and state courts have correctly taken a different view (extending privacy protection, for example, to consensual adult homosexuality),[95] *Roe* v. *Wade* is surely right.

=

Part 4
Killing and Letting Die

EVEN if one were to resolve the difficult issue of fetal personhood by determining that the fetus is a person, the abortion controversy would not thereby be settled. The act of abortion itself would still stand in need of characterization. Is it a case of active killing, or is it rather a case of passively refusing to aid, or of withdrawing voluntary aid? The difference is significant, for our legal and moral traditions tend to treat these classes of actions very differently. Just how the relevant distinction is to be drawn, however, and exactly what its moral and legal import are, are themselves troublesome questions.

In "Killing and Letting Die," Philippa Foot explores the nature and moral relevance of the distinction between killing and letting die. She argues that the morally interesting distinction is between deaths which occur as a result of causal chains initiated by the agent, on the one hand, and deaths which occur as a result of sequences not initiated by the agent, on the other. A complete understanding of the moral significance of this distinction, she argues, awaits a more complete theory of positive and negative duties. But in any case, if abortion is to be justified as a case of death resulting from the positive actions of an agent, it must be justified as a case of killing, and not as a case of a death resulting from inaction, as Judith Thomson would have it.

In "Abortion and Self-Defense," Nancy Davis challenges the view, widely shared by both defenders and opponents of abortion, that even if abortion turns out to be unjustifiable in all other cases, in cases where maternal life is threatened by continued pregnancy, abortion can always be justified on grounds of self-defense. She offers a careful examination both of the elements of a legitimate claim of self-defense and of the special relationship obtaining between a pregnant woman and the fetus she carries. The analysis suggests that abortion is the killing of one who poses a passive threat to the life of the woman. Davis argues that in such a case the agent-relative permission to preserve one's own life at the expense of that of another is insufficient to generate obligations (or even permissions) on the part of others (e.g., doctors) to intervene on one's behalf.

Davis also raises the question of the moral symmetry of the mother-fetus relationship. She concludes that the relation between the pregnant woman and the fetus is indeed morally asymmetric, but argues that this fact, though indeed morally relevant, is not in itself sufficient to form the basis of an unproblematic justification of abortion as self-defense.

Killing and Letting Die

Philippa Foot

Is there a morally relevant distinction between killing and allowing to die? Many philosophers say that there is not, and further insist that there is no other closely related difference, as for instance that which divides act from omission, whichever plays a part in determining the moral character of an action. James Rachels has argued this case in his well-known article on active and passive euthanasia, Michael Tooley has argued it in in his writings on abortion, and Jonathan Bennett argued it in the Tanner Lectures given in Oxford in 1980.[1] I believe that these people are mistaken, and this is what I shall try to show in this essay. I shall first consider the question in abstraction from any particular practical moral problem, and then I shall examine the implications my thesis may have concerning the issue of abortion.

The question with which we are concerned has been dramatically posed by asking whether we are as equally to blame for allowing people in Third World countries to starve to death as we would be for killing them by sending poisoned food? In each case it is true that if we acted differently—by sending good food or by not sending poisoned food—those who are going to die because we do not send the good food or do send the poisoned food would not die after all. Our agency plays a part in what happens whichever way they die. Philosophers such as Rachels, Tooley, and Bennett consider this to be all that matters in determining our guilt or innocence. Or rather they say that although related things are morally relevant, such as our reasons for acting as we do and the cost of acting otherwise, these are only contingently related to the distinction between doing and allowing. If we hold *them* steady and vary only the way in which our agency enters into the matter, no moral differences will be found. It is of no significance, they say, whether we kill others or let them die, or whether they die by our act or our omission. Whereas these latter differences may at first seem to affect the morality of action, we shall always find on further enquiry that some other difference—such as a difference of motive or cost—has crept in.

Now this, on the face of it, is extremely implausible. We are not inclined to think that it would be no worse to murder to get money for some comfort such as a nice winter coat than it is to keep the money back before sending a donation to Oxfam or Care. We do not think that we might just as well be called murderers for one as for the other. And there are a host of other examples which seem to make the same point. We may have to allow one person to die if saving him would mean that we could not save five others, as for instance when a drug is in short supply and he needs five times as much as each of them, but that does not mean that we could carve up one patient to get "spare parts" for five.

These moral intuitions stand clearly before us, but I do not think it would be right to conclude from the fact that these examples all seem to hang on the contrast between killing and allowing to die that this is precisely the distinction that is important from the moral point of view. For example, having someone killed is not strictly *killing* him, but seems just the same morally speaking; and on the other hand, turning off a respirator might be called killing, although it seems morally indistinguishable from allowing to die. Nor does it seem that the difference between 'act' and 'omission' is quite what we want, in that a respirator that had to be turned on each morning would not change the moral problems that arise with the ones we have now. Perhaps there is no locution in the language which exactly serves our purposes and we should therefore invent our own vocabulary. Let us mark the distinction we are after by saying that one person may or may not be 'the agent' of harm that befalls someone else.

When is one person 'the agent' in this special sense of someone else's death, or of some harm other than death that befalls him? This idea can easily be described in a general way. If there are difficulties when it comes to detail, some of these ideas may be best left unsolved, for there may be an area of indefiniteness reflecting the uncertainty that belongs to our moral judgments in some complex and perhaps infrequently encountered situations. The idea of agency, in the sense that we want, seems to be composed of two subsidiary ideas. First, we think of particular effects as the result of particular sequences, as when a certain fatal sequence leads to someone's death. This idea is implied in coroners' verdicts telling us what someone died of, and this concept is not made suspect by the fact that it is sometimes impossible to pick out a single fatal sequence—as in the lawyers' example of the man journeying into the desert who had two enemies, one of whom bored a hole in his water barrel while another filled it with brine. Suppose such complications absent. Then we can pick out the fatal sequence and go on to ask who initiated it. If the subject died by poisoning and it was I who put the poison into his drink, then I am the agent of his death; likewise if I shot him and he died of a bullet wound. Of course there are problems about fatal sequences which would have been harmless but for special circumstances, and those which although threatening would have run out harmlessly but for something that somebody did. But we can easily understand the idea that a death comes about through our agency if we send someone poisoned food or cut him up for spare parts, but not (ordinarily) if we fail to save him when he is threatened by accident or disease. Our examples are not problem cases from *this* point of view.

Nor is it difficult to find more examples to drive our original point home, and show that it is sometimes permissible to allow a certain harm to befall someone, although it would have been wrong to bring this harm on him by one's own agency, i.e., by originating or sustaining the sequence which brings the harm. Let us consider, for instance, a pair of cases which I shall call Rescue I and Rescue II. In the first Rescue story we are hurrying in our jeep to save some people —let there be five of them—who are imminently threatened by the ocean tide. We have not a moment to spare, so when we hear of a single person who also needs rescuing from some other disaster we say regretfully that we cannot rescue him, but must leave him to die. To most of us this seems clear, and I shall take it as clear, ignoring John Taurek's interesting if surprising argument against the obligation to save the greater number when we can.[2] This is Rescue I and with it I contrast Rescue II. In this second story we are again hurrying to the place where the tide is coming in in order to rescue the party of people, but this time it is relevant that the road is narrow and rocky. In this version the lone individual is trapped (do not ask me how) on the path. If we are to rescue the five we would have to drive over him. But can we do so? If we stop he will be all right eventually: he is in no danger unless from us. But of course all five of the others will be drowned. As in the first story our choice is between a course of action which will leave one man dead and five alive at the end of the day and a course of action which will have the opposite result. And yet we surely feel that in one case we can rescue the five men and in the other we cannot. We can allow someone to die of whatever disaster threatens him if the cost of saving him is failing to save five; we cannot, however, drive over *him* in order to get to *them*. We cannot originate a fatal sequence, although we can allow one to run its course. Similarly, in the pair of examples mentioned earlier, we find a contrast between on the one hand refusing to give to one man the whole supply of a scarce drug, because we can use portions of it to save five, and on the other, cutting him up for spare parts. And we notice that we may not originate a fatal sequence even if the resulting death is in no sense our object. We could not knowingly subject one person to deadly fumes in the process of manufacturing some substance that would save many, even if the poisoning were a mere side effect of the process that saved lives.

Considering these examples, it is hard to resist the conclusion that it makes all the difference whether those who are going to die if we act in a certain way will die as a result of a sequence that we originate or of one that we allow to continue, it being of course something that did not *start* by our agency. So let us ask how this could be? If the distinction—which is roughly that between killing and allowing to die— *is* morally relevant, because it sometimes makes the difference between what is right and what is wrong, how does this work? After all, it cannot be a magical difference, and it does not satisfy anyone to hear that what we have is just an ultimate moral fact. Moreover, those who deny the relevance can point to cases in which it seems to make no difference to the goodness or badness of an action having a certain result, as, for example, that some innocent person dies, whether due to a sequence we originate or because of one we merely allow. And if the way the result comes about *sometimes* makes no difference, how can it ever do so? If it sometimes makes an action bad that harm came to someone else as a result of a sequence we *originated*, must this not always contribute some element of badness? How can a consideration be a reason for saying that an action is bad in one place without being at least a reason for saying the same elsewhere?

Let us address these questions. As to the route by which considerations of agency enter the process of moral judgment, it seems to be through its connection with different types of rights. For there are rights to noninterference, which form one class of rights; and there are also rights to goods or services, which are different. And corresponding to these two types of rights are, on the one hand, the duty not to interfere, called a 'negative duty', and on the other the duty to provide the goods or services, called a 'positive duty'. These rights may in certain circumstances be overridden, and this can in principle happen to rights of either kind. So, for instance, in the matter of property rights, others have in ordinary circumstances a duty not to interfere with our property, though in exceptional circumstances the right is overridden, as in Elizabeth Anscombe's example of destroying someone's house to stop the spread of a fire.[3] And a right to goods or services depending, for example, on a promise will quite often be overridden in the same kind of case. There is, however, no guarantee that the special circumstances that allow one kind of right to be overridden will always allow the overriding of the other. Typically, it takes more to justify an interference than to justify the withholding of goods or services; and it is, of course, possible to think that nothing whatsoever will justify, for example, the infliction of torture or the deliberate killing of the innocent. It is not hard to find how all this connects with the morality of killing and allowing to die—and in general with harm which an agent allows to happen and harm coming about through his agency, in my special sense having to do with originating or sustaining harmful sequences. For the violation of a right to noninterference consists in interference, which implies breaking into an existing sequence and initiating a new one. It is not usually possible, for instance, to violate that right to noninterference, which is at least part of what is meant by 'the right to life' by failing to save someone from death. So if, in any circumstances, the right to noninterference is the only right that exists, or if it is the only right special circumstances have not overridden, then it may not be permissible to initiate a fatal sequence, but it *may* be permissible to withhold aid.

The question now is whether we ever find cases in which the right to noninterference exists and is not overridden, but where the right to goods or services either does not exist or *is* here overridden. The answer is, of course, that this is quite a common case. It often happens that whereas someone's rights stand in the way of our interference, we owe him no *service* in relation to that which he would lose if we interfered. We may not deprive him of his property, though we do not have to help him secure his hold on it, in spite of the fact that the balance of good and evil in the outcome (counting his loss or gain and the cost to us) will be the same regardless of how they come about. Similarly, where the issue is one of life and death, it is often impermissible to kill someone—although special circumstances having to do with the good of others make it permissible, or even required, that we do not spend the time or resources needed to save his life, as for instance, in the story of Rescue I, or in that of the scarce drug.

It seems clear, therefore, that there are circumstances in which it makes all the difference, morally speaking, whether a given balance of good and evil came about through our agency (in our sense), or whether it was rather something we had the ability to prevent but, for good reasons, did not prevent. Of course, we often have a strict duty to prevent harm to others, or to ameliorate their condition. And even where they do not, strictly speaking, have a *right* to our goods or services, we should often be failing (and sometimes grossly failing) in charity if we did not help them. But, to reiterate, it may be right to allow one person to die in order to save five, although it would not be right to kill him to bring the same good to them.

How is it, then, that anyone has ever denied this conclusion, so sympathetic to our everyday moral intuitions and apparently so well grounded in a very generally recognized distinction between different types of rights? We must now turn to an argument first *given*, by James Rachels, and more or less followed by others who think as he does. Rachels told a gruesome story of a child drowned in a bathtub in two different ways: in one case someone pushed the child's head under water, and in the other he found the child drowning and did not pull him out. Rachels says that we should judge one way of acting as bad as the other, so we have an example in which killing is as bad as allowing to die. But how, he asks, can the distinction ever be relevant if it is not relevant here? [4]

Based on what has been said earlier, the answer to Rachels should be obvious. The reason why it is, in ordinary circumstances, "no worse" to leave a child drowning in a bathtub than to push it under, is that both charity and the special duty of care that we owe to children give us a positive obligation to save them, and we have no particular reason to say that it is "less bad" to fail in this than it is to be in dereliction of the negative duty by being the agent of harm. The level of badness is, we may suppose, the same, but because a different kind of bad action has been done, there is no reason to suppose that the two ways of acting will always give this same result. In other circumstances one might be worse than the other, or only one might be bad. And this last result is exactly what we find in circumstances that allow a positive but not a negative duty to be overridden. Thus, it could be right to leave someone to die by the roadside in the story of Rescue I, though wrong to run over him in the story of Rescue II; and it could be right to act correspondingly in the cases of the scarce drug and the "spare parts."

Let me now consider an objection to the thesis I have been defending. It may be said that I shall have difficulty explaining a certain range of examples in which it seems permissible, and even obligatory, to make an intervention which jeopardizes people not already in danger in order to save others who are. The following case has been discussed. Suppose a runaway trolley is heading toward a track on which five people are standing, and that there is someone who can possibly switch the points, thereby diverting the trolley onto a track on which there is only one person. It seems that he should do this, just as a pilot whose plane is going to crash has a duty to steer, if he can, toward a less crowded street than the one he sees below. But the railway man then puts the one man newly in danger, instead of allowing the five to be killed. Why does not the one man's right to noninterference stand in his way, as one person's right to noninterference impeded the manufacture of poisonous fumes when this was necessary to save five?

The answer seems to be that this is a special case, in that we have here the *diverting* of a fatal sequence and not the starting of a new one. So we could not start a flood to stop a fire, even when the fire would kill more than the flood, but we could divert a flood to an area in which fewer people would be drowned.

A second and much more important difficulty involves cases in which it seems that the distinction between agency and allowing is inexplicably irrelevant. Why, I shall be asked, is it not morally permissible to allow someone to die deliberately in order to use his body for a medical procedure that would save many lives? It might be suggested that the distinction between agency and allowing is relevant when what is allowed to happen is itself aimed at. Yet this is not quite right, because there are cases in which it does make a difference whether one originates a sequence or only allows it to continue, although the allowing is with deliberate intent. Thus, for instance, it may not be permissible to deprive someone of a possession which only harms him, but it may be reasonable to refuse to get it back for him if it is already slipping from his grasp.[5] And it is arguable that nonvoluntary passive euthanasia is sometimes justifiable although nonvoluntary active euthanasia is not. What these examples have in common is that *harm* is not in question, which suggests that the 'direct', i.e., deliberate, intention of *evil* is what makes it morally objectionable to allow the beggar to die. When this element is present it is impossible to justify an action by indicating that no *origination* of evil is involved. But this special case leaves no doubt about the relevance of distinguishing between originating an evil and allowing it to occur. It was never suggested that there will *always and everywhere* be a difference of permissibility between the two.

Having defended the moral relevance of the distinction which roughly corresponds to the contrast between killing and allowing to die, I shall now ask how it affects the argument between those who oppose and those who support abortion. The answer seems to be that this entirely depends on how the argument is supposed to go. The most usual defense of abortion lies in the distinction between the destruction of a fetus and the destruction of a human person, and neither side in *this* debate will have reason to refer to the distinction between being the agent of an evil and allowing it to come about. But this is not the only defense of abortion which is current at the present time. In an influential and widely read article, Judith Jarvis Thomson has suggested an argument for allowing abortion which depends on denying what I have been at pains to maintain.[6]

Thomson suggests that abortion can be justified, at least in certain cases, without the need to deny that the fetus has the moral rights of a human person. For, she says, no person has an absolute right to the use of another's body, even to save his life, and so the fetus, whatever its status, has no right to the use of the mother's body. *Her* rights override *its* rights, and justify her in removing it if it seriously encumbers her life. To persuade us to agree with her she invents an example, which is supposed to give a parallel, in which someone dangerously ill is kept alive by being hooked up to the body of another person, without that person's consent. It is obvious, she says, that the person whose body was thus being used would have no obligation to continue in that situation, suffering immobility or other serious inconvenience, for any length of time. We should not think of him as a murderer if he detached himself, and we ought to think of a pregnant woman as having the same right to rid herself of an unwanted pregnancy.

Thomson's whole case depends on this analogy. It is, however, faulty if what I have said earlier is correct. According to my thesis, the two cases must be treated quite differently because one involves the initiation of a fatal sequence and the other the refusal to save a life. It is true that someone who extricated himself from a situation in which his body was being used in the way a respirator or a kidney machine is used could, indeed, be said to kill the other person in detaching himself. But this only shows, once more, that the use of "kill" is not important: what matters is that the fatal sequence resulting in death is not initiated but is rather allowed to take its course. And although charity or duties of care could have dictated that the help be given, it seems perfectly reasonable to treat this as a case in which such presumptions are overridden by other rights—those belonging to the person whose body would be used. The case of abortion is of course completely different. The fetus is not in jeopardy because it is in its mother's womb; it is merely dependent on her in the way children are dependent on their parents for food. An abortion, therefore, originates the sequence which ends in the death of the fetus, and the destruction comes about "through the agency" of the mother who seeks the abortion. If the fetus has the moral status of a human person then her action is, at best, likened to that of killing for spare parts or in Rescue II; conversely, the act of someone who refused to let his body to be used to save the life of the sick man in Thomson's story belongs with the scarce drug decision, or that of Rescue I.

It appears, therefore, that Thomson's argument is not valid, and that we are thrown back to the old debate about the moral status of the fetus, which stands as the crucial issue in determining whether abortion is justified.

Abortion and Self-Defense

Nancy Davis

WHAT I shall call the *Moderate* view about the morality of abortion is the view that abortion is often (though not necessarily always)[1] morally defensible (even) in circumstances in which the continuation of the pregnancy does not pose a threat to the pregnant woman's life.[2] I wish to distinguish Moderate views from two rivals: *Restrictive* views, which hold that abortion is morally defensible only when (though not necessarily always when) the continuation of the pregnancy poses a threat to the woman's life;[3] and *Permissive* views, which hold that abortion is generally morally defensible; although there may be (extreme) circumstances in which it should be overturned, there is a presumption that abortion is morally defensible.

The deepest, most intractable disagreement in the abortion dispute has been one that divides the Restrictives from the Moderates and Permissives, and the most difficult task confronting Moderates and Permissives has been that of producing a compelling defense of elective abortion. Permissives, Moderates, and Restrictives concur in the view that abortion is defensible when it is undertaken to preserve a pregnant woman's life, even when the performance of abortion would amount to the making of a choice between lives:[4] that is, when the death of the woman would not occur until after the safe (live) delivery of the fetus. (When I do not specify otherwise, this is the sort of case that I shall be discussing.)[5] Although it is conceded that "abortion is never a *paradigm* case of justified self-defense," [6] it is supposed nonetheless that it is the woman's right of self-defense that justifies abortion when it is undertaken to preserve her life.

That the *Restrictives'* proposed defense of abortion in such cases involves the appeal to the woman's right of self-defense appears to be obvious, for Restrictives make it clear that they do not think that a woman's desire to control her own body, or her interest in resisting what she sees as an unwelcome encroachment upon her bodily integrity, can possibly outweigh the fetus's right to life. They similarly reject more general appeals to the importance of personal autonomy and to individuals' rights to decide when they shall incur hardship to render life-preserving assistance to other persons. While Moderates and Permissives think that considerations such as these may often have decisive force, Restrictives do not agree: *they* hold the view that there is a strict prohibition against killing the innocent, one which cannot be overridden by appeals to the woman's autonomy. This is not to say that Restrictives suppose that the prohibition debars *all* killing as wrongful: we are not held to violate the prohibition when we kill another person in (justified) self-defense.[7] Given these two facts—that the Restrictives reject the appeal to autonomy, and that they allow killing in self-defense while forbidding it in other circumstances—it is quite plausible to suppose that it is self-defense that Restrictives appeal to as justification for permitting abortion when it is undertaken to preserve a pregnant woman's life.

What I shall argue is that it is doubtful that we can defend abortion—even in cases in which the woman's life is clearly at stake—by appealing to the right of self-defense. I shall argue this on two grounds. First, that the entitlement to self-defense is even more problematic than has been commonly supposed: its force in the abortion dispute has been misconstrued and overestimated because its structure has not been properly understood. Second, that the abortion dispute is, in some ways, a special one: there are features of the relationship between the pregnant woman and the dependent fetus that effectively preclude our regarding the problem of abortion as yet another (albeit complicated) problem of trying to find a just balance between two persons' conflicting rights.

I certainly believe that abortion is defensible when it is undertaken to preserve a woman's life,[8] and I believe that abortion can be justified without appealing to the right of self-defense; there are other options. But there may not be options that are readily available to the Restrictive, for it is not at all clear that one can produce a rationale for permitting abortion when it is undertaken to preserve a woman's life while forbidding it in all other circumstances. If I am correct in thinking this, then Restrictives face a dilemma: if they wish to allow abortions that are undertaken to preserve pregnant women's lives, then they must also allow them in less extreme circumstances. (Allowing this would effectively turn the Restrictive into some sort of Moderate.) On the other hand, if Restrictives wish to insist that abortion is indeed indefensible when the woman's *life* is not at stake, then I believe they must espouse an even more restrictive view, one that would deny the legitimacy of a woman's seeking to terminate her pregnancy even when she knows that continuing with it would kill her. This is a view that may have its advocates, but it is a hard view indeed and—at least on the face of it—an implausible one: we are entitled to ask that a strong, secular (that is, nonauthoritarian) argument be mustered in its defense.[9]

My argument thus involves a direct attack on the Restrictive view of abortion. But it also has bearing on the tenability of the Moderate view, for it uncovers serious problems with one of the strategies that has been widely deployed in defense of the Moderate position, what I shall call the *Thomson-strategy*.[10] Thomson-Moderates argue that even if the fetus is to be regarded as a person from the earliest stages of its development, it cannot be inferred that abortion is generally morally indefensible, or that it is defensible only when it is undertaken to preserve a woman's life. Not all of the things that we do to other persons that kill them, or otherwise cut short their lives, constitute wrongful assaults upon them, or violations of their rights to life: the prohibition against the killing of the innocent is not an absolute or an overriding one. There are cases in which it is morally defensible to kill a person, just as there are cases in which it is morally defensible to let a person die.[11] These include not only cases of self-defense—and plausible extrapolations of such cases—but also cases in which one person justifiably terminates another person's life-support, and in particular those cases of justifiable termination of life-support in which one person chooses not to continue to bear the burden of providing life-support to another person, even though this choice has foreseeably fatal consequences for the person whose life-support is thus terminated. A fetus is not only dependent upon the pregnant woman for the sustaining of its life (as a child or a patient or an invalid may be dependent upon her), it is (in a sense) parasitic upon the woman: its life-support is provided through the medium of the woman's own body.[12] The relationship between the woman and the fetus is thus one of asymmetrical dependency, and the termination of a pregnancy may be characterized as (or regarded as morally analogous to) the termination of life-support. We do not hold the view that people are, in general, under a strict obligation to undertake to provide life-support to other persons, or that they are not permitted to discontinue it when the burden of providing ongoing assistance proves to be onerous. It is therefore, on the face of it, quite implausible to suppose that pregnant women as a class constitute a special case, that *they* should be held to be under a strict obligation to provide the fetus with the necessary life-support. When a woman has sound reasons for wishing to cease providing life-support to the dependent fetus—reasons that would allow people in other life-support situations to discontinue providing it—then it would appear to be both unreasonable and unfair to deny her the right to terminate her pregnancy.[13]

I believe that Thomson-Moderates are able to offer a better explanation of why abortion is defensible when it is undertaken to preserve a woman's life than Restrictives are. I believe, moreover, their greater success in this regard derives from their emphasis on the fundamental asymmetry of the relationship between a pregnant woman and a dependent fetus, and not from an appeal to the woman's right of self-defense.[14] But, although I believe the Thomson strategy is superior to the Restrictives' strategy, I think there are serious problems with it. There is a tension between supposing—as Thomson-Moderates say they are supposing—that the fetus is a person and supposing that the asymmetry of the relationship between the woman and the fetus is in itself and by itself a morally substantive fact. There is also a tension between emphasizing the special nature of the relationship between the woman and the fetus—as Thomson-Moderates do—and attempting to defend elective abortion by modeling conflicts of interest between the woman and the fetus on conflicts of interest between postfetal persons.[15] If the relationship between the woman and the fetus is thought to be in itself a special one, then this undercuts the force of arguments by analogy: it is not at all clear that we can model conflicts of interest between the woman and the fetus on conflicts of interest between postfetal persons. (I shall return to this point later.) If I am correct in my diagnosis of the Thomson strategy's deficiency, then the Moderates' position too may require reformulation or emendation.

The line of argument that I wish to advance is complicated, and neither its comprehensive exposition nor its complete defense can be accomplished here. My aim in the present context is fairly limited: I shall argue that one cannot justify abortion undertaken to preserve a woman's life by appealing to the right of self-defense, and then indicate what are some of the important implications of this argument.

The crux of my argument is the claim that even in cases in which a woman seeks an abortion to preserve her own life, and is morally justified in so doing, it is not the right of self-defense that provides the ground of the justification. This may seem like a puzzling or even a paradoxical thing to say, especially since, as I have said, I mean to be attacking the Restrictive view of abortion: if Restrictives maintain that abortion is defensible only when the continuation of the pregnancy poses a threat to the woman's life, then is it not obvious that it is precisely the right of self-defense that is being advanced as the (only admissible) justification of abortion? Indeed, it might be thought that determining the range of defensible abortions *is* determining the bounds of the woman's right of self-defense, and so that the only real difference between the Thomson-Moderates and the Restrictives lies in their different understandings of precisely what entitlements the right of self-defense confers upon the woman. This conjecture is one that reflects claims that have been made in the literature. In *Abortion and Moral Theory*, L. W. Sumner, a Moderate, says, "The fetus' right to life is bounded by the mother's rights of self-defense and vice versa. To map the former is therefore also to map the latter" (p. 114).

In order to explain how my central claim is not paradoxical, I must explain why Sumner's claim is problematic. I believe that Sumner distorts both the right of self-defense and the right to life, and that this distortion renders the Thomson-Moderates' position unnecessarily problematic from the start. If we were to agree with Sumner, then we would have to suppose that Thomson-Moderates who assume that the fetus is a person, yet maintain that abortion is defensible in cases of rape or personal hardship, are putting forward at least one of two implausible claims: that the right of self-defense is (or includes) the right for us to kill other persons when not doing so would impose unwanted inconvenience or discomfort upon us; or that our having a right to life does not afford us protection against being killed by people who would have to endure discomfort or inconvenience if they were to refrain from killing us. Either of these claims might ultimately prove to be defensible, but neither seems at all acceptable *prima facie*: it is not plausible to claim that a woman who seeks an abortion to terminate a pregnancy arising from rape—automatically, and for that very reason—does not violate the fetus's right to life, or that she can be said—automatically, and for that very reason—to be exercising a right of self-defense.[16] It is reasonable to suppose that a right of self-defense entitles us to kill someone who is threatening our life,[17] not someone whose presence causes us inconvenience or embarrassment (however acute). It is reasonable to suppose that a fetal right to life is not something that can be nullified by the illicit circumstances of a fetus's conception: if a fetus has a right to life, then it has it in virtue of being the sort of entity that it is[18] (and the question of whether its existence arose from rape surely does not decide *that* issue). Thus Sumner's claim seems unpersuasive. It appears to distort the right to life or the right of self-defense, and to disenfranchise the Thomson-Moderate from the start.

I am not objecting to what Sumner says simply on the ground that what he says renders implausible a view that is attractive and widely held, namely, the Thomson-Moderates' view, or that it seems to conflict with commonsense intuitions about what is and what is not a case of self-defense. I think that Sumner's claim would be problematic even if it were made in the context of the Restrictive view, which circumscribes the right of self-defense far more narrowly. I believe that it is a mistake to approach the abortion dispute with the assumption that a satisfactory strategy for its resolution is one that attempts to resolve the conflict between the woman and the fetus by seeking to balance the rights of the one against the rights of the other.[19] Even if we believe—or assume for the sake of argument—that the fetus is a person, we should take seriously the suggestion that the relationship between the pregnant woman and the dependent fetus is, in important ways, a special one. But if we take such a suggestion seriously, then we must admit the possibility that it has repercussions on how the abortion dispute can be understood and gainfully discussed. We cannot insist that the relationship is a special one without calling into question the wisdom of seeking to resolve the abortion dispute by modeling conflicts of interest that arise between the woman and the fetus upon those that arise in other contexts between postfetal persons. We should not, then, assume at the outset that the problem of abortion is (or is well characterized as) a problem of balancing the rights of the pregnant woman against the rights of the fetus.

I am not suggesting merely that we cannot be confident about the adequacy of an appeal to rights, or that we are unclear about the details of applying the machinery of rights and interests to the problem of abortion. I am also raising a deeper worry. If we cannot happily apply the existing machinery of rights and interests to the conflict between the woman and the fetus, then we might surmise that we must modify or supplement our current (inchoate!) theory of rights in order to apply it to the problem of abortion. But we should consider, also, another hypothesis: the possibility that we have unearthed problems that have lain dormant in our theory of rights, problems that may arise clearly in, but are not special to, the problem of abortion.[20] Although I do not count myself as someone who is generally sympathetic to appeals to rights, I am not here taking the opportunity to rehearse the familiar skeptical worries. I am suggesting, rather, that once we have considered the possibility that the relationship between the woman and the fetus is a special one, we should recognize that it would be unwise to commit ourselves *a priori* (as Sumner would have us do) to the view that the problem of abortion is, or can be gainfully characterized as, a problem of balancing the rights of the pregnant woman against the rights of the fetus.

I shall now go on to argue that even if we were to accept the view that the problem of abortion can or should be seen as a problem of balancing rights, it is not the woman's right of *self-defense* that belongs in the scales.

It is widely conceded that "abortion is never a paradigm case of justified self-defense," [21] but this is not thought to present an insurmountable obstacle to defending abortion when it is undertaken to preserve a woman's life. The deviations from the paradigm are not thought to be telling. Though there is not agreement on just how abortion differs from the clearest cases of justified self-defense, the following differences are often noted:

1. The fetus whose continued presence in the woman's body poses a threat to her life is neither an aggressor nor an assailant: that is, it does not intend or foresee the harm that its presence causes, and it is not in any way morally at fault for causing it.[22] Nor does the threat that it poses to the woman's life even derive from any exercise of its agency, for the fetus is obviously not an agent at all.[23]

2. The clearest cases of justified self-defense are those in which the victim's response is quite spontaneous, and the deliberation, if there is any, is gone through under duress: there is not time to deliberate fully; there is no less violent response that is both effective and clearly available; and there is no readily apparent way for the victim to deflect the attack or evade it altogether. Although it is true that the pregnant woman whose life is threatened does not have the option of evading the attack or adopting less violent means in her

own defense, her course of action is usually one that she has had time to deliberate about. The killing of the fetus is thus, in a sense, premeditated.[24] This connects with the third difference between abortion and paradigm cases of justified self-defense.

3. The fact that the killing is premeditated undermines the characterization of it as an indirect, or merely foreseen-but-not-intended, killing. If one agrees that the killing of the fetus is premeditated, then it does not seem that one can plausibly maintain that the death of the fetus lies outside of the scope of the woman's intention: one cannot plausibly claim that the woman merely foresees the death, but does not intend it as a means or an end.[25] A case in which a woman seeks an abortion to preserve her life is thus not like a case of self-defense in which a victim shoots and kills an attacker who cannot effectively be repulsed by other means. It is more like a case in which we foresee that we will be attacked by a (temporarily) crazed assailant and—since escape is impossible—choose to poison the would-be attacker in order to forestall a confrontation that would be fatal to us. Whatever may be said about the defensibility of such conduct, it is not conduct that is comfortably characterized as justified self-defense.

4. The clearest cases of justified self-defense are those in which victims do not bear responsibility for their predicament. However, when victims find themselves in life-threatening circumstances because they have negligently or recklessly engaged in conduct that could have been foreseen to lead to such an outcome, their entitlement to kill to preserve their own lives is less clear-cut. When a woman is pregnant because she has voluntarily engaged in sexual intercourse without taking contraceptive measures, then she may bear some responsibility for her predicament. Although she may be entitled to seek an abortion to preserve her own life, it cannot be said that her doing so is clearly a case of justified self-defense.[26]

5. A pregnant woman does not perform the abortion herself; she engages a third party—a physician—to perform it for her. It may often be permissible for a third party to kill an assailant to assist an innocent victim—thus supporting the victim's desire not to succumb to a life-threatening attack—but it is not plausible to describe the *third party's* actions as undertaken in or justified by an appeal to self-defense. Perhaps the victim of a wrongful attack can claim some entitlement to assistance in repulsing it, but this is a claim to a corol-

lary right, not just a claim to the right of self-defense. If a third party is justified in assisting the victim, the justification comes from an appeal to that corollary right, not (only) from the victim's right of self-defense.

Although there is not a consensus between Moderates and Restrictives—or, for that matter, among Restrictives themselves—about which of these features create the most serious problems for the classification of abortion as justified self-defense, there is widespread confidence that it is not (5) that is the source of the difficulty. Says Baruch Brody, a staunch (ultra-) Restrictive, "To be sure, it is the abortionist, and not the mother, who will destroy the fetus, but this is irrelevant."[27] Sumner, a Moderate, claims that "if a woman has the right to defend herself against the fetus, then she has the right to invoke third-party assistance" (p. 112).[28] Donald Regan, whom I take to be a Permissive, says, "Surely if a woman can defend herself against the fetus, a doctor may help."[29]

I believe that this confidence is unwarranted. Even if we suppose that there is clearly a moral right of self-defense, when we apply it to the situation in which a woman wishes to abort a fetus whose continued presence in her body poses a threat to her life, we find that it is not a strong enough entitlement to support the claim that the woman is entitled to the doctor's (third-party) assistance. We cannot conclude even that it would be *permissible* for the doctor to choose to assist her. In saying this, I do not mean to cast doubt on the moral defensibility of a woman's seeking an abortion to preserve her life, or on the defensibility of a doctor's rendering her the necessary assistance. What I am doing, rather, is pointing out that there is a problem with appealing to the right of self-defense to justify the woman's and the doctor's course of action.

To see why this is so, we should look more closely at the question of the innocence of the fetus. It has been claimed that it is not the *moral* innocence of an attacker that is relevant to the question of whether or not we can claim justification in killing another person to preserve our own life. What matters is what has been termed *causal* or *technical innocence*: attackers are not technically innocent when their actions, behavior, or (in some instances) mere movements *qua* physical objects, or mere presence constitutes a threat to another person's life.[30] Thus we would be permitted to kill, and be justified in so doing by the right of self-defense, not only the morally guilty hostile aggressor, but also the following morally innocent persons: a psychotic assailant, a child who is about to trip the fuse wire of a dangerous explosive, and an epileptic whose violent convulsions threaten our life because we are confined together in a very small space and the epileptic is holding a sharp cleaver.[31] All of these attackers are morally innocent, but technically guilty: each is a threat to another person's life.

It is an interesting question why it should ever be thought justifiable for us to kill another person to preserve our own life.[32] Once it has been said that it is not attackers' *moral* innocence, but only their *technical* innocence, that is at issue, it becomes difficult to see why it should be *justifiable* for us to kill the person who (inadvertently) threatens our life. A person can pose a threat to another person's life and be deemed technically guilty without having done anything wrong —indeed, without having done anything at all. How then could the mere fact of posing a threat to another person's life be thought to be of any moral significance whatsoever? If we think that it is justifiable to kill in self-defense, then must we not be supposing that we can point to some morally relevant difference between the person who happens to be posing the merely technical threat and the person who happens to be the victim of it? What might such a difference be?

In some (but by no means in all) cases of self-defense, it seems that we can identify an asymmetry between attacker and victim. When the attacker is a hostile aggressor or a psychotic assailant, I can justify killing in self-defense by pointing out that there is in each case a difference between myself and the attacker that can be seen to be morally relevant. The aggressor is hostile (and thus has malign motives or bad intentions, however ineffective the aggressor may be in realizing them in action); the psychotic is dangerous (and thus is more likely to go on to harm other people than I am).[33] In both of these cases, it can be argued that my choice is clearly morally justified, for the grounds upon which it is defended—that the death of the attacker represents the lesser of two evils, or the smaller injustice[34]—are such that, if I am justified in making my choice, then any disinterested person would be justified in making the same choice: preferring my survival to that of my attacker.[35] These killings can be defended by any disinterested person, and justified by an appeal to a neutral moral point of view.

It is considerably less obvious how we are to justify killing to preserve our own life when the attacker has done nothing at all to threaten us but is, instead, a *passive threat*: someone whose mere movements *qua* physical object or mere presence constitutes a threat to our life.[36]

To see just why this is so, it will be helpful to bear some cases in mind: the one that we have been focusing on—the case in which the woman's life is threatened by the continuation of her pregnancy—and the following case:

Alice and Ben are mountain climbing when a rockslide occurs that threatens to sweep Ben off the ledge that he has been standing on. If Ben falls straight down—as he is virtually certain to do—he will fall onto Alice, for she is standing on the narrow ledge beneath his, and surely kill her. If Ben manages to land on Alice's ledge, however, he is unlikely to be killed: indeed, he is unlikely even to be seriously hurt. Alice can determine how Ben falls, for she can manipulate his rope if she chooses to do so. If she gives his rope a tug, she will deflect Ben's fall and thus preserve her life. But she will kill Ben in the process, for if he does not land on Alice's ledge, then he will tumble down the side of the mountain to his death. Alice cannot survive unless she deflects Ben's fall; Ben cannot survive if she does.[37]

We saw, in the cases of the hostile aggressor and the psychotic assailant, that we could point to a difference between the victim and the attacker, and argue that the difference would provide anyone with a reason for preferring the victim's survival. Moreover, since the difference in question constitutes a *moral* asymmetry, we might be able to appeal to it to explain why someone who chose to assist the victim would be acting rightly—or at least permissibly—while someone who chose to aid the attacker would not be; for it could be said that the very thing that supports the victim's right of self-defense also generates the victim's claim to preferential assistance. But this rationale fails on both counts when it is applied to the case of an attacker who is merely a passive threat.

It cannot plausibly be argued that Alice's entitlement to kill Ben derives from, or is to be explained by, the fact that it would be morally preferable that she should be the one to survive—that her survival would represent either the lesser of two evils or the fairer choice (by the lights of any disinterested person, from an impartial moral point of view). (The same holds true when we substitute "the pregnant woman" for "Alice," and "the fetus" for "Ben.") It is Ben who is falling on Alice, and thus Ben who is deemed to be technically guilty. But this is not in itself a sound basis upon which to claim that it is Alice rather than Ben who should survive, that there is a *morally* significant asymmetry between Alice and Ben.[38] We cannot reasonably suppose that people who happen to be falling through the air are generally more

dangerous or more hostile or less deserving than people who are standing still (and being fallen upon). Since who poses a passive threat to
whom may have nothing whatsoever to do with the morality of either
person's conduct (or, for that matter, with the morality of anyone
else's conduct either) and is, indeed, just a question of luck, we cannot reasonably suppose that the victims of passive attacks have, as
such, a stronger claim to the preservation of their lives than their
(merely passive) attackers do. If it is defensible for Alice to kill Ben
to preserve her own life, then the justification must derive from a different source, and have a different structure, than the one that was outlined above as a possible account of why a victim is justified in killing
a hostile aggressor or a psychotic assailant. For there is, in general, no
reason to suppose that it is morally preferable (from a neutral or disinterested standpoint) that it should be the *victim* who survives when
the attacker poses merely a passive threat to the victim's life. (To say
this is not to foreclose the possibility that we should reject the explanation of the defensibility of killing the assailant and the aggressor that is
outlined above. The point is rather that the rationale for killing the
assailant and the aggressor is not one that applies in the case of an
attacker who poses a passive threat.)

When I claim that I may be justified in killing a person who poses
a passive threat to my life, I am not claiming that my life has, or
should be thought to have, greater value than that of my attacker. Nor
am I claiming that it would be (more) unjust if I am the one who is
killed. I am, instead, merely calling for other peoples' recognition of
the fact that (by my lights) my life has the greater value to me. The
entitlement to defend our life against a passive threat is thus what has
been called an *agent-relative permission*.[39] Because of the greater value
that each of us understandably attaches to the continuation of his or
her own life, we are (in certain circumstances)[40] permitted to kill another person to preserve our own life, even though we acknowledge
that the other person's claim to life is not weaker than our own. Even
when I acknowledge that my preference is not one that would be en-
endorsed from a neutral moral standpoint—it is not better or fairer
that I should be the one to survive—it is permissible for me to kill
another person to preserve my own life.

Since the agent-relative permission to preserve one's own life appears
to be derived from the value each person assigns to his or her own life,
and not from whatever value may be assigned to its preservation from

some impartial point of view, it is obvious that peoples' agent-relative permissions may often conflict. When neither the victim nor the attacker is constrained by a special obligation, and neither is an aggressor, a psychotic assailant, or a criminal being justly punished for a crime,[41] then both may claim entitlement to preserve their lives at the expense of the other person's life. Each can defend this choice on the same ground: a person's life is of special value to the person whose life it is. Thus there may arise circumstances in which each person's entitlement effectively thwarts the other: each is entitled to attempt to kill the other person in the interest of securing his or her own preservation. It would be permissible for Alice to maneuver Ben's rope so that Ben falls down the mountain rather than directly onto her, and it would be permissible for Ben to try to bring it about that he falls directly onto Alice's ledge (and thus directly onto Alice) rather than down the mountain to his death.[42] In itself, this is not unduly problematic, for we recognize that permissions can conflict, and we do not think that the fact that we are unable to succeed in doing what we are permitted to do is morally worrying when we have not been wrongly prevented, or wrongly undermined in our attempts. (*Ex hypothesi*, since Ben and Alice may each appeal to the [same] agent-relative permission to preserve his or her own life at another person's expense [*the* other person's expense], neither is wrongfully undermining the other.) Morally worrying difficulties emerge when we consider the role of third-party intervention: there are problems with supposing that third parties are obliged to assist victims against attackers who pose merely a passive threat to the victims' lives, and problems, too, with supposing even that third parties are permitted to render assistance to such victims.

If having an agent-relative permission to preserve our life at the expense of another person's could, by itself, generate an obligation for a disinterested third party or bystander to intervene and render us assistance, then there could be circumstances in which bystanders would be faced with conflicting and even inconsistent obligations. A bystander would be obliged to help Alice deflect Ben, and also obliged to help Ben resist Alice's attempt. Although we are not disquieted by the observation that *two or more individuals* could find themselves in circumstances in which their agent-relative *permissions conflict* (and thus make it impossible for both to do what each is permitted to do), we are very much disturbed by the suggestion that *one person*—a disinterested third party—could have *inconsistent obligations*.[43] If so, then we must recognize that a victim's agent-relative permission to preserve his or her own life at the expense of the other person's life cannot by itself generate an obligation for a third party to intervene to render assistance to the victim.

There is another route to the same conclusion. While there is considerable disagreement on the question of its ultimate significance and on the details of its interpretation, most of the people who posit the existence of moral rights reject the view that the possession of a right is, in and of itself, something that devolves strong positive obligations on third parties. We may possess a right to life, but we cannot thereby claim entitlement to whatever it is that we need to stay alive.[44] If *rights* do not in and of themselves yield strong entitlements to positive assistance, then surely *permissions*—which are much weaker—do not do so. If the entitlement to kill a person who poses merely a passive threat to our life is, as I have been arguing, merely an agent-relative permission, then we cannot suppose that it devolves upon third parties the obligation to render assistance to the victims of such threats.

It is not much less problematic to suppose that agent-relative permissions, in and of themselves, yield *permissions* for third parties or bystanders to intervene to render assistance. Even when a third party has, in fact, a strong and morally unexceptionable preference that I not be killed by the person who is posing a passive threat to my life, the bystander cannot claim to have the same reason for his or her preference that I do. There is a logical point here (which is not to say that there is a deep one): a third party might not *want* to go on living if I am the one who is killed, but I *cannot* go on living if I am killed. A disinterested third party cannot justify rendering me assistance simply by appealing to my agent-relative permission. If a bystander is permitted to intervene to render assistance to someone who is the victim of a passive threat, this must be justified on some other ground.

There is another reason for being unhappy with the suggestion that, if we are permitted to kill to preserve our own lives, then a third party must be permitted to render us the assistance we need to secure our own survival. If it were permissible for a bystander to help Alice defend herself against Ben simply in virtue of her agent-relative permission to assign special importance to the preservation of her own life, then it seems that it would be permissible, for the same reason, for the bystander to help Ben defend himself against Alice. When the threat that is posed to a person's life is merely a passive threat, we cannot infer that there is any morally relevant difference between attacker and victim in virtue of which the victim can automatically be said to have the stronger claim. Ben has done nothing to impugn his status as Alice's moral peer; there is no difference between Ben and Alice in virtue of which the one person's agent-relative permission should be deemed any weaker than the other's. On the basis of this reasoning, we might be inclined to conclude that it would be permissible for a bystander to assist either Alice or Ben. But I am not at all sure that this is the proper conclusion to draw. When there are (on the face of it) equally strong reasons for helping A to thwart B and for helping B to thwart A, then we may doubt that a disinterested third party would be justified in choosing to help one of them rather than the other. If Ben's and Alice's agent-relative permissions are of equal weight (as they would appear to be), then it would seem to be *wrong* for us actively to prefer the one to the other.[45] To say this is not to suggest that morality requires that a disinterested third party refrain from intervention altogether; it is to suggest that any choice between a victim and an attacker who poses a passive threat must be shown to be a morally defensible one. (Where the claims of the victim and the attacker are of equal strength, then a distinterested third party might be obliged to decide whom to help by [for example] tossing a coin.) If this is right, then we must recognize that the role of third parties is not at all a transparent one. Even when we move from the question of what a victim may be entitled to request or receive, to the question of what a disinterested third party may be permitted to supply, we cannot infer that the victim has (as such) a stronger claim than the attacker who poses merely a passive threat to the victim's life. When an attacker's technical guilt consists simply in the fact that the attacker poses a passive threat to another person's life, there may be no morally relevant asymmetry between the attacker and the victim, and so disinterested third parties cannot claim to have a moral reason for systematically favoring the victim's claim to survival. We cannot conclude, then, that a bystander would be permitted to intervene on the victim's behalf.

The application of this reasoning to the case of 'abortion in self-defense' is straightforward enough. If this sort of case is thought to fall under the rubric of self-defense at all, then it must be because the fetus can be understood to be technically guilty. Since the fetus is obviously unlike a hostile aggressor or a deranged assailant, its technical guilt could only lie (at most) in its being a passive threat to the pregnant woman's life. I have suggested that when we seek permission to defend our life against a person who poses merely a passive threat to it, we can claim no stronger entitlement than an agent-relative permission to assign special weight to the preservation of our own life. And I have argued that this is, in itself, too weak a basis upon which to conclude that a disinterested third party would be permitted to intervene to render us assistance. It will thus be defensible for a physician to perform an abortion to save a pregnant woman's life just in case it can be argued that there is some other, stronger ground for the woman's claim than the agent-relative permission to preserve her own life. (For that is, indeed, all that her 'right of self-defense' comes to if she is thought to be seeking license to kill an attacker whose technical guilt consists merely in posing a passive threat to her life.) There certainly appear to be cases of self-defense in which one can appeal to some other, stronger ground than the victim's agent-relative permission to preserve his or her own life: when the attacker is a hostile aggressor or a deranged assailant, then one can argue that there is a morally relevant asymmetry that justifies our rendering assistance to the victim and our denying it to the attacker. But I have argued that this line of defense is closed to us in cases in which an attacker poses merely a passive threat to a victim's life. An attacker's right to life is not forfeited, nor is his or her status as moral peer undermined, by the fact of the attacker's posing a passive threat to another person's life. It would thus appear that we cannot explain a woman's entitlement to terminate a pregnancy that threatens her life by appealing to the right of self-defense. Or, to put the point another way, the appeal to the right of self-defense will not support the claim that abortion is virtually always, if not always, a defensible course of action for a woman and her doctor when the continuation of the pregnancy poses a threat to the woman's life.

If my argument is sound, then Restrictives are faced with what they may well regard as an unpalatable choice: they must adopt either a view that is quite a bit stricter than the Restrictive view or one that may be considerably less strict. If they agree that the appeal to self-defense is unsuccessful, then they can simply accept the conclusion that a woman is not entitled to terminate a pregnancy that threatens her life: although there may be cases in which it would be permissible for a woman to have an abortion (with the necessary medical assistance) in order to preserve her own life, this is not a course of action that can be defended generally, or on the basis of principle.

Although this conclusion is repugnant to common sense, it is a conclusion that some people would accept. Brody has argued that since there is no morally relevant asymmetry between the woman and the fetus, and since the fetus as a person has the same right to life that any other person has (and hence the same right to life that the woman has), it is not defensible for us to favor the woman's life over that of the fetus as a matter of course (or policy). What we should do instead is adopt a "fair random method" [46] to determine, on a case-by-case basis, whose life is to be saved and whose sacrificed: when the woman's life is threatened by the continuation of the pregnancy, but the fetus could survive and be born alive if the abortion is not performed, then what we should do is toss a coin to decide between them.

This view is sterner than the Restrictive view and, it seems to me, it is a doctrine that is difficult to defend on purely secular grounds. It is a very hard doctrine indeed if it is argued for as Brody argues for it. As we have seen, Brody thinks it does not matter morally that it is a third party—the doctor—and not the woman herself who performs the abortion. Brody's view thus has the consequence that it would be impermissible for a woman to abort the fetus to save her own life even if this were something that she could do by herself. She, like the physician, would be obliged to toss a coin. This is, I think, a most implausible view.

It is worth pointing out that Brody's conclusion does not gain any support from what I have said thus far, for I have been arguing that third-party permissions and entitlements may differ from those of the principals. I have suggested, moreover, that the case of 'self-defense against a passive threat' is one that presents us with an instance in which they clearly do differ. Although it is not a view that I hold (for reasons that will be made clearer as we proceed), I think that one could maintain that a woman would be entitled to perform an abortion upon herself while denying that a doctor would be permitted to help her.

The other alternative is to argue that abortion *is* a defensible course of action when the woman's life is at stake, but to claim that, although the fetus presents (only) a passive threat to a pregnant woman's life, there is nevertheless a morally relevant asymmetry between the woman and the fetus. This seems the more attractive line to take, but it is not one that Restrictives can readily opt for, since it is far from clear that it can be rendered consistent with the Restrictives' fundamental outlook—that the fetus is a person, and is thus fully protected by the 'natural law' forbidding homicide.

In *The Theory of Morality*, Alan Donagan suggests that the asymmetry might lie in the fact that the fetus "owes a debt of gratitude to its parents, in particular to its mother, for its very life" (p. 162). Since the pregnant woman is, of course, in no way beholden to the fetus, "in any threat to the mother's life arising out of her pregnancy, her status as victim is beyond serious question" (p. 163).[47] In *The Ethics of Homicide*, Philip Devine proposes that one might seek to justify abortion undertaken to preserve a woman's life by appealing to "the closer ties obtaining between the physician and the woman than between the physician and the unborn child" (p. 153).[48] Neither Devine's nor Donagan's proposal seems to me to resolve the Restrictives' dilemma satisfactorily.

Devine's proposal attempts to disadvantage the fetus systematically —to handicap fetuses as a class—on a basis that is both weak and arbitrary. A pregnant woman who needs an abortion to preserve her life might not have any significant ties with the physician who performs the surgery; she might, for example, be brought to a strange hospital in a coma. More to the point, however, is the fact that a fetus, in virtue of being what it is, is never in a position to have close ties with a physician or, for that matter, with anyone. Thus the appeal to the woman's closer ties to the physician seems neither decisive nor fair. It is wrongheaded in another way as well. Although we think that it is sometimes defensible to appeal to the closeness of our ties to another person to justify our giving that person's preferences and interests special weight (even when we admit that, from an impartial point of view, that person's claims are equal to a rival's), we are most reluctant to allow this sort of favoritism when the ties in question may be entirely financial or purely professional ones. We would not think that physicians would be acting rightly if they decided to let a pregnant woman die rather than perform the abortion that was needed to save her life because they had powerful senior colleagues serving on the local branch of the "Friends of the Fetus" committee. Nor would we think that they were acting rightly if they agreed to perform the abortion simply because they were offered a fee for doing so (whereas no one offered them a 'fee' for refusing).[49] If pregnant women, as such, have a stronger claim to the preservation of their lives than dependent fetuses do, it is not Devine's proposal that provides the foundation for the claim.

There is a different problem with the suggestion Donagan puts forward: it offers support to the Moderate rather than to the Restrictive view of abortion.[50] If we think the fetus owes the woman a debt of gratitude, then it appears that we are regarding pregnancy as a continuing act of supererogation: when a woman prefers to discontinue the pregnancy because the burden of providing fetal life-support has become too onerous, then she does not wrong the fetus, for she is merely declining to continue doing it a favor. This sort of reasoning will obviously permit abortion in a wide range of cases, not just those in which the woman's life is in danger. (Indeed, it is widely thought to be just the reasoning that underlies the Thomson-Moderates' position.) For it cannot plausibly be claimed that abortion violates a fetus's right to life if continuing with a pregnancy is regarded as an act of supererogation.

I believe it is problematic to regard the fetus as owing a debt of any kind to anyone. But if we ask ourselves what is plausible in the view that it does owe a debt to the woman who carries it, then I think that we find ourselves appealing to the very features of the relationship between the pregnant woman and the dependent fetus that many Moderates and Permissives have been at pains to stress.[51] A pregnant woman provides life-support to the developing fetus through her body, and the fetus is, in turn, parasitic upon her: a fetus thus survives off a woman (that is, at her expense), not in partnership with her. Since the life and well-being of the fetus are sustained through its physical dependence on the woman's body, the very fact of being pregnant undermines a woman's autonomy. She cannot choose what she shall do without thereby choosing for someone else, and she must therefore take into account the possible risks of even the most mundane sorts of activities: driving a car, lifting a bucket, taking an aspirin.[52] While providing assistance to a post-fetal person may involve a significant reduction of a benefactor's freedom of choice and action, pregnancy involves a physical invasion of the body. A pregnant woman is thus not in the position of someone who is (merely) reluctantly providing a time-consuming and exhausting service to another person. Nor is she (merely) in the position of someone whose body is regarded by others as a resource of the community, in the way that the possessor of a rare blood type might be so regarded in an emergency, or the possessor of two healthy kidneys might be regarded in a society beset by hereditary kidney disease. Pregnancy is, by its nature, a more intimate invasion, for it modifies a woman's *self*: it takes *her* over by hormonal alteration, as well as in more subtle ways.[53]

The relationship between the pregnant woman and the dependent fetus can thus be seen to be inherently asymmetrical. Given the nature of the connection, and how this connection affects the pregnant woman, it seems reasonable to suppose that the asymmetry is relevant and, indeed, morally significant. The supposition that the asymmetry is of moral significance may well underlie the widespread conviction that abortion is defensible whenever the pregnancy poses a threat to the woman's life. And it may figure in proposed justifications of preferring the woman's life to the fetus's life whenever it is necessary to choose between them. It is implausible, however, to suppose that this is all that can be justified by an appeal to the asymmetry. For the appeal to the special asymmetrical nature of the relationship between the woman and the fetus is not an argument that characterizes 'abortion in self-defense' as justified self-defense (for it does not involve characterizing it as self-defense at all). This may well pose a problem for a Restrictive who appeals to the asymmetry, for it is doubtful that this appeal provides a basis for defending abortion only when it is necessary to preserve a woman's life. It may have considerably more permissive implications.

The strategy that we have been considering—the appeal to the special asymmetrical nature of the relationship between the woman and the fetus—is not one that proceeds via any general argument to the effect that victims of passive threats have, as such, a stronger claim to third-party assistance than their attackers do. The asymmetry between the woman and the fetus is supposed (somehow) to be a special one,[54] a feature of the fetus's intimate biological dependence, not one that simply obtains in virtue of a person's posing a passive threat to another person's life. And the appeal to this special asymmetry is supposed to yield the conclusion that a woman whose life is threatened by the continuation of the pregnancy has a strong claim to the assistance of disinterested third parties, while, as I have argued, victims of passive threats do not generally have a claim to preferential assistance. In defending 'abortion in self-defense' by appealing to the asymmetrical relationship between the fetus and the woman, one is not involved in defending a *policy* of providing preferential assistance to the persons who are the victims of passive threats.

Nor can the appeal to this asymmetry be fit into the other model of self-defense sketched above. Although the appeal to the asymmetry is supposed to yield the conclusion that a pregnant woman may be entitled to preserve her life by aborting (and thus killing) the fetus and have a strong claim to the third-party assistance that she needs to preserve her life—a claim that is much stronger than the claim that victims of passive threats generally have—it does not subsume 'abortion in self-defense' under the model of self-defense that applies in the case of the hostile aggressor or deranged assailant. For the sort of asymmetry that is in question is importantly unlike the one that characterizes the relationship between an aggressor or an assailant and the persons who are their victims. As we have seen, the aggressor and the assailant have in some sense done something that has weakened, forfeited, or under-mined their prior claims to full moral parity with the persons who are now their victims. But a fetus cannot be so regarded, for a fetus has done nothing of the kind. Since the fetus has done nothing at all, any attribution of agency—however slight—seems problematic. (Perhaps this constitutes a partial explanation of why we encounter difficulties in supposing that a fetus owes its 'parents' a debt of gratitude, and in regarding the fetus who threatens the pregnant woman's life as a 'pur-suer.')[55] When the fetus poses a threat to the pregnant woman's life, it does not forfeit moral standing that it previously had. The appeal to the special asymmetrical nature of the relationship between the preg-nant woman and the dependent fetus appears to be a rival to, and not a mere extension of, the argument that characterizes 'abortion in self-defense' as a case of self-defense.

In light of the difficulties that have been raised regarding the at-tempt to apply the notions of self-defense to the case of abortion, I think that Restrictives would do better to agree that 'abortion in self-defense' is not a case of self-defense at all than to maintain that it is a case of self-defense that merely deviates somewhat from more familiar cases. For we do not have a model that fits the case of 'abortion in self-defense': the passive-threat model does not return conclusions that are strong enough to support 'abortion in self-defense' as a principle or policy, and the aggressor-assailant model mischaracterizes the nature and the role of the fetus's threat. Nor is it obvious that we could con-struct a workable model (by emendation, extrapolation, or some other non-*ad hoc* reasoning) without significantly distorting our views about the nature and structure of our entitlement to defend ourselves (and, perhaps, the nature and structure of rights in general). This may make an appeal to the special asymmetrical nature of the relationship be-tween the woman and the fetus a more attractive strategy to Restric-tives who recognize the difficulties of characterizing 'abortion in self-defense' as a case of justified self-defense, yet want to hold to the Restrictive view that abortion is permissible only when it is necessary to preserve the pregnant woman's life. But this attraction is only superficial.

If we wish to maintain that the appeal to the asymmetry is powerful enough to yield the conclusion that abortion is defensible whenever the continuation of the pregnancy poses a threat to a woman's life, then we must be able to explain *how* it is that the appeal yields *this* conclusion—how (exactly) the appeal provides support for the view that the claims of the woman outweigh the claims of the fetus when it is necessary to choose between them. As we saw in discussing self-defense, the supposition that the woman's claims are stronger is not based on the belief that anyone has done anything that can be construed as eroding the fetus's claims or as bolstering the woman's. The threat to the woman's life is not produced by the malign, incomplete, or defective exercise of the fetus's agency (for it is doubtful that the fetus [in its present stage of development] can be characterized as an agent at all). Nor can it properly be said that the threat to the woman's life arises from anything that the fetus does, for it is (merely) the ongoing connection of the fetus to the woman that poses the threat to her life. The appeal to the special asymmetrical nature of the relationship between the woman and the fetus seems to involve the view that it is the fetus's ongoing dependency that itself provides a basis for thinking that the fetus has the less substantial claim to have its life preserved. And so, if the appeal to the asymmetry between the woman and the fetus yields the conclusion that the woman's claims are stronger, it must do so by drawing upon a substantive moral view. It must embody the supposition that, because the fetus is (unilaterally) dependent upon the pregnant woman, different relative strengths are to be assigned to the woman's claims and the fetus's claims *ab initio*: the fetus is not (for it never was) the woman's moral peer.[56]

To say this is not to assert categorically that the woman and the fetus are not moral peers, but to suggest that the argument that appeals to the asymmetry between the woman and the fetus to defend 'abortion in self-defense' may well involve the assumption that the woman and the fetus are not moral peers. (Nothing else that we have considered thus far has allowed us to maintain that the woman is *entitled* to terminate a pregnancy in order to preserve her life and is *entitled* to receive assistance in killing a fetus who [passively] threatens her life; other avenues to defending 'abortion in self-defense' appear to be closed.) If this suggestion is correct, then we can see why the appeal to the asymmetry between the woman and the fetus is not likely to be a strategy that can be called upon to help defend the Restrictive view of abortion.

If it is necessary to posit some sort of moral asymmetry between the woman and the fetus in order to explain how 'abortion in self-defense' can be morally defensible as a policy, then we should recognize that there may be no reason to suppose that the case in which a woman seeks an abortion to preserve her life is morally exceptional: although it may be the clearest sort of case in which abortion is defensible, it need not be the only sort of case. The exact size of the gap (in moral status) between the woman and the fetus—the exact difference in the strengths of their competing claims—is certainly not something that non-Restrictives have made clear, nor is there any doubt that attempts at greater clarity and precision will continue to be the subject of much controversy. But Restrictives are not justified in assuming *a priori* that the gap is one that *must* be minimal; there is no reason in principle to suppose that the difference can only be great enough to decide a tie in the woman's favor. If the woman's claims are strong enough to justify abortion—with the assistance of a third party—when it is undertaken to preserve her life, then they *may* be strong enough to justify it in other cases as well. Although this is a view that Restrictives will reject, this rejection is something that must be argued for. If the line of argument I have been developing has force, then I believe that it succeeds in shifting the burden of proof onto those who would espouse a Restrictive view. For—as I hope I have shown—we should be wary of supposing that we can defend 'abortion in self-defense' by appealing to our usual models of justified self-defense, and skeptical of the claim that the appeal to the special asymmetrical nature of the relationship between the woman and the fetus yields the conclusion that the woman is to be accorded only marginal preference—that the woman's entitlement to preserve her life is strong enough to allow for 'abortion in self-defense,' but no stronger.

I have been focusing on the problems that confront Restrictives who appeal to the asymmetry between the woman and the fetus to defend 'abortion in self-defense,' but the conclusions I have reached have wider implications, for the appeal to the special asymmetrical nature of the relationship between the woman and the fetus is central to the Thomson-Moderates' position. Thomson-Moderates wish to appeal to this asymmetry, but also to maintain—if only for the sake of argument—that the fetus is a person, and hence the woman's moral peer. But it is far from obvious that these are compatible aims, for it is not at all clear that one can place the requisite moral weight—enough to return the conclusion that 'abortion in self-defense' is defensible as a policy—

without calling into question the assumption that the fetus is the woman's moral peer. If there is such a tension in the Thomson-Moderates' position, then it may represent a serious problem. For it may undercut the rationale behind the adoption of the Thomson strategy: that of showing that Moderate conclusions about the morality of abortion can be derived (even) from Restrictive assumptions about the moral status, indeed the personhood, of the fetus.

The difficulty that confronts Restrictives and Thomson-Moderates—that of explaining how the special asymmetrical nature of the relationship between the woman and the fetus provides support for the view that the woman's claims outweigh the claims of the fetus—is, I believe, a deep and serious one. The belief in the justifiability of 'abortion in self-defense' seems ultimately to involve—or to reflect—the conviction that the claims of the fetus are, as such, weaker than those of the pregnant woman, and that it is the special asymmetrical nature of the relationship between the woman and the fetus that (somehow) accounts for the moral disparity between them. But how these convictions are related is puzzlingly obscure, for it is not clear why the fact of fetal dependency should be thought to bear on the strength of the fetus's claims (and, ultimately, on the moral status of the fetus itself). We are inclined to think that a being's moral status depends, in some fundamental way, on what kind of thing it is,[57] and though we recognize that a fetus *is* a dependent (in this stage of its development), its dependence upon the pregnant woman is something that we recognize to be both temporary and contingent. Why, then, should the fact of the fetus's dependency be thought to be so important to the determination of its moral status? It is not the dependency in itself that can account for why the claims of the fetus count for less: a fetus developing *in vitro* is not dependent in the way that a fetus developing inside a pregnant woman is, but we do not suppose that the claims of the *in vitro* fetus are any stronger.[58] (Nor is it obvious that we would take the claims of the *in vitro* fetus to be on a par with those of any other [postfetal] person.)

More to the point, perhaps, is the question of *how* the dependency of the fetus is relevant. It does not seem to figure in the sort of case that we have been considering (that is, a case in which we must choose between the woman and the fetus), for it is a case in which either the woman or the fetus could survive, and (henceforth) do so independently of the other. Although our belief in the defensibility of 'abortion in self-defense' may involve the conviction that there is a moral disparity between the woman and the fetus which is to be explained by appealing to the special asymmetrical nature of the relationship between them, it is not a conviction that is firmly grounded, for it is an explanation that is really quite obscure.

I have not tried to show that abortion is morally defensible whenever it is undertaken to preserve a woman's life (though it is certainly a view that I hold). What I have tried to show is that, although this is a view that is widely held, it is one whose defense is neither straightforward nor unproblematic.

Part 5

Persons, Privacy, and Samaritanism

SINCE Judith Thomson's "A Defense of Abortion" raised the possibility of analyzing pregnancy and abortion in terms of Samaritanism, the nature of Samaritanism, its relevance to the abortion debate, and the use of analogies for shedding light on the abortion question have been hotly contested issues. King, Macklin, and Foot address these issues directly or indirectly. In this section, Meredith Michaels and Laurence Thomas direct their attention specifically to the Samaritanism argument, and to the use of a different analogy by opponents of abortion and the slavery analogy, respectively. The question of the nature and scope of privacy is thoroughly entangled with the Samaritanism issue. For as Michaels argues, the limits of the obligations society may impose on an individual are in an important sense the limits of privacy. Daniel Wikler's analysis of the right to privacy as it figures in the abortion decisions is hence an important component of the discussion contained in this section, though many of the issues Wikler raises are closely connected to those raised by Richards and Wertheimer.

Michaels discusses the distinction between public and private interests and the obligations that a society may impose on individuals in the context of the analysis of pregnancy as a case of Samaritanism. She attacks both the claim that a society can never impose Samaritan obligations on its citizens and the claim that this analysis demonstrates a real moral asymmetry in the relation of a woman to the fetus she carries. She concludes that the analysis is incapable of providing a defense of abortion.

Thomas, in "Abortion, Slavery, and the Law: A Study in Moral Character," replies to an argument frequently raised in support of legislative efforts to prohibit abortion: that abortion is the legal and moral equivalent of slavery. The argument suggests that in both cases a weak minority is oppressed by a powerful majority because that majority refuses to acknowledge that members of that minority are indeed persons, in the face of powerful evidence to the contrary. Thomas begins by developing a conception of a paradigm bearer of the right to life. He argues that whereas slaves fit this description, fetuses do not, despite the fact that they are potentially bearers of such a right.

Wikler distinguishes informational privacy from autonomy privacy. He argues that the right to abortion rests primarily on the right to autonomy privacy—the right to control the intimate affairs of one's life and to make one's own decisions regarding one's religious and metaphysical views. He argues that legislation which would restrict abortion would violate autonomy privacy not only by restricting women's control over their reproductive lives, but also through imposing a view of the status of the fetus upon them. This essay is hence closely related to those of Benshoof and Richards, and should also be read in the context of those discussions.

Abortion and the Claims of Samaritanism

Meredith W. Michaels

THERE are those who believe that fetuses are persons and there are those who do not. Then, there are those who think that the moral status of abortion depends upon the metaphysical status of the fetus, and there are those who, perhaps driven away by the apparent futility of settling the metaphysical issue, argue that it does not. The *locus classicus* of such arguments, is, of course, Judith Thomson's seminal (*sic*) paper, "A Defense of Abortion." [1] In addition to enjoying a serene independence from the personhood controversy, arguments like Thomson's have the advantage of hoisting the antiabortionist with his own petard. Suppose that the fetus is a person, fully fledged and fully righted, from the moment of conception. That alone does not entail that abortion is always morally impermissible. Indeed, if the woman, in carrying the fetus to term, can be construed as making a sacrifice of the Good Samaritan sort, she can be under no obligation to do so. We do not, in general, require Good Samaritanism of ourselves or of others. Hence, we are not justified in requiring it of unwillingly pregnant women.

My intention is to question whether the Good Samaritan tactic adopted by Thomson successfully maneuvers us to a resolution of the abortion issue. In fact, I will argue that it does not, due to two inherent flaws in its design. First, contrary to Thomson's supposition, it is not true that people never have Samaritan duties to one another. If so, Thomson's claim that unwillingly pregnant women are singled out for extra duty is unjustified. Second, if we are to take seriously both the notion that the unwillingly pregnant woman is being asked to make undue sacrifices for the fetus and that the fetus is a person, then we must also take seriously the possibility that in having an abortion the woman is requiring that the fetus make undue sacrifices for her. I shall begin by elucidating the particular nature of the relativism that underlies appeals to Samaritanism. I shall end by suggesting what I take to be the ultimate cause of the failure of Good Samaritan arguments, namely that they presuppose that we have a shared context for moral evaluation. Inasmuch as that is not something that we have, the appeal to Samaritanism is finally beyond assessment.

II

Thomson herself provides only the barest sketch of the standards by which Good Samaritanism is to be adjudicated. The following penultimate passage, which has always seemed to me more suitable as an introduction than as a conclusion to a paper, contains Thomson's preferred views on the matter:

... while I do argue that abortion is not impermissible, I do not argue that it is always permissible. There may well be cases in which carrying the child to term requires only Minimally Decent Samaritanism of the mother, and this is a standard we must not fall below. I am inclined to think it a merit of my account precisely that it does not give a general yes or a general no. It allows for and supports our view that a sick and desperately frightened fourteen-year-old schoolgirl, pregnant due to rape, may *of course* choose abortion, and that any law that rules this out is an insane law. And it also allows for and supports our sense that in other cases resort to abortion is even positively indecent. It would be indecent in the woman to request an abortion, and indecent in a doctor to perform it, if she is in her seventh month, and wants the abortion just to avoid the nuisance of postponing a trip abroad. [Thomson, p. 138]

But if, as Thomson goes on, it is wrong to treat all cases of abortion as morally on a par, then clearly we must have available to us some set of moral guidelines by means of which we can determine whether a woman seeking an abortion is indeed entitled to it, or whether she is falling below the standard of Minimally Decent Samaritanism. If we allow each woman to adopt her own guidelines, as presumably those in favor of abortion on demand would have it, then the standards appealed to by Thomson's seven-months-pregnant woman could not be dismissed as morally frivolous. When Thomson claims that her Good Samaritan argument supports "our sense" that abortion is wrong in such a case, we must suppose that the "our" quantifies not over everybody (for after all, the seventh-month woman herself cannot be included), but only over those who have an appropriately developed and enlightened moral sense. Once we remember that we are assuming the fetus is a person from the moment of conception, the problem seems particularly acute. Our moral sense must enable us to mediate and resolve disputes which in many cases involve weighing the (mere?) desires and interests of one party against the life of the other. (I am thinking of cases in which the woman's life is not at stake.) It is very easy, especially in light of the particular examples chosen by Thomson, to be taken in both by the plight of the seven-month-old fetus and by that of the fourteen-year-old girl. But if the fetus carried by the fourteen-year-old girl is as much a person as she is, then Thomson's "of course" is misplaced. Many Catholics, for example, would claim that the "of course" goes quite the other way. If the Good Samaritan standard is to help us resolve the abortion issue, then we need, I think, something more than an appeal to the moral intuitions of a narrowly circumscribed, historically located group of academicians. That is not to say that the views of the members of such a group are necessarily suspect. But neither are they, simply in virtue of being had, correct.

Thomson's position is compelling because it does indeed appear to be the case that the burden an unwillingly pregnant woman is required to bear is disproportionately large. Disproportionate, that is, to the size of the burdens the rest of us are required to bear. This is especially true in cases where the woman is expected to give up her life in order to save that of the fetus. We have, then, a context for the evaluation of Thomson's claim: If she is right, then it should be clear that no one else is compelled to sacrifice to the same degree. The appeal to Good Samaritanism is inherently relativistic. That is, we must judge the sacrifice of the woman relative to those expected of others in the woman's community, and not relative to some moral ideal. Thomson is not then claiming that the precise degree of Bad Samaritanism that is in fact legally or socially endorsed is morally justifiable. Her discussion of the Kitty Genovese case makes that altogether clear. The claim is simply that relative to existing Samaritan standards and the practices that fall within their sphere, antiabortion laws require of women unparalleled sacrifices. This, then, points to a solution to the problem of evaluation raised in the preceding paragraph. In judging whether a claim to unwarranted sacrifice is legitimate, we look not to the dictates of a moral sense enlightened by an awareness of some ideal moral code, but rather to one enlightened by an awareness of the de facto, or even de jure, moral code.

The inital plausibility and indeed simplicity of Thomson's argument has about it an aura of the inviolate. In fact, it is not clear what those who sanction abortion would do without it; it has played such a crucial role in the justification of abortion in recent years. There is a question, however, whether its central premise can emerge unscathed from an examination which takes seriously its relativistic claim. From that examination, to which I now turn, will emerge dangerous obstacles for those who have set their store by Good Samaritan arguments. Nevertheless, it has the advantage of shedding some light on the abortion issue's particular recalcitrance. Admittedly, the examination will take us through redoubtable territory. We begin with the military draft, and end with moral incommensurability.

III

Assuming that an unwillingly pregnant woman always has the option of giving up the child for adoption upon its delivery, what sorts of sacrifices does the pregnancy itself impose on her? There is the emotional trauma attendant upon carrying a fetus to term only to say goodbye to it. There are the obvious and inevitable physical changes, some of which are regularly associated with psychological changes of various sorts. In addition, in a certain percentage of cases, these changes are serious and irreversible. Moreover, when the woman is unmarried or very young, her pregnancy undoubtedly carries with it at least some degree of social stigma. That stigma frequently entails ostracism, loss of employment, interruption of education, or other undesirable material consequences. Childbirth itself is painful, especially when one does not anticipate with joy the product of one's labor. Clearly, this is a bare sketch. It does not take much in the way of imagination or insight to fill in the quotidian details in the life of a person who suffers through an unwanted pregnancy. The sum of these impositions and deprivations amounts to what must indeed be seen as a hardship of major proportions. The present question, however, is whether it is indeed unparalleled.

One need not travel far to find instances of people enduring what can only be described as considerable hardship. The actual society in which we live, for better or for worse, does not distribute its benefits and burdens equally. At present, we are enduring an unemployment rate of 10 percent, that rate being higher among those who are historically disadvantaged, namely, blacks and other racial minorities.

Some citizens enjoy enormous wealth, others enjoy none at all. Although there have been efforts in the direction of eliminating racial oppression, it remains a chronic and pernicious problem. Those who suffer its effects are required, in terms of employment, education, standard of living, and self-esteem, to endure lifelong hardship of an incalculable degree. Hardships of this sort are not typically thought of as instances of Good Samaritanism, but then neither (certainly not before Thomson) is the unwillingly pregnant woman so described. We are told that those who suffer economic and social deprivation do so for a just cause: freedom from governmental tyranny in the home and the marketplace. Like the suffering borne by the unwillingly pregnant woman, the suffering of the poor and oppressed is not borne by all.

In order to dismiss such hardships as irrelevant to the issue of abortion, one might argue that whatever their extent, they are nevertheless not endured as a result of a statutory imposition. Laws prohibiting abortion would impose on women a de jure and not simply a de facto compulsion to sacrifice. We are not legally required to give over nine months of our lives to needy violinists. Hence women ought not be required to give up nine months of their lives to needy fetuses. Though this maneuver strikes me as evading a moral question by introducing a legal one, for the moment we can leave it as it stands. Waiting at the sidelines is the military draft, a statutory requirement that young men between the ages of eighteen and twenty-four serve in the Armed Forces. In the name of God and Country, a young man must endure, in many cases against his will or at least his desires, a two-year-long process in which he is subjected to physical and psychological hardship, interruption of career and personal plans, separation from his family and community, and possible injury or even death. To suggest that some men enjoy making such sacrifices of liberty and privacy is beside the point. Undoubtedly, some of the women who find themselves pregnant but who, for moral reasons, do not seek abortions view their sacrifices to be worthy ones. They are not, for that reason alone, any less arduous. In any case, the only relevant consideration at this point is whether the fact that the draft imposes serious hardships on those who fall within its provenance establishes an invokable precedent.

Donald Regan argues that it does not.[2] He does so in the context of a larger argument to the effect that a Good Samaritan argument like Thomson's provides the basis for a constitutional claim to equal protection. Though Regan is not explicit on this point, the advantage of the Good Samaritan argument, namely its evasion of the personhood issue, is equally welcome in the legal sphere. The Court managed to evade that issue in *Roe* v. *Wade*; nevertheless, they left open the possibility that those better equipped to determine matters of personhood would discover that the fetus is indeed a person. Should that happen, the Court's appeal to privacy in *Roe* would surely be overturned, for the Court's interest would have to shift from protecting the woman from unnecessary governmental regulation to protecting the life of the fetus. From this derives the extraordinary appeal of any argument to the effect that even if the fetus is a person, abortion is permissible. Inasmuch as the Good Samaritan argument does just that, the only question that remains is exactly how to find a constitutional location for it. Regan hopes to persuade us that laws prohibiting abortion are "...at odds with the general tenor of samaritan law," and hence that they violate the pregnant woman's right to equal protection (Regan, p. 1570).

Although Regan is willing to grant that the draft does indeed require sacrifices equal in extent to those endured by pregnant women who are denied abortions, he claims that "the woman is being required to aid a specific other individual (the fetus); the draftee is not. Rightly or wrongly, our tradition distinguishes between obligations to aid particular individuals and obligations to promote a more broadly based public interest" (p. 1606). Against this claim it might be argued that "...every interest protected by state power becomes ipso facto a public interest" (p. 1607). In other words, the statutory enactment of a prohibition against abortion would itself create a public interest in the protection of the fetus, and so Regan's distinction between the two cases begs the question. If so, the suggestion that "...the draftee serves a public interest while the pregnant woman denied an abortion serves only the interest of the fetus" is simply false (p. 1607). Regan's response to this line of argument is best left in his own words:

There is something to this. I am protected by law against gratuitous physical assault, and that suggests that in some sense there must be a public interest in so protecting me. Still, the public interest involved is ultimately based on my private interest in physical integrity. Similarly, if the prohibition on abortion is justified on the ground that the fetus has a right to life (as it commonly is these days), then the ultimate public interest is in protecting the private interest of the fetus. This public interest is not enough to justify compelling the pregnant woman to carry the fetus. The reason is that in every potential samaritan case there is a public interest in protecting the person in need of aid which is precisely analogous to the public interest in saving the fetus. We cannot rely on this public interest in the abortion case and ignore it elsewhere. [P. 1607]

There are two things to be said here. First, Regan seems to be claiming, in response to the suggestion that every legally protected private interest becomes a matter of public interest, that it is equally arguable that every public interest is ultimately reducible to a private interest. Indeed, it is often claimed that the only legitimate purpose of government is the protection of the rights of its citizens. Certainly, a good deal of current governmental rhetoric attempts to persuade us that something akin to this is true, and such rhetoric has impressive historical roots. Yet, if this is so, then the public interest served by the draftee is ultimately reducible to private interest. Second, if indeed in every potential samaritan case there is a public interest in protecting the person in need of aid, then one wonders why that interest is ignored. Even if we cannot, for a variety of reasons, insure that every needy individual is paired with an appropriately equipped samaritan, we can do so in the case of every fetus. We would then be maximizing, to a greater extent than we are now, the public interest. In any case, we surely need a more adequate account of the relation between public and private interest if we intend to appeal to them in distinguishing between the respective obligations of draftees and unwillingly pregnant women. (Anyone wishing illumination on the difficulties involved in determining the boundaries of the concepts of privacy and the public good should consult Louis Henkin).[3]

Good Samaritanism is, according to Regan, a property had by one individual in virtue of a relationship she bears to another individual. I am not sure this is strictly true, or in any case how one might go about determining whether it is. Many of those historical figures who are arguably Good Samaritans (at least in spirit) saw themselves as having obligations to aid mankind as a whole. The discharge of such obligations frequently took the form of aiding particular individuals, or particular groups of individuals, but the obligation itself was seen as a general obligation to help those with a particular need or set of needs, whoever they might be. I am thinking of people such as Jesus, Gandhi, and Martin Luther King. Thus, there does not appear to be anything intrinsically misguided in characterizing the obligation of the military draftee as an obligation to come to the aid, not simply of his country, but of its citizens. Although it is true that the paradigm textbook case of Good Samaritanism involves two individuals, it does not follow that the original Good Samaritan himself is morally distinguishable from those who construe themselves to have obligations to aid groups of individuals or individuals in general.

Thus it appears that a crucial premise of Thomson's argument is mistaken: others *are* required to make sacrifices of the Samaritan kind that are at least prima facie morally comparable to those made by unwillingly pregnant women. I shall now turn to a consideration of the second claim I wish to defend, which is in fact a species of the first: namely, that Thomson's sacrificial arguments apply equally to the fetus, especially on the assumption that the fetus is a person.

IV

Let us grant, for the moment, that the paradigm case of Good Samaritanism is indeed definitive of it and hence that it is only exemplified in those cases where one individual comes to the aid of another. We have been asked to consider whether it is morally justifiable to compel a woman to make large sacrifices for the fetus. We are expected to conclude that it is not, given that nobody else is so compelled. Putting aside for the moment the cases of the draftee, and the poor and otherwise oppressed, there remains another individual, the fetus, whose interests have yet to be directly addressed. Whenever it is determined that the potential sacrifice of the pregnant woman crosses the boundary into Good Samaritanism and hence lies outside the boundary of that which we can morally require, we shift the burden to the fetus. Its burden, the loss of its life, is a particularly heavy one. If we cannot require Good Samaritanism of the pregnant woman, then how can we require that the fetus terminate the course of its life in order that the woman may pursue uninterruptedly the course of hers? Of course, we have hanging over us Thomson's graphic account of the unconscious violinist whose life suddenly depends on yours. May you unhook yourself so that your life can continue its uninterrupted course? Of course you may. But the violinist is not giving up his life to benefit yours. His life, or so the story goes, was soon to end, until the Society of Music Lovers found you. Not so, in the case of the fetus; its life has just begun. Whatever its consequences, there does seem to be a moral difference between terminating the life of someone who was about to die anyway and terminating the life of someone who wasn't.

It may be conceptually illicit to suggest that in granting a woman an abortion, we are requiring Good Samaritanism of the fetus, in that it is fairly clear that the fetus is incapable of agency, moral or otherwise. We are not requiring that the fetus do anything, only that it die. (Even granting that the fetus is a person, I do not think that a fetus can be said to "give up" its life in the sense in which a grown woman can.) The situation seems rather to be analogous to one in which the parents of a young child decide to make a radical change in the normal course of his life without regard for his needs. They might, for example, decide to move from Amherst to the Amazon jungle in order to pursue their passion for capturing poisonous snakes. It may be inappropriate to describe the child as "giving up" the safety and comfort of life in Amherst in order that his parents satisfy their frivolous desires, but it is nevertheless clear that in doing so, the parents are requiring of the child that he bear an unreasonable burden. (If my story is not persuasive, I am certain that one meeting your requirements can be fabricated.) The salient point is this: in the sort of case I have just described, it would be wrong, should we manage to persuade the child's parents not to haul him off to the jungle, to applaud their Good Samaritanism. What they give up for themselves in order to maintain "aid" for their child simply fails to constitute a Samaritan sacrifice. Nor does an appeal to the relative weight of their burden have any force here. Suppose that it has become a general practice to treat children cavalierly and hence that requiring these particular parents to "postpone their trip abroad" would impose on them an unequal burden. The mere fact that a practice has become fashionable does not insure that it has become morally defensible. Recall Thomson's remark that Minimally Decent Samaritanism is a standard we must not fall below.

We have before us two separate, though closely related questions. First, in denying an abortion to a pregnant woman are we requiring of her a degree of sacrifice not required of anyone else similarly situated (that is, situated within her community)? Second, by granting an abortion to a pregnant woman are we overvaluing the alleged burden of the woman relative to that of the fetus? The relationship between the questions emerges when we consider whether the fetus itself ought to be included as a full-fledged member of the relevant community. If it is, then both that which the woman is required to give up, if she is denied an abortion, and that which the fetus is required to give up, if she is granted it, must be evaluated within the context of the community of which they are both members. It is on this point that the Good Samaritan argument ultimately founders. But this requires some elaboration.

V

Let us return to the case of the draftee. When the draft is in force, young men have what might be called a prima facie obligation to join the armed services. Perhaps the prima facie obligation on the part of the young man is derived from an obligation on the part of the state to insure that its citizens are defended. The obligation is met by imposing a prima facie obligation on that subset of its citizens best suited to the task. The Selective Service allows exceptions to conscription in those cases where it judges a man to have a justifiable reason for overriding his obligation. He may be exempted from service if he is physically or psychologically unable to bear its burdens, or if, for reasons of conscience he objects to military service—albeit, the last exception is narrowly construed. The point of the exceptions is nevertheless clear. The community of which a young man is a member recognizes that in requiring that he bear the burdens of conscription, it thereby creates in itself an obligation not to impose on him any additional ones, be they physical, psychological, or burdens of conscience. Yet, in creating room for exceptions, the community presupposes that it is capable of judging when such exceptions can legitimately be granted, when, that is, a man's prima facie obligation to military service is indeed overridden. The requirement to sacrifice, then, has an upper limit.

Without suggesting that they are strictly analogous, it does seem that there are significant parallels between the case of the draftee and the case of the pregnant woman. Leaving aside those cases in which a woman is pregnant due to rape, we can perhaps characterize the woman as having a prima facie obligation to the fetus. (Though I do not at present want to make much of antecedent conditions, we may also wish to leave aside those cases in which a woman makes careful use of a statistically effective contraceptive measure but gets pregnant anyway. Such a case is rather like giving a block party, after which you discover that one of the guests has moved into your house.) Perhaps the prima facie obligation on the part of the woman is derived from an obligation on the part of the state to protect the fetus. That obligation is met by imposing a prima facie obligation on, in this case, the only subset of its citizens suited to the task. Yet, if the state does view itself as having a legitimate interest in the protection of the fetus, then, as with the case of conscription, it ought to allow that there may be cases in which the woman's prima facie obligation is overridden. In a discussion of civil disobedience (and tangentially of conscientious objection), Michael Walzer appeals to the concept of "moral seriousness." [4] Though he admits that "the term is not easy to define, nor the quality easy to measure," he nevertheless views it as crucial to the distinction between frivolous or criminal disobedience and civil disobedience (Walzer, p. 20). In that context, moral seriousness is evidenced by a willingness to respect those genuine goods that the state provides, to reflect upon and worry about the possible consequences of the action for the public as a whole (ibid.). Presumably, in the case of the conscientious objector, the grounds on which he makes his appeal for an exception to military service are ones which possess the quality of moral seriousness, that they are indeed the dictates of a reflective conscience. Yet, the success of the venture depends upon the capacity and the willingness of the larger community in which this individual or these groups reside to recognize and to grant the moral seriousness of their claims. In the absence of any shared sense of what is to count as moral seriousness, an appeal to it will inevitably founder, as did so many such claims during the Vietnam War.

Things are equally bleak in the case of abortion. In a society in which private rights and the public good are more often than not seen to be at odds, and in which we have no clear, let alone shared, sense of our individual obligations to one another, it is difficult to see how a general claim to Good Samaritanism is to be evaluated. If we lack what Alistair MacIntyre calls a "moral community," [5] then the claim that a woman is unduly and unfairly burdened by a particular pregnancy is bound to be met with varying degrees of scorn and suspicion. "In any society in which government does not express or represent the moral community of the citizens, but is instead a set of institutional arrangements for imposing a bureaucratised unity on a society which lacks genuine moral consensus, the nature of political obligation becomes systematically unclear" (MacIntyre, p. 236). Whether or not the prima facie obligation of the woman to the fetus is a political one, it seems nevertheless a clear instance of MacIntyre's claim. To those who hold the alleged rights of the fetus to be paramount, the isolated cries of women claiming to be forced into Good Samaritanism are bound to be dismissed as lacking in moral seriousness. Similarly, to those required to bear the burdens of an unwanted pregnancy, the charge that the life of the fetus takes precedence over everything else is equally liable to dismissal. In the absence of any consensus as to what counts as an instance of moral seriousness, there is little hope that the respective claims of the woman and fetus will ever be successfully arbitrated. As we have seen, the model of the draft, with its provisions for legitimate exceptions, presupposes that those who impose the obligation on the potential draftee have the capacity to acknowledge the moral seriousness of competing claims. It presupposes, that is, that the potential draftee and those who judge him are members of the same moral community. Without that community, the competing claims are, to borrow again from MacIntyre, morally incommensurable. Notice that the success of the model does not require that the competing claimants agree as to the correctness of the resolution of their claims, only that they agree as to its moral legitimacy. Given that in the case of abortion neither claimant takes the other to be morally serious, the draft model cannot apply. Thomson's contention that it is a merit of her account that it does not give a general yes or a general no holds only if we suppose that we have a consensus on the appropriate standards for determining the legitimacy of a woman's request for an abortion. And the possession or acquisition of standards requires first that everyone be willing to grant the possibility of the moral seriousness of such requests.

VI

Precisely why it is we find ourselves in this particular position is a subject for another paper, yet it might be worthwhile to sketch briefly a possible explanation. The case of abortion (and, for that matter, the draft) are instances of a general phenomenon that is eloquently described by MacIntyre in *After Virtue*. MacIntyre argues that the lack of moral community is in part a function of the fact that the "specifically modern self ... finds no limits set to that on which it may pass judgment for such limits could only derive from rational criteria for evaluation and (the modern) self lacks any such criteria. Everything may be criticized from whatever standpoint the self has adopted" (p. 30). Because she believes from her stance that she is entitled to criticize anything, the modern self believes that her moral stance is the only legitimate one; that it exists independently of any contingent state of affairs, in particular, the social and historical role she herself occupies. Her belief that hers is the only legitimate stance naturally allows her to dismiss without argument any that competes with it. As is so ably captured by Roger Wertheimer's analysis of the current controversy, the abortion issue is a particularly acute example of this.[6] On the one hand, "liberals habitually argue as though extreme conservatism were an invention of contemporary scholasticism with a mere century of popish heritage," and on the other, the conservative believes that "the issue is not, as the liberal supposes, one of religious ritual and self-regarding behavior, but of minority rights, the minority being not Catholics but the fetuses of all faiths, and the right being the right of an innocent human being to life itself" (Wertheimer, pp. 34, 36). The conservative comes to the debate armed with the innocence of the fetus, the liberal with the victimization of women. Each has, in addition, an impressive arsenal at the sidelines. From the conservative point of view, a woman who chooses an abortion in order not to interrupt her college career is playing fast and loose with the sanctity of human life. And despite strident liberal denials to the contrary, three-month-old fetuses do have an undeniable air of humanity about them. From the liberal point of view, it is entirely unfair that a woman should be burdened with the responsibilities of an unwanted pregnancy, especially in a society whose views about sexuality are so ambiguous as to produce open invitations to sexual activity in the media and active opposition to sex education in the schools. Women have good reason to be outraged by their plight, the roots of which are captured in Alice Walker's description of Nelda Hill—a character in her novel *Meridian*—who finds herself pregnant at the age of fourteen.[7] Several years later, "Nelda knew that the information she had needed to get through adolescence was information Mrs. Hill could have given her" (Walker, p. 88). It is the Nelda Hills who are required to bear (*sic*) the responsibility for the consequences of their ignorance, an ignorance for which they are not at fault.

The lack of any common ground between the moral stance of the liberal and that of the conservative precludes either side from viewing the other as morally serious. Similarly, the parties to the dispute are precluded from viewing each other as members of a single moral community. The claims to obligation, and the opposing claims to waivers therefrom, can neither be recognized nor viewed as legitimate without a shared framework for their evaluation. (That is perhaps why we accommodate most easily obligations to family members, and least easily those to citizens of faraway lands.) The Good Samaritan arguments we have considered attempt to concede some ground to the opponents of abortion by claiming that the woman does have a prima facie obligation to the fetus, one that can be overridden should her sacrifice be judged too extensive. Yet the concession does not forge a bridge between the two positions; it rather occupies some of the empty space between them. The incommensurability of the claims of the woman and the claims of the fetus's advocates is analogous to the following sort of case. Suppose there are two teen-aged boys, one from New York and one from Kenya. The Kenyan is brought to New York and asked to negotiate his way from the 125th Street bus station to Bleecker Street. The New Yorker is brought to Kenya and asked to track a wild boar through the bush. Afterward, the two boys meet and each claims that his task was the harder of the two. Given the respective frameworks within which each evaluates his task, their judgments are incommensurable. An enormous gulf separates their cultures and each one sees his own as providing the only accurate standard of judgment. Hence, neither can grant true legitimacy to the other's claim.

VII

Good Samaritan arguments, rather than resolving the abortion issue, cast its intransigence in the very starkest light. I have attempted to show that the appeal to undue sacrifice is far less straightforward than Thomson and her Good Samaritan successors have imagined. People other than pregnant women, including fetuses (assuming, as Thomson does, that they are people), are required to make sacrifices, and so pregnant women are not morally isolated. Perhaps more discouraging, though, is the recognition that Good Samaritan arguments presuppose a high degree of shared moral enlightenment. In an argument as compelling as Thomson's, we are bound to pass quickly over the implicit assumption that there is something answering to what she calls "our sense" and "our view." Yet, those who come to weigh the sacrifice of the woman against the right to life of the fetus will do so in two separate groups, each carrying its own set of scales. And each will insist that the other's scales fail to give the correct weight, that only its own are the scales of Justice. Nor can those who favor abortion retreat to the claim that the fetus, after all, is not a person; for that concept, too, is a moral one. As we have seen, the absence of a moral community precludes moral agreement, and a moral community is surely something we lack.

Abortion, Slavery, and the Law:
A Study in Moral Character

Laurence Thomas

ONCE upon a time there was slavery, and of it some people said: It is good. Today, we suppose that no one of sound moral character thinks that about slavery. Indeed, the practice is now forbidden by the Constitution of the United States. Antiabortionists would like to think that all of this militates in their favor. They would like to think that (a) just as persons who supported the practice of slavery thereby revealed a serious flaw in their moral character, so, too, are persons flawed who favor a woman's right to have an abortion in circumstances *other than* when the mother's life or health is jeopardized beyond the normal risks of childbearing. They would also like to think that (b) just as the legal prohibition of slavery is in order, so is the legal prohibition of abortion.[1]

Now, those of the pro-choice persuasion—moderates and liberals—think that the antiabortionists, that is, the conservatives, espouse a view which is utterly ludicrous. Accordingly, they tend to dismiss (a) and (b) out of hand. I think these two claims warrant a hearing, not because I believe either to be correct, but because it is important to see why, as I will show in this essay, they are both false.

I

It is a characteristic feature of persons of sound moral character that doing what is morally right is an abiding and overriding concern. It is of great import to them that their positions on moral matters are defensible from the moral point of view, and not merely an embodiment of their own propensities, preferences, and prejudices. Thus, of persons of good moral character the following can be said: (1) They are apt to be very good at discerning whether a given moral stance, taken by themselves or others, is defensible from the moral point of view; (2) If they were to have good reasons for believing that—with regard to some moral issue—they have adopted a position which is indefensible from the moral point of view, then they would both give up that position and alter their behavior accordingly. Put another way, persons of good moral character are not unwilling to acknowledge that something constitutes a moral wrong when they have every good reason for believing that it does. I take it for granted that being of sound moral character is compatible with doing what is morally wrong, at least from time to time, in that a person who has such a character does not thereby have perfect moral knowledge. The example of (2) gives us a general idea of what a person of sound moral character is like, though she or he should lack perfect moral knowledge.

Now, the wickedness generally associated with the practice of slavery has an awful lot to do with the fact that (2) seems not to have been satisfied by those who condoned the practice. What we do not suppose is that the condoners of the practice could have truly searched their souls and yet have arrived at the conclusion that slaves were merely little green things, children of a lesser God—indeed, anything but full-fledged persons. For, if we really thought that, then slavery simply could not have been the wicked practice we have made it out to be. The reason for this is that what makes a practice egregiously wicked is not only that it constitutes a serious moral wrong, but also that those who either engage in or support the practice—condoners of the practice, as I call them—are *unwilling* to acknowledge that it constitutes a serious moral wrong, although they have very good reasons for believing precisely that. A practice is egregiously wicked when we can say of the majority of those condoning it that in this way they thereby reveal a serious flaw in their moral character. This we can say of the majority of the condoners of slavery if, as it would seem, they were unwilling to regard slaves as full-fledged persons despite every good reason for doing so.

Let us now turn to the abortion issue. As I have remarked, the anti-abortionist would like to think that just as those who condoned the practice of slavery thereby revealed a significant flaw in their moral character, so do those who advocate a pro-choice view. Using criterion

(2) to judge what having a good moral character involves, they are right only if it is the case that pro-choice advocates are *unwilling* to acknowledge that the fetus is a full-fledged person although they have very good reasons for believing that it is. And precisely this would be so if, as the antiabortionists would like to maintain, the following is true: Just as we do not suppose that condoners of slavery could have truly searched their souls and nonetheless arrived at the conclusion that slaves were less than full-fledged persons, so it is today that a person cannot truly search her or his soul and nonetheless arrive at the conclusion that the fetus is less than a full-fledged person. However, as we shall see, this surmise is mistaken.

II

Let me begin this section by introducing the notion of a paradigm bearer of the right to life. For any being β, β is a paradigm bearer of the right to life during stage S. If, at any time during S, β's life were jeopardized by any other being, whether or not moral agency can be ascribed to it, then we would have a moral reason to come to β's assistance, cases of forfeiture and the like aside. An obvious consequence of what I have just said is that no nonhuman animal is thought to be a paradigm bearer of the right to life during any of its stages of development. For we are not of the mind that we have a moral reason to prevent animals from killing one another, including their own offspring. And I shall assume that being a paradigm bearer of the right to life comes in the wake of being a full-fledged person. Thus, as I am using it the term 'person' is a moral concept. Persons have certain moral rights, among them the right to life. As I shall use the term 'human being,' it refers to any creature with a human genetic code. Thus, any creature conceived only by humans is, at the very moment of conception, a human being.

Now, as a way of making good the claim that the cases of abortion and slavery are far from analogous, let me introduce the difference between parallel and linear stage comparisons of life lines. By the former, I mean the comparison of any two stages, actual or not, which are taken to be part of the same life line. By the latter, I mean the comparison of $1 + n$ ($n > 1$) life lines in order to determine whether or not each has stages which are the same in the relevant respects. In drawing upon this distinction, it will help to have a diagram before us:

Slave	stage 1	stage 2
		life lines
Condoner of slavery	stage 1	stage 2
Adult human	stage 1	stage 2
		life lines
Human fetus	stage 1	stage 2

_____ Realized life
_ _ _ _ Potential life

stage 2:
being is regarded
as paradigm bearer of the
right to life

Needless to say, slavery involved only a parallel comparison between the life lines of the slaves and the condoners of slavery. For the question concerning the condoners of slavery was not: Did the slaves form the beginning of a life line of beings which were unquestionably thought to be full-fledged persons during at least one of their developmental stages? Rather, it was: Were the life lines of the slaves sufficiently similar to the life lines of the condoners of slavery in the morally relevant respect that if the latter were full-fledged persons at a given stage, then so were the former at the parallel stage? These are logically distinct questions, for either can be answered affirmatively regardless of how the other is answered. And as history shows, the condoners of slavery were very much concerned to provide a negative answer to the second question.

By contrast, with the issue of abortion the question just is: If human beings, by which I mean simply creatures with forty-six chromosomes, have a right to life at stage 2, then do they also have this right at stage 1, it being understood that having this right comes in the wake of personhood? (I put the question this way, because the issue of fetuses having a right to life does not get off the ground in the absence of paradigm bearers of the right to life.) Conceptually, this question is about how to evaluate the same life line with respect to having the right to life; hence, we have linear stage comparison. This truth is obscured, though, by two facts. One is that the life line of those who take up this question cannot be the same as the life line of those who are affected by it. The other is that those who take up the question rightly regard themselves as paradigm bearers of the right to life. So, it can be very tempting to suppose that the abortion issue revolves around the comparison of two different life lines and that, in particular, the question is this: Are the life lines of the human fetus and a full-fledged person of sufficient similarity that if the latter has a right to life then so does the former? The obvious answer is that they are not, inasmuch as at the very outset of its existence, anyway, about the only thing a human fetus has in common with a full-fledged person is that it, too, is a human being.

A further consideration in support of the view that the abortion issue is as I have stated it, is that antiabortionists maintain that it is simply in virtue of being a human being that the fetus has a right to life. If this is their position, then they cannot be establishing that the fetus has this right by way of parallel stage comparisons. For, if it is in virtue of being a human being—that is, a creature with forty-six chromosomes—that a thing has a right to life, then one hardly needs to point to full-fledged persons in order to establish that human fetuses have a right to life. Comparisons with the life line of other human beings are thus rendered otiose.

We can now sharply delineate the difference between the issues of abortion and slavery. To successfully argue that condoners of slavery ought morally to have regarded slaves as full-fledged persons, we need the premise (a) that cases which are alike in morally relevant respects should be treated alike, it being understood that species membership does not define the morally relevant respects, and we need the premise (b) that the condoners of slavery regarded themselves as full-fledged persons. The premise we do not need is (c), if a being shall be a paradigm bearer of the right to life during stage Sn of its life line, then it is a paradigm bearer of this right during its entire life line or, in any case, during any stage prior to Sn. Whether or not (c) is true, we can by way of (a) and (b) establish that slavery was morally wrong. And when these two premises are taken in conjunction with criterion (2) of having a good moral character, we can establish that by engaging in the practice of slavery the condoners of slavery thereby revealed a deep flaw in their moral character.

But though its truth is irrelevant to the slavery issue, if (c) is true, then whereas it would not follow that all abortions are morally wrong, it would certainly follow that we should adopt a nonpermissive stance toward abortions. However, it is evident, I trust, that (c) cannot be established by way of (a), and (b') full-fledged persons regard themselves as paradigm bearers of the right to life. Nor will (a) and (b'), in conjunction with criterion (2) of having a good moral character, enable us to obtain the conclusion that only someone with a seriously defective moral character would fail to see that (c) is true and, therefore, fail to see that the fetus is a paradigm bearer of the right to life.

Now, we know that (c) hardly stands as a logical truth. For instance, a person could hold that (i) the fetus is merely an organic shell until birth, when it is provided with a soul by God, (ii) it is in virtue of this act by God that the fetus becomes a full-fledged person, and (iii) the fetus cannot become a full-fledged person in any other way. Whatever abortion amounted to in this view, it could not amount to killing a full-fledged person.[2]

The story I have just told gives away the lie to the claim, by antiabortionists, that anyone who truly searched her or his heart could not help but see that the fetus is a full-fledged person from the moment of conception. For versions of this story have seen the light of day; indeed, one version has been held by the Catholic church, itself. And it can hardly be thought that merely by taking God, or theology in general, out of the picture, the question of whether or not the fetus is a full-fledged person is settled affirmatively.

Of course, antiabortionists would be quick to point out that just as the story the condoners of slavery told about slaves was false, so is the story I have just told about the fetus. No doubt this is true enough. But there is a difference. The story the condoners of slavery told clearly did fly in the face of the evidence; it was clearly a rationalization on their part in order to continue the practice of slavery. Given that the condoners of slavery took themselves to be full-fledged persons, we are at a loss to see how they could have thought that the slaves were less than that. However, nothing of that sort is true of the story I told about when the fetus becomes a full-fledged person and so a paradigm bearer of the right to life. Given the difference between a fetus and an adult in terms of physical features, physiology, and realized capacities, the idea that there is no moral difference between the two does not immediately present itself. And it will not do for the antiabortionist to contend that anyone who maintains that the cases of slavery and abortion are not analogous is simply being arbitrary about what physical features and the like are irrelevant with respect to whether or not something is a full-fledged person. For what is at issue is precisely whether or not there is any difference among human beings which makes a difference with respect to their moral status. And there is nothing inconsistent about maintaining that some things do make a difference and other quite different things do not. In fact, if we perceive enough of a difference along the very same dimension, there is nothing inconsistent about maintaining that there is a morally relevant difference, as is shown by our treatment of the mentally insane who perform criminal acts.

Consider the following example. There is a cancerous disease which is such that if a fetus acquires it within the first two weeks of its existence, then it is certain to die by the fifth month of its fetal life. The disease prevents the fetus from assuming anything like a human form; its organs never develop properly, and by the third month, its entire brain is virtually consumed by the cancerous cells of the disease. Once the disease sets in, there is no stopping it: the fetus will die. Of course, when the fetus dies, the woman carrying it will have a miscarriage. Suppose, then, that during her first month of pregnancy a woman learns that the fetus she is carrying has this cancerous disease. Would it be morally wrong for her to have an abortion, it being understood that in no way will her health be jeopardized if she carries the fetus until she has a miscarriage—which she will most surely have in her sixth month?

It is obvious that a person who thinks that the fetus is a paradigm bearer of the right to life from the moment of conception on, is logically committed to the view that it would be morally wrong for the woman to have an abortion; whereas a person who does not think this can maintain that the woman does not commit a moral wrong in failing to carry the fetus until it miscarries. Now, the observation I wish to make is simply this. I am unable to see what kind of argument can be advanced to show that the woman is wicked if she treats the diseased fetus in accordance with the latter view. In particular, I do not see that an argument can be advanced to show that, on account of so treating the fetus, she fails to satisfy criterion (2) of what is involved in having a good moral character. These considerations receive support from another corner: Judges and juries are often reluctant to treat as full-fledged murderers those who have killed a loved one in order to spare the person great suffering.[3] To be sure, there are judges and juries who would regard such killings as instances of murder. That this is so is perfectly compatible with the aims of this essay. For my position is simply that there are competing and equally defensible conceptions of when a human being, that is, a creature with forty-six chromosomes, is a paradigm bearer of the right to life. And one might suppose that if the issue can be debated with respect to adult human beings, then *a fortiori* it can be debated with respect to human beings who are in a fetal stage.

Whatever else may be true, to accuse a person of having a bad moral character is to make a serious charge. Accordingly, if we so accuse others, that very accusation may itself be seen as an instance of cruelty on our part, if our only basis for it is that their view of the moral landscape differs from ours in an important respect. Indeed, an accusation so made has all the appearances of being arbitrary and capricious from the moral point of view. I have tried to give an example where it cannot be plausibly maintained that a person who had an abortion could be accused of having a bad moral character. If I am right about this, then there is a version of the view that the fetus is not a paradigm bearer of the right to life but only potentially such a being. A person can hold this view and yet not be accused of having a bad moral character.

III

In the introduction to this essay, I expressed my disagreement with antiabortionists who maintain just as the legal prohibition of slavery is in order, so, too, is the legal prohibition of abortion—excepting when the mother's life or health is jeopardized beyond the normal risks of childbearing. I should like to think that it is now somewhat evident why I disagree.[4]

Nothing is more important to the stability of a society than that its members have the conviction that they are not treated in an arbitrary and capricious manner by the social institutions of that society. This is especially so in the case of legal institutions—of which criminal law is a key element—inasmuch as they define the rights, freedoms, and privileges of the members of society; and they also provide a basis for legitimate expectations both in terms of support from, as well as noninterference on the part of, others. To this end, it is of tremendous importance that the members of society have the conviction that this or that behavior or practice is not declared criminal for arbitrary and capricious reasons.

The explanation for this is straightforward. The violation of criminal law generally constitutes grounds for punishing a person; to punish a person is to inflict a form of suffering upon him; and it goes without saying that people should not have suffering inflicted upon them for arbitrary and capricious reasons.

It is also true, however, that to punish a person is to cast aspersion upon his moral character both officially and publicly. Given the argument from stability this, too, should not be done for arbitrary and capricious reasons. If so, then the following principle would seem to hold. We may call it the Staying Hand Principle: (a) *If* there is widespread disagreement among the members of society as to whether or not an act or a practice is morally wrong, and (b) *if* a satisfactory case cannot be made for the view that there is every reason to believe that persons who so behave thereby reveal a serious flaw in their moral character (these are logically independent conditions), then the act or practice in question should not be declared criminal. This principle should be set aside only where uniformity of action (or nearly that) is necessary to avert disaster. When a society makes an act or practice criminal though *both* of these conditions obtain, then that society can be regarded as not respecting those citizens who fail to see that by engaging in such behavior, they do what is morally wrong.

It is important to note that the Staying Hand Principle does not amount to a form of legal moralism.[5] This principle does not state that nothing should be made a criminal act so long as the majority of people believe in their heart of hearts (or whatever) that there is nothing morally objectionable about it. For I have not supposed that the majority can never be egregiously wrong about matters of either morality or law. Nor, it should be noted, does this principle entail the clearly untenable view that the law should never punish a person for doing what he sincerely believes to be right.

If we find ourselves feeling somewhat uncomfortable about the principle, I suspect that part of the explanation has to do with the fact that by itself, each part of the principle obviously constitutes an unacceptable, and not just an insufficient, reason why a practice should not be made criminal. In general, at any rate, we are inclined to think that whether or not a practice should be made criminal has little to do with what most people think should be done. Again, we are inclined to think that whether or not a person should be punished for his criminal behavior has little to do with the fact that his behavior did or did not reveal a serious flaw in his moral character. For example, although it would probably be very difficult to show that a person who robbed her wealthy brother of a million dollars in order to save their mother's life thereby revealed a serious flaw in her moral character, it hardly seems to follow from this that she should go unpunished for the crime she committed; though, to be sure, leniency may be in order. So, given that the Staying Hand Principle is simply the conjunction of two unacceptable considerations for staying the law's hand, one naturally suspects a *leger de main*.

It must be remembered, however, that the Staying Hand Principle has been introduced to handle a very specific kind of problem, namely: What should society do when—because of widespread and fundamental disagreement over the morality of a practice—there is such disagreement over whether or not the practice should be allowed in society and when moral considerations, themselves, do not militate in favor of any particular moral assessment of the practice? The principle is not intended to handle those practices where it is very clear, on moral grounds, whether or not society should allow a practice to continue.

Now, when the Staying Hand Principle is applied to the issue of abortion, there is, I believe, no getting around the conclusion that society should adopt a nonrestrictive policy with respect to abortion. That is, it should not prohibit abortion even if that prohibition includes an exception for those cases when carrying the fetus seriously jeopardizes the mother's health. For, as I have tried to show by way of illustration, it is implausible to maintain that every case of having an abortion, other than when carrying the fetus so jeopardizes the mother's life, is indicative of having a bad moral character.

It goes without saying that the conclusion reached here is a limited one. The question of just how permissive an abortion policy should be is left wide open. Still, there has been progress, and on two accounts. First, if the conclusion reached is sound, then we do know that society should adopt a permissive abortion policy rather than a restrictive one, that is, which precludes abortion except when carrying the fetus would seriously jeopardize the mother's health. And that is important to know. Second, we have reached this conclusion in a somewhat surprising way, namely by way of reflections upon what is involved in having a good moral character.

It may be objected that this strategy would permit all sorts of moral horrors to occur. An adequate response would be a long one. An inadequate response is as follows: It cannot be reasonably supposed that as I have unpacked the idea, a person can be said to have a good moral character no matter what she or he is prepared to do. After all, remember that I argued against, and not for, slavery using the very same ideas about what is involved in having a good moral character. Finally, whether we like it or not, perfect moral knowledge does not come in the wake of having a good moral character. A society should not treat its members as if this were not so. I should like to think that the arguments of this essay are in keeping with this ideal.

A final comment: I should point out that even if the arguments of this essay are sound, there is another controversy which has not been settled, namely whether the state should fund abortions for those who cannot afford them. I have said nothing which bears on this issue; nor have I meant to.

Abortion, Privacy, and Personhood:
From *Roe* v. *Wade* to the Human Life Statute

Daniel Wikler

Roe, Privacy, and Abortion

THE Supreme Court, in *Roe* v. *Wade*,[1] held that termination of a
pregnancy through abortion in the early stages is an exercise of a
constitutional right of privacy. During the past decade, numerous legal
commentators have sought to understand what the Court meant by
privacy, whether such a right is in fact granted by the Constitution,
and whether the right in question should be understood as protecting
choices about abortion. Others have been concerned with the moral
rights at issue.

The Court's argument remains controversial. Its logic is difficult to
follow, and several of its key concepts—especially that of privacy—are
obscure. There is, as a result, no consensus on what *Roe's* privacy
argument was—if indeed it was any one argument—and hence on
whether it was successful.

This situation is bound to remain, for, in my view, *Roe's* notion
of privacy cannot be given a precise formulation. This ought not,
however, cause us to dismiss the argument out of hand. The concept
of privacy has been logically ill-behaved throughout the century in
which it has figured prominently in constitutional law, but its importance is felt to be greater than ever.

The best strategy may be to respect privacy's position in our conceptual field of vision, attempting all the while to reduce the vagueness of its boundaries, and to devote our energies to assessing its
bearing on other matters we care about. In what follows I review some
of the controversy over *Roe's* privacy argument in an attempt to bring

to it whatever clarity may be achievable. With the result, I attempt to uncover the logical relation between it and the concept of personhood, which stands with privacy at the center of the abortion debate. My goal is to demonstrate that these must be discussed in tandem; in particular, that our evaluation of *Roe*'s privacy argument is dependent on certain features of our concept of personhood.

Because the route taken here is circuitous, I will pause to provide a brief map of the argument. The first part of the essay takes note of the two chief conceptions of privacy: one involving information about the self, and the other, autonomy in certain "personal" affairs. I identify the latter as the kind of privacy figuring in *Roe*, though the two may be related at a deeper level. Precisely characterizing "autonomy privacy" is a difficult task, which I approach only long enough to motivate a discussion of the various ways that a ban on abortion might be thought to violate a woman's right of privacy. My reading of *Roe* v. *Wade* requires me to identify both the interests which the putative right of privacy is to protect, and the state interests it is to override.

Each of these privacy claims turns out to be problematic. The single most important question in assessing the privacy argument, however, turns out to be whether the protection of the right of privacy is to be denied on account of the Harm Principle. I interpret *Roe* as acknowledging that the relevance of the Harm Principle determines the success of the privacy argument, but as denying that it applies. This in turn derives from the Court's construal of the question of fetal personhood. Our assessment of the privacy argument thus leads us to reexamine this issue. To develop motivation I review some arguments used in the legislative review of the recent Human Life Statute, which presents a view of the personhood question quite at odds with that found in *Roe* v. *Wade*. Though I reach a negative verdict on that view, I find its case worthy of respect, and indeed demanding some important revisions in pro-choice argumentation. *Roe*'s privacy argument may be retained, but only at a cost.

Two Concepts of Privacy

It was known long before *Roe* that privacy is not a univocal concept, nor even one which, once partitioned, produces any notions clear enough for unproblematic legal or moral argument.[2] *Roe* did nothing to clarify matters. The result was that critics of *Roe* simply dismissed its privacy argument as incoherent, whereas its defenders provided numerous "clarifications" and reconstruals which were wholly inconsistent with each other.

"Privacy" ordinarily means something like control over certain kinds of observation of or information about oneself. This is the meaning assigned to the term in almost all of the recent philosophical literature on privacy, and is the only conception even considered in such large-scale treatments of the subject as Westin's *Privacy and Freedom*.[3]

It takes no profound analysis to reach the conclusion that if abortion rights follow upon privacy rights, the privacy in question is not primarily of the sensory or informational sort. Any attempt to fit *Roe's* privacy argument into this mold must necessarily be strained.[4] Thus, prosecution of a woman under an antiabortion law would reveal that the woman wanted an abortion, which might be as damaging as the kinds of disclosures which informational privacy rights prevent. But prosecution for all sorts of acts is embarrassing, whether these be income tax evasion or assault. We cannot judge these state actions wrong on this basis alone. We must take into account the propriety of the law and of the act which is held to be unlawful.

Again, it is true that some methods of enforcement of antiabortion laws might conceivably involve violation of the confidentiality of medical records, but a court bent on protecting informational privacy could bar these methods of enforcement instead of striking down the statutes. Similarly, the doctor-patient relationship may be, with that of confessor and penitent, among the most intimate, but fear of breach of this confidentiality supports abortion rights no more than they would a right to abuse children.

If these laws do abridge a right of privacy, then, it is not because they force unwanted disclosure about the self. From this premise any of three conclusions might be drawn. First, we might judge that inasmuch as privacy means informational privacy, and in that antiabortion laws need not compromise informational privacy in any fundamental way, privacy rights do not include abortion rights. Thus no argument like *Roe's* could be judged to be correct.

This conclusion is suggested by one reading of the sequence of opinions from *Griswold*[5] through *Eisenstadt*[6] to *Roe*. The first of these objected to the intrusion into the bedroom which might be necessary to obtain evidence that a married couple had used contraceptives. *Eisenstadt* insisted that single persons be given the same protection as married people, and thus struck down a statute forbidding the sale of contraceptives. It was a giant leap from the bedroom in *Griswold* to the drugstore in *Eisenstadt*, but only a small step from there to the doctor's office in *Roe*. Those who would dismiss the privacy argument insist that the Court at some point in this sequence simply forgot what privacy was all about. Thus, despite its precedent-citing behavior in *Roe*, it is a waste of time to try to salvage the Court's privacy argument or to support its conclusions with a better argument of that same genre.

The second response to the finding that the privacy argument for abortion rights is not about informational privacy is much more forgiving. Perhaps taking a cue from Humpty Dumpty, this approach permits the Court to choose its own jargon, concedes that "privacy" meant something else in *Roe*, and proceeds to take that something else seriously as an argument for abortion rights. If this maneuver renders the entire philosophical (and much of the legal) literature on privacy irrelevant to the job of assessing the privacy argument, so be it; there are other literatures to turn to. Besides, it is not fair to charge *Roe* with utter caprice, in that its use of "privacy" does connect with certain uses of the term in legal writing and in ordinary discourse. The task, then, is to achieve an unambiguous formulation of this concept and to determine whether there exists a right of privacy in that sense which extends to women the right to make decisions about abortion.

The third response to what we might call the "semantic" critique of *Roe*'s privacy argument is that there exists a more fundamental notion of privacy of which both informational privacy and the sort involved in privacy arguments for abortion are categories.[7] Alternately, some authors hold that, whereas the "privacy" in *Roe* is not privacy, both privacy and that which *Roe* meant by "privacy" protect the same set of fundamental interests. Inasmuch as, in this latter view, privacy rights exist derivatively, to protect these deeper interests, we may expect the same kinds of arguments for *Roe*-"privacy" that we ordinarily marshal in support of ordinary privacy.

Autonomy Privacy

Roe's privacy argument does not succeed unless the second or third of these approaches, or both, are correct. Even if they are, however, we will need to clarify the relevant notion of privacy. But what is it? Clearly, it is some sort of autonomy or liberty, and called for this reason "autonomy privacy." This has proven to be an elusive concept. In my opinion, it will of necessity remain so. Nevertheless, we can make a few clarifying observations.

If abortion rights are to be secured by a right of autonomy privacy, these rights must, first, be rights against the state. But more is involved than this. According to *Roe*, the class of acts covered under a right of privacy is something other than the totality of those left unregulated by the government. Privacy is something distinct from undifferentiated liberty, and not all state regulation compromises it. Instead,

only personal rights that can be deemed "fundamental" or implicit in the concept of ordered liberty . . . are included in this guarantee of personal privacy . . . the right has some extension to activities relating to marriage . . . procreation . . . contraception . . . family relationships . . . and child rearing and education.[8]

Aside from the list of examples, this passage provides little guidance as to what is to count as "personal" and "fundamental." "Personal" is little more than a synonym of "private" in this context. Nor does "private" amount to self-regarding. Many actions which are primarily self-regarding are far from fundamental, and, besides, as Professor Tribe notes,[9] the Court denied during the same term as *Roe*'s that "conduct involving consenting adults" is always placed by the Court beyond state regulation—footnoting Mill as a source for the rejected view.

The Court's language does suggest that rights of privacy are primarily for the nurturing of family life, thereby protecting individual autonomy only insofar as it is exercised in connection with family matters. Thus Professors Heymann and Barzelay find in *Roe* evidence of concern for

a sphere of interests—which the court now groups and denominates "privacy"—implicit in the "liberty" protected by the 14th Amendment. At the core of this sphere is the right of the individual to make for himself—except where a very good reason exists for placing the decision in society's hands—the fundamental decisions that shape family life: whom to marry; whether and when to have children; and with what values to rear these children. . . . Our political system is superimposed on and presupposes a social system of family units, not just of isolated individuals.[10]

This version of privacy, however, does not accommodate the fact that Ms. Roe was unmarried. A woman seeking an abortion may have no family of her own and indeed might be actively trying to prevent one from forming.

Professor Richards provides a more liberal version of this argument; rather than nurturing family life,

the Court may be working out the right to autonomy in deciding how or whether to love. . . . the prohibition of abortion limits the right to decide whether an act will have procreative consequences, and can affect whether or not one will enter into a new love relationship; thus, such prohibition violates the right of autonomy in love.[11]

(Richards notes that "other rights may be relevant to the sound disposition of the abortion issue.")

This view, however, is open to similar objections: the lover (if indeed the father ever was that) may be wholly removed from the pregnant woman's life when she opts for abortion, and the fate of the pregnancy may not affect their relationship at all. Similar difficulties arise in consideration of other construals of the privacy interest. If, as one account would have it, a right of privacy was required to moderate the effects upon the individual of the rise of the modern industrial state, it is not clear why it would include a right of abortion; for such a right might also have been an important protection against the social restrictions of preindustrial society.[12]

We are not likely, then, to arrive at a nicely delineated concept of privacy or of the privacy interest with which to begin an evaluation of the privacy argument in *Roe*. We can say only that, whatever else may be true of it, privacy involves matters which pertain to individuals as individuals; which, if they are to be protected by right, are of fundamental importance; and which are literally "personal," i.e., affecting the individual's power to define the kind of person he or she is, the basic goals and values which make up one's identity.

This will have to serve as our working formulation. I need not point out its vagueness. And its vagueness is plainly troublesome. The state invades privacy when it forbids early abortion, for example, but not when it drafts young men for war—or so much of liberal opinion holds; our formulation does not permit us to make sense of this pair of judgments. Other odd pairings come readily to mind. Still, this formulation is better than none, so long as we are prepared to make use of the concept while admitting its defects. We proceed, then, to determine whether abortion rights are protected by rights of privacy if the latter concept is construed in this way.

To determine the strength of the privacy argument for abortion rights, we must identify the privacy interests at stake; survey the state's interests, if any, which would be served by a ban on abortions; and try to determine the proper outcome in case these two sets of interests conflict.

Abortion: Privacy Interests

In which respects would laws restricting the practice of abortion compromise a woman's interest in privacy? The literature on the privacy argument has not been as precise as one might wish on this key question. In my view, those who press the privacy argument for abortion rights might list at least three specific intrusions, ranging from obvious to subtle.

Pregnancy interest   First, a ban on abortion requires that women who want to terminate their pregnancies must undergo an unwanted pregnancy. The specific interest in this instance is that of power over the disposition of one's body. Being pregnant is, *inter alia*, a disability and a discomfort. It may also be distressing for its effects on social relations and on self-image. The state does not ordinarily command its citizens to tolerate such bodily conditions if something can be done to ameliorate them, and if it did, its action would likely be viewed as intruding on autonomy privacy.

Family planning interest   Second, a ban on abortion compromises the woman's interest in being able to control the number and timing of childbirths. This has a strong impact on life plans of almost any sort. Choice of careers, and success in the chosen field, may depend on optimal timing of children. So may success in finding a suitable mate, or in maintaining distance from an unsuitable one. Indeed, the presence of children affects most choices and activities of parents, and the absence of children too has pervasive effect.

Moral autonomy interest   The third conflict between antiabortion laws and autonomy privacy derives from the state's attempt to take over the individual's task of defining her own morality. This is, perhaps, the most "personal" and the most fundamental of the interests which autonomy privacy would protect. At the same time, the moral autonomy interest is less tangible than the pregnancy or family planning interests, and some explication is in order.

There is some intrusion into a woman's moral autonomy in denying in respect to the first two interests. The decision to have children, or to remain childless, is based in some cases on particular ideals, goals, and values which might be moral in nature; the same might be occasionally true with respect to being pregnant. Indirectly, any number of moral and personal norms are involved, such as those concerning sexuality and independence. In these respects the debate over abortion, and particularly over rights of privacy, really is a contest over women's emancipation.

The central moral question which the state decides for the woman in restricting abortion, however, is what her actions toward the fetus should be. The immediate question, of course, is whether the woman should be compelled to supply the fetus with a nurturing environment in her own body. This is closely related to the pregnancy interest.

But there is an even more basic issue involved: whether or not the woman should relate to the fetus as if it were a person. In effect, this is simply the issue of fetal personhood, for if the fetus, at a given stage of development, is a person, then it should be treated like one. The question then, is whether the woman is to be empowered to use her own sense of the fetus's moral status or will be required to act on a view adopted by the state. In this sense, the state interferes with autonomy privacy by taking a stand on whether the fetus is a person.

Thus the privacy argument becomes something like a complaint against the state's adoption of an official morality, i.e., against legal moralism. It need not oppose all legal moralism, but, on this reading, it opposes the attempt to dictate to women which moral beliefs, personal ideals, goals, and standards should govern their choices regarding pregnancy and childbearing.

Abortion: State Interests

What is the state interest in banning abortions? Any number of potential state interests might be imagined, from encouraging population growth to discouraging illicit sexual behavior; but neither of these, nor any like them, were taken seriously by the Court in Roe.

The only state interest which was given prominence in the opinion was that of protecting potential life. This was the interest which took precedence over the woman's right of privacy after viability. This part of Roe, however, remains wholly inscrutable to many commentators, including this one. It is not clear why the state should have this interest at all (given the lack of any need to spur population growth), and in any case would seem to be just as strong during the early stages of pregnancy (or even before conception) as it is toward the end.

The most significant feature of *Roe* in this regard is the state interest which it disavowed, that of preventing harm to others. The apparent rationale for the antiabortion laws of the past was the Harm Principle, with the harm in question being the death visited upon the fetus during abortion. *Roe* v. *Wade* rejected this position. Yet it did not put the privacy interest of the pregnant woman before the interests of the developing fetus. In keeping with its refusal to accept Texas's definition of human life, it refused to consider the fetus's interests at all.

At the same time, the Court recognized the importance of this issue. In particular, it held that if abortion were to be viewed as involving harm to persons, Ms. Roe's case would "collapse." If the fetus were to be regarded as a person, the pregnant woman's privacy interest would be insufficient to guarantee any right of abortion. In this crucial respect, the Court took a position quite opposed to that embodied in the well-known defense of abortion by Judith Thomson.[13] Thomson argued that women had the right to terminate unwanted pregnancies even if fetuses were persons, essentially on the ground that the fetus had no automatic claim on the woman's body.

Thomson's is a much stronger claim on behalf of the woman's privacy (if indeed that is what is at stake in her argument) than is *Roe*'s. Her argument champions the woman's right to control her body over the fetus's full-blown right to life. The right of privacy in *Roe*, in contrast, hardly has an opponent; the obscure "state interest in preserving potential life" is a relative pushover.

Interests in Conflict?

I have listed three interests of the pregnant woman which might be protected under the banner of a right of privacy, and two state interests which might conflict with them. An evaluation of the claims made on behalf of these interests will take us closer to the heart of the privacy argument.

Pregnancy interest   This would seem to be the most clear-cut instance of violation of autonomy privacy. One's body is one's own, if anything is, and the right of property begins with it. Nevertheless, we can raise some troubling questions concerning the role of this interest in the privacy argument for abortion rights.

It is significant, for example, that a ban on abortion does not subject the body to intervention by the state. It is less invasive, in this sense, than the law requiring blood tests before marriage, or vaccination in case of epidemic. Antiabortion laws limit the liberty of the woman to do with her body as she sees fit, but in this respect the laws are far from unique: neither may the woman inject heroin or other dangerous drugs, or seek health care from an unlicensed practitioner. In any case, the Court states that the pregnant woman "cannot be isolated in her privacy" due to the effect of abortion on the fetus; as far as *Roe* was concerned, abortion was less private than these purely self-regarding acts.

This observation provides a reason for caution in simply declaring a right over one's body which must include a right of abortion. But against this there may be grounds for distinguishing abortion from these other dispositions of a woman's body. Abortion is more "important" than, say, the use of recreational drugs, and it is ordinarily more closely linked with success in carrying out major life projects.

For these reasons, the ban on abortion provides a greater burden on a woman who wishes one than some of the other prohibitions regarding the body. Still, it is not wholly clear that the notion of a burden, whether or not unfair, necessarily involves privacy. A special tax, for example, would not. Granted that the burden, being a bodily one, is more obviously related to the "personal"; what then stands out in relation to privacy is that "personal" quality rather than the burden itself. It is significant that the argument concerning the pregnancy interests turned up in one well-known account as an equal-protection argument.[14] If successful, that account would show that a ban on abortion unfairly requires sacrifices of women which are never required of men; but this does not invoke the notion of a privacy right.

A more fundamental objection to linking the pregnancy interest to rights of privacy is that the pregnancy interest is not, in many cases, the important one—important, that is, to the woman herself. The principle reason for desiring abortion in many (I suspect most) cases is that of not bearing a child: that is, not being a parent at that time; or, if adoption is considered, of not bringing a child into the world, to coexist without acquaintance.

The claim, then, is that many women seek abortions not primarily because they wish not to be pregnant but because they do not wish to become biological and/or social parents. This supposition is, I repeat, one which can be settled by empirical research. If it is true, then the pregnancy interest loses much of its significance. Even if an argument for protecting the pregnancy interest were successful, and even if it were regarded as a kind of privacy argument, it would in a sense be deprived of its point. Though the woman would have a right not to be burdened by pregnancy, she would assert that right not because she cared so much about that burden, but because she wanted to avoid becoming a parent.

To be sure, this indirect legal path toward securing one's interests is nothing unusual. A property owner may use her property rights to prevent an ugly building to be constructed, even though she may have no particular right to an architecturally beautiful environment. Nor should the exercise of the person's right be denied when done to secure further goals.

Still, if women seeking abortion do not do so primarily to protect the pregnancy interest, the intuitive appeal of the privacy argument would be lost if the privacy claim extended only to that interest. Perhaps the woman's constitutional right would be protected. The key moral issue, however, is the degree to which the privacy argument succeeds in protecting the other two "privacy" interests independently of the pregnancy interest.

The several privacy interests are mutually involved in many, if not most, attempts to secure abortions. But they may be considered separately for analytical purposes. And the issues are sharply separated in practice under certain unusual conditions. In embryo transfer, for example, the embryo is removed from the woman who became pregnant and is placed in the womb of another woman, who continues the pregnancy and bears the child. In the not-too-distant future, there may exist an artificial womb capable of sustaining fetal life from just after conception all the way to term. It would then be possible for a woman wishing not to be pregnant to arrange to have the fetus removed from her body to the artificial womb. These actions would protect the pregnancy interest just as surely as does abortion. If the pregnancy interest is all that is at stake, the woman will not want or seek to prevent the fetus's transfer to the artificial womb. If, on the other hand, the primary interest is the family planning interest, then the disposal of the fetus after removal from the woman's body becomes the key issue. My guess is that the latter will ordinarily be the case. If so, a privacy argument which proceeds from the pregnancy interest will not support the action which is most urgently desired.

Family planning interest The case for linking this interest with rights of privacy is more tenuous. To be sure, the family planning interest is a strong one; and it generally falls within the realm of the "personal" and the private. The question is whether it is protected by a right of privacy. In the case of offspring that are acknowledged persons, the family planning interest certainly provides no right of termination of life to either parent. No woman should be empowered to direct physicians to end the life of a small child, for example, simply because the woman no longer wishes to be a parent; nor should the father have this right. The family planning interest, then, is not secured by a right of privacy if the planning requires the killing of persons. Here we are merely restating the remark made in *Roe* concerning the dependence of Ms. Roe's case upon the finding that fetuses are not to count as persons.

Moral autonomy interest Would the state violate a woman's privacy interest by ascribing to fetuses the status of person? It is this aspect of antiabortion laws that Professor Tribe identified as an establishment of religion. His argument proceeds from the observation that views on fetal personhood are propounded by various faiths as dogma. However, this approach fails for the simple reason that sentiments underlying a given view on fetal personhood, including that which regards fetuses as persons from the moment of conception, may be and sometimes are wholly secular.

Professor Richards's analysis, in his contribution to this volume, corrects this defect. He urges a broadened interpretation of the language prohibiting an establishment of religion, according to which the state's neutrality would extend to what we might call the "spiritual" as well as the narrowly religious. If he is right, then the state should be proscribed from establishing an official morality, whether that morality is secular or religious in its origin. It is in this respect that antiabortion laws might be said to violate the moral autonomy interest of women, and therefore to violate privacy.

However, Richards's argument does not fit comfortably in this harness. A ban on abortion based on an ascription of personhood to fetuses would violate a right of privacy possessed by women no more than the ban on slavery violated such a right on the part of slaveowners. There does seem to be a sense in which the state interferes with moral autonomy in such rulings, but this particular kind of intrusion (as contrasted with, say, the denial of the pregnancy interest) is visited on the population-at-large. A ban on abortion would in this respect be interpretable as run-of-the-mill legal moralism (at most) rather than as a special intrusion into the privacy of pregnant women.

The Tribe-Richards argument speaks directly to the privacy argument, but at a different locus. Its most natural use is in determining the proper scope of the Harm Principle. The Court, as we have seen, was prepared to completely subordinate the woman's right of privacy to the Harm Principle; if it had recognized the fetus as a person, privacy would not have been protected. State definitions of personhood, then, determine the scope of that principle—and, simultaneously, that of privacy. If the state recognized fetuses as persons, the right of privacy would not include a right of abortion.

If this judgment is correct, the importance of privacy in settling the outcome of the abortion problem is wholly dependent upon our definition of personhood. The reason that arguments like those of Tribe and Richards support the privacy argument is that they give it some scope. Unless the state is warded off (e.g., through arguments like Richards's) from defining personhood, the privacy argument fails. Our assessment of the privacy argument, then, leads us to an examination of the construal of state definitions of personhood as involving legal moralism.

Personhood: Objectivity and Legal Moralism

Given that *Roe*'s privacy argument (and the outcome of the decision itself) was to turn in large part on the matter of the fetus's personhood, the Supreme Court's understanding of the nature of that issue was of key significance. It had several choices to make. Either the fetus's personhood was "objectively" (in some suitable sense of this term) decidable, or not. If so, the fetus was objectively a person or objectively a nonperson. And in either case, the burden of proof of the fetus's status could be placed on the state, or it could be placed on Ms. Roe.

The Court refused to uphold Texas's finding that the fetus is a person. Wertheimer, in his contribution to this volume, suggests that *Roe* also refrained from ruling that the fetus objectively lacked personhood (indeed, that this lack of objective answer dictated the conclusion of the opinion). And the Court certainly placed the burden of proof upon the state.

In doing so, it gave the high ground to the pro-choice side. Ms. Roe did not have to prove anything concerning the fetus's status as a person, and she would win even if the state could prove that the pro-choice forces' denial of fetal personhood was merely a subjective opinion or feeling. As construed by *Roe* v. *Wade*, then, abortion rights are mandated by a constitutional right of privacy unless the state could demonstrate that the fetus's status as a person was an objective truth.

This was a heavy burden to place on the state, and it is not surprising that the Court, in its review of centuries of debate, found the state's case lacking. Nevertheless, *Roe* is not the last word on this matter. In my view, the Court's discussion of the nature of the personhood issue was too cursory and invites extended discussion. An opportunity for such an investigation arose seven years later when the right-to-life forces introduced a bill in Congress which undertook the Court's implicit challenge. Their "Human Life Statute" claimed that the personhood of the fetus was objectively determinable; it was scientific fact; and the fact was that personhood began at conception.

The Human Life Statute Construed As a Challenge to *Roe*

The thesis of those supporting the Human Life Statute was that fetal personhood, from the moment of conception, is a matter of scientific fact; governmental affirmation of the status of fetuses as persons is no more than acceptance of the assurances of scientific experts. Accordingly, the state neither establishes religion nor any official morality in treating fetuses as persons, even though such treatment implies at a minimum that destructive abortion is not justified on grounds of privacy (construed as the family-planning interest).

Though the Human Life Statute seems at this writing to be destined for oblivion, and indeed was not taken very seriously at the time except as a dubious political expedient, its thesis is consequential. If sustained, it would threaten to undermine the claim of both the moral autonomy and the family-planning interests as bases for abortion rights. It may have more interest in prompting a theoretical argument than it did as a political phenomenon or legal ploy, and as such deserves examination in this essay. Indeed, I wish to argue that the Human Life Statute presents a quite plausible claim, and that the derision with which it was greeted by scholars proceeded in certain respects from mistaken premises. In the end my verdict on that claim is negative, but its rejection can be shown to require the sacrifice of some treasured premises on the part of "pro-choice" advocates.

The Human Life Statute represented a legal strategy for banning abortions. It consisted of little more than an affirmation that science has demonstrated that human life is present from the moment of conception (and that all human lives are persons). The statute would require only a majority in the Congress, unlike the proposed constitutional amendments, and would not have to be ratified by the states. Its provisions would permit the extension to fetuses of the Constitution's Equal Protection Clause. Individual states would then be free to pass laws banning abortion.

The key question, of course, was whether the statute would, in light of *Roe* v. *Wade*, survive review by the Supreme Court. According to the law review article which inspired the statute, the Court would, or should, recognize Congress's legitimate role as fact-finder. The problem is what sort of "fact" the definition of life and personhood constitutes. The testimony solicited by the statute's backers portrayed the statute's thesis as a report from the laboratory. Eminent scientists detailed the biochemical processes at work in the fertilized egg and stressed the completeness of the embryo's genetic complement.

The ensuing debate, carried on in the popular press, the pages of *Science*, and elsewhere, did not engage the issue at this level. The scientific testimony was not challenged. Instead, critics denied that the embryologists and geneticists were expert in determining the beginnings of human life. Individual scholars and prestigious bodies, including most of the membership of the National Academy of Sciences, declared that definition to be a matter of personal, moral, or religious belief, and not a matter for scientific exploration or demonstration. Accordingly, those scientists testifying as experts in favor of the statute were viewed as exceeding their authority; their remarks were indicative of the sentiments of a few individuals on a question of sentiment, and nothing more.

This rebuttal was imported into the official testimony by the only witness critical of the statute to be included in the first, and most visible, group of experts (indeed, even his appearance would not have occurred without intensive political maneuvering by the statute's senatorial opponents). The testimony of this witness, Leon Rosenberg, chairman of Yale's genetics department, is of considerable interest, for it went farther than other commentaries in focusing the charge that the other experts had paraded their own personal values as objective science.[15]

Rosenberg stated that he knew of no scientific data which could be used to determine when human life began. The issue was not whether he lacked access to data available to the scientists testifying in favor of the bill; it was what to count as "science." Rosenberg proposed a criterion: an issue was a scientific one if it could be settled by observation or experiment. Insofar as this had not been done in the case of defining human life, and in that no determinative observations or experiments had been proposed, Rosenberg concluded that the definition lay outside his expertise and that of his colleagues.

The fate of the privacy argument for abortion rights, then, had come to depend in part on the resolution of an issue in philosophy of science: the definition not of personhood or human life but of science itself. Rosenberg's testimony attracted a great deal of favorable comment. Indeed, numerous observers portrayed it as successfully ripping away the façade of scientific objectivity from the statute and its antiabortion backers. The statute did, after all, merely assert one set of personal convictions, and its passage would, in this view, constitute legal moralism.

Yet a closer examination of Rosenberg's argument does not lend comfort to the pro-choice side. A problem with his rule for distinguishing science from personal conviction is that it threatens to disenfranchise a good deal of orthodox science. In particular, it is ill-suited to judging the enterprise of scientific classification. The periodic table of the elements, for example, is an achievement of the science of chemistry. But its scientific validity is predicated upon its scientific utility, the help it offers in formulating generalizations and laws and in fostering inquiry. There is no observation or experiment which can "prove" the table to be correct, but that is no argument against counting it as science. And similar conclusions apply to other broad classifications and categories of mainline science.

One question of importance for the abortion debate, then, is whether the classification of fetal life as "human life" might deserve similar status as a scientific fact. I do not want to attempt a final judgment on this matter in the present essay. The challenge, however, is clear. If categories such as "gold" and "whale" are defined by science, why should science be ruled out as a source of a definition of human life? Why should "living individual of the species *Homo sapiens*" be incapable of being defined by scientific criteria meeting the usual tests of scientific utility?

If these questions meet no satisfactory reply, we may conclude that although some scientists may in fact merely be voicing personal, moral, or religious conviction in testifying that human life begins at conception, their expertise cannot be denied on principle. The definition of human life, i.e., of which entities are to count as individual living *Homo sapiens*, is the sort of issue science *might* settle.

Whether science *does* define human life (in this sense), however, depends on the answer to a further question: Does such a definition have the needed scientific utility? A positive answer may be indicated in the case of species about which we have less powerful feelings. It is at least imaginable that a definition of life (and its beginning) for fruit flies might be useful: geneticists count the distribution of genotypes in successive generations, and must know whether to count unhatched fertilized eggs. It may be that a definition of fruit fly life as beginning from conception would be standard in genetic science. Or it could be that such a definition would have no particular utility, and thus would not be enshrined as science.

If a definition of human life possessed the necessary scientific utility, then it would count as a scientific "fact"; otherwise not. Either way, however, it would be within the province of science, and not necessarily a matter of personal, moral, or religious belief. And scientists would be the appropriate experts to consult, for the utility of such a definition is a scientific question, and one which only scientists can answer.

The Human Life Statute is not yet vindicated by these observations, but the chief argument of its critics is put into question. And that argument, which construes the status of the fetus as a question which the state must not attempt to answer, lies at the heart of the defense of abortion rights by the privacy argument.

Biology and Personhood

My argument concerning science and the definition of human life may seem to have an obvious flaw: personhood is not necessarily a biological concept. The issue is not whether fetuses are alive, according to this argument; they are. Nor need we question that they are of the species *Homo sapiens*. "Personhood," in this view, is a moral category; it is of little importance whether scientists can produce a scientific definition of "living individual *Homo sapiens*." "Personhood" is a social, or perhaps a psychological category, not a biological one. Indeed, nonhumans, such as advanced computers or aliens, may someday be encountered who would have to be regarded as persons; and they have no human biology at all. The most that the argument thus far advanced can demonstrate, according to this objection, is that *if* the important sense of "person" simply is the biological category of *Homo sapiens,* then a state definition of human life might be recognition of fact and hence in no sense any abridgment of privacy. If, however, "person" is a category distinct from the biological one, the privacy argument remains unscathed. I believe that this objection is right, and will argue for it, though only briefly, at the conclusion of the paper.

I also want to claim, however, that most of those who might endorse this objection—found among the ranks of those favoring freedom of choice over abortion—*also endorse premises which imply its negation.* In other words, given other claims of the pro-choice side, this objection cannot be consistently advanced. Either the objection must be foregone, or the other claims abandoned. I believe that the latter is the most reasonable course. I will attempt to identify these conflicting claims and to measure the conceptual cost of achieving consistency.

My suggestion is that pro-choice advocates, whether or not they realize it, generally trade on definitions of personhood which are biological. Thus they cannot meet the argument of the Human Life Statute by declaring the biological definition of human life irrelevant to the abortion issue.

This thesis needs to be laid out in a series of steps:

1. *Pro-choice advocates generally believe that the onset of fetal personhood occurs sometime after conception.* There is no logical necessity in this association of views, but there is a definite congeniality. Persons simply cannot be treated as fetuses are in abortions, and pro-choice advocates who believe that fetuses are persons from the start are bound to feel the tension between these positions.

2. *Most of the developmental milestones which are most commonly proposed as the beginning of personhood have significance only if understood as marking the beginning of biological personhood, i.e., as the moment at which a fetus becomes a living individual* Homo sapiens. A list of the usual milestones will demonstrate the point. Viability, the most common, is an inscrutable criterion; but surely the suggestion is that of an organism which is *biologically* self-sufficient and independent of the mother's body. Though moral significance may be attached to it, the milestone is one of physical development (and of the development of medical technique) and does not involve the

achievement of any particular social or psychological status. The same is true of birth, which is the latest milestone ordinarily encountered among pro-choice advocates, and of heartbeat and quickening, which are the earliest.

It is true that some pro-choice advocates have argued that the beginning of personhood occurs when brain activity begins; and others have dated it from the appearance of a self-concept in the young child. These are indeed psychological milestones, and my argument does not apply to them. But my sense is that most pro-choice advocates who have declared themselves on the matter have settled on one of the biological milestones.

3. *The choice of a developmental milestone as the beginning of biological personhood is* not *a matter of personal, religious, or moral conviction.* According to a philosophical doctrine known as the "division of semantic labor," the definition of certain kinds of terms in ordinary linguistic communities is literally left to the experts. What we mean by "water," for example, is *whatever water experts say water is;* the same with gold, whales, and integers. The experts define water independently of the various and sundry subjective notions of water which may exist in the minds of different members of the community; water has a real essence (its atomic structure), and this defines it; and this is known to the experts (if there are any experts).

Similarly in the case of biological personhood—that is, if the tentative analysis of that concept's claim to scientific status is sustained. Though different members of the community may "mean" different things by the term "person," even when using it to refer to the biological category, there would, if the argument I have advanced is correct, be but one *correct* definition. Informed scientists would know it, and others not. If science supported a definition of individual living *Homo sapiens* which marked its onset from conception, then people who regarded it as beginning at viability, or at birth, or at some other developmental point would be simply and flatly wrong.

4. *Dating personhood from viability, or from birth, or from one of the other milestones which have at most biological significance, then, requires a bow to scientific authority. There is no possibility of dismissing the biologists by mention of the psychological or social character of personhood, for the choice of milestone has betrayed a lack of endorsement in that understanding of the personhood concept.*

5. *If my tentative argument concerning biology's authority is correct, and if biology does in fact support a definition of human life as be-*

ginning at conception (both are admittedly large assumptions), then the pro-choice position crumbles once the biological conception of personhood is adopted. The thesis of the Human Life Statute would be endorsed by the implications of the pro-choice advocate's own premises. And it follows from that thesis, together with common views of how persons ought to be treated, that abortion should not be permitted in most circumstances.

Women's Privacy and the Concept of Personhood

I have tentatively advanced an argument which purports to show that the opinion even of pro-choice advocates contains premises which support an antiabortion position which may be surprisingly invulnerable to key elements of the privacy argument. But pro-choice advocates need not interpret this argument, even if its many premises were all accepted, as requiring their capitulation to the antiabortion side. It does suggest, however, that the premises which may undermine the pro-choice position be abandoned.

Concretely, this requires that those defending on privacy grounds the woman's right to choose abortion abandon that fidelity to the biological conception of personhood which their views on abortion may imply. A pro-choice position on abortion requires, if the argument is correct, the moral position that developing humans do not become persons until (and unless) they become persons in some suitable social or psychological sense.

This requirement does not sound difficult—until the alternative conception of personhood is explicitly characterized. At that point, moral intuition may balk. For not just any social or psychological conception of personhood will do. The choice cannot be purely arbitrary, but must cohere with the basic premises of our moral outlook. The organisms to be accorded the status of person must have properties which signal that they deserve the treatment accorded to beings with that status. These properties will not be merely biological; and if they are psychological ones, they may not appear in the developing human for some time—in particular, until some time *after* birth.

We are led, then, to a dilemma which has bedeviled pro-choice advocates all along. If conception and other biological milestones of development are rejected as indicators of personhood, and psychological traits serve instead, the definition must take account of the fact that fetuses and infants may not have enough psychology. And this raises the bogey of infanticide. Philosophers who have defended psychological definitions of personhood have had to face up to this difficulty. Some have simply endorsed infanticide, undoubtedly at the cost of being rejected by all but a few unflinching colleagues. Others have conjured up reasons for disapproving of infanticide independent of any wrong done to the infant, but their arguments often appear to be rationalizations.

Fear of being portrayed as advocates of parents' rights to commit infanticide, then, may cause some pro-choice advocates to balk at these conclusions. Perhaps certain of the premises of my argument can be rejected. If so, fine: I do not like the direction which the argument took, and would be glad to be convinced that it is mistaken.

If a refutation is not forthcoming, however, the privacy argument seems to require a major change in popular thinking about what constitutes a person. This change, as with many revisions in fundamental moral categories, produces some highly unintuitive and unpleasant implications.

This outcome is easier to contemplate, however, if we keep in mind the unintuitive and unpleasant implications of rival views. The position of the Human Life Statute, for example, which accords the status of person to fertilized eggs, seems committed to absurd policies of fetal rescue. Two-thirds of all fertilized eggs are spontaneously aborted, and if they are to be treated on a par with other persons we should redirect almost all our research and treatment funds from heart disease and other health problems of those with few years to live. The Senate testimony and questioning produced a host of other absurdities as well.[16]

Continued debate, then, may sharpen the public's sense of the conflict of arguments as well as the conflict of positions. If none of the arguments proves to be in perfect harmony with ordinary morality, some of the less attractive implications of the pro-choice premises may be easier to admit to.

Conclusion

What, then, are we to think of the privacy argument for rights of abortion? Our first observation must be that the privacy argument, especially as expressed in *Roe* v. *Wade*, is very difficult to make out. The difficulty is compounded by the lack of clarity in the notion of privacy itself.

The chief difficulties lie, however, in determining the precise sense in which rights of abortion are to be understood as protecting the privacy interest. In this essay I have suggested three distinct points of contact between privacy and abortion. The pregnancy interest, I have suggested, may merit legal protection and serve as a vehicle for protection of other interests. The family-planning interest is less deserving, unless the status of a fetus is determined not to be that of a person.

Finally, state action in the determination of that status might itself be considered to bear on the woman's privacy in abridging her interest in moral autonomy; alternatively, it might constitute an unwelcome and burdensome form of legal moralism in reducing the scope of her right to privacy by providing an application for the Harm Principle. But this would not be so if the definition of personhood were a question of biological science, for this would, in important respects, remove the issue from the moral realm. The thesis of the Human Life Statute, which claimed scientific status, is, I have argued, much more plausible than has generally been acknowledged. If it ultimately fails, its rejection may require revision of some important elements in the typical pro-choice view of the morality of abortion, bringing changes which are intuitively unpleasant and unlikely to win over new adherents. Yet such is the moral and intellectual difficulty of the debate over abortion that neither side is entitled to escape substantial discomfort.

Appendix: Selected Supreme Court Decisions Concerning Abortion and Contraception

City of Akron v. Akron Center for Reproductive Health, _____ U.S. _____, 103 S. Ct. 2481, 76 L.Ed.2d 687 (1983) struck down a city ordinance which required: (1) that all second-trimester abortions be performed in a hospital; (2) that a minor obtain written consent from one parent, or a court order prior to obtaining an abortion; (3) that a woman be recited "a lengthy and inflexible list of information" (including a constitutionally impermissible statement that "the unborn child is a human life from the moment of conception"); and additional requirements.

Bellotti v. Baird, 443 U.S. 622, 99 S. Ct. 3035, 61 L.Ed.2d 797 (1979) struck down a Massachusetts statute which required an unmarried minor to obtain the consent of her parents, prior to obtaining an abortion.

Carey v. Population Services International, 431 U.S. 678, 97 S. Ct. 2010, 52 L.Ed.2d 675 (1977) struck down, on the grounds of privacy, a New York statute restricting minors' access to contraceptives.

Colautti v. Franklin, 439 U.S. 379, 99 S. Ct. 675, 58 L.Ed.2d 596 (1979) struck down, on the grounds of vagueness, a Pennsylvania law which subjected doctors to criminal penalties for failing to use the abortion technique most likely to result in live birth at the stage of pregnancy when the fetus "is viable" or "may be viable."

Doe v. Bolton, 410 U.S. 179, 93 S. Ct. 739, 35 L.Ed.2d 201 (1973) decided with *Roe v. Wade* (Chap. 1, above), struck down Georgia's "reform" criminal abortion statute which provided that women could obtain abortions for a number of health reasons.

Eisenstadt v. Baird, 405 U.S. 438, 92 S. Ct. 1029, 31 L.Ed.2d 349 (1972) struck down a Massachusetts law which prohibited the distribution of contraceptives except to married persons by prescription.

Griswold v. Connecticut, 381 U.S. 479, 85 S. Ct. 1678, 14 L.Ed.2d 510 (1965) struck down a Connecticut statute which made it a crime to obtain contraceptives, or for doctors to counsel their use.

H. L. v. Matheson, 450 U.S. 398, 101 S. Ct. 1164, 67 L.Ed.2d 388 (1981) upheld a Utah statute which requires doctors to notify a minor's parents before the minor could obtain an abortion, if the minor is dependent and living with parents and the minor does not provide a reason why notification would not be in her best interest.

Maher v. *Roe*, 432 U.S. 464, 97 S. Ct. 2376, 53 L.Ed.2d 484 (1977) *Beal* v. *Doe*, 432 U.S. 438, 97 S. Ct. 2366, 53 L.Ed.2d 464 (1977) upheld a Connecticut regulation and a Pennsylvania statute which limited state medical financial assistance to "medically necessary abortions."

McRae v. *Harris*, 448 U.S. 297, 100 S. Ct. 2671, 65 L.Ed.2d 784 (1980) upheld the constitutionality of a congressional statute which prohibited the use of federal Medicaid funds to pay for abortions in almost all circumstances.

Planned Parenthood of Central Missouri v. *Danforth*, 428 U.S. 52, 96 S. Ct. 2831, 49 L.Ed.2d 788 (1976) struck down a Missouri statute which required a married woman to obtain her husband's consent prior to obtaining an abortion, and a similar requirement that an unmarried minor obtain the consent of one parent prior to obtaining an abortion.

Planned Parenthood of Kansas City v. *Ashcroft*, _____ U.S. _____, 103 S. Ct. 2517, 76 L.Ed.2d 733 (1983) decided with *Akron Center for Reproductive Health*, struck down a Missouri statute which required that all second-trimester abortions be performed in hospitals; and upheld provisions of the Missouri statute which required: (1) a second physician attend the abortion of any viable fetus; (2) a pathology report for all abortions; and (3) that a minor obtain parental consent or a judicial authorization prior to obtaining an abortion.

Roe v. *Wade*, 410 U.S. 113, 93 S. Ct. 705, 35 L.Ed.2d 147 (1973) is excerpted in Chapter 1, above,

Poelker v. *Doe*, 432 U.S. 519, 97 S. Ct. 2371, 53 L.Ed.2d 528 (1977) decided with *Maher* v. *Roe* and *Beal* v. *Doe*, upheld the refusal of a public hospital in St. Louis, Missouri, to perform abortions.

Simopoulos v. *Virginia*, _____ U.S. _____, 103 S. Ct. 2532, 76 L.Ed.2d 755 (1983) decided with *Akron Center for Reproductive Health and Planned Parenthood of Kansas* v. *Ashcroft*, affirmed the criminal conviction of a Virginia physician for performing a second-trimester abortion outside a licensed hospital. (The court noted that the Virginia statute's definition of hospital was constitutionally different from the definitions in *Akron* and *Ashcroft*.)

==

Notes

Introduction

1 Judith J. Thomson, "A Defense of Abortion," *Philosophy and Public Affairs*
   1 (1971): 47–66.
2 D. H. Regan, "Rewriting *Roe* v. *Wade*," *Michigan Law Review* 77 (1979):
   1569.

Roe v. *Wade*, 410 U.S. 113 (1973)

The notes to this chapter correspond to those of the original decision. Lacunae
are noted in those instances where the editors have deleted the citations. No citations are given for those portions of the decision not reprinted here, and all the
notes have been omitted from the dissenting opinion of William Rehnquist.

1 "Article 1191. Abortion
   "If any person shall designedly administer to a pregnant woman or knowingly
   procure to be administered with her consent any drug or medicine, or shall
   use towards her any violence or means whatever externally or internally applied, and thereby procure an abortion, he shall be confined in the penitentiary not less than two nor more than five years; if it be done without her
   consent, the punishment shall be doubled. By 'abortion' is meant that the life
   of the fetus or embryo shall be destroyed in the woman's womb or that a
   premature birth thereof be caused.
   "Art. 1192. Furnishing the means
   "Whoever furnishes the means for procuring an abortion knowing the purpose intended is guilty as an accomplice.
   "Art. 1193. Attempt at abortion
   "If the means used shall fail to produce an abortion, the offender is nevertheless guilty of an attempt to produce abortion, provided it be shown that
   such means were calculated to produce that result, and shall be fined not less
   than one hundred nor more than one thousand dollars.
   "Art. 1194. Murder in producing abortion

"If the death of the mother is occasioned by an abortion so produced or by an attempt to effect the same it is murder.

"Art. 1196. By medical advice

"Nothing in this chapter applies to an abortion procured or attempted by medical advice for the purpose of saving the life of the mother."

The foregoing Articles, together with Art. 1195, compose Chapter 9 of Title 15 of the Penal Code.

Article 1195, not attacked here, reads:

"Art. 1195. Destroying unborn child

"Whoever shall during parturition of the mother destroy the vitality or life in a child in a state of being born and before actual birth, which child would otherwise have been born alive, shall be confined in the penitentiary for life or for not less than five years."

4   The name is a pseudonym.

8   A. Castiglioni, A History of Medicine 84 (2d ed. 1947), E. Krumbhaar, translator and editor (hereinafter Castiglioni).

9   J. Ricci, The Genealogy of Gynaecology 52, 84, 113, 149 (2d ed. 1950) (hereinafter Ricci); L. Lader, Abortion 75–77 (1966) (hereinafter Lader); K. Niswander, Medical Abortion Practices in the United States, in Abortion and the Law 37, 38–40 (D. Smith ed. 1967); G. Williams, The Sanctity of Life and the Criminal Law 148 (1957) (hereinafter Williams); J. Noonan, An Almost Absolute Value in History, in The Morality of Abortion 1, 3–7 (J. Noonan ed. 1970) (hereinafter Noonan); Quay, Justifiable Abortion— Medical and Legal Foundations (pt. 2), 49 Geo. L. J. 395, 406–422 (1961) (hereinafter Quay).

10   L. Edelstein, The Hippocratic Oath 10 (1943) (hereinafter Edelstein). But see Castiglioni 227.

11   Edelstein 12; Ricci 113–114, 118–119; Noonan 5.

12   Edelstein 13–14.

13   Castiglioni 148.

14   *Id.*, at 154.

15   Edelstein 3.

16   *Id.*, at 12, 15–18.

17   *Id.*, at 18; Lader 76.

18   Edelstein 63.

19   *Id.*, at 64.

20   Dorland's Illustrated Medical Dictionary 1261 (24th ed. 1965).

21   E. Coke, Institutes III *50; 1 W. Hawkins, Pleas of the Crown, c. 31 § 16 (4th ed. 1762); 1 W. Blackstone, Commentaries *129–130; M. Hale, Pleas of the Crown, 433 (1st Amer. ed. 1847). For discussions of the role of the quickening concept in English common law, see Lader 78, Noonan 223–226; Means, The Law of New York Concerning Abortion and the Status of the Foetus, 1664–1968: A Case of Cessation of Constitutionality (pt. 1), 14 N.Y.L.F. 411, 418–428 (1968) (hereinafter Means I); Stern, Abortion: Reform and the Law, 59 J.Crim. L. C. & P. S. 84 (1968) (hereinafter Stern); Quay 430–432; Williams 152.

22   Early philosophers believed that the embryo or fetus did not become formed

and begin to live until at least 40 days after conception for a male, and 80 to 90 days for a female. See, for example, Aristotle, Hist. Anim. 7.3.583b; Gen. Anim. 2.3.736, 2.5.741; Hippocrates, Lib. de Nat. Puer., No. 10. Aristotle's thinking derived from his three-stage theory of life: vegetable, animal, rational. The vegetable stage was reached at conception, the animal at "animation," and the rational soon after live birth. This theory, together with the 40/80 day view, came to be accepted by early Christian thinkers.

The theological debate was reflected in the writings of St. Augustine, who made a distinction between *embryo inanimatus*, not yet endowed with a soul, and *embryo animatus*. He may have drawn upon Exodus 21:22. At one point, however, he expressed the view that human powers cannot determine the point during fetal development at which the critical change occurs. See Augustine, De Origine Animae 4.4 (Pub. Law 44.527). See also W. Reany, The Creation of the Human Soul, c. 2 and 83–86 (1932); Huser, The Crime of Abortion in Canon Law 15 (Catholic Univ. of America, Canon Law Studies No. 162, Washington, D.C., 1942).

Galen, in three treatises related to embryology, accepted the thinking of Aristotle and his followers. Quay 426–427. Later, Augustine on abortion was incorporated by Gratian into the Decretum, published about 1140. Decretum Magistri Gratiani 2.32.2.7 to 2.32.2.10, in 1 Corpus Juris Canonici 1122, 1123 (A. Friedburg, 2d ed. 1879). This Decretal and the Decretals that followed were recognized as the definitive body of canon law until the new Code of 1917.

For discussions of the canon-law treatment, see Means I, pp. 411–412; Noonan 20–26; Quay 426–430; see also J. Noonan, Contraception: A History of Its Treatment by the Catholic Theologians and Canonists 18–29 (1965).

23 Bracton took the position that abortion by blow or poison was homicide "if the foetus be already formed and animated, and particularly if it be animated." 2 H. Bracton, De Legibus et Consuetudinibus Angliae 279 (T. Twiss ed. 1879), or, as a later translation puts it, "if the foetus is already formed or quickened, especially if it is quickened," 2 H. Bracton, On the Laws and Customs of England 341 (S. Thorne ed. 1968). See Quay 431; see also 2 Fleta 60–61 (Book 1, c. 23) (Selden Society ed. 1955).

24 E. Coke, Institutes III *50.

25 1 W. Blackstone, Commentaries *129–130.

26 Means, The Phoenix of Abortional Freedom: Is a Penumbral or Ninth Amendment Right About to Arise from the Nineteenth-Century Legislative Ashes of a Fourteenth-Century Common-Law Liberty?, 17 N.Y.L.F. 335 (1971) (hereinafter Means II). The author examines the two principal precedents cited marginally by Coke, both contrary to his dictum, and traces the treatment of these and other cases by earlier commentators. He concludes that Coke, who himself participated as an advocate in an abortion case in 1601, may have intentionally misstated the law. The author even suggests a reason: Coke's strong feelings against abortion, coupled with his determination to assert common-law (secular) jurisdiction to assess penalties for an offense that traditionally had been an exclusively ecclesiastical or canon-law crime. See also Lader 78–79, who notes that some scholars doubt that the common

law ever was applied to abortion; that the English ecclesiastical courts seem to have lost interest in the problem after 1527; and that the preamble to the English legislation of 1803, 43 Geo. 3, c. 58, § 1, referred to in the text, *infra*, at 136, states that "no adequate means have been hitherto provided for the prevention and punishment of such offenses."

27 *Commonwealth* v. *Bangs*, 9 Mass. 387, 388 (1812); *Commonwealth* v. *Parker*, 50 Mass. (9 Metc.) 263, 265–266 (1845); *State* v. *Cooper*, 22 N.J.L. 52, 58 (1849); *Abrams* v. *Foshee*, 3 Iowa 274, 278–280 (1856); *Smith* v. *Gaffard*, 31 Ala. 45, 51 (1857); *Mitchell* v. *Commonwealth*, 78 Ky. 204, 210 (1879); *Eggart* v. *State*, 40 Fla. 527, 532, 25 So. 144, 145 (1898); *State* v. *Alcorn*, 7 Idaho 599, 606, 64 P. 1014, 1016 (1901); *Edwards* v. *State*, 79 Neb. 251, 252, 112 N.W. 611, 612 (1907); *Gray* v. *State*, 77 Tex. Cr. R. 221, 224, 178 S.W. 337, 338 (1915); *Miller* v. *Bennett*, 190 Va. 162, 169, 56 S.E.2d 217, 221 (1949). *Contra, Mills* v. *Commonwealth*, 13 Pa. 631, 633 (1850); *State* v. *Slagle*, 83 N.C. 630, 632 (1880).

28 See *Smith* v. *State*, 33 Me. 48, 55 (1851); *Evans* v. *People*, 49 N.Y. 86, 88 (1872); *Lamb* v. *State*, 67 Md. 524, 533, 10 A. 208 (1887).

29 Conn. Stat., Tit. 20, § 14 (1821).

30 Conn. Pub. Acts, c. 71, § 1 (1860).

31 N.Y. Rev. Stat., pt. 4, c. 1, Tit. 2, Art. 1, § 9, p. 661, and Tit. 6, § 21, p. 694 (1829).

32 Act of Jan. 20, 1840, § 1, set forth in 2 H. Gammel, Laws of Texas 177–178 (1898); see *Grigsby* v. *Reib*, 105 Tex. 597, 600, 153 S.W. 1124, 1125 (1913).

33 The early statutes are discussed in Quay 435–438. See also Lader 85–88; Stern 85–86; and Means II 375–376.

34 Criminal abortion statutes in effect in the States as of 1961, together with historical statutory development and important judicial interpretations of the state statutes, are cited and quoted in Quay 447–520. See Comment, A Survey of the Present Statutory and Case Law on Abortion: The Contradictions and the Problems, 1972 U. Ill. L.F. 177, 179, classifying the abortion statutes and listing 25 states as permitting abortion only if necessary to save or preserve the mother's life.

35 Ala. Code, Tit. 14, § 9 (1958); D.C. Code Ann. § 22-201 (1967).

36 Mass. Gen. Laws Ann., c. 272, § 19 (1970); N. J. Stat. Ann. § 2A:87-1 (1969); Pa. Stat. Ann., Tit. 18, §§ 4718, 4719 (1963).

37 Fourteen States have adopted some form of the ALI statute. . . . The precise status of criminal abortion laws in some states is made unclear by recent decisions in state and federal courts striking down existing state laws, in whole or in part.

38 "Whereas, Abortion, like any other medical procedure, should not be performed when contrary to the best interests of the patient since good medical practice requires due consideration for the patient's welfare and not mere acquiescence to the patient's demand; and

"Whereas, The standards of sound clinical judgment, which, together with informed patient consent should be determinative according to the merits of each individual case; therefore be it

"RESOLVED, That abortion is a medical procedure and should be performed only by a duly licensed physician and surgeon in an accredited hospital acting only after consultation with two other physicians chosen because of their professional competency and in conformance with standards of good medical practice and the Medical Practice Act of his State; and be it further

"RESOLVED, That no physician or other professional personnel shall be compelled to perform any act which violates his good medical judgment. Neither physician, hospital, nor hospital personnel shall be required to perform any act violative of personally-held moral principles. In these circumstances good medical practice requires only that the physician or other professional personnel withdraw from the case so long as the withdrawal is consistent with good medical practice." Proceedings of the AMA House of Delegates 220 (June 1970).

39   "The Principles of Medical Ethics of the AMA do not prohibit a physician from performing an abortion that is performed in accordance with good medical practice and under circumstances that do not violate the laws of the community in which he practices.

"In the matter of abortions, as of any other medical procedure, the Judicial Council becomes involved whenever there is alleged violation of the Principles of Medical Ethics as established by the House of Delegates."

42   Note omitted.

43   Note omitted.

44   Potts, Postconceptive Control of Fertility, 8 Int'l J. of G. & O. 957, 967 (1970) (England and Wales); Abortion Mortality, 20 Morbidity and Mortality 208, 209 (June 12, 1971) (U.S. Dept. of HEW, Public Health Service) (New York City); Tietze, United States: Therapeutic Abortions, 1963–1968, 59 Studies in Family Planning 5, 7 (1970); Tietze, Mortality with Contraception and Induced Abortion, 45 Studies in Family Planning 6 (1969) (Japan, Czechoslovakia, Hungary); Tietze & Lehfeldt, Legal Abortion in Eastern Europe, 175 J.A.M.A. 1149, 1152 (April 1961). Other sources are discussed in Lader 17–23.

45   See Brief of Amicus National Right to Life Committee; R. Drinan, The Inviolability of the Right to Be Born, in Abortion and the Law 107 (D. Smith ed. 1967); Louisell, Abortion, The Practice of Medicine and the Due Process of Law, 16 U.C.L.A.L.Rev. 233 (1969); Noonan 1.

46   See, e.g., Abele v. Markle, 342 F. Supp. 800 (Conn. 1972), appeal docketed, No. 72-56.

47   See discussions in Means I and Means II.

48   See, e.g., State v. Murphy, 27 N.J.L. 112, 114 (1858).

49   Watson v. State, 9 Tex. App. 237, 244–245 (1880); Moore v. State, 37 Tex. Cr. R. 552, 561, 40 S.W. 287, 290 (1897); Shaw v. State, 73 Tex. Cr. R. 337, 339, 165 S.W. 930, 931 (1914); Fondren v. State, 74 Tex. Cr. R. 552, 557, 169 S.W. 411, 414 (1914); Gray v. State, 77 Tex. Cr. R. 221, 229, 178 S.W. 337, 341 (1915). There is no immunity in Texas for the father who is not married to the mother. Hammett v. State, 84 Tex. Cr. R. 635, 209 S.W. 661 (1919); Thompson v. State (Ct. Crim. App. Tex. 1971), appeal docketed, No. 71-1200.

50   See *Smith* v. *State*, 33 Me. at 55; *In re Vince*, 2 N. J. 443, 450, 67 A.2d 141, 144 (1949). A short discussion of the modern law on this issue is contained in the Comment to the ALI's Model Penal Code § 207.11, at 158 and nn. 35–37 (Tent. Draft No. 9, 1959).

51   Tr. of Oral Rearg. 20–21.

52   Tr. of Oral Rearg. 24.

53   We are not aware that in the taking of any census under this clause, a fetus has ever been counted.

54   When Texas urges that a fetus is entitled to Fourteenth Amendment protection as a person, it faces a dilemma. Neither in Texas nor in any other state are all abortions prohibited. Despite broad proscription, an exception always exists. The exception contained in Art. 1196, for an abortion procured or attempted by medical advice for the purpose of saving the life of the mother, is typical. But if the fetus is a person who is not to be deprived of life without due process of law, and if the mother's condition is the sole determinant, does not the Texas exception appear to be out of line with the Amendment's command?

There are other inconsistencies between Fourteenth Amendment status and the typical abortion statute. It has already been pointed out, no. 49, *supra*, that in Texas the woman is not a principal or an accomplice with respect to an abortion upon her. If the fetus is a person, why is the woman not a principal or an accomplice? Further, the penalty for criminal abortion specified by Art. 1195 is significantly less than the maximum penalty for murder prescribed by Art. 1257 of the Texas Penal Code. If the fetus is a person, may the penalties be different?

55   Note omitted.

56   Edelstein 16.

57   Lader 97–99; D. Feldman, Birth Control in Jewish Law 251–294 (1968). For a stricter view, see I. Jakobovits, Jewish Views on Abortion, in Abortion and the Law 124 (D. Smith ed. 1967).

58   Amicus Brief for the American Ethical Union et al. For the position of the National Council of Churches and of other denominations, see Lader 99–101.

59   L. Hellman & J. Pritchard, Williams Obstetrics 493 (14th ed. 1971); Dorland's Illustrated Medical Dictionary 1689 (24th ed. 1965).

60   Hellman & Pritchard, *supra*, n. 59, at 493.

61   For discussions of the development of the Roman Catholic position, see D. Callahan, Abortion: Law, Choice, and Morality 409–447 (1970); Noonan 1.

62   See Brodie, The New Biology and the Prenatal Child, 9 J. Family L. 391, 397 (1970); Gorney, The New Biology and the Future of Man, 15 U.C.L.A.L. Rev. 273 (1968); Note, Criminal Law—Abortion—The "Morning-After Pill" and Other Pre-Implantation Birth-Control Methods and the Law, 46 Ore. L. Rev. 211 (1967); G. Taylor, The Biological Time Bomb 32 (1968); A. Rosenfeld, The Second Genesis 138–139 (1969); Smith, Through a Test Tube Darkly: Artificial Insemination and the Law, 67 Mich. L. Rev. 127 (1968); Note, Artificial Insemination and the Law, 1968 U.Ill.L.F. 203.

63   W. Prosser, The Law of Torts 335–338 (4th ed. 1971); 2 F. Harper & F. James, The Law of Torts 1028–1031 (1956); Note, 63 Harv. L. Rev. 173 (1949).

64   See cases cited in Prosser, *supra*, n. 63, at 336–338; Annotation, Action for Death of Unborn Child, 15 A.L.R. 3d 992 (1967).

65   Prosser, *supra*, n.63, at 338; Note, The Law and the Unborn Child: The Legal and Logical Inconsistencies, 46 Notre Dame Law, 349, 354–360 (1971).

66   Louisell, Abortion, The Practice of Medicine and the Due Process of Law, 16 U.C.L.A.L.Rev. 233, 235–238 (1969); Note, 56 Iowa L. Rev. 994, 999–1000 (1971); Note, The Law and the Unborn Child, 46 Notre Dame Law, 349, 351–354 (1971).

67   [I]n this opinion we [do not] discuss the father's rights, if any exist in the constitutional context, in the abortion decision. No paternal right has been asserted in either of the cases, and the Texas . . . statute on [its] face take[s] no cognizance of the father. We are aware that some statutes recognize the father under certain circumstances. North Carolina . . . requires written permission for the abortion from the husband when the woman is a married minor, that is, when she is less than 18 years of age; if the woman is an unmarried minor, written permission from the parents is required. We need not now decide whether provisions of this kind are constitutional.

The Legacy of *Roe* v. *Wade*

1   These cases, *City of Akron* v. *Akron Reproductive Health Center*, 103 S. Ct. 2481 (1983); *Planned Parenthood of Kansas City* v. *Ashcroft*, 103 S. Ct. 2517 (1983), and *Simopolous* v. *Virginia*, 103 S. Ct. 2532 (1983) were decided by the Supreme Court on June 15, 1983.

2   The Supreme Court struck down the key provisions of the Akron ordinance: (1) the second trimester hospitalization requirement; (2) the 24-hour waiting period; (3) the mandated statement by the physician; and (4) the parental consent requirement. *City of Akron* v. *Akron Reproductive Health Center*, 103 S. Ct. 2481, 2504 (1983).

   The opinion strongly affirmed the principles of *Roe* v. *Wade*, and its progeny, in which "the Court repeatedly and consistently has accepted and applied the basic principle that a woman has a fundamental right to make the highly personal choice whether or not to terminate her pregnancy." 103 S. Ct. at 2487, n.1 (citations omitted).

   A sharp dissenting opinion, written by Justice O'Connor and joined by Chief Justice Burger and Justice White, challenged the trimester/compelling state interest analysis of *Roe* v. *Wade*. The dissenters would have upheld the Akron ordinance on the grounds that none of its provisions imposed a sufficient burden on the "limited" fundamental right to choose abortion to warrant invalidation. *City of Akron* v. *Akron Reproductive Health Center*, 103 S. Ct. 2481, 2505–16. Some of the arguments of the dissent are similar to those made by the Justice Department in its *amicus* brief.

Roe v. Wade: A Study in Male Ideology

1   See my article, "Feminism, Marxism, Method and the State," *Signs* 8 (1983):
    635–58.

2   This is not to suggest that the decision should have gone the other way, or to
    propose individual hearings to determine coercion prior to allowing abortions.
    Nor is it to criticize Justice Blackmun, author of the majority opinion in *Roe*,
    who probably saw legalizing abortion as a way to help women out of a desper-
    ate situation, which it has done.

3   D. H. Regan, "Rewriting *Roe v. Wade.*" 77 *Michigan Law Review* 1569
    (1979), in which the Good Samaritan happens in the fetus.

4   As of 1973, ten states that made abortion a crime had exceptions for rape and
    incest; at least three had exceptions for rape only. Many of these exceptions
    were based on Model Penal Code Section 230.3 (Proposed Official Draft
    1962), quoted in *Doe v. Bolton*, 410 U.S. 179, 205–7, App. B (1973), per-
    mitting abortion, *inter alia*, in cases of "rape, incest, or other felonious inter-
    course." References to states with incest and rape exceptions can be found in
    Roe v. Wade, 410 U.S. 113 n.37 (1973). Some versions of the Hyde Amend-
    ment, which prohibits use of public money to fund abortions, have contained
    exceptions for cases of rape or incest. All require immediate reporting of the
    incident.

5   Kristin Luker, *Taking Chances: Abortion and the Decision Not to Contracept*
    (Berkeley and Los Angeles: University of California Press, 1976).

6   *Roe v. Wade*, 410 U.S. 113 (1973).

7   *Griswold v. Connecticut*, 381 U.S. 479 (1965).

8   *Eisenstadt v. Baird*, 405 U.S. 438 (1972).

9   *Harris v. McRae*, 448 U.S. 297 (1980).

10 T. Gerety, "Redefining Privacy," *Harvard Civil Rights Civil Liberties Law
    Review* 12 (1977): 233–96, at 236.

11 Kenneth I. Karst, "The Freedom of Intimate Association," *Yale Law Journal*
    89 (1980): 624; "Developments—The Family," *Harvard Law Review* 93
    (1980): 1157–1383; *Doe v. Commonwealth Atty*, 403 F. Supp. 1199 (E.D.
    Va. 1975), *aff'd without opinion*, 425 U.S. 901 (1976) but cf. *People v.
    Onofre*, 51 N.Y.2d 476 (1980), *cert. denied* 451 U.S. 987 (1981).

12 Tom Grey, "Eros, Civilization and the Burger Court," *Law and Contempo-
    rary Problems* 43 (1980): 83.

13 Susan Sontag, "The Third World of Women," *Partisan Review* 40 (1973):
    188.

14 See Adrienne Rich, *Of Women Born: Motherhood As Experience and Insti-
    tution* (New York: Bantam Books, 1977), ch. 3, "The Kingdom of the
    Fathers," esp. pp. 47, 48: "The child that I carry for nine months can be
    defined *neither* as me or as not-me" (emphasis in the original).

15 Kristin Booth Glen, "Abortion in the Courts: A Lay Women's Historical
    Guide to the New Disaster Area," *Feminist Studies* 4 (1978): 1.

16 Judith Jarvis Thomson, "A Defense of Abortion," *Philosophy and Public
    Affairs* 1 (1971): 47–66.

17 Andrea Dworkin, *Right Wing Women* (New York: Perigee, 1983). You

must read this book. See also Friedrich Engels arguing on removing private housekeeping into social industry, *Origin of the Family, Private Property and the State* (New York: International Publishers, 1942).

18 *H. L. v. Matheson,* 450 U.S. 398 (1981); *Poe v. Gerstein; Bellotti v. Baird,* 443 U.S. 622 (1979); but cf. *Planned Parenthood of Central Missouri v. Danforth,* 428 U.S. 52 (1976).

19 See Dworkin, *Right Wing Women,* pp. 98–99.

20 S. Warren and L. Brandeis, "The Right to Privacy," *Harvard Law Review* 4 (1890); 190, p. 205; but note that the right of privacy under some *state* constitutions has been held to *include* funding for abortions: *Committee to Defend Reproductive Rights v. Meyers,* 29 Cal. 3d 252 (1981); *Moe v. Society of Admin. and Finance,* 417 N.E.2d 387 (Mass. 1981).

The Juridical Status of the Fetus

1 The moral status of the fetus has been extensively discussed. See generally D. Callahan, *Abortion: Law, Choice and Morality* (1970); *The Morality of Abortion: Legal and Historical Perspectives* (J. Noonan ed. 1970) (hereinafter cited as *Morality of Abortion*); *The Problem of Abortion* (J. Feinberg ed. 1973); Wertheimer, "Understanding the Abortion Argument," 1 *Phil. & Pub. Aff.* 67 (1971).

2 In 1974 Congress passed the National Research Act, which established the National Commission for the Protection of Human Subjects of Biomedical and Behavioral Research. The National Commission was given a mandate to investigate and study research involving the living fetus, and to recommend whether and under what circumstances such research should be conducted or supported by the Department of Health, Education, and Welfare. National Research Act, Pub. L. No. 93-348, § 213, 88 Stat. 342 (1974). Congress was concerned that unconscionable acts involving the fetus might have been performed in the name of scientific inquiry.

3 See "All About That Baby," *Newsweek,* August 7, 1978, at 66; "The First Test Tube Baby," *Time,* July 31, 1978, at 58.

4 See note 154 *infra* and accompanying text.

5 See, e.g., *Roe v. Wade,* 410 U.S. 113 (1973).

6 See, e.g., the following statutes and regulations, all of which regulate fetal research: National Research Act, Pub. L. No. 93-348, § 213, 88 Stat. 342 (1974) (congressionally mandated moratorium on research on the living human fetus); HEW Additional Protections Pertaining to Research, Development, and Related Activities Involving Fetuses, Pregnant Women, and Human In Vitro Fertilization, 45 C.F.R. §§ 46.201-11 (1978); Ariz. Rev. Stat. Ann. § 36-2302 (West Supp. 1978); Cal. Health & Safety Code § 25956 (West Supp. 1978); Ill. Ann. Stat., ch. 38, §§ 81-18, -26, -32 (Smith-Hurd 1977); Ind. Code Ann. § 35-1-58.5-6 (Burns 1977); Ky. Rev. Stat. § 436.026 (1975); La. Rev. Stat. Ann. § 14:87.2 (West 1974); Me. Rev. Stat. tit. 22, § 1593 (Supp. 1978); Mass. Ann. Laws, ch. 112, § 12J (Michie Law. Co-op 1975); Minn. Stat. Ann. § 145.422 (1973); Mo. Ann. Stat. § 188.035 (Vernon Supp. 1979); N.D. Cent. Code §§ 14-02-2.01, -02 (Supp. 1977); 35 Pa.

Stat. Ann. tit. 35, § 6605 (Purdon 1974); S.D. Comp. Laws Ann. § 34-23A-17 (1976); Utah Code Ann. § 76-7-310 (1978).

7   See note 3 *supra*; see also text at notes 123–33 *infra*.

8   410 U.S. 113 (1973).

9   This article does not address the problems of constitutional interpretation raised by *Roe*. These issues have been explored in several excellent articles. See, e.g., Ely, "The Wages of Crying Wolf: A Comment on *Roe v. Wade*," 82 *Yale L.J.* 920 (1973); Heymann and Barzelay, "The Forest and the Trees: *Roe v. Wade* and Its Critics," 53 *B.U. L. Rev.* 765 (1973); Tribe, "The Supreme Court, 1972 Term—Foreword: Toward a Model of Roles in Due Process of Life and Law," 87 *Harv. L. Rev.* 1 (1973).

10 The Ethics Advisory Board of the Department of Health, Education, and Welfare studied this research and has issued a report and recommendations concerning the conditions under which such research should be conducted and supported. 44 Fed. Reg. 35,033 (1979).

11 The Court in *Roe* stated that "[i]f the State is interested in protecting fetal life after viability, it may go so far as to proscribe abortion during that period, except when it is necessary to preserve the life or health of the mother." 410 U.S. at 163–64. However, the Court did not explain what it meant by "health."

Two years earlier, the Court faced this issue in *United States* v. *Vuitch*, 402 U.S. 62 (1971). In *Vuitch* the Court held that a District of Columbia statute prohibiting abortion except as "necessary for the preservation of the mother's life or health" was not unconstitutionally vague. 402 U.S. at 68, 72. Although the Court did not define health, it said, on the basis of dictionary definition, that the term included mental health. 402 U.S. at 72.

Justice Douglas, however, disagreed. He felt that the imprecision of the term "health" made the statute unconstitutionally vague. He illustrated the lurking ambiguities by posing the following questions:

May [the doctor] perform abortions on unmarried women who want to avoid the "stigma" of having an illegitimate child? Is bearing a "stigma" a "health" factor? Only in isolated cases? Or is it such whenever the woman is unmarried?

Is any unwanted pregnancy a "health" factor because it is a source of anxiety?

Is an abortion "necessary" in the statutory sense if the doctor thought that an additional child in the family would unduly tax the mother's physical well-being by reason of the additional work which would be forced upon her?

Would a doctor be violating the law if he performed an abortion because the added expense of another child in the family would drain its resources, leaving an anxious mother with an insufficient budget to buy nutritious food?

Is the fate of an unwanted child or the plight of the family into which it is born relevant to the factor of the mother's "health"? [402 U.S. at 76 (Douglas, J., dissenting in part)]

These questions remain unanswered.

12 410 U.S. at 113, 120.

13 410 U.S. at 120.

14 410 U.S. at 129.

15   410 U.S. at 156.

16   410 U.S. at 122.

17   Plaintiff Doe and intervenor Hallford also appealed from a denial of the injunction. Plaintiff Doe alleged that she was married, suffered from a disorder, had been advised by her physician to avoid pregnancy, and on medical advice had discontinued use of birth control pills. She alleged that she would desire a legal abortion should she become pregnant. The district court dismissed her complaint because she did not have standing. This action was upheld by the Supreme Court. 410 U.S. at 129. Hallford was a licensed physician who sought to intervene in Roe's action. He alleged that he had been arrested for violation of the statutes at issue and that two prosecutions were pending against him. The district court found that Hallford had standing to sue. The Supreme Court reversed, 410 U.S. at 126–27, relying on its decisions in *Samuels* v. *Mackell*, 401 U.S. 66 (1971), and *Younger* v. *Harris*, 401 U.S. 37 (1971).

18   410 U.S. at 153.

19   410 U.S. at 154, 155.

20   410 U.S. at 147–52.

21   410 U.S. at 148.

22   Brief for Appellants at 30–32, *Roe* v. *Wade*, 410 U.S. 113 (1973).

23   Motion and Brief Amicus Curiae of Certain Physicians, Professors and Fellows of the American College of Obstetrics and Gynecology in Support of Appellees at 32–40 *Roe* v. *Wade*, 410 U.S. 113 (1973). Amici pointed out that most abortions in Eastern Europe were performed in the first trimester of pregnancy and that fact might account for the very low mortality rates of those countries. They further contended that higher mortality rates in Western and Northern Europe might be the result of the performance of abortions after the first trimester. *Id.* at 39. Appellants also argued that abortion was without significant psychiatric sequellae. Brief for Appellant, *supra* note [22], at 33–34. This assertion was also contested. Motion and Brief Amicus Curiae of Certain Physicians, at 55–58.

24   410 U.S. at 149.

25   410 U.S. at 163. The Court's reasoning indicates that the state's compelling interest in the woman's health is dependent upon mortality data. If the data changed, presumably the point at which the state's interest would attach would also change. Recent data suggest that mortality from abortions during the first twelve weeks of pregnancy is declining while mortality associated with childbirth is increasing. This suggests that some second trimester abortions may be safer than childbirth, and thus, a state's compelling interest in the mother's health would not justify legislation until later in pregnancy. Tietze, "New Estimates of Mortality Associated with Fertility Control," 9 Family Plan. Perspec. 74 (1977).

26   410 U.S. at 163. The Court had a somewhat narrow view of what constituted appropriate implementations of that compelling state interest in maternal health after the first trimester. As examples, the Court would have permitted

requirements as to the qualifications of the person who is to perform the abortion; as to the licensure of that person; as to the facility in which the procedure is to be performed, that is, whether it must be a hospital or may be a clinic or some other place of less-than-hospital status; as to the licensing of the facility; and the like. [410 U.S. at 163]

The Court, however, did not convincingly explain why the state does not have a similar interest in maternal health during first trimester abortions. Presumably, the state is interested in licensure and quality of facilities whenever its citizens undergo surgery. The reliance on comparative mortality rates between normal childbirth and first trimester abortion does not justify the absence of all regulation in the first trimester, although it might justify a lesser degree of regulation.

27   410 U.S. at 163. The consultation requirement constitutes a minimal regulation for first trimester abortions, ensuring only that abortions are performed under safe conditions. By precluding other regulation of first trimester abortions, the Court may have been trying to prevent state interference with a woman's interests during the first three months of pregnancy. That hope, however, was soon shattered. In the year after *Roe*, many state legislatures enacted restrictive legislation. See Moss, "Abortion Statutes after Danforth: An Examination," 15 *J. Fam. L.* 537 (1976–1977).

The Court itself has subsequently conceded that states may otherwise restrict a woman's access to abortion. For example, Missouri's statute requiring the written consent of the woman as well as certain recordkeeping requirements for hospitals and physicians was held to be constitutional. *Planned Parenthood* v. *Danforth*, 428 U.S. 52, 65–69, 79–81 (1976). The decision of the Court in *Maher* v. *Roe*, 432 U.S. 465 (1977), holding that the failure of states to pay abortion expenses while paying costs related to childbirth was not a violation of the equal protection clause, also burdens a woman's decision to seek an abortion. See *Beal* v. *Doe*, 432 U.S. 438 (1977); *Poelker* v. *Doe*, 432 U.S. 519 (1977).

28   410 U.S. at 150.

29   For an overview of fetal development, see text at notes 123–29 *infra*.

30   410 U.S. at 161–62. The Constitution of the United States does not discuss the time at which a developing entity acquires rights, and nothing indicates that the founders intended "person" to include the unborn. No court had so assumed. Furthermore, every state, including Texas, had statutorily endorsed some abortions through exceptions to its criminal abortion provisions. 410 U.S. at 157–58.

31   410 U.S. at 158.

32   410 U.S. at 159.

33   410 U.S. at 160 (footnote omitted).

34   410 U.S. at 162–63.

35   410 U.S. at 160.

36   410 U.S. at 163.

37   410 U.S. at 160.

38   410 U.S. at 160. Some commentators have suggested that viability should be linked to weight as well as gestational age. See Behrman and Rosen, "Report on Viability and Nonviability of the Fetus," in *Research on the Fetus: Appendix* 12-1, 12-6, 12-9 (Natl. Comm. for the Protection of Human Sub-

jects of Biomedical and Behavioral Research ed. 1975) (HEW Publication No. (OS) 76-128). See also Gordon, "Neonatal and 'Perinatal' Mortality Rates by Birth Weight," 2 *Brit. Med. J.* 1202 (1977); Stewart, Turcan, Rawlings, and Reynolds, "Prognosis for infants weighing 1000 g or less at birth," 52 *Archives of Disease in Childhood* 97 (1977) (hereinafter cited as Stewart).

39   See Noonan, "An Almost Absolute Value in History," in *Morality of Abortion, supra* note 1, at 52; North and McDonald, "Why Are Neonatal Mortality Rates Lower in Small Black Infants Than in White Infants of Similar Birth Weight?," 90 *J. Pediatrics* 809 (1977) (suggests black babies are genetically endowed with greater capacity to survive than whites, and females are more likely to survive than males).

40   The Supreme Court has reexamined the definition of viability in two subsequent cases. In *Planned Parenthood v. Danforth*, 428 U.S. 52 (1976), the Court sustained the constitutionality of a Missouri statute's definition of viability: "Viability [is] that stage of fetal development when the life of the unborn child may be continued indefinitely outside the womb by natural or artificial life-supportive systems." Mo. Ann. Stat. § 188.015(3) Vernon Supp. (1975). The Supreme Court held that the Missouri definition was compatible with the definition of viability in *Roe*, 428 U.S. at 63. In fact, said the Court,

one might argue . . . that the presence of the statute's words "continued indefinitely" favor, rather than disfavor, the [challengers], for, arguably, the point when life can be "continued indefinitely outside the womb" may well occur later in pregnancy than the point where the fetus is "potentially able to live outside the mother's womb." [428 U.S. at 64]

The Court apparently believed that the Missouri abortion statute did not cover the entire area of permissible regulation (24–28 weeks), but apparently regulated only abortions of fetuses with an estimated gestational age of twenty-eight weeks or longer.

The Court has recently made another effort to clarify its concept of viability. In *Colautti v. Franklin*, 439 U.S. 379 (1979), the Court held unconstitutional on grounds of vagueness a Pennsylvania statute that subjected a physician to criminal penalties for failure to conform to a statutorily prescribed standard of care following a determination that the fetus "is viable" or "may be viable." 439 U.S. at 381. The Court found two problems with the statute. First, it did not clarify whether the physician's determination would be judged by a subjective or objective standard, or a mixture of the two. Second, the Court was not sure whether the phrase "may be viable" incorporated *Roe*'s viability standard or whether the phrase referred to a period prior to viability. 439 U.S. at 391.

To the first concern, the Court stated that the determination of viability was a subjective assessment to be made by the attending physician. However, the Court appears to have changed the *Roe* definition of viability in stating: "Viability is reached when, in the judgment of the attending physician on the particular facts of the case before him, there is a reasonable likelihood of the fetus's sustained survival outside the womb, with or without artificial support." 439 U.S. at 388. The apparent departure from *Roe* was noted in the dissenting opinion of Justice White. He argues that *Roe* used the term "potentially able," and for that reason the *Roe* definition of viability "reaches an earlier point in the development of the fetus than that stage at which a doctor could say with assurance that the fetus *would* survive outside the womb." 439 U.S. at 402 (emphasis in original).

Second, the Court considered whether the phrases "may be viable" and "viable" had different meanings. Pennsylvania argued that the two phrases meant the same thing. 99 S. Ct. at 684. The Court rejected that contention, finding two possible interpretations for the distinction. Under either interpretation, the Court found the statute ambiguous and therefore unconstitutionally vague. 439 U.S. at 393–94.

41   410 U.S. at 163.

42   Omenn, "Prenatal Diagnosis of Genetic Disorders," 200 *Science* 952 (1978).

43   *Id.*

44   Humans with severe malformations of the central nervous system, such as those without brains (anencephaly), severe and grotesque multiple system malformations (cyclops), and severe fetal asphyxia or anoxia would not be considered biologically viable. Behrman and Rosen, *supra* note 38, at 12–26.

45   410 U.S. at 163.

46   Ely, *supra* note 9, at 924.

47   This article stresses capability rather than actual independence. Even a newborn is not actually independent; it would die without the care of others. Actual ability to feed and clothe oneself only occurs well after birth.

48   2 Paige Ch. 24 (N.Y. 1830).

49   The historical use of live birth is traced from Roman law to the present in 4 R. Pound, *Jurisprudence* § 127, at 384–94 (1959). The civil law principle, later adopted by the common law, was that fetal existence was a legal fiction used to protect fetal interests in property until live birth occurred. *Id.* at 387–90. Louisell takes a different view. He asserts that all of these cases accidentally involve live-born children. He argues: "Under such circumstances it is understandable, but really gratuitous and superfluous, for the court to observe that the child must have been born alive. The observation is only dictum; it does not necessarily require a different result in those cases where the observation is inappropriate." Louisell, "Abortion, The Practice of Medicine and the Due Process of Law," 16 *UCLA L. Rev.* 233, 237 (1969).

50   2 Paige Ch. at 40.

51   2 Paige Ch. at 41 (emphasis added).

52   In civil law, a child born within the first six months after conception was presumed incapable of living. This presumption had to be rebutted before these newborns could inherit and transmit property to others. 2 Paige Ch. at 41.

53   E.g., *Tomlin v. Laws*, 301 Ill. 616, 618, 134 N.E. 24, 25 (1922); *Swain v. Bowers*, 91 Ind. App. 307, 316–17, 158 N.E. 598, 601–2 (1927); *Harper v. Archer*, 12 Miss. (4 S. & M.) 99, 109 (1845); *In re Will of Wells*, 129 Misc. 447, 457, 221 N.Y.S. 714, 725 (Sur. Ct. 1927); *Kimbro v. Harper*, 113 Okla. 46, 49, 238 P. 840, 842 (1925). Whether a living but previable fetus *ex utero* can be the subject of homicide remains undecided. An early case

illustrates the difficulty in determining whether death was caused by the previability itself or by the criminal assault. "Want of hair, nails, &c. or other circumstances of premature birth, must be evidence in favor of the prisoner [indicted for the murder of her child]. Circumstances of maturity, marks of violence, etc. are evidence against her." *Pennsylvania* v. *McKee*, 1 Addison 1 (Allegheny County Ct. Pa. 1791). But see *Morgan* v. *State*, 148 Tenn. 417, 421, 256 S.W. 433, 434 (1923) (if the fetus is criminally injured while previable and dies of its injuries after birth, the offense constitutes homicide).

54 43 Iowa at 519 (1876).

55 43 Iowa at 520 (emphasis in original).

56 43 Iowa at 521.

57 43 Iowa at 521.

58 43 Iowa at 521–22.

59 43 Iowa at 521–22.

60 *Shedd* v. *State*, 178 Ga. 653, 654–55, 173 S.E. 847, 847 (1934); *State* v. *O'Neall*, 79 S.C. 571, 573, 60 S.E. 1121, 1122 (1908); *Morgan* v. *State*, 148 Tenn. 417, 420–21, 256 S.W. 433, 434 (1923).

61 *Shedd* v. *State*, 178 Ga. 653, 655, 173 S.E. 847, 848 (1934); *Morgan* v. *State*, 148 Tenn. 417, 420–21, 256 S.W. 433, 434 (1923).

62 See *Wallace* v. *State*, 7 Tex. Crim. 570, 573 (1880) (total expulsion required).

63 *Allen* v. *State*, 128 Ga. 53, 57 S.E. 224 (1907). The transcript of the trial record is discussed in *Shedd* v. *State*, 178 Ga. 653, 656, 173 S.E. 847, 848–49 (1934). But see *State* v. *Osmus*, 73 Wyo. 183, 194, 276 P.2d 469, 472 (1954) ("Not every baby cries when born").

64 *People* v. *Chavez*, 77 Cal. App. 2d 621, 623, 176 P.2d 92, 94 (1947).

65 *Jackson* v. *Commonwealth*, 265 Ky. 295, 296, 96 S.W.2d 1014, 1014 (1936); *State* v. *O'Neall*, 79 S.C. 571, 572, 60 S.E. 1121, 1122 (1908); *Morgan* v. *State*, 148 Tenn. 417, 419, 256 S.W. 433, 433 (1928); *Harris* v. *State*, 28 Tex. Crim. 308, 309, 12 S.W. 1102, 1103 (1889).

66 See notes 123–29 *infra* and accompanying text.

67 See note 133 *infra*.

68 65 F. Supp. 138 (D.D.C. 1946).

69 *Dietrich* v. *Inhabitants of Northampton*, 138 Mass. 14 (1884), was the first American case to consider whether a fetus injured *in utero* and born alive could recover from a negligent defendant. This case involved a woman who miscarried after falling on a negligently maintained highway. The infant was previable and lived for a few minutes before dying. The court, in an opinion by then-Judge Holmes, stated that a child subsequently born alive would have no cause of action for injuries sustained while *in utero*, because the child did not have independent existence apart from the mother. 138 Mass. at 16. This was the law until *Bonbrest* v. *Kotz* was decided. However, the *Dietrich* position was challenged as early as 1900 in a dissenting opinion in *Allaire* v. *St. Luke's Hosp.*, 184 Ill. 359, 56 N.E. 638 (1900). This case involved the negligent operation of an elevator in which the pregnant mother was a passenger. The fetus was injured while viable. The majority followed *Dietrich*, but a dissent by Judge Boggs argued persuasively that fetuses injured while viable

and subsequently born alive should be able to recover. 184 Ill. at 368–74, 56 N.E. at 640–42.

70   W. Prosser, *Handbook of the Law of Torts* § 55 (4th ed. 1971). Courts also quickly established that live birth followed closely by death would not preclude a cause of action under a wrongful death statute. *Id.*

Courts disagree whether a fetus must be viable at the time of injury to recover. In *Bonbrest v. Kotz*, 65 F. Supp. 138 (D.D.C. 1946), the fetus was viable and some courts retained that requirement. However, where the injured fetus is born alive there seems to be little point in drawing an arbitrary line about when injury must occur. If the objective of recovery is to compensate a living person who bears injuries caused by another's negligence, the timing of the injury is irrelevant. For a listing of states still adhering to viability and those who have abandoned it, see Comment, "Negligence and the Unborn Child: A Time for Change," 18 *S.D. L. Rev.* 204 n.7, 213 n.74 (1973). Since the date of that publication, Florida has abandoned the viability requirement. *Day v. Nationwide Mut. Ins. Co.*, 328 So. 2d 560 (Fla. Dist. Ct. App. 1976).

71   The recognition of the fetus as a separate entity has led some commentators to argue that it should be entitled to legal protection from a point at or near conception. See e.g., Noonan, *supra* note 39; Ramsey, "Reference Points in Deciding About Abortion," in *Morality of Abortion, supra* note 1, at 60. This was the point selected by the West German Constitutional Court in holding a permissive abortion statute unconstitutional. Judgment of Feb. 25, 1975, Bundesverfassungsgericht, 39 BVerfGE 1. (An English translation appears in Gorby and Jonas, "West Germany Abortion Decision: A Contrast to *Roe v. Wade*," 9 *J. Mar. J. Prac. & Pro.* 551, 605 (1976)).

The special reliance in tort law on the fact that the fetus is genetically separate from the mother from conception is causing current difficulty. In suits seeking recovery for preconception injuries where the fetus is born alive, it is argued that no duty is owed to one not yet in being. These suits involve negligent conduct which occurs prior to the conception of the child. The injury occurs to the parent(s), but they are not harmed. The harm attaches to the fetus at conception. These injured children will be unable to recover if it is required that the fetus be a separate entity at the time of the negligent conduct. Such a result seems unjust. The traditional elements of the tort of negligence can be applied to allow recovery. "If there is a human life, proved by subsequent birth, then that human life has the same rights at the time of conception as it has at any time thereafter. There cannot be absolutes in the minute to minute progress of life from sperm and ovum to cell, to embryo to foetus, to child." *Zepeda v. Zepeda*, 41 Ill. App. 2d 240, 249–50, 190 N.E.2d 849, 853 (1963), *cert. denied*, 379 U.S. 945 (1964).

In at least one case a cause of action for a preconception injury has been permitted. In *Renslow v. Mennonite Hosp.*, 40 Ill. App. 3d 234, 351 N.E.2d 870 (1976), the plaintiff's mother had been given two blood transfusions when she was thirteen. These transfusions were the wrong blood type and caused sensitization of her blood. This was discovered eight years later through routine testing of her blood while she was pregnant with the plaintiff. Since the plaintiff's life was in danger, labor was induced. The plaintiff was born, but suffered injuries including permanent damage to the brain and nervous system.

72 229 Minn. 365, 38 N.W.2d 838 (1949).

73 229 Minn. at 370–71, 38 N.W.2d at 841.

74 Alabama: *Eich v. Town of Gulf Shores*, 293 Ala. 95, 300 So. 2d 354 (1974); Connecticut: *Gorke v. LeClerc*, 23 Conn. Supp. 256, 181 A.2d 448 (1962); *Hatala v. Markiewicz*, 26 Conn. Supp. 358, 224 A.2d 406 (1966); Delaware: *Worgan v. Greggo & Ferrara, Inc.*, 50 Del. 258, 128 A.2d 557 (1956); District of Columbia: *Simmons v. Howard Univ.*, 323 F. Supp. 529 (D.D.C. 1971) (mem.); Georgia: *Porter v. Lassiter*, 91 Ga. App. 712, 87 S.E.2d 100 (1955); Illinois: *Chrisafogeorgis v. Brandenburg*, 55 Ill. 2d 368, 304 N.E.2d 88 (1973); Indiana: *Britt v. Sears*, 150 Ind. App. 487, 277 N.E.2d 20 (1971); Kansas: *Hale v. Manion*, 189 Kan. 143, 368 P.2d 1 (1962); Kentucky: *Rice v. Rizk*, 453 S.W.2d 732 (Ky. 1970); Maryland: *State ex rel. Odham v. Sherman*, 234 Md. 179, 198 A.2d 71 (1964); Massachusetts: *Mone v. Greyhound Lines, Inc.*, 368 Mass. 354, 331 N.E.2d 916 (1975); Michigan: *O'Neill v. Morse*, 385 Mich. 130, 188 N.W.2d 785 (1971); Minnesota: *Verkennes v. Corniea*, 229 Minn. 365, 38 N.W.2d 838 (1949); Mississippi: *Rainey v. Horn*, 221 Miss. 269, 72 So. 2d 434 (1954); Nevada: *White v. Yup*, 85 Nev. 527, 458 P.2d 617 (1969); New Hampshire: *Poliquin v. MacDonald*, 101 N.H. 104, 135 A.2d 249 (1957); Ohio: *Stidam v. Ashmore*, 109 Ohio App. 431, 167 N.E.2d 106 (1959); Oklahoma: *Evans v. Olson*, 550 P.2d 924 (Okla. 1976); Oregon: *Libbee v. Permanente Clinic*, 268 Or. 258, 518 P.2d 636 (1974); Rhode Island: *Presley v. Newport Hosp.*, 117 R.I. 177, 365 A.2d 748 (1976); South Carolina: *Fowler v. Woodward*, 244 S.C. 608, 138 S.E.2d 42 (1964); *Todd v. Sandidge Constr. Co.*, 341 F.2d 75 (4th Cir. 1964) (South Carolina law); Washington: *Moen v. Hanson*, 85 Wash. 2d 597, 537 P.2d 266 (1975) (*en banc*); West Virginia: *Baldwin v. Butcher*, 155 W. Va. 431, 184 S.E.2d 428 (1971); Wisconsin: *Kwaterski v. State Farm Mut. Auto. Ins. Co.*, 34 Wis. 2d 14, 148 N.W.2d 107 (1967).

The following states expressly deny recovery under wrongful death statutes for injury to the fetus *in utero* that results in stillbirth: Arizona: *Kilmer v. Hicks*, 22 Ariz. App. 522, 529 P.2d 706 (1974); California: *Justus v. Atchison*, 19 Cal. 3d 564, 565 P.2d 122, 139 Cal. Rptr. 97 (1977); Florida: *Stern v. Miller*, 348 So. 2d 303 (Fla. 1977); Iowa: *McKillip v. Zimmerman*, 191 N.W.2d 706 (Iowa 1971); Louisiana: *Wascom v. American Indem. Corp.*, 348 So. 2d 128 (La. App. 1977); Missouri: *State ex rel. v. Sanders*, 538 S.W.2d 336 (Mo. 1976) (*en banc*); Nebraska: *Egbert v. Wenzl*, 199 Neb. 573, 260 N.W.2d 480 (1977); New Jersey: *Graf v. Taggert*, 43 N.J. 303, 204 A.2d 140 (1964); New York: *Endresz v. Friedberg*, 24 N.Y.2d 478, 248 N.E.2d 901, 301 N.Y.S.2d 65 (1969); North Carolina: *Cardwell v. Welch*, 25 N.C. App. 390, 213 S.E.2d 382, *cert. denied*, 287 N.C. 464 (1975); Pennsylvania: *Marko v. Philadelphia Transp. Co.*, 420 Pa. 124, 216 A.2d 502 (1966); Tennessee: *Hamby v. McDaniel*, 559 S.W.2d 774 (Tenn. 1977); Virginia: *Lawrence v. Craven Tire Co.*, 210 Va. 138, 169 S.E.2d 440 (1969).

Two states, however, have indicated that they would allow recovery for injuries resulting in stillbirth even without proof that the fetus was viable when the injury occurred. See *Presley* v. *Newport Hosp.*, 117 R.I. 177, 188–189, 365 A.2d 748, 753 (1976) (dictum stating that recovery would be allowed for previable injury resulting in subsequent stillbirth); *Porter* v. *Lassiter*, 91 Ga. App. 712, 87 S.E.2d 100 (1955) (allowing recovery for injury to a woman one and one-half months pregnant which resulted, after quickening, in a stillborn infant at four and one-half months).

75   Most states required live birth to convict an offender of homicide for the infliction of fatal prenatal injuries. See e.g., *Keeler* v. *Superior Ct.*, 2 Cal. 3d 619, 470 P.2d 617, 87 Cal. Rptr. 481 (1970); *State* v. *Cooper*, 22 N.J.L. 52, 54 (1849); *State* v. *Dickinson*, 23 Ohio App. 2d 259, 263 N.E.2d 253 (1970), *aff'd*, 28 Ohio St. 2d 65, 275 N.E.2d 599 (1971); *Morgan* v. *State*, 248 Tenn. 417, 256 S.W. 433 (1928).

In *People* v. *Chavez*, 77 Cal. App. 2d 621, 626, 176 P.2d 92, 94 (1947), the court said that a child killed while being born could be the subject of homicide. The court's statement, however, was dictum since it affirmed the defendant's conviction on the ground that there was sufficient evidence to support jury findings that the child was born alive and removed from the mother.

Louisiana by statute makes criminal "killing a child during delivery" by the "intentional destruction, during parturition of the mother, of the vitality of life of a child in a state of being born and before actual birth, which child would otherwise have been born alive." La. Rev. Stat. Ann. § 14.87.1 (West 1974).

In a few states killing a fetus before it was quick constituted a lesser crime than manslaughter. See *Evans* v. *People*, 49 N.Y. 86 (1872); *Foster* v. *State*, 182 Wis. 298, 196 N.W. 233 (1923). Other cases that outlawed abortion from conception forward did not equate abortion with murder. See e.g., *State* v. *Reed*, 45 Ark. 333 (1885); *Smith* v. *State*, 33 Me. 48 (1851); *State* v. *Elliott*, 206 Or. 82, 289 P.2d 1075 (1955). However, some states did make illegal abortion a felony. See *State* v. *Reed*, 45 Ark. 333, 334 (1885) (prequickening attempted abortion a felony; postquickening attempt a misdemeanor); *Smith* v. *State*, 33 Me. 48, 57 (1851) (felony if intent to destroy fetus, otherwise a misdemeanor).

76   2 Cal. 3d 619, 470 P.2d 617, 87 Cal. Reptr. 481 (1970).

77   Cal. Penal Code § 187 (West Supp. 1979) (emphasis added).

78   *People* v. *Smith*, 59 Cal. App. 3d 751, 129 Cal. Rptr. 498 (1976).

79   59 Cal. App. 3d at 757, 129 Cal. Rptr. at 502. A California court recently affirmed a conviction for the murder of a viable fetus between 22-24 weeks in development. *People* v. *Apodaca*, 76 Cal. App. 3d 479, 142 Cal. Rptr. 830 (1978). The defendant was convicted of murder in the second degree against the fetus, and rape and assault against the mother. The court held that multiple punishment was warranted because each conviction "was [for] a crime of violence against a different victim: the murder was a crime against the fetus, while the rape was a crime against [the mother]." 76 Cal. App. 3d at 493, 142 Cal. Rptr. at 840.

80   U.S. Const. amends. V, XIV § 1. *Cf. Dred Scott* v. *Sanford*, 60 U.S. (19

How.) 393, 451–52 (1856) (denying rights to blacks after holding that blacks are mere property).

81   See generally U.S. Const. amends. XIII-XV. These amendments, ratified between 1865 and 1870, were designed primarily to protect fundamental rights of blacks who had recently been emancipated from years of slavery and treatment as something less than human. See *Dred Scott v. Sanford*, 60 U.S. (19 How.) 393 (1856). Today, however, these amendments protect all humans of any race. See *Regents of the Univ. of Cal. v. Bakke*, 438 U.S. 265, 289–95 (1978) (opinion of Powell, J.).

Apart from the questions of who is human, or of how we determine who is a member of the species, there is the more interesting question of what, if anything, distinguishes humans from some of the more intelligent animals. One of the characteristics thought to distinguish humans from animals has been the ability to communicate through language. This distinction may become blurred, however, since there is evidence that some animals can be taught language skills. See, Hayes "The Pursuit of Reason," *N.Y. Times*, June 12, 1977, Sec. 6 (Magazine), p. 21. This in turn raises the issue of whether some animals ought to have rights. See Feinberg, "The Rights of Animals and Unborn Generations," in *Philosophy and Environmental Crisis*, 43, 45–51, 55–57 (W. Blackstone ed. 1974).

82   Children, for example, do not have the right to trial by jury in juvenile delinquency hearings. *McKeiver v. Pennsylvania*, 403 U.S. 528 (1971).

83   See text at notes 92–104, *infra.*

84   *Carey v. Population Servs. Intl.*, 431 U.S. 678, 687–89 (1977) (plurality opinion); *Griswold v. Connecticut*, 381 U.S. 479 (1965). In *Griswold* the Court invalidated a Connecticut statute prohibiting distribution of contraceptives to married couples. The Court stated that a zone of privacy, emanating from the Bill of Rights, encompasses the marital relation. 381 U.S. at 484–86. That zone of privacy can be regulated only upon a showing of compelling state interest. Despite the Court's denial, *Griswold* extends the substantive due process approach adopted by the Court in *Lochner v. New York*, 198 U.S. 45 (1905). For a discussion of the right to privacy and substantive due process, see Tribe, *supra* note [9]; Ely, *supra* note [9].

85   *Eisenstadt v. Baird*, 405 U.S. 438, 453 (1972).

86   381 U.S. 479 (1965) (the Court struck down a Connecticut statute banning the use of contraceptives by married people).

87   405 U.S. 438 (1972) (right of access to contraceptives the same for single and married individuals).

88   410 U.S. 113 (1973).

89   428 U.S. 52 (1976).

90   431 U.S. 678 (1977) (plurality opinion).

91   431 U.S. at 687. The Court distinguished the right to privacy from a more expansive notion of a right to autonomy that might, for example, protect homosexual relations between consenting adults. As Justice Goldberg stated in his *Griswold* concurrence, "[T]he Court's holding today . . . in no way interferes with a State's proper regulation of sexual promiscuity or misconduct." 381 U.S. at 498–99. See also *Carey v. Population Servs. Intl.*, 431

U.S. at 694 n.17; 431 U.S. at 702–3 (White, J., concurring in part and concurring in the judgment). It has been argued persuasively, however, that the
right of privacy as used in *Roe* embraces the notion of autonomy rather than
traditional notions of privacy. See e.g., Friendly, "The Courts and Social Policy: Substance and Procedure," 33 *U. Miami L. Rev.* 21, 35–36 (1978); Note,
Roe and *Paris*, "Does Privacy Have a Principle?," 26 *Stan. L. Rev.* 1161
(1974).

92 See *Carey* v. *Population Servs. Intl.*, 431 U.S. 678, 693 (1977) (minors have
a right to privacy that protects procreation).

93 See *Planned Parenthood* v. *Danforth*, 428 U.S. 52, 74 (1976) (the state may
subject minors' constitutional rights to greater regulation than that permissible for adults).

94 The Supreme Court has often held that specific constitutional guarantees extend to minors as well as adults. See, e.g., *In re Winship*, 397 U.S. 358
(1970) (proof beyond a reasonable doubt required in delinquency hearing);
In re Gault, 387 U.S. 1 (1967) (extending the Due Process Clause to juvenile
delinquency hearings and specifically requiring notice of charges, right to
counsel, and a right to cross examination); *Haley* v. *Ohio*, 332 U.S. 596
(1948) (plurality opinion) (due process requires suppression of minor's involuntary confession). But see *McKeiver* v. *Pennsylvania*, 403 U.S. 528
(1971) (refusing to extend right of trial by jury to juvenile delinquency
hearings).

95 *Carey* v. *Population Servs. Intl.*, 431 U.S. at 692 (plurality opinion).

96 *Carey* v. *Population Servs. Intl.*, 431 U.S. 678 (1977).

97 *Planned Parenthood* v. *Danforth*, 428 U.S. 52 (1976).

98 431 U.S. at 91–96 (plurality opinion). The decision in *Carey* is a majority
opinion except upon the issue of prohibiting the distribution of contraceptives
to minors under the age of 16. That portion of the opinion, referred to in the
text, is a plurality opinion written by Justice Brennan and joined by Justices
Stewart, Marshall, and Blackmun. Justice White concurred in the judgment
on this issue because he found that the state had not demonstrated that the
prohibition against distribution of contraceptives to minors had a deterrent
effect on premarital intercourse. 431 U.S. at 702. Justices Powell and Stevens
based their concurrences in part on the statute's unconstitutional prohibition
of distribution of contraceptives to married females between the ages of 14
and 16. 431 U.S. at 707–8 (Powell, J., concurring in part and concurring in
the judgment); 431 U.S. at 713 (Stevens, J., concurring in part and concurring in the judgment).

99 The concurring opinions to that part of the opinion in *Carey* declaring the
statute unconstitutional emphatically make that point. Justice Stevens, in a
statement with which Justice White explicitly concurred, 431 U.S. at 702–3,
wrote: "Indeed, I would describe as 'frivolous' appellees' argument that a
minor has the constitutional right to put contraceptives to their intended use,
notwithstanding the combined objection of both parents and the State." 431
U.S. at 713. Justice Powell stated that the New York statute was unconstitutional because "this provision prohibits parents from distributing contracep-

tives to their children, a restriction that unjustifiably interferes with parental interests in rearing their children." 431 U.S. at 708.

100 99 S. Ct. 3035 (1979). In *Planned Parenthood* v. *Danforth*, 428 U.S. 52 (1976), all of the Justices indicated that a requirement of parental consultation might well be constitutional. Justice Stewart believed the Missouri statute to be unconstitutional primarily because of the absolute limitation that it created to a minor's access to abortion. However, citing *Bellotti*, he held open the possibility that a requirement only of parental consultation, as opposed to parental consent, would be constitutional. 428 U.S. at 90–91 (Stewart, J., concurring). The remaining Justices would have upheld the Missouri requirement of parental consent and would undoubtedly have held the less restrictive requirement of parental consultation constitutional as well. 428 U.S. at 95 (White, J., with Burger, C. J., and Rehnquist, J., concurring in part and dissenting in part) (parental consent furthers valid state interest in ensuring that unmarried minor makes abortion decision in her own best interests); 428 U.S. at 103 (Stevens, J., concurring in part and dissenting in part) (parental consent maximizes probability that abortion decisions will be made with full understanding of consequences).

101 99 S. Ct. at 3050.

102 In *Bellotti* Justice Powell offered three reasons: "The peculiar vulnerability of children; their inability to make critical decisions in an informed, mature manner; and the importance of the parental role in child-rearing." 99 S. Ct. at 3043.

103 Pilpel, "Minors' Rights to Medical Care," 36 *Alb. L. Rev.* 462, 463–64 (1972).

104 See *Planned Parenthood* v. *Danforth*, 428 U.S. at 102–3 (Stevens, J., concurring in part and dissenting in part).

105 See Areen, "Intervention between Parent and Child: A Reappraisal of the State's Role in Child Neglect and Abuse Cases," 63 *Geo. L. J.* 887 (1975). Areen traces the history of child abuse and neglect and points out, for example, that children were forced to be indentured servants both in England and the United States. *Id.* at 894–903. That suggests that children were treated like property.

106 *Prince* v. *Massachusetts*, 321 U.S. 158, 165 (1944).

107 Feinberg argues that beings must have interests if they are logically to be subjects of rights. He suggests that interests are composed of conations ("conscious wishes, desires, and hopes; or urges and impulses; . . . or latent tendencies, direction of growth, and natural fulfillments"). Feinberg, *supra* note 81, at 49. Interests are necessary because a right-holder must be capable of being represented (a being cannot be represented if it has no interest), and because a right-holder must be capable of being a beneficiary in its own person. In the usual case a right-holder is a normal adult human being. Feinberg contends that children are also right-holders because they have interests, or in the case of newborns because they have a capacity to acquire interests. Emerging interests are sometimes in need of protection, otherwise they might never come into existence. These interests may be protected by

representatives. He further argues that the same principle can be extended to the unborn. The unborn a day prior to birth are "not strikingly different" from the newborn in the first hour after birth. *Id.* at 62. In a later article, he argues that the unborn have no right to be born. Feinberg, "Is There a Right to Be Born?," in *Understanding Moral Philosophy*, 346 (J. Rachels ed. 1976).

108   *Ginsberg* v. *New York*, 390 U.S. 629, 649–50 (1968) (Stewart, J., concurring in the result).

109   Feinberg, *supra* note 81, at 62. The argument that beings have rights because they have the potential to be competent adults raises disturbing questions, however, with respect to the severely mentally retarded and the mentally disabled. We can argue that to the extent that they are potentially curable they should have rights. However, it might be extremely difficult to regard some humans as potentially curable—those in irreversible comas, for example. Should these beings have rights? I am inclined to think not. I hasten to add that the fact that perhaps they should not have rights does not imply that they are to be treated cavalierly. There may be many reasons we should treat them as though they had rights. For Feinberg's discussion of this issue, see *id.* at 60–61.

110   The legal rights of children must often be asserted by representatives, because that is the only practical means of assuring that those rights will be protected. The same principle could extend to the unborn.

111   For example, at common law death ended the contract. Restatement of Contracts §§ 35(1)(d), 48 (1932).

112   Blackstone argues that the ability to pass title to property is not a natural right. He writes: "[T]here is no foundation in nature or in natural law why a set of words upon parchment should convey the dominion of land. . . ." 2 W. Blackstone, *Commentaries* 2. However, Blackstone concedes that humans have always been permitted to devise property.

[T]he universal law of almost every nation (which is a kind of secondary law of nature) has either given the dying person a power of continuing his property, by disposing of his possession by will; or, in case he neglects to dispose of it, or is not permitted to make any disposition at all, the municipal law of the country then steps in, and declares who shall be the successor. [*Id.* at 10–11]

In the United States, the Supreme Court has stated that although validly created wills will be enforced, enforcement is not necessarily a matter of constitutional rights. *Irving Trust Co.* v. *Day*, 314 U.S. 556, 562 (1942). *Contra Nunnemacher* v. *State*, 129 Wis. 190, 108 N.W. 627 (1906).

113   *In re Estate of Johnson*, 169 Misc. 215, 217–20, 7 N.Y.S.2d 81, 83–86 (Sur. Ct. 1938).

114   The prevailing concept of the human body was a temple for the Holy Spirit, from which a person's soul was temporarily separated at death. It would have been repugnant to common law society to attach to such a holy vessel the commercial values that attend legal property rights. *In re Estate of Johnson*, 169 Misc. 215, 218, 7 N.Y.S.2d 81, 84 (Sur. Ct. 1938). Therefore, until the time of Henry VIII, the place and manner of burial were controlled by

the ecclesiastical courts. See Groll and Kerwin, "The Uniform Anatomical Gift Act: Is the Right to a Decent Burial Obsolete?," 2 *Loy. Chi. L. J.* 275 (1971). Bodies, according to law and custom, were buried intact in the community churchyard. Any attempt by the decedent to control the manner of his burial by testamentary direction failed because the body was not "property." *Id.* at 275–76.

115 *Fidelity Union Trust Co. v. Heller*, 16 N.J. Super. 285, 290, 84 A.2d 485, 487 (1951).

116 *Diebler v. American Radiator & Standard Sanitary Corp.*, 196 Misc. 618, 620, 92 N.Y.S.2d 356, 358 (1949).

117 The New York statute, which made it a crime to interfere with the decedent's wishes for his own burial, was repealed upon enactment of the Uniform Anatomical Gift Act, 1970 N.Y. Laws ch. 466, § 2.

118 In disputes between executors or administrators attempting to carry out the decedent's directions and decedent's next-of-kin having other plans for interment, courts have held that the wishes of the deceased for the disposition of the remains are paramount to all other considerations. E.g., *In re Estate of Henderson*, 13 Cal. App. 2d 449, 57 P.2d 212 (1936); *In re Harlam*, 57 N.Y.S.2d 103 (1945); *In re Herskovits*, 183 Misc. 411, 48 N.Y.S.2d 906 (1944); *In re Estate of Eichner*, 173 Misc. 644, 18 N.Y.S.2d 573 (1940). Even when the decedent's testamentary directives contravene the religious beliefs of his family (e.g., where a Jewish decedent leaves instruction that he should be cremated), courts still have often upheld the wishes of the deceased. See generally *In re Herskovits*, 183 Misc. 411, 412, 48 N.Y.S.2d 906, 907 (1944); *In re Estate of Johnson*, 169 Misc. 215, 7 N.Y.S. 81 (1938).

A majority of courts, however, refuse to allow a body, once buried, to be exhumed. E.g., *Yome v. Gorman*, 242 N.Y. 395, 403, 152 N.E. 126, 128 (1926). Moreover, since a decision in disputes between a decedent's executor and surviving relations is an exercise of equitable powers, the courts have not hesitated to violate the decedent's directions where the directives offend the court's conception of family responsibility or community interest. See *Herold v. Herold*, 16 Ohio Dec. 303, 3 Ohio N.P. (n.s.) 405 (C.P. Butler Co. 1905).

119 Codifications for all participating jurisdictions are collected in Groll and Kerwin, *supra* note 114, at 290 n.49.

120 Uniform Anatomical Gift Act §§ 2(10), 4(a).

121 See Uniform Anatomical Gift Act §§ 2(a), 4(a).

122 The problem of choosing where on the continuum of human potentiality we wish to acknowledge significant legal protection is analogous to the issue of how far into the future we want to permit the wishes of the dead to control disposition of property. From the earliest times, the common law sought to balance the power to bind land indefinitely against the desire for free alienability of property. The Rule Against Perpetuities, first announced in The Duke of Norfolk's Case, 22 Eng. Rep. 931 (Ch. 1682), attempted to strike a balance between these competing concerns. The Rule is, without doubt, somewhat arbitrary and is certainly difficult to understand and apply, but it

does attempt a balance between competing, equally valid concerns. For an interesting account of the Rule and its origins, see Haskins, "Extending the Grasp of the Dead Hand: Reflections on the Origins of the Rule Against Perpetuities," 126 *U. Pa. L. Rev.* 19 (1977).

123   See Hellegers, "Fetal Development," 31 *Theo. Stud.* 3, 3–4 (1970). This article is a particularly vivid and nontechnical description of fetal development which highlights stages of development and the importance that has been attached to them historically.

124   *Id.* at 6. Normally, implantation occurs in the endometrium, the lining of the uterine cavity. However, extrauterine implantation sometimes occurs, most commonly in the fallopian tubes, resulting in an ectopic pregnancy.

125   *Id.* at 7. Pregnancy can be diagnosed at this stage by chemical tests that measure hormones secreted to stop the menstrual cycle. However, these chemicals tests indicate only that pregnancy has probably occurred. The positive signs of pregnancy are: "(1) identification of the fetal heartbeat separately and distinctly from that of the mother; (2) perception of active fetal movements by the examiner; and (3) recognition of the fetus radiologically or sonographically." J. Pritchard and P. MacDonald, *Williams' Obstetrics* 204 (15th ed.) ([East Norwalk, Conn: Appleton-Century-Crofts,] 1976). Menstrual extraction, the morning-after pill, and the intrauterine device, commonly used as contraceptives, might technically be considered "abortifacients" since they interrupt pregnancy before it can be diagnosed.

126   Hellegers, *supra* note 123, at 4.

127   See J. Pritchard and P. MacDonald, *supra* note 125, at 89.

128   *Id.* at 212. In the early criminal law, this was a significant point before which abortion was sometimes permitted. Later criminal abortion statutes prohibited abortion from conception. Since quickening is a matter of maternal perception rather than fetal development, it has no modern legal significance.

129   Hellegers, *supra* note 123, at 8–9. Hellegers asserts that the fetus between the 20th and 28th weeks may have approximately a 10 percent chance of survival. This view is not universally accepted. Behrman and Rosen report that a worldwide survey revealed that no infant weighing less than 601 grams and less than 24 weeks in gestational age has survived. Behrman and Rosen, *supra* note 38, at 12–9.

130   See Brans, "Advances in Perinatal Care: 1970–1980," 19 *J. Reproductive Med.* 111 (1977). Brans discusses the significant advances in selected areas —hemolytic disease, hyperbilirubinemia, maternal diabetes, hyaline membrane disease, nutrition of the tiny premature neonate, infections, and monitoring mother-child interaction.

131   See Manniello and Farrell, "Analysis of United States neonatal mortality statistics from 1968 to 1974," 129 *Am. J. Obstetrics & Gynecology* 667 (1977). That article analyzes neonatal statistics with specific reference to changing trends in major casualties. The authors conclude that the data show a fall in the annual newborn mortality rate from 16.1 to 12.3 per 1,000 births. *Id.* at 669. They attribute this decline to advances in perinatology. *Id.* at 673. See also Stewart, *supra* note 38. That article concludes that provided intensive

care methods are available, the prognosis for infants weighing less than 1,000 grams is better than in the past. *Id.* at 103. However, the costs of providing for perinatal intensive care are high. One investigator reports a $40,000 figure per infant less than 1,000 grams. Pomerance, Ukrainski, and Ukra, "The Cost of Living for Infants ≦ 1,000 Gms. at Birth," abstracted in 11 *Pediatric Research* 381 (1977). These high costs suggest that guidelines should be developed concerning problems such as when to withdraw intensive perinatal care.

132   See Omenn, *supra* note 42. The most common technique employed is amniocentesis. Amniocentesis involves the insertion of a needle through the abdominal wall into the amniotic sac to withdraw amniotic fluid. The fluid and fetal cells found in the fluid are analyzed to detect the presence of genetic diseases. Currently most chromosomal anomalies and more than sixty inborn errors of metabolism can be identified through that technique. Littlefield, Milunsky, and Atkins, "An Overview of Prenatal Genetic Diagnosis," in *Birth Defects* 221 ([ed. A. Motulsky (New York: Elsevier Science Publication)] 1974). Other techniques are visualization of the fetus by a fetoscope, radiography and ultrasound, and sampling of fetal and maternal blood. For an explanation of these techniques and their current level of development see Omenn, *supra* note 42.

133   See J. Pritchard and P. MacDonald, *supra* note 125, at 204–5, 537–40, 274–77.

134   This is a relatively new concept for medicine. Until about twenty-five years ago the mother was regarded as the patient. The fetus was regarded as another maternal organ. The physician, therefore, always acted in the best interests of the mother, believing that doing so was in the best interest of the unborn. See J. Pritchard and P. MacDonald, *supra* note 125, at 265.

135   See *id.* at 809–11.

136   See Liggins and Howie, "The Prevention of RDS by Maternal Steroid Therapy," in *Modern Perinatal Medicine* (ed. L. Gluck [Chicago: Year Book Medical Publishers,] 1974); *Id.,* "A Controlled Trial of Antepartum Glucocorticoid Treatment for Prevention of the Respiratory Distress Syndrome in Premature Infants," 50 *Pediatrics* 515 (1972).

137   Investigators are removing primate fetuses from the womb, performing complicated neurosurgery, replacing the fetuses, and delivering them at term. It is hoped that such research will increase knowledge about nervous system damage in humans. "Primate Neurobiology: Neurosurgery with Fetuses," 199 *Science* 960 (1978).

138   An analogous change is occurring in the determination of when a person is legally dead. The traditional criterion for determining whether death has occurred was cessation of the heartbeat. Modern medicine has made it possible, however, artificially to sustain the heart even while the patient is in an irreversible coma. See Capron and Kass, "A Statutory Definition of the Standards for Determining Human Death: An Appraisal and a Proposal," 121 *U. Pa. L. Rev.* 87, 89 (1972). In light of this achievement, our reliance on cessation of the heartbeat to indicate death has been seriously challenged. As a consequence, new criteria for determining death have been proposed. See Ad Hoc Committee of the Harvard Medical School to Examine the

Definition of Brain Death, "A Definition of Irreversible Coma," 205 *J.A.M.A.*
337 (1968); Task Force on Death and Dying, Institute of Society, Ethics
and Life Science, "Refinements in Criteria for the Determination of Death:
An Appraisal," 221 *J.A.M.A.* 48 (1972). Adoption of new criteria has not
meant that our concept of dying has changed. It means only that we must
consider new medical data and new technological innovations in determining
when death occurs.

139   One court permitting recovery for injury to a viable stillborn infant stated:

Suppose . . . viable unborn twins suffered simultaneously the same prenatal
injury of which one died before and the other after birth. Shall there be a
cause of action for the death of the one and not for that of the other? Surely
logic requires recognition of causes of action for the deaths of both, or for
neither. [*Stidham* v. *Ashmore*, 109 Ohio App. 431, 434, 167 N.E.2d 106,
108 (1959)]

140   *In re Peabody*, 5 N.Y.2d 541, 158 N.E.2d 841, 186 N.Y.S.2d 265 (1959).
The court stated:

Because of the necessity in medieval England always to have available a living
person who could be charged with the performance of feudal duties, the
common law developed the rule that a remainder estate was destroyed if the
heir or devisee was not alive when the prior estate came to an end. [5
N.Y.2d at 546, 158 N.E.2d at 844, 186 N.Y.S.2d at 269]

141   See *Trustees of Dartmouth College* v. *Woodward*, 17 U.S. (4 Wheat.) 518,
636 (1819).

142   The Supreme Court acknowledged that complexity in *Colautti* v. *Franklin*:

As the record in this case indicates, a physician determines whether or not
a fetus is viable after considering a number of variables: the gestational age
of the fetus, derived from the reported menstrual history of the woman;
fetal weight, based on an inexact estimate of the size and condition of the
uterus; the woman's general health and nutrition; the quality of the available
medical facilities; and other factors. Because of the number and the imprecision of these variables, the probability of any particular fetus' obtaining
meaningful life outside the womb can be determined only with difficulty.
[439 U.S. 379, 395–96 (1979) (footnote omitted)]

143   Indeed, between the 20th and 28th weeks there is no reliable technique to
make the determination of viability. See Kass, "Determining Death and Viability in Fetuses and Abortuses," in *Research on the Fetus: Appendix supra*
note 38, at 11–1, 11–15. A competent examiner using a stethoscope can detect a heartbeat that suggests fetal life and age at approximately 20 weeks of
pregnancy. Even *ex utero*, determining viability is not entirely free of difficulty. One author suggests that a fetus *ex utero* is to be considered viable if
it shows all five of the following signs: (1) spontaneous muscular movement,
(2) response to external stimuli, (3) elicitable reflexes, (4) spontaneous respiration, and (5) spontaneous heart function. *Id.* Behrman suggests that a
fetus is viable *ex utero* if it has a minimum number of basic integrative
physiologic functions. In 1975 he listed the following: (1) perfusion of tis-
sues with adequate oxygen and the prevention of the increasing accumulation
of carbon dioxide and/or lactic and other organic acids, and (2) neurologic

regulation of the components of the cardiorespiratory perfusion function, of the capacity to ingest nutrients, and of spontaneous and reflex muscle movements. Behrman and Rosen, *supra* note 38, at 12–26. He suggests, however, that these functions cannot be reliably assessed in all cases. He argues that there is a correlation of these functions with gestational age and weight. Delivered infants weighing less than 601 grams and/or less than 24 weeks gestational age should be considered nonviable. At this stage signs of life, such as a beating heart, pulsation of the umbilical cord, etc., are not adequate in and of themselves to indicate the presence of the basic minimum functions. See *id.*

144 See Behrman and Rosen, *supra* note 38, app. A at 12–51. Their study has comprehensive data on premature survival rates by gestational age. Although this study does not represent a statistical sampling of total world, U.S., or Canadian births, it represents the best available data at the time the study was done. The study shows the percent of survivors among those born at 28 weeks is 46.2 percent.

145 "Verified" means substantiated in the manner that new medical information is substantiated by acceptance and publication in an established medical journal. Earliest verified survival refers to survival in the United States. Historically, American physicians have been held to a standard of practice in a particular locality. See W. Prosser, *supra* note 70, § 32 at 164. However, accreditation of medical schools, better methods of communication and transportation, and availability of medical literature and consultation have contributed to a breakdown of the locality rules. In some jurisdictions the locality rule has been entirely discarded. *Id.* There of course will be babies who will not live although born well after the earliest verified survival, because viability is in part a function of available medical resources, and these babies will not be born in or near hospitals with the resources to keep them alive. See text at note 39, *supra.* In the future, earliest verified survival will ideally be determined by some national body, applicable in the entire United States, and subject to periodic review. See text at notes 163–64, *infra.* This national body might decide to take into account survival data from other countries in arriving at a national standard of viability for the United States. Information from foreign countries was taken into account by the National Commission when making its recommendations concerning fetal research. See Behrman and Rosen, *supra* note 38, at 12–2, 12–4.

146 Because our ability to sustain life earlier in gestation will probably move faster than common acceptance of this information by physicians, legislatures, and courts, perhaps a state should be able to create a zone in which we have no verified fetal survival but in which abortion is prohibited. Kass argues that we should treat every fetus with an audible heartbeat (which occurs at about twenty weeks) as if it were viable, although some will not be. See Kass, *supra* note 143, at 11–14. The National Commission adopted this approach in its report. It recommended that the "possibly viable infant," who is likely to be between 20 and 24 weeks and between 500 and 600 grams, could be involved in research only under stringent conditions. Natl. Commn. for the Protection

of Human Subjects of Biomedical and Behavioral Research, Research on the Fetus: Report and Recommendations 75 (1975) (HEW Publication No. [OS] 76–127).

147 The Court has never considered a carefully drafted statute or a statute that incorporated the *Roe* definition of viability. At least one state legislature attempted to prohibit abortion on demand 24 weeks after conception. This statute was declared unconstitutional in *Floyd* v. *Anders*, 440 F. Supp. 535 (D.S.C. 1977) (three-judge panel), *vacated and remanded per curiam*, 440 U.S. 445 (1979). "Because the District Court may have reached this conclusion on the basis of an erroneous concept of 'viability' which refers to potential, rather than actual, survival of the fetus outside the womb," the Court remanded in light of *Colautti* v. *Franklin*, 439 U.S. 379 (1979). The Court also suggested that the district court give further consideration to abstention.

148 428 U.S. 52 (1976).

149 428 U.S. at 64.

150 439 U.S. 379 (1979).

151 Under the Court's position presumably the physician could determine that a fetus older than 28 weeks was not viable. The physician might however have a difficult time sustaining that position if the finding were contested.

152 439 U.S. at 396 (footnote omitted).

153 See *Roe* v. *Wade*, 410 U.S. 113, 163–64 (1973).

154 Current research suggests that there is a relationship between maternal use of alcohol and fetal abnormality. See Ouellette, Rosett, Rosman, and Weiner, "Adverse Effects of Maternal Alcohol Abuse During Pregnancy," 297 *New Eng. J. Med.* 528 (1977). At least one female has been indicted for child abuse for giving birth to a child addicted to heroin. *In re Baby X*, No. 77–1557 (6th Jud. Cir. Oakland Cty., Mich.). However, another case has held that a mother cannot be punished in such circumstances. *Reyes* v. *Superior Court*, 75 Cal. App. 3d 214, 141 Cal. Rptr. 912 (1977).

155 Some will argue that this approach places too great a constraint on a woman's right to terminate her pregnancy. This is true only if termination of pregnancy means that a woman is entitled to a method of termination that will result in a dead fetus. There seems to be no justification for permitting termination of pregnancy after viability by a method likely to kill the fetus. We do not permit infanticide. There seems to be no logic in permitting the death of an entity that, like the newborn, is capable of living independently of its mother, on the ground that it has not been physically detached from the mother. We are simply extending the rationale behind proscriptions against infanticide to viable but unborn entities. Since viability will probably continue to occur earlier in pregnancy, at some future point some fetuses may be viable very early in the gestational period. If that event comes to pass, it may also become possible to separate mothers and fetuses upon request at minimal risk to both.

156 It appears that there are relatively few instances where continued pregnancy implies certain death for the mother. The threat to her life is relative and

may depend on whether she has the financial resources to permit her to be hospitalized, to hire domestic help, etc. See Ryan, "Humane Abortion Laws and the Health Need of Society, 17 W. *Res. L. Rev.* 422, 430 (1965).

157   Health is a difficult concept to define. See note 11, *supra*.

158   See *Raleigh Fitkin-Paul Morgan Mem. Hosp.* v. *Anderson*, 42 N.J. 421, 201 A.2d 537, *cert. denied*, 377 U.S. 985 (1964). In this case, the court ordered that a blood transfusion should be administered contrary to a woman's religious beliefs as a Jehovah's Witness, if needed to save the life of her unborn 32-week-old fetus.

159   But see *Colautti* v. *Franklin*, 439 U.S. 379, 386 n.7 (1979) (prior to viability, state may not impose criminal sanctions to protect fetal life).

160   I do not suggest here that the mother should be punished rather than treated in such circumstances. However, persons have often been punished for involuntary behavior, and a similar result here would be consistent with that legal tradition.

161   Viability has been criticized as a criterion for that reason. See Krimmel and Foley, "Abortion: An Inspection into the Nature of Human Life and Potential Consequences of Legalizing Its Destruction," 46 *U. Cin. L. Rev.* 725, 741–42 (1977). Some commentators have emphasized biological properties. Some argue for conception as the most relevant point in fetal development, because it dates the creation of a unique genetic makeup. See Noonan, *supra* note 39, at 57. Others select a period up to fourteen days after conception or when we are assured that individualization has occurred. This point was selected by the Constitutional Court of West Germany. See note 71, *supra*. Still others select viability. See Engelhardt, "The Ontology of Abortion," 84 *Ethics* 217, 228–30 (1974). Another view suggests that, rather than looking to a point in fetal development such as viability in defining when full legal protection is appropriate, we should look to the presence or absence of certain unique human characteristics, though there is little consensus as to what those characteristics should be. Some examine the degree of social and personal concern invested in an entity in defining when life begins. See *id.* at 230–32. Others emphasize the entity's intellectual and cognitive functions. See Lederberg, "A Geneticist Looks at Contraception and Abortion," 67 *Annals Internal Med.*, Supp. 7, at 26 (1976). Still others emphasize the possession of self-consciousness or a capacity for self-consciousness. See Fletcher, "Indicators of Humanhood: A Tentative Profile of Man," *Hastings Center Report*, Nov. 1972, at 1. These approaches share the same defect. Since they are all the product of philosophical views and social influences prevalent in different sectors of society at any given time, they are subject to prejudicial and subjective applications. In the past, such approaches have justified unjust treatment of persons based upon color, racial, sexual, religious, or cultural difference. By excluding blacks from the slave owners' definition of human (based upon "scientific" data of biological inferiority that often was falsified), the slave owners were able to rationalize slavery. See G. Myrdal, *The Negro in America* 31–36 ([Boston: Beacon Press,] 1956). Such justifications even permeated the Supreme Court in the *Dred Scott* decision, where it stated:

[T]he right of property in a slave is distinctly and expressly affirmed in the Constitution. The right to traffic in it, like an ordinary article of merchandize and property, was guarantied [sic] to the citizens of the United States. ...And no word can be found in the Constitution which gives Congress a greater power over slave property, or which entitles property of that kind to less protection than property of any other description. [*Dred Scott v. Sanford*, 60 U.S. (19 How.) 393, 451–52 (1856)]

Blacks in America are not the only persons discriminated against because of supposed biological inferiority. The Chinese in America and the Jews in Europe as well as others have suffered similar fates. See *People v. Hall*, 4 Cal. 339, 404–5 (1854) (Chinese, as well as blacks, excluded from testifying in action where any party is white because marked by nature as inferior and incapable of progress of intellectual development beyond a certain point); International Military Tribunal: Nuremberg 14 Nov. 1945–1 Oct. 1946 Trial of the Major War Criminals.

162 *Planned Parenthood v. Danforth*, 428 U.S. 52, 64 (1976).

163 Natl. Commn. for the Protection of Human Subjects of Biomedical and Behavioral Research, *supra* note 146, at 5, 75.

164 Note, however, that suggestions for new criteria for determining death originated with nongovernmental groups. See note 156, *supra*.

165 See note 132, *supra*.

166 Some commentators who look to the possession of certain unique characteristics in defining when life begins have been forced to consider the legality of infanticide as well as that of abortion. Some would allow infanticide in some circumstances. See, e.g., J. Fletcher, *The Ethics of Genetic Control* [Garden City, N.Y.: Anchor Press, 1974], 152–54, 185–87; Tooley, "Abortion and Infanticide," 2 *Phil. Pub. Aff.* 37 (1972). Other commentators reach different conclusions. Paul Ramsey, for example, advises against the abortion of defective fetuses but supports a withdrawal of medical treatment that would lead to the fetus's death. Ramsey, *supra* note 71, at 97–100.

Understanding Blackmun's Argument: The Reasoning of *Roe v. Wade*

1 *Roe v. Wade*, 410 U.S. 113 at 159 (1973).

2 For a critical review of Blackmun's apologists up to 1978, see John T. Noonan, Jr., *A Private Choice*, (New York: The Free Press, 1979). Noonan's criticisms of the apologists are generally fair; his criticisms of Blackmun are of the common sort I shall be scouting.

3 Wertheimer, "Understanding the Abortion Argument," *Philosophy and Public Affairs* 1, no. 1 (Fall 1971). (Lest the point of the present essay be misunderstood, I should add that I harbor no fantasy that the Court was familiar with or influenced by the earlier essay.)

4 *Roe v. Wade*, 410: U.S. 113, 150.

5 Ibid., pp. 156–57.

6 Ibid., p. 158.

7 Ibid., p. 162.

8 Ibid., pp. 163–64.

9 Ibid.

10 Cf. my "Philosophy on Humanity," in Edward Manier et al., eds., *Abortion* (South Bend, Ind.: University of Notre Dame Press, 1977).

11 No doubt the legal status of the neonate is in *some* ways special. In particular, our legal system has often—in practice, if not in judicial pronouncements —been more permissive about "euthanasia" with neonates. However, where courts have ruled on this, the permission has not been predicated on a denial that the neonate is legally a person, and still less on the idea that the neonate lacks some psychological attributes requisite for having legal rights.

12 *Roe v. Wade*, 410 U.S. 113, 162.

13 Ibid., pp. 156–59.

14 Ibid., p. 156.

15 Admittedly, Blackmun's locating the abortion decision within a woman's "right of privacy" is not unproblematic. But whatever difficulties there may be in defining the general right which encompasses the abortion decision or in tracing its constitutional roots, still—absent any suppositions attributing some kind of personhood to the fetus—doubts about the abortion decision being within a woman's rights seem quite far-fetched. In any case, the focus of this essay is not on establishing the existence of the constitutional right, but on the larger argument that assumes its existence.

16 Ibid., p. 162.

17 Cf. the opinion of Judge Charles Breitel in *Byrn* v. *New York City Health and Hospitals Corp.*, 31 N.Y.2d 194, 286 N.E.2d 887 (1972); *appeal dismissed*, 410 U.S. 940 (1973).

18 *Contra* Noonan, *Private Choice*, pp. 13–19.

19 Obviously, granting corporations the status of (artificial) persons for restricted purposes of civil law is an altogether distinct matter.

20 *Roe v. Wade*, 410 U.S., 157–59, 161–62.

21 Ibid., pp. 155–56.

22 Still, the reasons properly governing judicial pronouncements differ from those governing our judgments unfettered by the internal demands of a legal system. The interesting question, which I cannot pursue here, is whether we in the community ought to talk as the judges do when they talk as they ought to.

23 Ibid., p. 159.

24 Ibid.

25 Ibid., p. 160.

26 Ibid., p. 116.

27 "A Candid Talk with Justice Blackmun," *New York Times Magazine*, February 20, 1983, p. 26.

28 *Contra* the opinion of Judge Raymond Pettine in *Doe* v. *Israel*, 358 F. Supp. 1197 (D.R.I., 1973).

29 *Roe v. Wade*, 410 U.S. 113, 116.

30 Ibid., pp. 116–17.

31 Ibid., pp. 129–50, 160–61.

32 Cf. "Woman Speak Out," *Life*, vol. 4, no. 11, November 1981, p. 52. To the question, "When do you think a fetus becomes a human being?", 30 percent

answered yes to, "Or is this a question that can't really be determined one way or another."

33 In addition to Wertheimer, "Understanding the Abortion Argument," see also my "Misunderstanding the Abortion Argument," presented to the Senate Judiciary Subcommittee on Separation of Powers hearings on S. 158, 1981.

34 This misleadingly oversimplifies the situation. Something more subtle and complex needs to be said about the diversity of attitudes toward the fetus at its various stages of development.

35 This date would have to shift if the Court were to accept the argument many have urged that advances in medical technology have made second-trimester abortions far safer than they were a decade ago and generally safer than childbirth.

36 *Roe v. Wade*, 410 U.S. 113, 163.

37 Ibid.

38 Ibid., pp. 164–65.

39 *Doe v. Bolton*, 410 U.S. 179, 221–22.

40 Ibid.

41 Ibid., p. 215.

A Human Life Statute

1 410 U.S. 113 (1973). For a critique of the Court's reasoning by a commentator not opposed to abortions, see Ely, "The Wages of Crying Wolf: A Comment on *Roe v. Wade*," 82 *Yale L.J.* 920 (1973) (reprinted in *The Human Life Review*, vol. 1, no. 1, Winter 1975). A stinging attack on the widespread taking of unborn life since *Roe v. Wade* has been delivered by the cofounder of the National Association for Repeal of Abortion Laws (now the National Abortion Rights Action League). See B. Nathanson, *Aborting America* ([Los Angeles: Right to Life,] 1979).

2 "We hold these truths to be self-evident, that all men are created equal, that they are endowed by their Creator with certain unalienable Rights, that among these are Life, Liberty and the pursuit of Happiness." The Declaration of Independence.

3 See *Roe v. Wade*, 410 U.S. at 157–58.

4 *Id.* at 162.

5 *Id.* at 152–54.

6 *Id.* at 156–57.

7 *Id.* at 160.

8 *Id.* at 159.

9 U.S. Const., amend. XIV, § 5.

10 *Chicago & Southern Air Lines, Inc. v. Waterman S. S. Corp.*, 333 U.S. 103, 111 (1948).

11 *Id.* The "dominant considerations" in the political question doctrine are "the appropriateness under our system of government of attributing finality to the action of the political departments and also the lack of satisfactory criteria for a judicial determination," *Coleman v. Miller*, 307 U.S. 433, 454–55 (1939).

12 *Baker* v. *Carr*, 369 U.S. 186, 217 (1962).

13 *Chicago & Southern Air Lines, Inc.* v. *Waterman S. S. Corp.*, 333 U.S. 103, 111 (1948).

14 Clark, "Religion, Morality, and Abortion: A Constitutional Appraisal," 2 *Loyola U. of L.A.L. Rev.* 1, 9 (1969).

15 *Harris* v. *McRae*, 100 S. Ct. 671, 2692 (1980).

16 See, e.g., *Gulf, C. & S. F. Ry.* v. *Ellis*, 165 U.S. 150, 154 (1897).

17 Cong. Globe, 39th Cong., 1st Sess. 1089 (1866) (statement of Cong. Bingham).

18 Cong. Globe, 39th Cong., 1st Sess. 2766 (1866) (statement of Sen. Howard). See also Cincinnati Commercial, Aug. 27, 1866, at 1, col. 3 (address of Cong. Bingham at Bowerstown, Ohio, Aug. 24, 1866).

19 See, e.g., 12 Transactions of A.M.A. 73–77 (1859). See J. Mohr, *Abortion in America: The Origins and Evolution of National Policy, 1800–1900*, at 165 (1978); J. Noonan, *A Private Choice: Abortion in America in the Seventies*, 52 (1979) (quoting minutes of A.M.A. annual meeting of 1859).

20 The Fifteenth Amendment provides:

> Section 1. The right of citizens of the United States to vote shall not be denied or abridged by the United States or by any State on account of race, color, or previous condition of servitude.
> Section 2. The Congress shall have power to enforce this article by appropriate legislation.

21 See *Fullilove* v. *Klutznick*, 100 S. Ct. 2758, 2774 (1980); *City of Rome* v. *United States*, 100 S. Ct. 1548, 1578 n.1 (1980) (Rehnquist, J. dissenting); *United States* v. *Guest*, 383 U.S. 745, 784 (1966) (opinion of Brennan, J.).

22 360 U.S. 45 (1959).

23 See *id.* at 50–53. Appellant also raised a Seventeenth Amendment argument against the literacy test, with equal lack of success. See *id.* at 46, 50.

24 *Id.* at 51.

25 See *id.* at 50, 53.

26 See 42 U.S.C. § 1973b(a)–(d) (1976). Most of the areas covered by this formula turned out to be in the South. The *Lassiter* case also involved a southern state, North Carolina.

27 383 U.S. 301 (1966).

28 See *id.* at 310–15, 333–34.

29 See *id.* at 329.

30 See *id.* at 333–34.

31 See *City of Rome* v. *United States*, 100 S. Ct. 1548, 1561 (1980). See also *id.* at 1575 (Powell, J., dissenting).

32 See 42 U.S.C. § 1973b(e) (1976). Although the section speaks generally of American flag schools teaching in languages other than English, it refers in effect to Puerto Rican schools. The state that used a literacy test to exclude graduates of such schools was New York.

33 Because Section 4(e) was introduced as an amendment to the Voting Rights Act on the floor of the Senate, it was debated only briefly and was not considered in congressional hearings. See 111 Cong. Rec. 11027–28, 11068–74 (1965).

34   384 U.S. 641 (1966).

35   *Id.* at 649 (emphasis added).

36   U.S. Const., Art. I, § 8.

37   See *Katzenbach* v. *Morgan*, 384 U.S. at 650–53.

38   See *id.* at 652–53.

39   See *id.* at 653–56.

40   *Id.* at 656 (emphasis added).

41   See *id.* at 650–51.

42   See *id.* at 648 and no.7. "It is the power of Congress which has been enlarged." *Id.* at 648 (quoting *Ex parte Virginia*, 100 U.S. 339, 345 (1880)).

43   See, e.g., Cox, "The Supreme Court 1965 Term, Foreword: Constitutional Adjudication and the Promotion of Human Rights," 80 *Harv. L. Rev.* 91, 106–7 (1966); Burt, "Miranda and Title II: A Morganatic Marriage," 1969 *Sup. Ct. Rev.* 81.

44   Pub. L. No. 91-285, 84 Stat. 314, 318 (1970).

45   400 U.S. 112 (1970).

46   See *Oregon* v. *Mitchell*, 400 U.S. 112, 216 (1970) (opinion of Harlan, J.).

47   See *id.* at 131–34 (opinion of Black, J.); *id.* at 147 (opinion of Douglas, J.); *id.* at 233–36 (opinion of Brennan, White, and Marshall, J. J.); *id.* at 282–84 (opinion of Stewart and Blackmun, J. J., and Burger, C. J.). See also *Gaston County* v. *United States*, 395 U.S. 285 (1969).

48   See *Oregon* v. *Mitchell*, 400 U.S. at 240 (1970) (opinion of Brennan, White, and Marshall, J. J.).

49   100 S. Ct. 2758, 2774 (1980).

50   *Id.* (quoting *Katzenbach* v. *Morgan*, 384 U.S. at 651).

51   100 S. Ct. 1548 (1980).

52   See *id.* at 1553–54.

53   See *id.* at 1559.

54   See *id.* at 1560.

55   *Id.* at 1562.

56   *Katzenbach* v. *Morgan*, 384 U.S. at 649.

57   Cohen, "Congressional Power to Interpret Due Process and Equal Protection," 27 *Stan. L. Rev.* 603, 618–19 (1975). Another commentator describes this congressional role as "interpretive filling-out of the underlying constitutional guarantee." Monaghan, "The Supreme Court 1974 Term, Foreword: Constitutional Common Law," 89 *Harv. L. Rev.* 1, 23 (1975).

58   *Id.* at 619.

59   *Id.*

60   See *id.* at 620.

61   See Bickel, "The Original Understanding and the Segregation Decision," 69 *Harv. L. Rev.* 1, 63 (1955).

62   See *Katzenbach* v. *Morgan*, 384 U.S. at 667–68 (Harlan, J., dissenting).

63   See *Oregon* v. *Mitchell*, 400 U.S. at 295–96 (opinion of Stewart, J. & Burger, C. J.).

64 See *City of Rome* v. *United States*, 100 S. Ct. at 1577–79, 1584–85 (Rehnquist, J., dissenting).

65 *Katzenbach* v. *Morgan*, 384 U.S. at 668 (Harlan, J., dissenting).

66 See *Oregon* v. *Mitchell*, 500 U.S. at 205–7 (opinion of Harlan, J.); *id.* at 294 (opinion of Stewart, J.).

67 See *City of Rome* v. *United States*, 100 S. Ct. at 1581 (Rehnquist, J., dissenting).

68 Justice Harlan discussed the relevance of this evidence to the constitutional determination in his later *Morgan* dissent. See 384 U.S. at 667–68 (Harlan, J., dissenting).

69 *Katzenbach* v. *Morgan*, 384 U.S. at 668 (Harlan, J., dissenting).

70 370 U.S. 530 (1962).

71 See *Ex parte Bakelite Corp.*, 279 U.S. 438 (1929); *Williams* v. *United States*, 289 U.S. 553 (1933).

72 See *Glidden Co.* v. *Zdanok*, 370 U.S. at 536–37, 541–43.

73 *Id.* at 542.

74 See *id.* at 542–43.

75 The Thirteenth Amendment reads as follows:

>   Section 1. Neither slavery nor involuntary servitude, except as punishment for a crime whereof the party shall have been duly convicted, shall exist within the United States, or any place subject to their jurisdiction.
>   Section 2. Congress shall have power to enforce this article by appropriate legislation.

76 392 U.S. 409 (1968).

77 See *id.* at 440–41.

78 *Id.* at 440.

79 427 U.S. 160 (1976).

80 See *id.* at 170 (opinion of the Court); *id.* at 186–87 (Powell, J., concurring); *id.* at 189–91 (Stevens, J., concurring); *id.* at 208 n.13 (White, J., joined by Rehnquist, J., dissenting).

81 See *Fullilove* v. *Klutznick*, 100 S. Ct. at 2786 (Powell, J., concurring).

82 *Oregon* v. *Mitchell*, 400 U.S. at 206–7 (opinion of Harlan, J.).

83 There are, of course, areas of constitutional interpretation apart from the Civil War amendments in which Congress has taken the lead and the courts have followed. One recurring example is found when Congress differs from the Supreme Court in interpreting the extent to which the Commerce Clause prohibits certain kinds of state regulation or taxation. See, e.g., *Prudential Ins. Co.* v. *Benjamin*, 328 U.S. 408, 423 (1946). Compare *Leisy* v. *Hardin*, 135 U.S. 100 (1890) with *In re Rahrer*, 140 U.S. 545 (1891).

84 347 U.S. 483 (1954).

85 163 U.S. 537 (1896).

86 See Cox, "The Role of Congress in Constitutional Determinations," 40 U. Cin. L. Rev. 199, 227 n.100 (1971).

87 See *South Carolina* v. *Katzenbach*, 383 U.S. at 326.

88 See 384 U.S. at 652–53.

89 100 S. Ct. at 1562 (emphasis added).

90   See L. Tribe, "The Supreme Court, 1972 Term, Foreword: Toward a Model of Roles in the Due Process of Life and Law," 87 *Harv. L. Rev.*, 1, 18–25 (1973).

91   See L. Tribe, *American Constitutional Law* 928 (1978).

92   *Harris* v. *McRae*, 100 S. Ct. 2671, 2689 (1980) (quoting *McGowan* v. *Maryland*, 366 U.S. 420, 442 [1961]).

93   *Katzenbach* v. *Morgan*, 384 U.S. at 651 n.10.

94   *Id.*

95   For example, if Congress enacted a federal criminal statute to prohibit abortion, its action would collide with the right to privacy. On one occasion Congress has taken action arguably contrary to the ratchet theory. In the Omnibus Crime Control and Prevention Act of 1967, Congress differed from the Supreme Court's view that police interrogation of a person in their custody is inherently coercive. See S. Rep. No. 1097, 90th Cong., 2d Sess., 60–61 (1968). The Supreme Court has not reviewed this provision.

96   See *Harris* v. *McRae*, 100 S. Ct. 2671, 2685–89 (1980).

97   See *id.* at 2688–89.

98   See *United States* v. *Guest*, 383 U.S. 745 (1966); Frantz, "Congressional Power to Enforce the Fourteenth Amendment Against Private Acts," 73 *Yale L.J.* 1353 (1964).

99   See *Roe* v. *Wade*, 410 U.S. at 156–57.

100   *United States* v. *Vuitch*, 402 U.S. 62, 80 (1971) (Douglas, J., dissenting in part).

101   See Cohen, *supra* note 59 and accompanying text.

102   *Proposed Amendments to the U.S. Constitution to Protect Unborn Children: Hearings on S. J. Res. 119 & S. J. Res. 130 before the Subcomm. on Constitutional Amendments of the Senate Judiciary Comm.*, 93d Cong., 2d Sess., pt. I, at 6 (1974) (statement of Sen. Hatfield).

103   See *Prudential Ins. Co.* v. *Benjamin*, 328 U.S. 408 (1946).

104   *Id.* at 439. See generally Koenig, "Federal and State Cooperation Under the Constitution," 36 *Mich. L. Rev.* 752 (1938).

105   See 42 U.S.C. § 1973h (1976).

106   *Katzenbach* v. *Morgan*, 348 U.S. at 651.

107   The Fifth Amendment does not confer power on Congress to enforce its terms, but Congress may well have power to influence judicial interpretations of the Fifth Amendment's protection of life by informing the judiciary of its view on the beginnings of life.

108   *Roschen* v. *Ward*, 279 U.S. 337, 339 (1929), quoted in *Katzenbach* v. *Morgan*, 384 U.S. at 657.

109   *Semler* v. *Oregon State Board of Dental Examiners*, 294 U.S. 608, 610 (1935), quoted in *Katzenbach* v. *Morgan*, 384 U.S. at 657.

110   *Williamson* v. *Lee Optical Co.*, 3´8 F. U.S. 483, 489 (1955), quoted in *Katzenbach* v. *Morgan*, 384 U.S. at (57.

111   *Abele* v. *Markle*, 342 F. Supp. 80(803–4 (D. Conn. 1972) (three judge court).

112   *Id.* at 804.

Constitutional Privacy, Religious Disestablishment, and the Abortion Decisions

1   410 U.S. 113 (1973).

2   *Doe* v. *Commonwealth's Attorney*, 403 F. Supp. 1199 (E.D. Va. 1975), *aff'd without opinion*, 425 U.S. 901 (1976).

3   See, e.g., *People* v. *Onofre*, 51 N.Y.2d 476 (1980), *cert. denied*, 451 U.S. 987 (1981).

4   J. H. Ely, *Democracy and Distrust: A Theory of Judicial Review* (Cambridge: Harvard University Press, 1982).

5   Francis Hutcheson, *A System of Moral Philosophy* (New York: Augustus M. Kelley, Publishers, 1968), p. 299.

6   James Witherspoon, *Lectures on Moral Philosophy*, ed. Jack Scott (London and Toronto: Associated University Presses, 1982), p. 123.

7   See Kenneth I. Karst, "The Freedom of Intimate Association," 89 *Yale L.J.* 624 (1980).

8   381 U.S. 449 (1958).

9   See J. H. Ely, "The Wages of Crying Wolf: A Comment on *Roe* v. *Wade*," 82 *Yale L.J.* 920 (1973).

10   See Learned Hand, *The Bill of Rights* (New York: Atheneum, 1968).

11   See R. M. Dworkin, *Taking Rights Seriously* (Cambridge: Harvard University Press, 1977), pp. 131–49.

12   John Stuart Mill, *On Liberty*, ed. Alburey Castell (New York: Appleton-Century-Crofts, 1947).

13   See ibid.; James Fitzjames Stephen, *Liberty, Equality, Fraternity*, ed. R. J. White (Cambridge: Cambridge at the University Press, 1967).

14   See H.L.A. Hart, *Law, Liberty and Morality* (Stanford, Calif.: Stanford University Press, 1963); Patrick Devlin, *The Enforcement of Morals* (London: Oxford University Press, 1965), pp. 1–25.

15   Devlin, *Enforcement of Morals*.

16   The closest approximation to a purely conventional form of moral appraisal is some form of conventional rule—utilitarianism, of the kind that Stephen, for example, appears to assume; see Stephen, *Liberty, Equality, Fraternity*. However, such a perspective is still importantly committed to the crucial relevance of utilitarian consequences in the moral assessment of actions and institutions, and thus convention, as such, has no controlling independent moral weight.

17   See note 8, above.

18   See note 1, above.

19   See note 2, above.

20   *Naim* v. *Naim*, 350 U.S. 935 (1956) (dismissing on spurious jurisdictional grounds the appeal from a Virginia judgment dissolving a racially mixed marriage under the state's antimiscegenation statute, statutes later held squarely unconstitutional in *Loving* v. *Virginia*, 388 U.S. 1 (1967)).

21   See note 2, above.

22   See Gerald Gunther, "The Subtle Vices of the 'Passive Virtues'," 64 *Colum. L. Rev.* 1 (1964).

23 See Mill, *On Liberty*.
24 Ibid., chap. 2.
25 Ibid., chaps. 3–5.
26 See, especially, Alexis de Tocqueville, *Democracy in America*, vol. 1, ed. P. Bradley (New York: Vintage Books, 1945), chaps. 15–16.
27 See Mill, *On Liberty*, p. 10.
28 See, e.g., David A. J. Richards, *The Moral Criticism of Law* (Encino, Calif.: Dickenson-Wadsworth, 1977), chaps. 5–6.
29 I phrase Mill's argument in the terms later to be elaborated in this study. The express terms of his own argument are an appeal to "individuality"; see Mill, *On Liberty*, p. 55; and, chap. 3, *circa*.
30 See John Stuart Mill, *Utilitarianism*, ed. Oskar Piest (Indianapolis–New York: Liberal Arts Press, 1957), chap. 2.
31 For an elaboration of this criticism of Mill, *see* David A. J. Richards, *Sex, Drugs, Death and the Law* (Totowa, N.J.: Rowman and Littlefield, 1982), chap. 1.
32 See Stephen, *Liberty, Equality, Fraternity*.
33 See, for example, John Gray, *Mill on Liberty: A Defence* (London: Routledge and Kegan Paul, 1983); and Fred Berger, in his important forthcoming study, *Happiness, Justice and Freedom* (University of California Press). I am grateful to Fred Berger for allowing me to see his manuscript before publication.
34 See D. Richards, *A Theory of Reasons for Action* (Oxford: Clarendon Press, 1971), pp. 114–15.
35 See C. L. Ten, *Mill on Liberty* (Oxford: Clarendon Press, 1980).
36 See, e.g., Ely, "Wages of Crying Wolf."
37 63 *Colum. L. Rev.* 391 (1961).
38 See, e.g., *Committee for Pub. Ed. & Rel. Lib. v. Regan*, 100 Sup. Ct. 840 (1980).
39 See, e.g., Bernard Williams, *Obscenity and Film Censorship* (Cambridge: Cambridge University Press, 1981), pp. 80–85; *Report of the Commission on Obscenity and Pornography* (Washington, D.C.: U.S. Government Printing Office, 1970), pp. 230–32.
40 See, e.g., Richards, *Sex, Drugs, Death and Law*, chap. 2.
41 My understanding is that Henkin would justify *Roe* on the general ground of privacy as an autonomy right. See, e.g., Louis Henkin, "Privacy and Autonomy," 74 *Colum. L. Rev.* 1410 (1974). I am grateful to Professor Henkin for comments on an earlier draft of this paper, which clarified his views on these matters for me.
42 *McRae v. Califano*, 491 F. Supp. at 741 (1980).
43 *Harris v. McRae*, 448 U.S. 297, 319 (1980).
44 See notes 5 to 8, above, and accompanying text.
45 These remarks are sketchy and highly incomplete, and will be further explicated and defended in a book-length study of the place of the religion clauses in American constitutional law.
46 See *Reynolds v. United States*, 98 U.S. 145 (1878).
47 In cases like *Sherbert v. Verner*, 374 U.S. 398 (1963), and others.
48 See John Locke, A *Letter Concerning Toleration*, in *Treatise of Civil Gov-*

ernment and A Letter Concerning Toleration (New York: Appleton-Century-Crofts, 1937), pp. 185, 198, 201, 207.

49 Thomas Jefferson, *Notes on the State of Virginia*, ed. William Penden (Chapel Hill: University of North Carolina Press, 1955), p. 159.

50 This idea is, I believe, implicit in Mill's argument for the harm principle, and is a thought central to the familiar theme in contemporary philosophy that that conception of the person, as essentially contemplative, deeply distorts the central place of agency in the lives of humans. Kant's conception of the primacy of practical over theoretical reason makes this point, I believe. See I. Kant, *Critique of Practical Reason*, trans. L. W. Beck (Indianapolis–New York: Liberal Arts Press, 1956), pp. 124–26. For more recent statements, see John Dewey, *The Quest for Certainty* (New York: Perigee Book, 1929); Richard Rorty, *Philosophy and the Mirror of Nature* (Princeton: Princeton University Press, 1979); Bernard Williams, *Descartes: The Project of Pure Enquiry* (Harmondsworth: Penguin, 1978).

51 See, e.g., *Everson v. Board of Educ.*, 330 U.S. 1 (1947).

52 For pertinent commentary, see Joseph Lecler, *Toleration and the Reformation*, vol. 1, trans. T. L. Westow (New York: Association Press, 1960), pp. 107–33; id., vol. 2, pp. 168–77.

53 See Pierre Bayle, *Commentaire Philosophique*, in *Oeuvres Diverses de Mr. Pierre Bayle*, vol. 2 (A La Haye: Chez P. Husson et al., 1727), pp. 357–560.

54 See Locke, *Letter Concerning Toleration*. For Locke's latitudinarian conception of legitimate religious differences over moral questions, see John Locke, *The Reasonableness of Christianity*, ed. I. T. Ramsey (Stanford, Calif.: Stanford University Press, 1957).

55 See Roger Williams, "The Bloody Tenent of Persecution," in *The Complete Writings of Roger Williams*, vol. 3, ed. S. L. Caldwell (New York: Russel & Russel, 1963).

56 For pertinent commentary, see Lecler, *Toleration*, vol. 1, pp. 336–60, 369–76. For relevant original texts, see Sebastian Castellio, *Concerning Heretics*, ed. R. H. Bainton (New York: Columbia University Press, 1935); Jacobus Acontius, *Darkness Discovered (Satan's Strategems)*, ed. R. E. Field (Delmar, N.Y.: Scholars' Facsimiles & Reprints, 1978).

57 See Plato, *Euthyphro*, trans. L. Cooper, in E. Hamilton and H. Cairns, *Plato: the Collected Dialogues* (New York: Pantheon, 1961), pp. 169–85.

58 For the evolution of this idea and its impact on early American thought both in the seventeenth and eighteenth centuries, see Norman Fiering, *Moral Philosophy at Seventeenth-Century Harvard* (Chapel Hill: University of North Carolina Press, 1981); Norman Fiering, *Jonathan Edwards's Thought and Its British Context* (Chapel Hill: University of North Carolina Press, 1981).

59 See Witherspoon, *Lectures on Moral Philosophy*, pp. 85–86, 103–4; but cf. pp. 91–94.

60 Reprinted, Jefferson, *Notes on Virginia*, p. 223.

61 See Locke, *Letter Concerning Toleration*, pp. 212–13. Locke, of course also exempted Catholics from toleration on the ground that they were themselves rootedly intolerant; id., pp. 210–12.

62 See Bayle, *Commentaire*, p. 431. Bayle, like Locke, would not extend tolerance to intolerant Catholics as well, id., pp. 410–15.

63 See excerpts from Joseph Story's *Commentaries on the Constitution of the United States*, pp. 128–30; Philip Schaff, "Church and State in the United States," in *Papers of the American Historical Association*, vol. 2, no. 4 (New York: Putnam's, 1888).

64 See, e.g., *Engel* v. *Vitale*, 370 U.S. 421 (1962).

65 See, e.g., *Epperson* v. *Arkansas*, 393 U.S. 97 (1968).

66 See Richards, *Sex, Drugs, Death and Law*, chap. 4.

67 367 U.S. 488 (1961).

68 See, e.g., *United States* v. *Seeger*, 380 U.S. 163 (1965).

69 See, e.g., *Doe*, note 2, above, 403 F. Supp. 1201; and Devlin, *Enforcement of Morals*.

70 See James C. Mohr, *Abortion in America* (Oxford: Oxford University Press, 1978).

71 *Griswold* v. *Connecticut*, 381 U.S. 449 (1958).

72 St. Thomas elaborates Augustine's conception of the exclusive legitimacy of procreative sex in a striking way. Of the emission of semen apart from procreation in marriage, he wrote: "[A]fter the sin of homicide whereby a human nature already in existence is destroyed, this type of sin appears to take next place, for by it the generation of human nature is precluded." T. Aquinas, *On the Truth of the Catholic Faith: Summa Contra Gentiles*, pt. 2, chap. 122(9), trans. V. Bourke (New York: Image, 1956), p. 146. For Augustine, see Augustine, *The City of God*, trans. H. Bettenson (Harmondsworth: Penguin, 1972), pp. 577–94.

73 For pertinent discussion, see H. L. A. Hart, *Essays on Bentham* (Oxford: Clarendon Press, 1982), chap. 3. Price is discussed at pp. 60–61.

74 Jean-Jacques Rousseau, *The Social Contract*, in *The Social Contract and Discourses*, trans. G. D. H. Cole (London: Dent, 1950).

75 Immanuel Kant, *Foundations of the Metaphysics of Morals*, trans. L. W. Beck (New York: Liberal Arts Press, 1959), pp. 49–51.

76 See W. Godwin, *Enquiry Concerning Political Justice*, ed. I. Kramnick (Harmondsworth: Penguin, 1976); R. P. Wolff, *In Defense of Anarchism* (New York: Harper and Row, 1970).

77 See notes 42 to 43, above, and text accompanying.

78 See L. W. Sumner, *Abortion and Moral Theory* (Princeton: Princeton University Press, 1981), pp. 115–23.

79 See Baruch Brody, *Abortion and the Sanctity of Human Life: A Philosophical View* (Cambridge: MIT Press, 1976); Joel Feinberg, "Abortion," in Tom Regan, ed., *Matters of Life and Death* (New York: Random House, 1980), pp. 202–14.

80 See J. J. Thomson, "A Defense of Abortion," 1 *Phil. & Pub. Aff.* 547–66 (1971); D. H. Regan, "Rewriting *Roe* v. *Wade*," 77 *Mich. L. Rev.* 1569 (1979).

81 See Feinberg, "Abortion," pp. 209–14. But see Frances Myrna, "The Right to Abortion," in *Ethics for Modern Life*, ed. R. Abelson and M. L. Friquegnon (New York: St. Martin's Press, 2d ed. 1980) at pp. 103–16.

82   If the fetus at fertilization has a lesser moral status than that of a full person, the claims made on its behalf could not constitute claims of rights in the required sense. Cf. Warren Quinn, "Abortion: Identity and Loss," 13 *Phil. & Pub. Aff.* 24 (1984). However, even claims of a lesser moral status may be based on metaphysical assumptions which crucially confuse the conditions of moral personality with biological individuation, as Quinn may.

83   James J. McCartney, "Some Roman Catholic Concepts of Person and their Implications for the Ontological Status of the Unborn," in *Abortion and the Status of the Foetus*, ed. W. B. Bondeson, H. Tristram Engelhardt, Jr., S. F. Spicker, & D. H. Winship (Dordrecht: Reidel 1983), pp. 313–23.

84   See Daniel Callahan, *Abortion: Law, Choice and Morality* (New York: Macmillan 1970), pp. 409–41; A. S. Morczewski, "Human Personhood," in Bondeson et al., *Abortion and Status of Foetus*, pp. 301–11.

85   See Feinberg, "Abortion," pp. 184–202; Paul Bassen, "Present Sakes and Future Prospects: The Status of Early Abortion," 11 *Phil. & Pub. Aff.* 314 (1982).

86   See Bondeson et al., *Abortion and Status of Foetus*, pp. xvi–xvii.

87   See McCartney, "Roman Catholic Concepts."

88   On the moral conscientiousness of an abortion decision for women, see Carol Gilligan, *In a Different Voice* (Cambridge: Harvard University Press, 1982), pp. 70–71.

89   See Beverly W. Harrison, *Our Right to Choose* (Boston: Beacon Press, 1983).

90   See Michael Tooley, "Abortion and Infanticide", 2 *Phil. & Pub. Aff.* 37 (1972); Feinberg, "Abortion."

91   See Bassen, "Present Sakes and Future Prospects"; Cf. Sumner, *Abortion and Moral Theory*; Brody, *Abortion and Sanctity of Life*; E. W. Kluge, *The Practice of Death* (New Haven and London: Yale University Press, 1975).

92   See, e.g., H. Tristram Engelhardt, Jr., "Viability and the Use of the Fetus," in Bondeson et al., *Abortion and Status of Foetus*, pp. 183–208.

93   See Richards, *Sex, Drugs, Death and Law*, chaps. 3–5.

94   See note 2, above.

95   See note 3, above.

Killing and Letting Die

1   James Rachels, "Active and Passive Euthanasia," *New England Journal of Medicine* 292 (January 9, 1975): 78–80; Michael Tooley, "Abortion and Infanticide," *Philosophy and Public Affairs* 2, no. 1 (Fall 1972); Jonathan Bennett, "Morality and Consequences," in *The Tanner Lectures on Human Values*, vol. 2, ed. Sterling McMurrin (Cambridge: Cambridge University Press, 1981).

2   John Taurek, "Should the Numbers Count?" *Philosophy and Public Affairs*, no. 4 (Summer 1977): 293–316.

3   G. E. M. Anscombe, "Modern Moral Philosophy," *Philosophy* 33 (1958): 1–19.

4   Rachels, "Active and Passive Euthanasia."

5   Cf. Philippa Foot, "Killing, Letting Die, and Euthanasia: A Reply to Holly
    Smith Goldman," *Analysis* 41, no. 4 (June 1981).
6   Judith Jarvis Thomson, "A Defense of Abortion," *Philosophy and Public
    Affairs* 1 (1971): 44.

Abortion and Self-Defense

1   There are many factors that bear on any particular abortion decision, thus
    the statement of the three positions must be qualified, and that is what the
    phrases in parentheses are meant to indicate. But recognizing the need for
    qualification should not incline us to suppose that none of the three posi-
    tions (or my statements of them) can possibly be satisfactory, since they are
    not meant to represent formulas that can be mechanically applied to cases,
    but rather (different) approaches to the question of how we are to determine
    the range of morally defensible abortions.
2   I shall refer to the prospective abortion candidate not as "the mother," but
    as "the pregnant woman," or, where context permits, "the woman." This en-
    cumbers both phraseology and syntax, but it seems to me that the benefits
    outweigh the costs. "Mother" is used to refer both to the person who is the
    female biological/genetic parent, and to the person who takes on the task of
    raising and nurturing a child. Since the person who bears a child may play no
    role whatsoever in raising it, it is clear that "mother" is ambiguous. In which
    of these senses—if either—is a pregnant woman accurately characterized as
    a mother? Not the first, for she does not become a biological mother until
    and unless the pregnancy issues in the live birth of a child: if abortion is per-
    formed, or the fetus simply dies *in utero*, this precludes her becoming a bio-
    logical mother. Nor is it entirely accurate to describe her as a nurturing
    mother. For there are significant differences between nurturing a postfetal
    child—something that one *does*, and does by *choice* (even if the choice is dic-
    tated by necessity, or made under duress)—and nurturing a *fetus*; for the
    fetus is a sort of parasite and the pregnant woman may be an unwilling—and
    even an unwitting—provider of fetal nurturance. Thus, since "mother" is an
    ambiguous term, and one whose criteria of application are not altogether
    clear, it is wise to avoid using it to refer to a pregnant woman. One does not
    want to charge the abortion dispute with more emotional high voltage than
    is necessary.
        This point has not been taken to heart by philosophers who discuss abor-
    tion: even when the ambiguity is noted (and conceded to be obvious), the
    prospective abortion candidate is still deemed "the mother." See, for example,
    Steven L. Ross, "Abortion and the Death of the Fetus," *Philosophy & Public
    Affairs* 11, no. 3 (Summer 1982): 232–45; see especially pp. 232, 239, 241.
3   How stringent the Restrictive view is is greatly affected by how the notion of
    a 'threat to life' is to be understood. If abortion is held to be defensible only
    when there is a clear and direct threat to a woman's life, then the Restrictive
    view will emerge as very strict indeed. On the other hand, if Restrictives
    allow abortion when the threat to life is marginal—a mere consequence of

there being some risk to the woman's health—then the Restrictive view will emerge as much more liberal than it appears to be. It is probable that secular Restrictives favor a middle interpretation, but the characterization of the notion of a 'threat to life' is far from straightforward. There are conditions that pose a threat to health—for example, diabetes and kidney disease—that may have severe, even fatal, repercussions, but they cannot comfortably be regarded as threats to life. Does the secular Restrictive allow or disallow abortion in such cases? The division between threats to life and threats to health is not likely to be easy to characterize or to draw with any precision, but it appears to be a division that Restrictives must rely on. It may also be one that non-Restrictives must rely on. See below, note 17.

4   It is important to recognize that the 'choice between lives' situation is one that can arise at *any* stage of a pregnancy. *Pace* Baruch Brody ("Abortion and the Sanctity of Human Life," reprinted in *The Problem of Abortion*, ed. Joel Feinberg [Belmont, Calif.: Wadsworth, 1973], pp. 104–20), the situation is not one that is "possible only at the very end of pregnancy"; we can know early on that we are faced with a case in which "if we do nothing the fetus will survive and the mother will die" (p. 115). The clearest example of such a case is that in which a woman is diagnosed early in her pregnancy as suffering from cervical cancer. The cancer poses a threat to the woman's life, but it does not in itself constitute a threat to the well-being of the fetus. The danger to the woman consists largely in the fact that the pregnancy accelerates the growth of the cancer and contraindicates the preferred sorts of treatment (for they are dangerous to the fetus).

5   I am not, of course, suggesting that other sorts of cases present no problems. But I think that the 'choice between lives' cases are the most worrying: they are the most pressing and, in a sense, the clearest.

6   L. W. Sumner, *Abortion and Moral Theory* (Princeton: Princeton University Press, 1981), p. 108, emphasis added.

7   See Brody, "Abortion and the Sanctity of Human Life"; Philip E. Devine, *The Ethics of Homicide* (Ithaca: Cornell University Press, 1977), chap. 5, sec. 22; Alan Donagan, *The Theory of Morality* (Chicago: University of Chicago Press, 1977), chap. 5, sec. 3. See also Sumner's helpful discussion of natural law theories in *Abortion and Moral Theory*, chap. 3.

8   I shall sometimes adopt a bit of shorthand and speak of the case in which abortion is undertaken to preserve the woman's life as 'abortion in self-defense.' Since I shall argue that 'abortion in self-defense' is not aptly characterized as a case of self-defense at all, I shall flag the expression with scare quotes.

9   The request is for an argument that is both strong and secular: it will not do simply to cite the longevity of the natural law tradition and point out that the 'natural law forbidding homicide' has been understood as applying only to the direct killing of the innocent, rather than as having a wider scope. Even if such an interpretation can be supported by historical evidence, and buttressed by the presentation of some sort of rationale, this is not enough. What is needed is not historical exegesis of a fundamentally religious perspective, or articulation of the rationale underlying it, but a defense of the

substantive view that it embodies: an argument to the effect that the substantive view that it embodies is defensible.

10   See Judith Jarvis Thomson, "A Defense of Abortion," *Philosophy & Public Affairs* 1, no. 1 (Fall 1971): 47–66. I do not mean to imply that Thomson herself would agree with my formulation of the Thomson-strategy. Nor do I mean to suggest that those who espouse a Thomson-Moderate position would agree among themselves, either on the finer points of their interpretation of Thomson's position, or in their own substantive conclusions.

11   There are cases of 'letting die' that are also cases of killing—for example, withholding food from one's infant child; and cases of 'killing' that are also cases of letting die—for example, turning off the life-support system of someone who is terminally ill to enable him or her to die of 'natural causes.' See Jonathan Bennett, "Morality and Consequences," in *The Tanner Lectures on Human Values*, Vol. II, ed. Sterling McMurrin (Cambridge: Cambridge University Press, 1981), pp. 45–116, especially Lectures I and III; Nancy Davis, "The Priority of Avoiding Harm," in *Killing and Letting Die*, ed. Bonnie Steinbock (Englewood Cliffs, N.J.: Prentice-Hall, 1980), pp. 172–214; Jonathan Glover, *Causing Death and Saving Lives* (Harmondsworth: Penguin, 1977), chaps. 6 and 7; Susan Teft Nicholson, *Abortion and the Roman Catholic Church* (Knoxville: *Journal of Religious Ethics Monograph*, 1978), chaps. 4 and 5; Judith Jarvis Thomson, "A Defense of Abortion," and "Rights and Deaths," *Philosophy & Public Affairs* 2, no. 2 (Winter 1973): 146–59; and "Killing, Letting Die and the Trolley Problem," *The Monist* 59, no. 2 (1976): 204–17.

To say this is not, of course, to claim that cases of killing are *always* describable as cases of letting die (or *vice versa*), nor is it to say that killing and letting die are *always* on a par. It is merely to point out that "the" distinction between killing and letting die is problematic: it is not exhaustive, exclusive, or evaluatively neutral. Nor is there anything like one clear distinction: there are several rather muddled ones.

It is surprising how many people assume that the *denial* of the tenability of "the" distinction between killing and letting die (on the ground that we cannot find a clear distinction here, and so cannot posit an intrinsic, morally significant asymmetry between the two) is an assertion of the absolute and universal moral equivalence of killing and letting die. It is, of course, no such thing.

12   People sometimes object to the use of "parasite" in this context. Three different objections are raised: that it involves the use of a term of opprobrium; that it involves a misrepresentation of the relationship between the fetus and the pregnant woman (on the ground that the relationship is better described as "symbiotic" than as "parasitic"); that it involves a misuse of the biological term "parasite" (on the ground that the term applies only when the two organisms involved are members of different species).

The first two objections simply fail. Those who take "parasite" to be a term of opprobrium are confusing the biological sense and the original sense ("one frequenting the tables of the rich and earning welcome by flattery," *Webster's New Collegiate Dictionary*, 7th ed. [Springfield, Mass.: Merriam, 1963],

p. 611). Those who call the relationship between the woman and the fetus "symbiotic" are mistaken: when continuation of the pregnancy poses a clear threat to a woman's life, the relationship between the woman and the fetus cannot be described as "symbiotic": this is simply a misuse of the biological term. The third objection is the most forceful. Some dictionaries and biological texts define "parasite" functionally in terms of the relationship between individual organisms, while others define it in terms of the relationship between members of two different species (that is, *a* is parasitic upon *b* versus *A's* are parasitic upon *B's*). To accommodate the discrepancy in usage, I have described the fetus as "(in a sense) parasitic upon the woman." It is worth noting, however, that my usage is the one preferred by many sources, and that Webster's offers a third entry that vindicates this usage entirely: "something that resembles a biological parasite in dependence upon something else without making a useful or adequate return" (p. 611).

13 See Thomson, "A Defense of Abortion." For legal argument that parallels Thomson's moral argument at many points, see Donald H. Regan, "Rewriting *Roe v. Wade*," *Michigan Law Review* 77, no. 7 (1979): 1569–1646, especially sec. III.

14 Sometimes it is claimed that the appeal to self-defense is, or involves, an appeal to this asymmetry. Both Sumner and Regan explicitly make such claims. Thus Sumner says, "The appeal to self-defense stresses an asymmetry in the mother/fetus relation; since the fetus is the intruder and the parasite, it is the mother who is defending herself against a threat" (*Abortion and Moral Theory*, p. 121; see also p. 112). Regan says, "The law of self-defense is shaped in part by the notion that there is an asymmetry between the attacker and the attacked (even when the attacker is innocent) which justifies the attacked in protecting himself or herself even in some cases where the cost to the attacker is greater than the harm from which the attacked is spared" (p. 1618). But the asymmetry that distinguishes the attacked from the attacker in cases of justified self-defense is different from the asymmetry in the relationship between the woman and the fetus. I argue this point in the text. (See also George Fletcher, *Rethinking Criminal Law* [Boston: Little, Brown, 1978], p. 863; Sanford Kadish, "Respect for Life and Regard for Rights in the Criminal Law," *California Law Review* 64, no. 4 [1976]: 871–901, especially sec. I.)

15 In speaking of "postfetal persons" I do not mean to be claiming categorically that the fetus is a person, but rather adopting a neutral way of speaking, one that neither asserts nor denies that the fetus is a person.

16 I think that both Regan and Sumner would disagree. But even if one agrees with Sumner in thinking that "the right of self-defense is a special case of the right to autonomy" (*Abortion and Moral Theory*, p. 114, note 46), and thinks also that abortion is defensible whenever pregnancy has arisen from rape, it is not plausible to suppose that one is thereby claiming that abortion (when the pregnancy has arisen from rape) is to be justified by an appeal to the woman's right of self-defense.

17 As I understand it, a right of self-defense is, in essence, a right of self-preservation: it entitles us to take action against someone who threatens to

put an end to us without justification. To say this is not to say that we are entitled to kill an attacker only when the attacker threatens to *kill* us (there are, after all, other ways of effectively destroying people). Nor is it to say that we are entitled to kill whenever an attacker threatens to kill us. But since this does not bear on the text footnoted here, I shall not discuss it. See below, note 42.

How broad is the entitlement? When may we appeal to the right of self-defense to justify killing an attacker who is not threatening to kill us? As most writers on the subject point out, two things seem to be material: the nature of the threat, and the nature of the harm. Other things being equal, we are entitled to be more aggressive in repelling a threat that is a clear instance of hostile or malevolent conduct than we are in repelling an innocent threat. And other things being equal, we are entitled to adopt more drastic measures against attackers who threaten us with serious and abiding harm than we are against those who threaten to cause us (merely) annoyance, inconvenience, or embarrassment.

It is not altogether clear what counts as serious and abiding harm, and so it is difficult to say precisely what the entitlement to self-defense (or self-preservation) actually amounts to. This is a serious problem, but it does not undermine the point in the text. Unless it can be shown that *every* woman who is pregnant due to rape suffers a serious and abiding harm if she is obliged to carry the fetus to term, it cannot be maintained that *any* woman who seeks to terminate a pregnancy arising from rape is justified in doing so *by virtue of her right of self-defense.*

18   The view that we can explain a being's possession of rights by appealing to the sort of being it is (the individual's properties, or the essential properties of the class of which it is a member) is an attractive and natural view. Even if we think of rights as things that are conferred (rather than discovered), and thus reject the suggestion that a fetus could be determined to have 'rights' simply by virtue of its possession of certain biological properties, we are inclined to believe that the properties of the fetus (or of *Homo sapiens* as a class) form the basis of the conferral. That is, we look to see what sort of entity the fetus is, and justify or explain conferring rights upon it by appealing to these biological (or descriptive) properties. Although the view is natural and attractive, it is problematic in a number of ways. (See Derek Parfit, "Later Selves and Moral Principles," in *Philosophy and Personal Relations,* ed. Alan Montefiore [London: Routledge and Kegan Paul, 1973] pp. 137–69.) And it still leaves us supposing that—somehow—it is the descriptive properties of the fetus that *determine* its personhood (or nonpersonhood), that necessitate our conferral of the rights and privileges of personhood upon it.

19   John Finnis remarks that "it is convenient and appropriate to speak of 'rights' for [some] purposes and in [some] contexts . . . [but] it is most inconvenient and inappropriate when one is debating the moral permissibility of types of actions—types such as 'abortions performed without the desire to kill' . . ." ("The Rights and Wrongs of Abortion," *Philosophy & Public Affairs* 2, no. 2 [Winter 1973]: 117–45; p. 117). Presumably, then, there

will be problems with speaking about rights not just in the case of abortion, but in any case that shares (what Finnis would agree to be) its relevant features: abortions are certainly not the only sorts of killings that may be, and often are, performed without the desire to kill.

20 Some of the problems that have lain dormant within our theory of rights emerge with great force when we appeal to our framework of rights and interests to try to answer the question of what is owed to future generations. See Derek Parfit, "Future Generations: Further Problems," *Philosophy & Public Affairs* 11, no. 2 (Spring 1982): 113–72, and *Reasons and Persons* (forthcoming).

21 Sumner, *Abortion and Moral Theory*, p. 108. See also Brody, "Abortion and the Sanctity of Human Life"; Joel Feinberg, "Abortion," in *Matters of Life and Death*, ed. Tom Regan (New York: Random House, 1980), pp. 183–217, especially sec. II, part 7; Fletcher, *Rethinking Criminal Law*, p. 863; Kadish, "Respect for Life," p. 876; Regan, "Rewriting *Roe v. Wade*," sec. III.

22 As I am using the terms, one who does not intend or foresee the harm that he or she will cause, and bears no moral fault for causing it (or being in the position of causing it), is merely an *attacker*, not an aggressor or an assailant.

23 See Feinberg, "Abortion," sec. II, pt. 7, especially pp. 207–8; Fletcher, *Rethinking Criminal Law*, p. 863; Kadish, "Respect for Life," p. 876.

24 See Regan, "Rewriting *Roe v. Wade*," pp. 1617–18.

25 This is very slippery ground, for as critical discussion of the Doctrine of Double Effect has shown, we are really not clear how the distinction between intended means and merely foreseen concomitant is to be drawn. The issue has been further obscured by a widespread tendency to confuse the question of whether a *death* is a means with the question of whether a *killing* is a means. (I argue that there are two different notions of 'means' at work in our thinking in "Means, Ends, and Double Effect," unpublished.) My suspicion is that those who hold the view that the death of the fetus is not a means (on the ground that the woman who undergoes abortion may not actually want the fetus dead) are confusing questions of intention with questions of motivation. But, again, this is very slippery ground.

26 Although this may be relevant to the question of whether abortion in such circumstances is justified or merely excused, it does not seem relevant to the question of whether or not it is defensible. A woman bears some responsibility for being pregnant if she negligently or recklessly engages in voluntary intercourse without taking contraceptive precautions. But unless she knew beforehand that pregnancy would pose a threat to her life, she cannot be said to be responsible for her predicament: that is, being pregnant when pregnancy poses a threat to her life. So the objection embodied in (3) does not straightforwardly apply to the case at hand.

27 "Abortion and the Sanctity of Human Life," p. 105.

28 *Abortion and Moral Theory*, p. 112. I am not sure whether Sumner wishes this claim to be understood within the narrow context of the case he has just been discussing (a case in which the woman is pregnant due to rape, the pregnancy will kill the woman, and the fetus cannot survive in any case), or more generally. Others make similar claims about the woman's right to

third-party assistance, but qualify them. Cf. Thomson, "A Defense of Abortion," pp. 52–6; Nicholson, *Abortion and the Roman Catholic Church*, pp. 52, 64, 71; Regan, "Rewriting *Roe* v. *Wade*," p. 1613.

29 *Ibid* [Regan, "Rewriting *Roe* v. *Wade*," p. 1613]. It should be noted that Regan's principal argument is not a self-defense argument, but a 'no duty to aid' argument. I think it is doubtful that the two arguments are as independent as Regan thinks they are, but this is a point that requires detailed argument, and I cannot pursue it here.

30 See Brody, "Abortion and the Sanctity of Human Life"; Devine, *The Ethics of Homicide*, chap. 5; Donagan, *The Theory of Morality*, chap. 3; Robert Nozick, *Anarchy, State and Utopia* (New York: Basic Books, 1974), pp. 34–35; Thomson, "Rights and Deaths."

31 The example is a slight adaptation of an example of Regan's: "Rewriting *Roe* v. *Wade*," p. 1611.

32 See Kadish, "Respect for Life."

33 There is, of course, a tacit "other things being equal" clause here.

34 Feinberg says that "if it comes down to an inescapable choice between the innocent party suffering a serious harm or the culpable party suffering a still more serious harm, then the latter is the lesser of two evils" ("Abortion," p. 207). He thus conflates the question of whether some choice represents the lesser injustice with the question of whether it represents the lesser of two evils. Many people—consequentialists especially, but not exclusively— would prefer to separate these questions.

35 To say this is not to say that any person would be obliged to make that choice. If we have a special obligation or stand in a special relation to one of the parties, then we may be permitted or even obligated not to act as a purely disinterested bystander would be obliged to act: we may be permitted—or even obligated—to support our friend's claim even though a disinterested third party would not be permitted to do so. Exactly what is the content, or the force, of our "agent-relative permissions" is, of course, of great importance to moral theory and moral life. But it is a complicated and highly controversial matter that I cannot pursue here. See Davis, "Utilitarianism and Responsibility"; Thomas Nagel, "The Limits of Objectivity," in *The Tanner Lectures on Human Values*, vol. I, ed. Sterling McMurrin (Cambridge: Cambridge University Press, 1980), pp. 77–139; Derek Parfit, "Innumerate Ethics," *Philosophy & Public Affairs* 7, no. 4 (Summer 1978): 285–301, and "Prudence, Morality, and the Prisoner's Dilemma," *Proceedings of the British Academy for 1979* (London: Oxford University Press, 1981), pp. 539–64; Amartya Sen, "Rights and Agency," *Philosophy & Public Affairs* 11, no. 1 (Winter 1982): 3–39; John Taurek, "Should the Numbers Count?" *Philosophy & Public Affairs* 6, no. 4 (Summer 1977): 293–316.

36 What renders someone a passive threat is not his or her immobility or inactivity, but his or her lack of agency: at least at the time of the attack, the person whose movements or presence poses a threat to someone's life is not an agent, but (in the old terminology) a patient. I think it is the lack of agency and not the mere lack of movement or activity that is relevant to

the question of the moral permissibility of killing someone who poses a threat to our life. On the basis of conversation and correspondence (respectively), I think that Thomson and Regan would disagree (though the real disagreement may be over how the notion of agency is to be understood).

37 Some people may think that the mountain-climbers case is special and atypical, for mountain climbing is a highly dangerous activity, and one in which the participants can be said to have 'assumed the risk.' While this may affect some peoples' intuitions, it does not affect mine: I would be inclined to say the same things about the case of Alice and Ben as I would about the case of Claire and David: Claire is a pedestrian who is about to be crushed by the falling David, who has been swept off a roof by a sudden explosion or freak gust of wind. David can survive his fall only if he lands squarely on Claire: Claire can survive only if she succeeds in deflecting David's fall by tugging on an available bit of rope (or shrubbery). I gather from conversation with Judith Thomson that she would not be inclined to say the same thing about the two cases.

38 This seems to me to be a corollary of Thomson's denial of the Principle of Moral Inertia. Says Thomson, "There is no Principle of Moral Inertia: there is no duty to refrain from interfering with existing states of affairs just because they are existing states of affairs" ("Killing, Letting Die and the Trolley Problem," p. 209).

39 See Davis, "Utilitarianism and Responsibility"; Nagel, "The Limits of Objectivity"; Parfit, "Innumerate Ethics," and "Prudence, Morality, and the Prisoner's Dilemma"; Sen, "Rights and Agency."

40 Exactly what circumstances, of course, is a burning question, but not one that can be pursued here (see note 35).

41 This is not to say that these are the only relevant factors; it is merely to point to a set of factors that are—at least on the face of it—relevant.

42 I am here discussing effective conflicts between Alice's and Ben's permissions; I am not suggesting that their permissions must be formulated in just the way that I have formulated them. It is difficult to determine the boundaries of our agent-relative permissions, and more difficult still to produce compelling explanations of the boundaries that one finds intuitively plausible. Some people would see the scope of Ben's permission as determined by the fine details of the example's causal structure (perhaps because they see these details as bearing on the form of Ben's intention). Thus it might be said that what matters is what is needed to break Ben's fall: does he need (only) to land on Alice's *ledge*, or does he need actually to land on *Alice*? Even when it is understood that the two are causally bound together—Ben cannot do the one without doing the other—Ben's agent-relative permission may divide them: he may be permitted to try to land on Alice's ledge, but not permitted to try to land on Alice. I am not inclined to share these intuitions, and I believe, moreover, that the attempt to appeal to them leads straight to the quagmire of double effect. But I am not suggesting that the agent-relative permission to preserve our own lives should be interpreted extensionally as granting us license to do whatever is causally necessary to preserve our own lives. Suppose that Ben's fall causes Alice injury but—miraculously!—does not kill her. It is far

from obvious that Ben could appeal to the agent-relative permission to preserve his life to justify hastening Alice's death by (for example) appropriating her warm clothing or her share of the food. Nor would he be permitted to leave her injuries untended if his fall left him capable of rendering her assistance.

43   See Thomas Nagel, "War and Massacre," *Philosophy & Public Affairs* 1, no. 2 (Winter 1972): 123–44.

44   Thomson makes this claim explicitly in "Rights and Deaths" (p. 148). Obviously, it is a view that Restrictives—who think that the fetus has a right to life but also suppose that the pregnant woman has *some* right of self-determination—also accept.

45   To say this is not to say that it must be wrong to actively prefer one to the other, but to point out that when it is agreed that two persons' moral claims are of equal weight, any basis that is used for discriminating between the two people must be shown to be one that morality endorses. Cf. Elizabeth Anscombe, "Who is Wronged?" *Oxford Review* 5 (Trinity 1967): 16–17; Taurek, "Should the Numbers Count?"

46   "Abortion and the Sanctity of Human Life," p. 119.

47   It is not clear that what Donagan says here is consistent with what he says in other places in the book. See Sumner's criticism, *Abortion and Moral Theory*, pp. 109–10.

48   The fetus has close *biological* ties with the pregnant woman, of course, but this cannot be the sort of thing that Devine has in mind when he speaks of close ties. Perhaps Devine's suggestion is as vague (and as weak) as it is because the view he attempts to rationalize is not one that he himself seems at all inclined to hold. This is more evident in the tone of his discussion than it is in any easily quotable extract, but see p. 153.

49   Indeed, this seems rather like blackmail.

50   Since Donagan seems in other respects to be a Restrictive, this is not a result that he would welcome. (But see note 47.)

51   See Feinberg, "Abortion," sec. II; Nicholson, *Abortion and the Roman Catholic Church*, chaps. 3 and 4; Regan, "Rewriting *Roe* v. *Wade*," sec. I; Thomson, "A Defense of Abortion."

52   Pregnant women in California were recently urged to stay out of hot tubs during the first trimester of pregnancy. (What next?)

53   See Regan "Rewriting *Roe* v. *Wade*," sec. IBI, and Nicholson, *Abortion and the Roman Catholic Church*, chaps. 3 and 4.

54   To say this is not to say that the asymmetry between the woman and the fetus is so special that nothing could possibly be morally analogous; it is rather to remind us that while other sorts of situations may exhibit features that render them to some degree morally parallel to pregnancy, pregnancy is *characterized* by these features.

55   See Brody, "Abortion and the Sanctity of Human Life," and Devine, *The Ethics of Homicide*, chap. 5, sec. 22.

56   I am not maintaining that the admission that the claims of one person are weaker than the claims of another requires the admission that the two are not moral peers. It matters why someone's claims are thought to be weaker.

The claims of the fetus are held to be weaker *ab initio*: their assessment as such is in no way related to anything that the fetus has done (and, quite possibly, in no way related to anything that anyone has done). In this case, then, it seems that the relative weakness of the claims of the fetus is predicated on the belief that the fetus simply is not the woman's moral peer: what content is there to the claim that the fetus is a person if its claims are *systematically* discounted? The question is obviously one that requires more sustained treatment than can be given here.

57   See note 18.

58   Indeed, the *in vitro* fetus may be less of a dependent than a house pet is: if the fetus is supplied with the proper conditions, it can develop on its own (though it requires monitoring, it does not necessarily require tending).

Abortion and the Claims of Samaritanism

1   Judith Jarvis Thomson, "A Defense of Abortion," *Philosophy and Public Affairs* 1, no. 1 (Fall 1971); reprinted in Joel Feinberg, ed., *The Problem of Abortion* (Belmont, Calif.: Wadsworth, 1973).

2   Donald Regan, "Rewriting *Roe* v. *Wade*," *Michigan Law Review* 77 (August 1979): 1569.

3   Louis Henkin, "Privacy and Autonomy," *Columbia Law Review* 74 (1974): 1410.

4   Michael Walzer, "The Obligation to Disobey," in *Obligations: Essays on Disobedience, War and Citizenship*, ed. M. Walzer (Cambridge: Harvard University Press, 1982).

5   Alistair MacIntyre, *After Virtue* (Notre Dame, Ind.: Notre Dame University Press, 1981).

6   Roger Wertheimer, "Understanding the Abortion Argument," in Feinberg, *Problem of Abortion.*

7   Alice Walker, *Meridian* (New York: Washington Square Press, 1977).

Abortion, Slavery, and the Law:
A Study in Moral Character

In writing this essay, conversations with Thomas Hill, Jr., Terrance McConnell, Holly Smith, and Lance Stell were extremely helpful at various points along the way. The writing of this essay was supported by an off-campus assignment from the University of North Carolina (Chapel Hill) and a fellowship from the National Humanities Center, both during the 1982–83 academic year.

1   Cf. Roger Wertheimer, "Understanding the Abortion Argument," in Thomas Nagel et al., eds., *The Rights and Wrongs of Abortion* (Princeton: Princeton University Press, 1974). He writes, "Catholics who are antiabortionist can no more think it wrong for themselves but permissible for Protestants to destroy a fetus than liberals can think it wrong for themselves but permissible for racists to victimize blacks" (p. 29).

2 On the topic of ensoulment, see John T. Noonan, Jr., ed., *The Morality of Abortion: Legal and Historical Perspectives* (Cambridge: Harvard University Press, 1970). The index contains numerous page references under "ensoulment."

3 For such an act Woodrow Wilson Collums was given a ten-year probationary sentence and assigned work in a senior home (5 March 1982, *Washington Post*), and Billy Ray Clore's charge was downgraded from murder to attempted murder (16 July 1983, *Washington Post*).

4 The arguments in this section draw upon my "Law, Morality, and Our Psychological Nature," in Michael Bradie and David Braybrooke, eds., *Social Justice* (Bowling Green, Ohio: Bowling Green Studies in Applied Philosophy, 1982).

5 I have in mind the legal moralism developed by Lord Patrick Devlin, *The Enforcement of Morals* (London: Oxford University Press, 1965). My thinking about the topic of abortion owes very much to L. W. Sumner, *Abortion and Moral Theory* (Princeton: Princeton University Press, 1981). Rarely have I learned so much from a book with which I have so sharply disagreed. See my review of the book in *Nous* 17 (1983).

Abortion, Privacy, and Personhood

The author thanks Norman Fost, Elliott Sober, and Alan Weisbard for useful and enjoyable repartee.

1 410 U.S. 113 (1973).

2 Hyman Gross, "The Concept of Privacy," *NYU L. Rev.* 42 (March 1967): 34–54.

3 Alan Westin, *Privacy and Freedom* (New York: Atheneum, 1967).

4 But see L. Tribe, "Foreword, Toward a Model of Roles in the Due Process of Life and Law," *Harvard L. Rev.* 87 (1) (November 1973), at n. 83, listing ways in which antiabortion legislation invades informational privacy.

5 *Griswold* v. *Connecticut*, 381 U.S. 479 (1965).

6 *Eisenstadt* v. *Baird*, 405 U.S. 438 (1972).

7 Professor D.A.J. Richards speaks of "persuasive analogies" between these two sorts of privacy; see his "Unnatural Acts and the Constitutional Right to Privacy: A Moral Theory," *Fordham L. Rev.* 45 (1977): 1312–48.

8 *Roe* v. *Wade*, 410 U.S. 113 (1973).

9 Tribe, "Foreword."

10 Philip Heymann and Douglas Barzelay, "The Forest and the Trees: *Roe* v. *Wade* and Its Critics," *Boston U. L. Rev.* 53 (July 1973): 765–84.

11 Richards, "Unnatural Acts," p. 1317.

12 Glenn Negley, "Philosophical Views on the Value of Privacy," *Law & Contemp. Problems*, 31 (1966): 319–25.

13 Judith J. Thomson, "A Defense of Abortion," *Philosophy and Public Affairs* 1, no. 1 (Fall 1971).

14 Donald Regan, "Rewriting *Roe* v. *Wade*," *Mich. L. Rev.* 77 (7) (August 1979): 1569–1646.

15 Testimony of Leon Rosenberg, M.D., Hearings before the Subcommittee on Separation of Powers, Committee on the Judiciary, U.S. Senate, April 24, 1981: U.S. Government Printing Office, 1982, pp. 48–72.

16 Philip Devine, in his *The Ethics of Homicide* (Ithaca: Cornell University Press, 1978), considers this sort of *ad hominem* argument in some detail (pp. 88–90).

=

Bibliography

Algeo, Donald. "Abortion, Personhood and Moral Rights." *The Monist* 64 (1981): 543–49.

Annas, George J. "Law and the Life Sciences." *Hastings Center Report* 10 (1980): 8–10.

———. "The Supreme Court and Abortion: The Irrelevance of Medical Judgment." *Hastings Center Report* 10 (1980): 23–24.

Appleton, S. F. "Beyond the Limits of Reproductive Choice: The Contributions of the Abortion Funding Cases to Fundamental Rights Analysis and the Welfare Rights Thesis." *Columbia Law Review* 81 (1981): 721–58.

Asaro A. "Judicial Portrayal of the Physician in Abortion and Sterilization Decisions: The Use and Abuse of Medical Discretion." *Harvard Women's Law Journal* 6 (1983): 51–102.

Atkinson, G. M. "Persons in the Whole Sense." *American Journal of Jurisprudence* 22 (1977): 86–117.

Bajema, Clifford E. *Abortion and the Meaning of Personhood.* Grand Rapids, Mich.: Baker Book House, 1974.

Bassen, Paul. "Present Stakes and Future Prospects: The Status of Early Abortion." *Philosophy and Public Affairs* 11 (1982): 314.

Beauchamp, T. L. "Abortion." In *Contemporary Issues in Bioethics*, edited by T. L. Beauchamp and L. Walters. Encino, Calif.: Dickenson Publishing Co., 1978.

Benda, E. "Impact of Constitutional Law on the Protection of Unborn Human Life: Some Comparative Remarks." *Human Rights* 6 (1977): 223–43.

Benjamin, Dick. *Abortion Is Murder.* Anchorage, Ak.: Abbottt Loop, 1980.

Bennett, Jonathan. "Morality and Consequences." In *The Tanner Lectures on Human Values*, vol. 2, edited by Sterling McMurrin. Cambridge: Cambridge University Press, 1981.

Bennett, Philip W. "A Defense of Abortion: A Question for Judith Jarvis Thomson." *Philosophical Investigations* 5 (1982): 142–45.

Bennett, R. W. "Abortion and Judicial Review: Of Burdens and Benefits, Hard Cases and Some Bad Law." *Northwestern University Law Review* 75 (1981): 978–1017.

Benshoof, Janet. "Mobilization for Abortion Rights." *Civil Liberties Review* 4 (1977): 76–79.

Bereday, George Z. F. "The Right to Live and the Right to Die: Some Considerations of Law and Society in America." *Values and Ethics in Health Care* 4 (1979) 233–56.

Berger, Fred. *Happiness, Justice and Freedom.* Berkeley and Los Angeles: University of California Press, 1984.

Bolner, J., and Jacobsen, R. "Right to Procreate: The Dilemma of Overpopulation and the United States Judiciary." *Loyola Law Review* 25 (1979): 235–62.

Bowes, W. A., and Selgestad, B. "Fetal versus Material Rights: Medical and Legal Perspectives." *Obstetrics and Gynecology* 58 (1981): 209–14.

Boyle, J. M. "That the Fetus Should Be Considered a Legal Person." *American Journal of Jurisprudence* 24 (1979): 59–71.

Brody, Baruch. *Abortion and the Sanctity of Human Life: A Philosophical View.* Cambridge: MIT Press, 1975.

———. "On the Humanity of the Fetus." In *Abortion: Pro and Con,* edited by Robert L. Perkins. Cambridge, Mass.: Schenkman Publishing Company, 1974.

———. "On the Humanity of the Fetus." In *Contemporary Issues in Bioethics,* edited by T. L. Beauchamp and L. Waters. Encino, Calif.: Dickenson Publishing Co., 1978.

———. "Thomson on Abortion." *Philosophy and Public Affairs* 1 (1972): 3.

Bryant, M. D., Jr. "State Legislation after *Roe* v. *Wade*: Selected Constitutional Issues." *American Journal of Law and Medicine* 2 (1976): 101–32.

Buchanan, E. "The Constitution and the Anomaly of the Pregnant Teenager." *Arizona Law Review* 24 (1982): 553–610.

Budner, Stanley. "Value Conflicts and the Uses of Research: The Example of Abortion." *Values and Ethics in Health Care* 1 (1975): 29–41.

Burtchaell, James T., ed. *The Abortion Parley.* Fairway, Kans. Andrews and McMeel, Inc., 1980.

Butler, P. A. "Right to Medicaid Payment for Abortion." *Hastings Law Journal* 28 (1977): 931–77.

Byrn, R. M., and Hellegers, A. "*Wade* and *Bolton*: Fundamental Legal Errors and Dangerous Implications." *Catholic Lawyer* 19 (1973): 243–58.

Callahan, Daniel. *Abortion: Law, Choice and Morality.* New York: Macmillan Company, 1970.

Canby, Jr., W. C. "Government Funding, Abortions, and the Public Forum." *Arizona State Law Journal* 1979: 11–21.

Caron, W. R.; Horan, D. J.; Noonan, J. S.; Wardle, L. D.; and Robinson, J. "Human Life Federalism Amendment." *Catholic Lawyer* 28 (1983): 111–28.

Carrier, L. S. "Abortion and the Right to Life." *Social Theory and Practice* 3 (1975): 4.

Chemerinsky, E. "Rationalizing the Abortion Debate: Legal Rhetoric and the Abortion Controversy." *Buffalo Law Review* 31 (1982): 107–64.

Churchill, Larry R., and Siman, Jose Jorge. "Abortion and the Rhetoric of Individual Rights: Why the Abortion Debate Is Sterile." *Hastings Center Report* 12 (1982): 9–12.

Cincotta, J. "Quality of Life from *Roe* to *Quinlan* and Beyond." *Catholic Lawyer* 25 (1979): 13–31.

Cohen, M., ed. *Rights and Wrongs of Abortion*. Philosophy and Public Affairs Reader. Princeton: Princeton University Press, 1974.

Conley, P. T., and McKenna, R. J. "The Supreme Court on Abortion: A Dissenting Opinion." *Catholic Lawyer* 19 (1973): 19–28.

Connery, John. *Abortion: The Development of the Roman Catholic Perspective*. Chicago: Loyola University Press, 1977.

Daniels, Charles B. "Abortion and Potential." *Dialogue* 18 (1979): 2.

Davis, Nancy. "The Priority of Avoiding Harm." In *Killing and Letting Die*, edited by Bonnie Steinbuck. Englewood Cliffs, N.J.: Prentice-Hall, 1980.

Delgado, R. "Parental Preferences and Selective Abortion: A Commentary on *Roe* v. *Wade* and *Doe* v. *Bolton* and the Shape of Things to Come." *Washington University Law Quarterly* 1974: 203–26.

Dellapenna, J. W. "History of Abortion: Technology, Morality, and the Law." *University of Pittsburgh Law Review* 40 (1979): 359–428.

———. "Nor Piety nor Wit: The Supreme Court on Abortion." *Columbia Human Rights Law Review* 6 (1974/1975): 379–413.

Dembitz, N. "The Supreme Court and a Minor's Abortion Decision." *Columbia Law Review* 80 (1980): 1251–63.

Destro, Robert A. "Abortion and the Constitution: The Need for a Life Protective Amendment." *California Law Review* 63 (1975): 1250–352.

Devine, Philip E. *The Ethics of Homicide*. Ithaca and London: Cornell University Press, 1978.

Devlin, Patrick. *The Enforcement of Morals*. London: Oxford University Press, 1965.

Donagan, Alan. *The Theory of Morality*. Chicago: University of Chicago Press, 1977.

Donceel, Joseph F. "Immediate Animation and Delayed Hominization." *Theological Studies* 31 (1970): 1.

Dorsen, Norman. "Crushing Freedom in the Name of Life." *Human Rights* 10 1981): 198–208.

Dourien-Rollier, A. M. "Legal Problems Related to Abortion and Menstrual Regulation." *Columbia Human Rights Law Review* 7 (1975): 120–35.

Drinan, Robert F. "The Inviolability of the Right to Be Born." In *Abortion and the Law*, edited by David T. Smith. Cleveland: Western Reserve University Press, 1967.

———. "The Right of the Fetus to Be Born." *Dublin Review* 1967–68: 514.

Duffy, M. A. "Abortion Decisions—How Will the United States Supreme Court Define 'Necessary'?" *Women's Lawyers' Journal* 64 (1978): 3–16.

Dunlap, Mary C. "*Harris* v. *McRae*." *Women's Rights Law Reporter* 6 (1980): 166–68.

Durham, W. C. "Counseling, Consulting, and Consent: Abortion and the Doctor-Patient Relationship." *Brigham Young University Law Review* 1978: 783–845.

Durham, W. C., Jr.; Wood, M. A. Q.; and Condie, S. J. "Accommodation of Conscientious Objection to Abortion: A Case Study of the Nursing Profession." *Brigham Young University Law Review* 1982: 253–370.

Dworkin, Andrea. *Right Wing Women*. New York: Perigee Books, 1983.

Dworkin, R. M. *Taking Rights Seriously*. Cambridge: Harvard University Press, 1977.

Ely, J. H. *Democracy and Distrust: A Theory of Judicial Review*. Cambridge: Harvard University Press, 1982.

————. "The Wages of Crying Wolf: A Comment on *Roe v. Wade.*" *Yale Law Journal* 82 (1973): 920.

Emerson, Thomas I. "The Power of Congress to Change Constitutional Decisions of the Supreme Court: The Human Life Bill." *Northwestern University Law Review* 77 (1982): 129–42.

Engelhart, H. Tristam, Jr. "The Ontology of Abortion." *Ethics* 84 (1974): 3, 217.

English, Jane. "Abortion and the Concept of a Person." *Canadian Journal of Philosophy* 5 (1975): 2.

Epstein, Richard A. "Substantive Due Process by Any Other Name: The Abortion Cases." *Supreme Court Review* 1973: 159–85.

Erickson, N. S. "Women and the Supreme Court: Anatomy Is Destiny." *Brooklyn Law Review* 41 (1974): 209–82.

Estreicher, S. "Congressional Power and Constitutional Rights: Reflections on Proposed 'Human Life' Legislation." *Virginia Law Review* 68 (1982): 333–458.

Etzioni, A. "Husband's Rights in Abortion." *Trial* 12 (1976): 56–58.

Fahy, C. "The Abortion Funding Cases: A Response to Professor Perry." *Georgetown Law Journal* 66 (1979): 1205–8.

Falik, Marilyn. *Ideology and Abortion Policy Politics*. New York: Praeger Publishers, 1983.

Feinberg, Joel. "Is There a Right to Be Born?" In *Understanding Moral Philosophy*, edited by J. Rachels. Encino, Calif.: Dickenson Publishers, 1976.

————. *The Problem of Abortion*. Belmont, Calif.: Wadsworth Publishing Co., 1973.

————. "The Rights of Animals and Unborn Generations." In *Philosophy and Environmental Crisis*, edited by William T. Blackstone. Athens: University of Georgia Press, 1974.

————. *Social Philosophy*. Englewood Cliffs, N.J.: Prentice-Hall, 1973.

————. "Voluntary Euthanasia and the Inalienable Right to Life." *Philosophy and Public Affairs* 7 (1978): 2.

Finnis, John. "The Rights and Wrongs of Abortion." In *The Rights and Wrongs of Abortion*, edited by Marshall Cohen, et al. Princeton: Princeton University Press, 1974.

Fletcher, George. *Rethinking Criminal Law*. Boston: Little Brown, 1978.

Fletcher, J. C. "The Fetus As Patient: Ethical Issues." *Journal of American Medical Association* 246 (1981): 772–73.

————. "Four Indicators of Humanhood: The Enquiry Matures." *Hastings Center Report* 4 (1974): 407.

————. *Humanhood: Essays in Biomedical Ethics*. Buffalo, N.Y.: Prometheus Books, 1979.

Foot, Philippa. "The Problem of Abortion and the Doctrine of the Double Effect." *Oxford Review* 1967.

Ford, N. "The Evolution of a Constitutional Right to an Abortion: Fashioned in the 1970s and Secured in the 1980s." *Journal of Legal Medicine* 4 (1983): 271–322.

Friendly, Henry J. "The Courts and Social Policy: Substance and Procedure." *University of Miami Law Review* 233 (1978): 21.

Frohock, Fred M. *Abortion: A Case Study in Law and Morals*. Westport, Conn.: Greenwood Press, 1983.

Fugua, D. "Justice Harry A. Blackmun: The Abortion Decisions." *Arkansas Law Review* 34 (1980): 276–96.

Geary, P. F. "Analysis of Recent Decisions involving Abortions." *Catholic Lawyer* 23 (1978): 237–42.

Gilligan, Carol. *In a Different Voice*. Cambridge: Harvard University Press, 1982.

Glen, K. "Abortion in the Courts: A Laywoman's Historical Guide to the New Disaster Area." *Feminist Studies* 4 (1978): 1.

Glenn, Gary. "Abortion and Inalienable Rights in Classical Liberalism." *American Journal of Jurisprudence* 20 (1975): 62–80.

Glover, Jonathan. *Causing Death and Saving Lives*. Harmondsworth: Penguin, 1977.

Gold, J. A. "Does the Hyde Amendment Violate Religious Freedom? *Harris* v. *McRae* and the First Amendment." *American Journal of Law and Medicine* 6 (1980): 361–72.

Golding, Martin P. "Towards a Theory of Human Rights." *The Monist* 52 (1968): 4.

Goldstein, L. F. "Critique of the Abortion Funding Decisions: On Private Rights in the Public Sector." *Hastings Constitutional Law Quarterly* 8 (1981): 313–42.

Goodpaster, Kenneth E. "On Being Morally Considerable." *Journal of Philosophy* 75 (1978): 6.

Gordy, J. D. " 'Right' to an Abortion, the Scope of the Fourteenth Amendment, 'Personhood', and the Supreme Court's Birth Requirement." *Southern Illinois University Law Journal* (1979): 1–36.

Govier, Trudy. "What Should We Do about Future People?" *American Philosophical Quarterly* 16 (1979): 2.

Granberg, Donald. "The Abortion Controversy: An Overview." *Humanist* 41 (1981): 28.

Granfield, David. *The Abortion Decision*. Garden City, N.Y.: Doubleday and Company, 1969.

Gray, John. *Mill On Liberty: A Defence*. London: Routledge and Kegan Paul, 1983.

Greenglass, Esther. *The Grounds for Moral Judgment*. Cambridge: Cambridge University Press, 1967.

Grey, Thomas. "Eros, Civilization and the Burger Court." *Law and Contemporary Problems* 43 (1980): 83.

Grisez, Germain. *Abortion: The Myths, the Realities, and the Arguments*. New York and Cleveland: Corpus Books, 1970.

———. "Toward a Consistent Natural-Law Ethics of Killing." *American Journal of Jurisprudence* 15 (1970).

Gross, Hyman. A *Theory of Criminal Justice*. New York: Oxford University Press, 1974.

Gunther, Gerald. "The Subtle Vices of 'Passive Virtues'." *Columbia Law Review* 64 (1964): 1.

Gunty, S. "Hyde Amendment and Medicaid Abortions." *Forum* 16 (1981): 825–40.

Gusfield, Joseph. *Symbolic Crusade*. Urbana: University of Illinois Press, 1963.

Gustafson, J. "Genetic Engineering and the Normative View of the Human." In *Ethical Issues in Biology and Medicine*, edited by P. N. Williams, pp. 46–58. Cambridge, Mass.: Schenkman, 1973.

Gutmann, Amy. "Moral Philosophy and Political Problems." *Political Theory* 10 (1982): 33–48.

Guttmacher, Alan F. *The Case for Legalized Abortion Now*. Berkeley: Diablo Press, 1967.

Hand, Learned. *The Bill of Rights*. New York: Atheneum, 1968.

Hardy, D. T. "*Harris* v. *McRae*: Clash of a Nonenumerated Right with Legislative Control of the Purse." *Case Western Reserve Law Review* 31 (1981): 465–508.

————. "Privacy and Public Funding: *Maher* v. *Roe* As the Interaction of *Roe* v. *Wade* and *Dandridge* v. *Williams*." *Arizona Law Review* 18 (1976): 903–38.

Haring, Bernard. *Medical Ethics*. Edited by Gabrielle L. Jean. Notre Dame, Ind.: Fides Publishers, 1973.

Harris, Harry. *Prenatal Diagnosis and Selective Abortion*. Cambridge: Harvard University Press, 1975.

Harrison, Beverly W. *Our Right To Choose*. Boston: Beacon Press, 1983.

Harrison, S. M. "The Supreme Court and Abortional Reforms: Means to an End." *New York Law Forum* 19 (1974): 685–701.

Hart, H. L. A. *The Concept of Law*. Oxford: Oxford University Press, 1961.

————. *Law, Liberty and Morality*. Stanford, Calif.: Stanford University Press, 1963.

Harvard Medical School, Ad Hoc Committee to Examine the Definition of Brain Death. "A Definition of Irreversible Coma." *Journal of the American Medical Association* 205 (1968).

Henkin, Louis. "Privacy and Autonomy." *Columbia Law Review* 74 (1974): 1410–33.

Henson, Richard G. "Utilitarianism and the Wrongness of Killing." *Philosophical Review* 80 (1971): 3.

Heymann, P. B., and Barzelay, D. E. "Forest and Trees: *Roe* v. *Wade* and Its Critics." *Boston University Law Review* 53 (1973): 765–84.

Hilgers, Thomas W., ed. *New Perspectives on Human Abortion*. Frederick, Md.: University Publications of America, Inc., 1981.

Hilgers, Thomas W., and Horan, Dennis J., eds. *Abortion and Social Justice*. Thaxton, Va.: Sun Life, 1980.

Hogan, J. E. "Conscience and the Law." *Catholic Lawyer* 21 (1975): 190–96.

Horan, D. J. "Abortion and the Conscience Clause: Current Status." *Catholic Lawyer* 20 (1974): 289–302.

————. "Abortion and Euthanasia: Recent Developments of Law." *Forum* 12 (1977): 960–79.

————. "Critical Abortion Litigation." *Catholic Lawyer* 26 (1981): 198–208.

————. "Dignity of Life Developments." *Catholic Lawyer* 27 (1982): 239–45.

————. "Viability, Values and the Vast Cosmos." *Catholic Lawyer* 22 (1976): 1–37.

Hutcheson, Francis. *A System of Moral Philosophy.* New York: Augustus M. Kelley Publishers, 1968.

Hutchinson, D. S. "Utilitarianism and Children." *Canadian Journal of Philosophy* 12 (1982): 61–73.

Isaacs, S. L. "Law of Fertility Regulation in the United States: A 1980 Review." *Journal of Family Law* 19 (1980): 65–96.

Jaffe, Frederick S.; Lindheim, Barbara L.; and Lee, Philip R. *Abortion Politics.* New York: McGraw-Hill, 1981.

Jones, C. J. "Abortion and Consideration of Fundamental Irreconcilable Interests." *Syracuse Law Review* 33 (1982): 565–613.

Jones, Gary E. "Rights and Desires." *Ethics* 92 (1981): 52–56.

Kadish, Sanford. "Respect for Life and Regard for Rights in the Criminal Law." *California Law Review* 64 (1976): 871–901.

Kapp, M. B. "Father's (Lack of) Rights and Responsibilities in the Abortion Decision: An Examination of Legal-Ethical Implications." *Ohio Northern Law Review* 9 (1982): 369–83.

Kavka, Gregory. "The Futurity Problem." In *Obligations to Future Generations,* edited by R. I. Sikora and Brian Barry. Philadelphia: Temple University Press, 1978.

Keeton, G. W. *The Elementary Principles of Jurisprudence,* 2d ed. London: Sir Isaac Pitman and Sons, Ltd., 1949.

Kelly, Gerald. *Medico-Moral Problems.* St. Louis: Catholic Hospital Association, 1958.

Kenny, John P. *Principles of Medical Ethics.* 2d ed. Tenbury Wells: Thomas More Books, 1962.

Kindregan, Charles P. *Quality of Life: Reflections on the Moral Values of American Law.* New York: Macmillan Publishing Co., Inc. 1969.

Kluge, E-H. W. *The Practice of Death.* New Haven and London: Yale University Press, 1975.

————. "St. Thomas, Abortion and Euthanasia: Another Look." *Philosophy Research Archives* 7 (1981): 14–72.

Kohl, Marvin. *The Morality of Killing: Euthanasia, Abortion and Transplants.* Highlands, N.J.: Humanities Press, Inc., 1974.

Kolb, C. E. M. "Proposed Human Life Statute: Abortion as Murder?" *American Bar Association Journal* 67 (1981): 1123–26.

Koop, Everett C., and Schaeffer, Francis A. *Whatever Happened to the Human Race?* Westchester, Ill.: Good News Publications, 1983.

Kremer, Elmar J. "Abortion and Pluralism." In *Death before Birth,* edited by E. J. Kremer and E. A. Synan. Toronto: Griffin House, 1974.

Krimmel, H. T., and Foley, M. J. "Abortion: An Inspection into the Nature of Human Life and Potential Consequences of Legalizing Its Destruction." *University of Cincinnati Law Review* 46 (1977): 725–821.

Lader, Lawrence. *Abortion.* Indianapolis: Bobbs-Merrill, 1966.

———. *Abortion II: Making the Revolution.* Boston: Beacon Press, Inc., 1974.

Latstra, H. *Abortion: The Catholic Theological Debate in America.* New York: Irvington Publishers, 1983.

Lee, L. T., and Paxman, J. M. "Pregnancy and Abortion in Adolescence: A Comparative Legal Survey and Proposals for Reform." *Columbia Human Rights Law Review* 6 (1974/1975): 307–55.

Lenow, J. L. "The Fetus As a Patient: Emerging Rights As a Person?" *American Journal of Law and Medicine* 9 (1983): 1–29.

Locke, John. "A Letter concerning Toleration." In *Treatise of Civil Government and A Letter Concerning Toleration.* New York: Appleton-Century-Crofts, 1931.

Loewy, A. H. "Abortive Reasons and Obscene Standards: A Comment on Abortion and the Obscenity Cases." *North Carolina Law Review* 52 (1973): 223–43.

Louisell, David W., and Noonan, John T., Jr. "Constitutional Balance." In *The Morality of Abortion: Legal and Historical Perspectives,"* edited by John Noonan. Cambridge: Harvard University Press, 1970.

Lowe, N. V. "Wardship and Abortion Prevention." *Law Quarterly Review* 95 (1980): 29–31.

Luker, Kristin. *Abortion and the Politics of Motherhood.* Berkeley and Los Angeles: University of California Press, 1984.

———. *Taking Chances: Abortion and the Decision Not to Contracept.* Berkeley and Los Angeles: University of California Press, 1976.

Lynch, R. N. "National Committee for a Human Life Amendment Inc.: Its Goals and Origins." *Catholic Lawyer* 20 (1974): 303–8.

Lynn, Suzanne M. "Technology and Reproductive Rights: How Advances in Technology Can Be Used to Limit Women's Reproductive Rights." *Women's Rights Law Reporter* 7 (1982): 223–27.

Lyon, C. M., and Benett, G. J. "Abortion—the Female, the Foetus and the Father." *Current Legal Problems* 32 (1979): 217–22.

Lyons, David. *Forms and Limits of Utilitarianism.* Oxford: Clarendon Press, 1965.

———. "Human Rights and the General Welfare." *Philosophy and Public Affairs* 6 (1977): 2.

———. "Liberty and Harm to Others." In *New Essays on John Stuart Mill and Utilitarianism,* edited by Wesley E. Cooper et al. Guelph: Canadian Association for Publishing in Philosophy, 1979.

———. "Mill's Theory of Morality." *Nous* 10 (1976): 2.

MacDougal, D., and Nasser, W. P. "Abortion Decision and Evolving Limits on State Intervention." *Hawaii Bar Journal* 11 (1974): 51–72.

McFadden, Charles J. *Medical Ethics.* 6th ed. Philadelphia: F. A. Davis Co., 1967.

McKernan, M. F., Jr. "Compelling Hospitals to Provide Abortion Services." *Catholic Lawyer* 20 (1974): 317–27.

Mackie, J. L. *Ethics*. Harmondsworth: Penguin, 1977.

Mahowald, Mary B. "Concepts of Abortion and Their Relevance to the Abortion Debate." *Southern Journal of Philosophy* 20 (1982): 195–208.

———. "Feminism and Abortion Arguments." *Kinesis* 11 (1982): 57–68.

Mall, David. *In Good Conscience: Abortion and Moral Necessity*. Libertyville, Ill.: Kairos Books, 1982.

Marcin, J. J. R. and Marcin, R. B. "Physician's Decision Making Role in Abortion Cases." *Jurist* 35 (1975): 66–76.

Marzen, T. J. "The Supreme Court on Abortion Funding: The Second Time Around." *St. Louis University Law Journal* 25 (1981): 411–27.

Mechanic, David. "The Supreme Court and Abortion: Side-Stepping Social Realities." *Hastings Center Report* 10 (1980): 17–19.

Melden, A. I. *Rights and Persons*. Oxford: Basil Blackwell, 1977.

Michel, A. E. "Abortion and International Law: The Status and Possible Extension of Women's Rights to Privacy." *Journal of Family Law* 19 (1981): 745–58.

Milby, T. H. "The New Biology and the Question of Personhood: Implications for Abortion." *American Journal of Law and Medicine* 9 (1983): 31–41.

Mill, John Stuart. *On Liberty*, edited by Alburey Castell. New York: Appleton-Century-Crofts, 1947.

———. *On Liberty*. New York: Bobbs-Merrill, 1956.

———. *Utilitarianism*, edited by Oskar Piest. Indianapolis and New York: Liberal Arts Press, 1957.

Mohr, James. *Abortion in America: The Origins and Evolution of National Policy, 1800–1900*. New York: Oxford University Press, 1978.

Montmarquet, James A. "Messing With Mother Nature: Fleck and the Omega Pill." *Philosophical Studies* 41 (1982): 407–20.

Morreall, John. "Of Marsupials and Men: A Thought Experiment on Abortion." *Dialogos* 18 (1981): 7–18.

Mumford, Stephen D. "Abortion: A National Security Issue." *Humanist* 42 (1982): 12–13.

Myrna, Frances. "The Right to Abortion." In *Ethics for Modern Life*, edited by R. Abelson and M. L. Friguegnon. New York: St. Martin's Press, 1980.

Nagel, Thomas. "War and Massacre." In *War and Moral Responsibility*, edited by Marshall Cohen et al. Princeton: Princeton University Press, 1974.

Narveson, Jan. "Future People and Us." In *Obligations to Future Generations*, edited by R. I. Sikora and Brian Barry. Philadelphia: Temple University Press, 1978.

———. *Morality and Utility*. Baltimore: Johns Hopkins University Press, 1967.

———. "Moral Problems of Population." *The Monist* 57 (1973): 1.

———."Utilitarianism and New Generations." *Mind* 76 (1967): 301.

Nathanson, Bernard, and Ostling, Richard N. *Aborting America*. Los Angeles, Calif.: Pinnacle Books, 1981.

Newton, Lisa. "Humans and Persons: A Reply to Tristam Engelhardt." *Ethics* 85 (1975): 4.

Nicholson, Linda. "Abortion: What Kind of Moral Issue?" *Journal of Value Inquiry* 15 (1981) 235–42.

Nicholson, Susan Teft. *Abortion and the Roman Catholic Church.* Knoxville, Tenn.: Religious Ethics, 1978.

Nielsen, H. A. "Toward a Socratic View of Abortion." *American Journal of Jurisprudence* 18 (1973): 105–13.

Noonan, John T., Jr. "An Almost Absolute Value in History." In *The Morality of Abortion: Legal and Historical Perspectives,* edited by J. Noonan. Cambridge: Harvard University Press, 1970.

————. *Contraception.* Cambridge: Harvard University Press, 1965.

————. "Deciding Who Is Human." *Natural Law Forum* (1968): 13.

————. "The Hatch Amendment and the New Federalism." *Harvard Journal of Law and Public Policy* 6 (1982): 93–102.

————. "How To Argue about Abortion." In *Contemporary Issues In Bioethics,* edited by T. L. Beauchamp and L. Walters. Encino, Calif.: Dickenson Publishing Co., 1978.

————. *A Private Choice: Abortion in America in the Seventies.* New York: Free Press, 1979.

O'Connor, J. M. "On Humanity and Abortion." *Natural Law Forum* (1968).

O'Meara, J. "Abortion: The Court Decides a Non-Case." *Supreme Court Review* 1974: 337–60.

Orenduff, J. M. "Abortion: A Plea for Moral Sensitivity." *Southwest Philosophical Studies* 6 (1981): 69–74.

Parfit, Derek. "Future Generations: Further Problems." *Philosophy and Public Affairs* 11 (1982): 113–72.

————. "Later Selves and Moral Principles." In *Philosophy and Personal Relations,* edited by Alan Montefiore. London: Routledge and Kegan Paul, 1973.

————. "On Doing the Best for Our Children." In *Ethics and Population,* edited by Michael D. Bayles. Cambridge, Mass.: Schenkman Publishing Company, 1976.

————. "Rights, Interests, and Possible People." In *Moral Problems in Medicine,* edited by Samuel Gorovitz. Englewood Cliffs, N.J.: Prentice-Hall, 1976.

Parness, J. A. "Social Commentary: Values and Legal Personhood." *West Virginia Law Review* 83 (1981): 487–503.

Parness, J. A. and Pritchard, S. K. "To Be or Not To Be: Protecting the Unborn's Potentiality of Life." *University of Cincinnati Law Review* 51 (1982): 257–98.

Paul, Eve W. "Legal Rights of Minors to Sex Related Medical Care." *Columbia Human Rights Law Review* 6 (1974/1975): 357–67.

Paul, Eve, and Schaap, Paula. "Abortion and the Law in 1980." *New York Law School Law Review* 25 (1980): 497–525.

Peffer, Rodney. "A Defense of Rights to Well-Being." *Philosophy and Public Affairs* 8 (1978): 1.

Perry, M. J. "Abortion Funding Cases: A Comment on the Supreme Court's Role in American Government." *Georgetown Law Journal* 66 (1978): 1191–245.

————. "Abortion, the Public Morals and the Police Power: The Ethical Function of Substantive Due Process." *U.C.L.A. Law Review* 23 (1976): 689–736.

————. "Substantive Due Process Revisited: Reflections On (and Beyond) Recent Cases." *Northwestern University Law Review* 71 (1976): 417–69.

————. "Why the Supreme Court Was Plainly Wrong in the Hyde Amendment Case: A Brief Comment on *Harris v. McRae.*" *Stanford Law Review* 32 (1980): 1113–28.

Petchesky, Rosalind P. *Abortion and Woman's Choice: The State, Sexuality and the Conditions of Reproductive Freedom.* New York: Longman, Inc., 1984.

————. "Antiabortion, Antifeminism, and the Rise of the New Right." *Feminist Studies* 7 (1981): 206–46.

————. "Reproductive Freedom and Beyond." *Signs* 5 (1980): 661–685.

Pilpel, Harriet, F. "Abortion, Conscience and the Constitution: An Examination of Federal Institutional Conscience Clauses." *Columbia Human Rights Law Review* 6 (1974/1975): 279–305.

Pluhar, Werner S. "Abortion and Simple Consciousness." *Journal of Philosophy* 74 (1977): 3.

Polityka, T. "From *Poe* to *Roe*: A Bickelian View of the Abortion Decision—Its Timing and Principle." *Nebraska Law Review* 53 (1974): 31–57.

Pottenham, T. O.; Peterson, D. M.; and Marzen, T. J. "Texas Abortion Law: Consent Requirements and Special Statutes." *Houston Law Review* 18 (1981): 819–48.

Potts, Malcolm. *Abortion.* Cambridge: Cambridge University Press, 1977.

Prosser, W. *Handbook of The Law of Torts.* 4th Ed., St. Paul, Minn.: West Publishing Co., 1971.

Purdy, Laura, and Tooley, Michael. "Is Abortion Murder?" In *Abortion: Pro and Con*, edited by Robert L. Perkins. Cambridge, Mass.: Schenkman Publishing Company, 1974.

Quinn, Warren. "Abortion: Identity and Loss." *Philosophy and Public Affairs* 13 (1984): 24.

Ramsey, P. "The Morality of Abortion." In *Moral Problems*, edited by J. Rachels. New York: Harper and Row, 1975.

Regan, Donald. "Rewriting *Roe v. Wade.*" *Michigan Law Review* 77 (1979): 1569.

Regan, Tom. "Feinberg on What Sorts of Beings Can Have Rights." *Southern Journal of Philosophy* 14 (1976): 4.

————. "The Moral Basis of Vegetarianism." *Canadian Journal of Philosophy* 5 (1975): 2.

Rice, C. E. "The Dred Scott Case of the Twentieth Century." *Houston Law Review* 10 (1973): 1059–86.

Rich, Adrienne. *Of Woman Born: Motherhood As Experience and Institution.* New York: Bantam Books, 1977.

Richards, David A. J. *The Moral Criticism of Law.* Encino, Calif.: Dickenson-Wadsworth, 1977.

————. *Sex, Drugs, Death and the Law.* Totowa, N.J.: Rowman Littlefield, 1982.

————. *A Theory of Reasons for Action.* Oxford: Clarendon Press, 1971.

Riga, P. J. "*Byrn* and *Roe*: The Threshold Question and Judicial Review." *Catholic Lawyer* 23 (1978): 308–81.

Roberts, B., and Skelton, K. D. "Abortion and the Courts." *Environmental Law* 1 (1971): 225–37.

Robertson, J. A. "The Right to Procreate and *In Utero* Fetal Therapy." *Journal of Legal Medicine* 3 (1982): 333–66.

Ross, Steven L. "Abortion and the Death of the Fetus." *Philosophy and Public Affairs* 11 (1982): 232–45.

Roupas, T. G. "The Value of Life." *Philosophy and Public Affairs* 7 (1978): 2.

Rubin, E. R. "Abortion Cases: A Study in Law and Social Change." *North Carolina Central Law Journal* 5 (1979): 215–53.

———. *Abortion, Politics and the Courts: Roe v. Wade and His Aftermath.* Westport, Conn.: Greenwood Press, 1982.

Ruddick, W., and Wilcox, W. "Operating on the Fetus." *Hastings Center Report* 12 (1982): 10–14.

Sarat, Austin. "Abortion and the Courts: Uncertain Boundaries of Law and Politics." In *American Politics And Public Policy*, edited by Allan Sindler. Washington, D. C.: Congressional Quarterly, Inc., 1982.

Sartorius, Rolf E. *Individual Conduct and Social Norms.* Encino and Belmont, Calif.: Dickenson, 1975.

Sarvis, Betty, and Hyman, Rodman. *The Abortion Controversy.* 2d ed. New York and London: Columbia University Press, 1974.

Scanlan, A. L. "Recent Developments in the Abortion Area." *Catholic Lawyer* 21 (1975): 315–21.

Schneider, Carl, and Vinovskis, Maris A., eds. *The Law and Politics of Abortion.* Lexington, Mass.: Lexington Books, D.C. Heath and Co., 1980.

Segers, Mary C. "Can Congress Settle the Abortion Issue?" *Hastings Center Report* 12 (1982): 20–28.

Sher, George. "Subsidized Abortion: Moral Rights and Moral Compromise." *Philosophy and Public Affairs* 10 (1981): 361–72.

Sheraine, H. "Beyond *Roe* and *Doe*: The Rights of the Father." *Notre Dame Law Review* 50 (1975): 483–95.

Sherwin, Susan. "The Concept of a Person in the Context of Abortion." *Bioethics Quarterly* 3 (1981): 21–34.

Shuite, E. J. "Tax-supported Abortions: The Legal Issues." *Catholic Lawyer* 21 (1975): 1–7.

Siegel, Mark A., and Jacobs, Nancy R., eds. *Abortion: An Eternal Social and Moral Issue.* Texas: Instruction Aides, 1982.

Silverstein, E. "From Comstockery through Population Control: The Inevitability of Balancing." *North Carolina Central Law Journal* 5 (1974): 8–47.

Simson, G. I. "Abortion, Poverty and the Equal Protection of the Laws." *Georgia Law Review* 13 (1979): 505–14.

Singer, Peter. "A Utilitarian Population Principle." In *Ethics and Population*, edited by Michael D. Bayles. Cambridge, Mass.: Schenkman Publishing Company, 1976.

Sneideman, B. M. "Abortion: A Public Health and Social Policy Perspective." *N.Y.U. Review of Law and Social Change* 7 (1978): 187–213.

Steiner, Gilbert Y., ed. *The Abortion Dispute and the American System.* Washington, D.C.: Brookings Institution, 1983.

Stephen, James FitzJames. *Liberty, Equality, Fraternity.* Edited by R. J. White. Cambridge: Cambridge University Press, 1967.

Stith, Richard. "The Problem of Public Pretense." *Indiana Philosophical Quarterly* 8 (1980): 13–30.

———. "World as Reality, as Resource, and as Pretense." *American Journal of Jurisprudence* 30 (1975): 141–53.

Stone, I. F. "Modern Problems in Ancient Dress." *Tulane Law Review* 54 (1980): 812–29.

Sumner, L. W. *Abortion and Moral Theory.* Princeton: Princeton University Press, 1981.

———. "Classical Utilitarianism and the Population Optimum." In *Obligations to Future Generations,* edited by R. I. Sikora and Brian Barry. Philadelphia: Temple University Press, 1978.

———. "A Matter of Life and Death." *Nous* 10 (1976): 2.

———. "Toward a Credible View of Abortion." *Canadian Journal of Philosophy* 4 (1974): 1.

Swan, G. S. "Abortion on Maternal Demand: Paternal Support Liability Implications." *Valpariso University Law Review* 9 (1975): 243–72.

———. "Compulsory Abortion: The Next Challenge to Liberated Women?" *Ohio Northern Law Review* 3 (1975): 152–75.

Szasz, Thomas S. "The Ethics of Abortion." In *Everywoman's Guide to Abortion,* edited by Martin Ebon. Richmond Hill, Ontario: Simon and Schuster of Canada, Ltd., 1971.

Ten, C. L. *Mill on Liberty.* Oxford: Clarendon Press, 1980.

Thomson, Judith Jarvis. "A Defense of Abortion" and "Rights and Deaths." In *The Rights and Wrongs of Abortion,* edited by Marshall Cohen, et al. Princeton: Princeton University Press, 1974.

———. "Killing, Letting Die and the Trolley Problem." *The Monist* 59 (1976): 204–17.

Tooley, Michael. "Abortion and Infanticide." *Philosophy and Public Affairs* 2 (1972): 1.

———. "A Defense of Abortion and Infanticide." In *The Problem of Abortion,* edited by Joel Feinberg. Belmont, Calif.: Wadsworth Publishing Company, 1973.

Torrey, Theodore W., and Feduccia, Alan. *Morphogenesis of the Vertebrates.* 4th ed. New York: John Wiley and Sons, 1979.

Tribe, Laurence. *American Constitutional Law.* Mineola, N.Y.: Foundation Press, 1978.

———. "Forward to the Supreme Court—1972 Term: Toward a Model of Roles in the Due Process of Life and Law." *Harvard Law Review* 87 (1973): 1–53.

Uddo, B. J. "Human Life Bill: Protecting the Unborn through Congressional Enforcement of the Fourteenth Amendment." *Loyola Law Review* 27 (1981): 1079–97.

Veatch, Robert M. *Death, Dying, and the Biological Revolution.* New Haven and London: Yale University Press, 1976.

Wade, Francis C. "Potentiality in the Abortion Discussion." *Review of Metaphysics* 29 (1975): 2.

Walbert, David F., and Butler, J. Douglas, eds. *Abortion, Society and the Law.* New York: University Press Books, 1973.

Wardle, Lynn D. *The Abortion Privacy Doctrine: A Compendium and Critique of Federal Abortion Cases.* Buffalo, N.Y.: William S. Hein and Co., Inc., 1980.

———. "The Gap between Law and Moral Order: An Examination of the Legitimacy of the Supreme Court Abortion Decisions." *Brigham Young University Law Review* 1980: 811–35.

Wardle, Lynn D., and Wood, Mary A. *A Lawyer Looks at Abortion.* Provo, Utah: Brigham Young University Press, 1982.

Warren, Mary Anne. "On the Moral and Legal Status of Abortion. In *Contemporary Issues in Bioethics,* edited by T. L. Beauchamp and L. Walters. Encino, Calif.: Dickenson Publishing Company, Inc., 1978.

Watters, Wendell W. *Compulsory Parenthood: The Truth about Abortion.* Toronto: McClelland and Stewart, 1976.

Weinberg, Roy D. *Family Planning and the Law.* 2d ed. Dobbs Ferry, N.Y.: Oceana Publishers, 1979.

Wertheimer, Roger. "Understanding the Abortion Argument." In *The Rights and Wrongs of Abortion,* edited by Marshall Cohen, et al. Princeton: Princeton University Press, 1974.

Westfall, David. "Beyond Abortion: The Potential Reach of a Human Life Amendment." *American Journal of Law and Medicine* 8 (1982): 97–135.

Wheeler, L. A. "*Roe v. Wade*: The Right of Privacy Revisited." *Kansas Law Review* 21 (1973): 527–48.

Wicclair, Mark R. "The Abortion Controversy and the Claim That This Body Is Mine." *Social Theory and Practice* 7 (1981): 337–46.

Williams, Glanville. *The Sanctity of Life and the Criminal Law.* New York: Alfred A. Knopf, 1974.

Williamson, M. "Rawls and Children." *Journal of Libertarian Studies* 2 (1978): 109–14.

Witherspoon, J. P. "Impact of the Abortion Decisions upon the Father's Role." *Jurist* 35 (1975): 32–65.

———. "New Pro-Life Legislation: Patterns and Recommendations." *St. Mary's Law Journal* 7 (1976): 637–97.

Wood, M. A., and Hawkins, L. B. "State Regulation of Late Abortion and the Physician's Duty of Care to the Viable Fetus." *Missouri Law Review* 45 (1980): 394–422.

Yarbrough, T. E. "Abortion Funding Issue: A Study in Mixed Constitutional Cues." *North Carolina Law Review* 59 (1981): 611–27.

Zaitchik, Alan. "Viability and the Morality of Abortion." *Philosophy and Public Affairs* 10 (1981): 18–26.

=

Contributors

Janet Benshoof is Director of the Reproductive Freedom Project of the American Civil Liberties Union. She has written a number of articles on reproductive rights, and has submitted important briefs in numerous reproductive rights cases.

Nancy Davis is Assistant Professor of Philosophy at the University of Colorado at Boulder, and a member of the Center for the Study of Values and Social Policy at the University of Colorado. She specializes in Ethics and Political Philosophy.

Philippa Foot is Professor of Philosophy at the University of California at Los Angeles and at Somerville College, Oxford University. Many of her essays in moral philosophy, including "The Problem of Abortion and the Doctrine of the Double Effect" are collected in her recent volume, *Virtues and Vices*, Oxford University Press, 1978.

Stephen H. Galebach is an attorney formerly associated with the firm of Covington and Burling in Washington, D.C. He now serves in the White House as Deputy Assistant Director for Legal Policy in the Office of Policy Development.

Jay L. Garfield is Assistant Professor of Philosophy in the School of Communications and Cognitive Science, Hampshire College.

Patricia Hennessey was the first director of the Civil Liberties and Public Policy Program at Hampshire College. She practices law at Kaye, Scholer, Fierman, Hays & Handler in New York.

Patricia A. King is Associate Professor of Law at Georgetown University Law Center. She is a fellow of the Hastings Institute and a Senior Research Scholar at the Kennedy Institute of Ethics. She is coauthor of *Law, Science, and Medicine*, forthcoming from Foundation Press. Professor King has served on the National Committee for the Protection of Human Subjects and on the President's Commission on Ethics.

Catharine MacKinnon is Assistant Professor of Law at the University of Minnesota Law School. She is the author of *Sexual Harassment of Working Women*, Yale University Press, 1979.

Ruth Macklin is Associate Professor of Bioethics in the Department of Community Health at the Albert Einstein College of Medicine. She is a fellow at the Hastings Center, and is formerly on the staff of that center. Professor Macklin is the author of numerous articles in biomedical ethics, and of *Man, Mind, and Morality: The Ethics of Behavior Control*. She is the coeditor of *Moral Problems in Medicine*, 2d. ed. Prentice Hall, 1983.

Meredith W. Michaels is Assistant Professor of Philosophy at Mount Holyoke College. Her interests lie in moral philosophy, reproductive rights, and social and political philosophy.

David A. J. Richards is Professor of Law at New York University School of Law where he teaches constitutional law, jurisprudence, and criminal law. He is the author of numerous articles and books, most recently, *Sex, Drugs, Death and the Law: An Essay on Overcriminalization*, Rowman and Littlefield, 1982.

Laurence Thomas is Associate Professor of Philosophy at the University of North Carolina at Chapel Hill. He has written extensively in moral philosophy, political philosophy, and moral psychology.

Roger Wertheimer, presently a Visiting Professor of Philosophy at the University of Houston, is the author of *The Significance of Sense* and numerous articles in social and political philosophy. His writings on abortion include "Understanding the Abortion Argument," "Misunderstanding the Abortion Argument," "Philosophy on Humanity," "In Defense of Speciesism," and a book-in-progress entitled *The Importance of Being Human*.

Daniel Wikler is Associate Professor of Philosophy at the University of Wisconsin, and Associate Professor of the History of Medicine at the University of Wisconsin Medical School. He has served as staff philosopher for the President's Council for the Study of Ethical Problems in Medicine in Washington, D.C. Among his publications in bioethics is "Brain Death and Personal Identity."

Library of Congress Cataloging in Publication Data
Main entry under title:
Abortion, moral and legal perspectives.

Bibliography: p.
1. Abortion—Law and legislation—United States—
Addresses, essays, lectures. 2. Abortion—United States—
Moral and ethical aspects—Addresses, essays, lectures.
I. Garfield, Jay L., 1955–   II. Hennessey,
Patricia, 1954–   .
KF3771.A75A27   1984   344.73′0419   84–8739
ISBN 0–87023–440–4   347.304419
ISBN 0–87023–441–2 (pbk.)